ATLAS OF
RUSSIAN HISTORY

ATLAS OF RUSSIAN HISTORY

Martin Gilbert
Fellow of Merton College, Oxford

Cartographic consultant ARTHUR BANKS

DORSET PRESS

1984 Dorset Press

This edition published by Dorset Press, a division of MARBORO BOOKS Corp., by arrangement with the proprietor.

Originally published as *Russian History Atlas*.

Russian History Atlas was first published in Great Britain in 1972.

Library of Congress Catalog Card Number: 72-80174

ISBN 0-88029-018-8

Printed in the United States of America

Contents

Preface

List of Maps

Section One—Ancient and Early Modern Russia

Section Two—Imperial Russia

Section Three—The Soviet Union

Bibliography of Works Consulted

Index

Preface

I have designed this Atlas in the hope that it is possible to present—
within the span of 146 maps—a survey of Russian history from the
earliest times to the present day. In drafting each map, I drew upon
material from a wide range of published works—books, articles, atlases
and single sheet maps—each of which I have listed in the bibliography.

On the maps themselves I have included much factual material not
normally associated with historical geography, such as the text of one of
Stalin's few surviving personal communications—the postcard to his sister-
in-law (printed on map 54), and Lenin's telegram to the Bolsheviks in
Sweden (printed on map 87). I have drafted each map individually, in such
a way as to enable the maximum factual information to be included
without making use of a separate page of text; and I have compiled the
index in order that it may serve as a means of using the Atlas as if it were a
volume of narrative.

I wish to acknowledge the help of many colleagues and friends. In 1962
I began research into Russian history under the supervision of Dr George
Katkov, whose insatiable curiosity about elusive historical facts, and whose
enthusiasm in tracking them down, have influenced all my subsequent
work. I also benefitted from the teaching and encouragement of Mr David
Footman, Mr Max Hayward, Dr Harry Willetts and the late Mr Guy Wint.
When I was preparing the first sketches for this Atlas, the maps I had
drawn and the facts I had incoporrated on them were scrutinized by three
friends—Mr Michael Glenny, Mr Dennis O'Flaherty and Dr Harry
Shukman—to each of whom I am most grateful for many detailed
suggestions, and for giving up much time to help me. At the outset of my
research I received valuable bibliographical advice from Dr J. L. I.
Simmons, and suggestions for specific maps from Mr Norman Davies,
Dr Ronald Hingley, Mr John B. Kingston and Mr Ewald Uustalu.
Jane Cousins helped me with bibliographical and historical research;
Mr Arthur Banks transcribed my sketches into clear, printable maps, and
Kate Fleming kept a vigilant eye on the cartography. Susie Sacher helped
me to compile the index: Sarah Graham, as well as undertaking all the

secretarial work, made many important suggestions, factual and cartographic.

I should welcome any suggestions for new maps which could be incorporated in subsequent editions, and any note of errors or obscurities.

Note on Transliteration

I have tried to adopt a uniform system of transliteration from the Russian. But where a place is familiar to English readers in an anglicized form, I have used the familiar form (thus Archangel, not Arkhangelsk; Caucasus, not Kavkaz; Moscow, not Moskva). Towns in the frontier area between eastern Europe and Russia are in general given their Russian transliteration: I have given alternate spellings in the index. In the case of the Polish towns of Belzec, Bialystok and Przemysl, I have retained the Polish forms (rather than the less familiar Russian, Belzhets, Belostok and Peremyshl.)

List of Maps

SECTION ONE: ANCIENT AND
EARLY MODERN RUSSIA

1 The Slavs by 800 BC
2 The Asian Migrations 800–600 BC
3 Scythians, Greeks and Slavs 600 BC–
   300 BC
4 Romans and Sarmatians 200 BC–
   200 AD
5 The Triumph of the Goths 200–400
   AD
6 The Empire of the Huns 450 AD
7 The First Slav Expansion 450–550 AD
8 The Avar Conquests 560–600 AD
9 The Slav Recovery 600–700 AD
10 The Khazar Kingdom 650–750 AD
11 The Scandinavian Migrations 800–
   1000 AD
12 The Slavs and the Norsemen by 880
   AD
13 Kievan Russia 880–1054
14 Rivers and Trade in 1000 AD
15 Christianity and the Slavs by 1000 AD
16 The Flourishing of Russian
   Monasticism 1200–1600
17 The Fragmentation of Kievan Russia
   1054–1238
18 The Republic of Novgorod 997–1478
19 The Eastern Trade Routes of
   Novgorod 1000–1450
20 German Eastward Expansion and the
   Baltic 900–1500
21 The Mongol Empire by 1300
22 The Mongol Conquest of Russia
   1219–1241

23 The Lithuanian Conquests 1240–1462
24 The Eastward Spread of Catholicism
   by 1462
25 The Rise of Moscow 1261–1533
26 The Expansion of Russia 1533–1598
27 Moscow and the Rivers of European
   Russia 1460–1860
28 The Expropriation of Land by Ivan IV
   1565–1571
29 Russia in the Time of Troubles
   1598–1613
30 The Polish and Swedish Invasions
   1610–1618
31 The Westward Expansion of Russia
   1640–1667
32 Social Unrest 1648 and 1670
33 Russian Eastward Expansion 1478–
   1710
34 Trade and Industry 1700–1800
35 The Cossacks 1500–1916
36 Russian Westward Expansion and the
   Baltic 1721–1945

SECTION TWO: IMPERIAL RUSSIA

37 War and Revolt under Peter the Great
   1695–1723
38 The Provinces and Population of
   Russia in 1724
39 The Germans of Russia 1710–1959
40 The Expansion of China 1720–1760
41 Russian Expansion under Catherine
   the Great 1762–1796
42 The Destruction of Polish
   Independence 1768–1795

43 The Russian Annexations of Poland 1772–1795
44 Russia in America 1784–1867
45 Russia in the Mediterranean 1798–1907
46 Russia and Turkey 1721–1829
47 Russia and Sweden 1700–1809
48 Russia in the Caucasus 1800–1900
49 Russia and Europe 1789–1815
50 Russia and Europe 1801–1825
51 Russia under Nicholas I 1825–1855
52 The Polish Revolt in 1831
53 The Polish Revolt in 1861
54 The Siberian Exiles 1648–1917
55 The Anarchists 1840–1906
56 Russian Industry by 1860
57 Peasant Discontent 1827–1860
58 Serfs in 1860
59 Russian Trade with China 1850–1870
60 The Far East 1850–1890
61 Anglo-Russian Conflict and Expansion in Central Asia 1846–1907
62 The Trans-Siberian Railway 1891–1917
63 Russia and the European Powers 1872–1887
64 Russia and the Balance of Power in Europe 1890–1907
65 China and the European Powers 1898–1904
66 Russia and Japan in the Far East 1860–1895
67 The Russian Response in the Far East 1895–1905
68 Prelude to Revolution 1894–1904
69 The Jews and their Enemies 1648–1917
70 The Jewish Response to Persecution 1827–1917
71 Russian Industry by 1900
72 The Socialist Revolutionaries 1902–1922
73 Lenin, Iskra, and the Bolsheviks 1900–1917
74 The Provinces and Population of European Russia in 1900
75 The 1905 Revolution in the Countryside
76 The 1905 Revolution in the Towns
77 The Moscow Uprising 1905

78 Russia and the Balkans 1876–1885
79 Russia, the Balkans, and the Coming of War 1912–14
80 German War Aims in Western Russia 1914–1918
81 The Eastern Front 1914
82 The Eastern Front 1915
83 The Eastern Front 1916
84 Russia in Turmoil 1914–1917
85 Russia and Turkey 1914–1921
86 The Fall of the Monarchy 1917
87 Lenin's Return to Russia 1917
88 The Location of the Bolshevik Leaders During the First Revolution of 1917
89 The War and Revolution July and August 1917
90 The October Revolution in Petrograd

SECTION THREE: THE SOVIET UNION

91 The Russian Revolution November 1917–March 1918
92 The War Against Bolshevism 1918–1919
93 The Anti-Bolshevik Attack on Petrograd 1919
94 Foreign Intervention in Northern Russia 1918–1919
95 Makhno and the Anarchists 1917–1920
96 The Russo-Polish War 1920
97 The Ukraine 1917–1921
98 Ukrainian Communities in Soviet Asia by 1937
99 The Ukrainians in North America by 1937
100 The Border States 1919–20
101 Soviet Diplomacy 1920–1940
102 Famine and Relief 1921
103 The Spread of Soviet Rule in Central Asia 1917–1936
104 Independent Transaucasia 1917–1921
105 The Kara Sea Expeditions of 1920 and 1921
106 The Independent Far Eastern Republic 1920–1922
107 The Russian Exodus 1917–1923

108 The Failure of World Revolution 1917–1927
109 Labour Camps in European Russia 1917–1936
110 Labour Camps in European Russia 1937–1957
111 Labour Camps East of the Urals 1918–1958
112 The Northern Sea Route 1920–1970
113 The Soviet Union under Stalin 1922–1953
114 The Partition of Poland 1939
115 The Russo-Finnish War 1939–1940
116 Soviet Annexations 1939–40
117 Europe on 22 June 1941
118 The German Invasion of the Soviet Union 1941
119 Soviet Wealth Controlled by Germany in 1942
120 United States Aid to the Soviet Union 1941–1945
121 Soviet Industry and Allied Aid 1941–1945
122 A German Plan for the Partition of the Soviet Union 1941
123 The German Administration in the East 1941–1944
124 German Plans and Conquests in 1942
125 The Siege of Stalingrad, September 1942–February 1943
126 The Siege of Leningrad 1941–1943
127 Soviet Partisans South of Leningrad 1941–1942
128 The German Drive to the Caucasus 1941–1943
129 The Advance of the Red Army 1943–1944
130 The Defeat of Germany 1944–1945
131 The Soviet Deportation of Nationalities 1941–1945
132 Flight and Expulsion 1939–1946
133 The Soviet Union in Eastern Europe 1945–1948
134 The Soviet Union in Eastern Europe 1949–1968
135 Birobidzhan 1928–1968
136 The Virgin Lands 1953–1961
137 Soviet Heavy Industry and Its Raw Materials
138 Cities and Railways in the Soviet Union 1917–1959
139 The Changing Names of Soviet Cities
140 The Cuban Missile Crisis 1962
141 Soviet Naval Strength 1970
142 The Soviet Union and China 1860–1970
143 The Soviet–Chinese Borderlands 1970
144 The Republics and Autonomous Regions of the Soviet Union in 1970
145 Russia's Western Frontier since 1700
146 The Invaders of Russia 1240–1945

Section One

ANCIENT AND EARLY MODERN RUSSIA

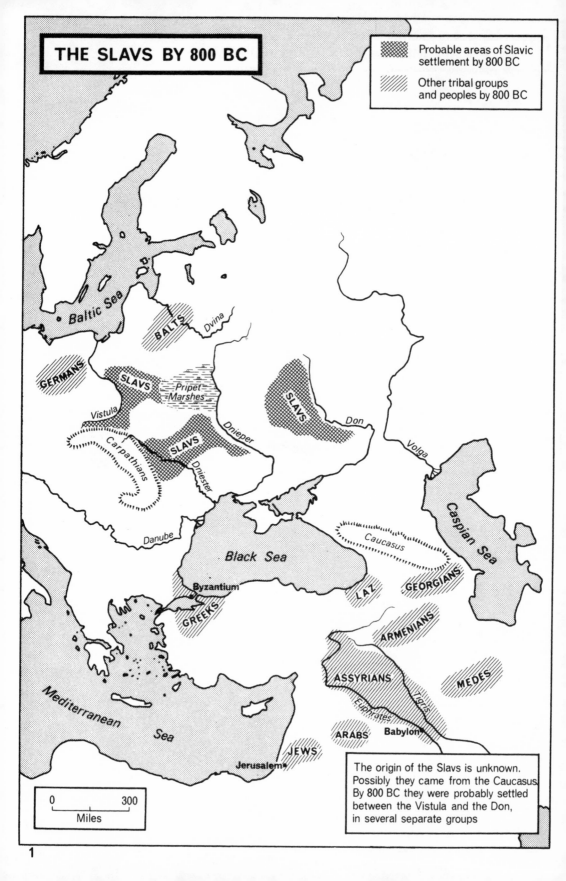

THE SLAVS BY 800 BC

Probable areas of Slavic settlement by 800 BC

Other tribal groups and peoples by 800 BC

Baltic Sea

BALTS

Dvina

GERMANS

SLAVS

Pripet Marshes

SLAVS

Vistula

Carpathians

SLAVS

Dnieper

Don

Volga

Dniester

Caspian Sea

Danube

Caucasus

Black Sea

Byzantium

LAZ

GEORGIANS

GREEKS

ARMENIANS

Mediterranean Sea

ASSYRIANS

MEDES

Euphrates

Tigris

ARABS

Babylon

JEWS

Jerusalem

0   300
Miles

The origin of the Slavs is unknown. Possibly they came from the Caucasus. By 800 BC they were probably settled between the Vistula and the Don, in several separate groups

1

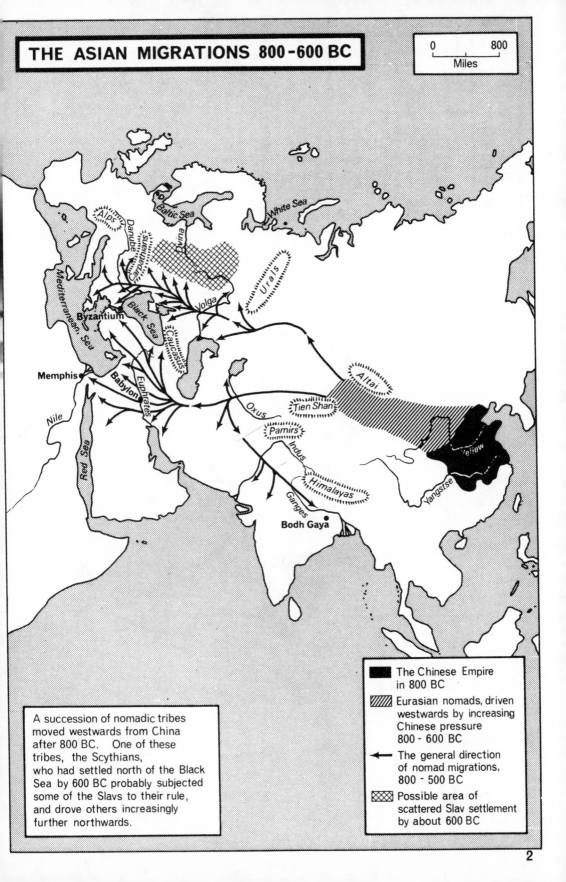

THE ASIAN MIGRATIONS 800-600 BC

0   800
Miles

Alps

Baltic Sea

White Sea

Danube

Carpathians

Dvina

Urals

Volga

Byzantium

Black Sea

Caucasus

Mediterranean Sea

Memphis

Babylon

Euphrates

Nile

Red Sea

Altai

Oxus

Tien Shan

Pamirs

Indus

Himalayas

Ganges

Bodh Gaya

Yellow

Yangtse

A succession of nomadic tribes
moved westwards from China
after 800 BC.   One of these
tribes, the Scythians,
who had settled north of the Black
Sea by 600 BC probably subjected
some of the Slavs to their rule,
and drove others increasingly
further northwards.

The Chinese Empire
in 800 BC

Eurasian nomads, driven
westwards by increasing
Chinese pressure
800 - 600 BC

The general direction
of nomad migrations,
800 - 500 BC

Possible area of
scattered Slav settlement
by about 600 BC

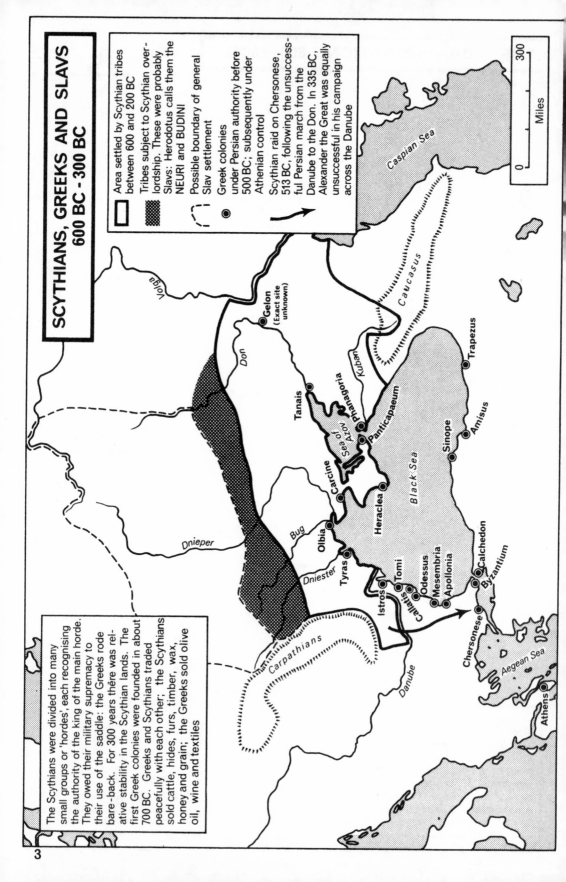

SCYTHIANS, GREEKS AND SLAVS
600 BC - 300 BC

☐ Area settled by Scythian tribes between 600 and 200 BC

▨ Tribes subject to Scythian over-lordship. These were probably Slavs: Herodotus calls them the NEURI and BUDINI

- - - Possible boundary of general Slav settlement

⊙ Greek colonies

Greek colonies under Persian authority before 500 BC; subsequently under Athenian control

→ Scythian raid on Chersonese, 513 BC, following the unsuccessful Persian march from the Danube to the Don. In 335 BC, Alexander the Great was equally unsuccessful in his campaign across the Danube

300 | Miles | 0

The Scythians were divided into many small groups or 'hordes', each recognising the authority of the king of the main horde. They owed their military supremacy to their use of the saddle: the Greeks rode bare-back. For 300 years there was relative stability in the Scythian lands. The first Greek colonies were founded in about 700 BC. Greeks and Scythians traded peacefully with each other; the Scythians sold cattle, hides, furs, timber, wax, honey and grain; the Greeks sold olive oil, wine and textiles

Caspian Sea

Volga

Caucasus

Gelon (Exact site unknown)

Don

Kuban

Trapezus

Tanais

Phanagoria

Sea of Azov

Panticapaeum

Amisus

Carcine

Sinope

Black Sea

Heraclea

Dnieper

Bug

Olbia

Dniester

Tyras

Tomi

Odessus

Mesembria

Apollonia

Calchedon

Byzantium

Istros

Callatis

Carpathians

Danube

Chersonese

Aegean Sea

Athens

3

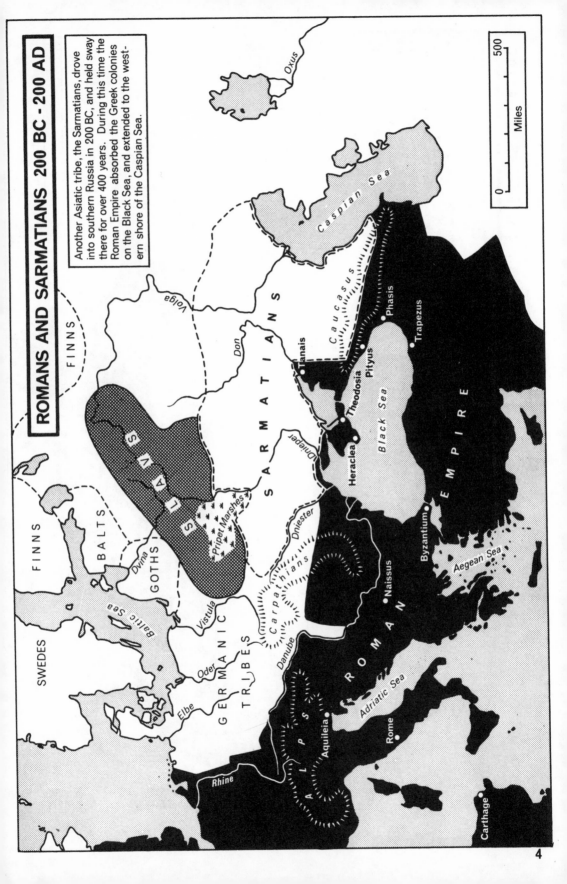

ROMANS AND SARMATIANS 200 BC - 200 AD

Another Asiatic tribe, the Sarmatians, drove into southern Russia in 200 BC, and held sway there for over 400 years. During this time the Roman Empire absorbed the Greek colonies on the Black Sea, and extended to the western shore of the Caspian Sea.

500

Miles

0

Oxus

Caspian Sea

FINNS

Volga

Don

FINNS

Caucasus

Phasis

Trapezus

Pityus

Tanais

SARMATIANS

Theodosia

Dnieper

BALTS

SLAVS

Heraclea

Black Sea

Dvina

GOTHS

Pripet Marshes

Byzantium

EMPIRE

Aegean Sea

FINNS

Vistula

Dniester

Carpathians

Naissus

SWEDES

Baltic Sea

Oder

GERMANIC TRIBES

Danube

ROMAN

Elbe

ALPS

Adriatic Sea

Aquileia

Rome

Rhine

Carthage

4

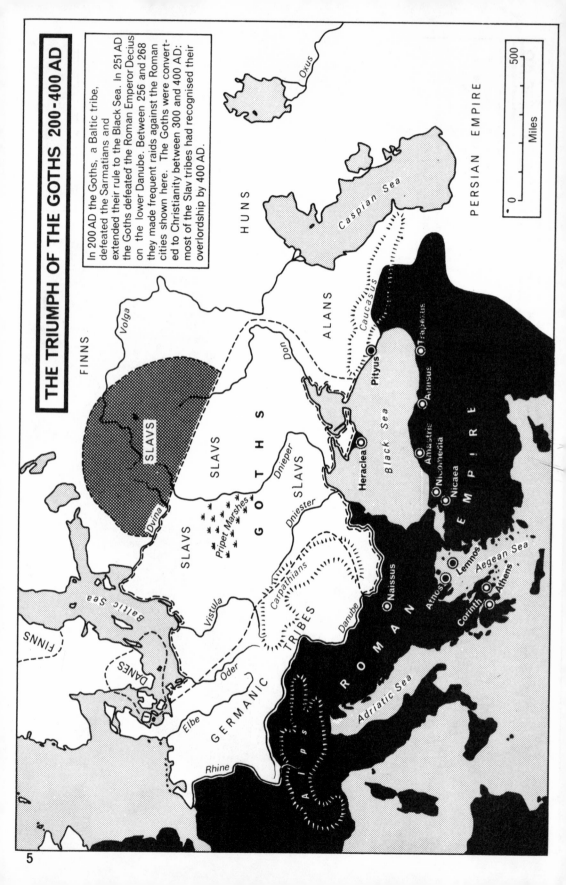

THE TRIUMPH OF THE GOTHS 200-400 AD

In 200 AD the Goths, a Baltic tribe, defeated the Sarmatians and extended their rule to the Black Sea. In 251 AD the Goths defeated the Roman Emperor Decius on the lower Danube. Between 256 and 268 they made frequent raids against the Roman cities shown here. The Goths were converted to Christianity between 300 and 400 AD: most of the Slav tribes had recognised their overlordship by 400 AD.

500

Miles

0

PERSIAN EMPIRE

HUNS

ALANS

Caspian Sea

Oxus

Volga

Don

Caucasus

Pityus

Trapezus

Amisus

Amastris

Nicomedia

Nicaea

Black Sea

Heraclea

Dnieper

Dniester

SLAVS

SLAVS

SLAVS

SLAVS

G O T H S

FINNS

Pripet Marshes

Vistula

Carpathians

Danube

Naissus

Athos

Lemnos

Aegean Sea

Corinth

Athens

R O M A N   E M P I R E

T R I B E S

G E R M A N I C

Oder

Elbe

Rhine

A l p s

Adriatic Sea

Baltic Sea

FINNS

DANES

Dvina

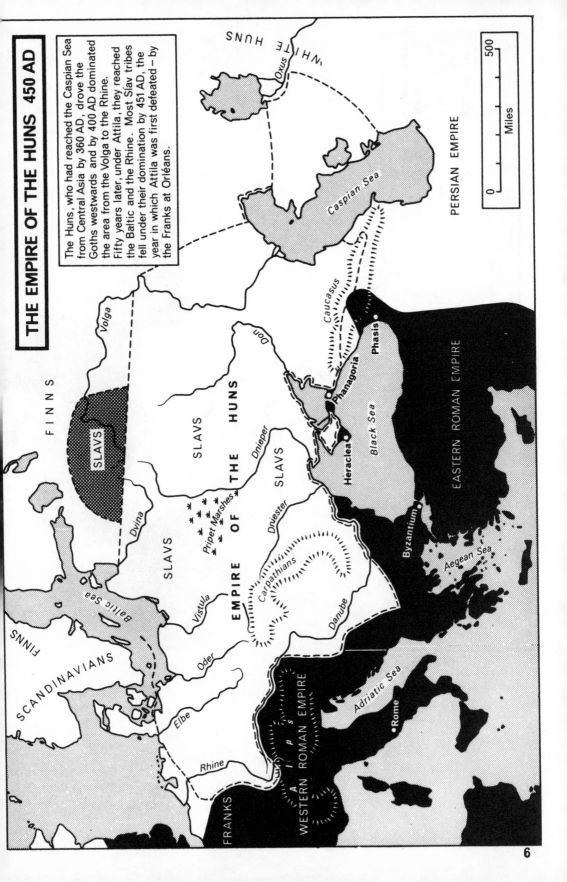

THE EMPIRE OF THE HUNS 450 AD

The Huns, who had reached the Caspian Sea from Central Asia by 360 AD, drove the Goths westwards and by 400 AD dominated the area from the Volga to the Rhine. Fifty years later, under Attila, they reached the Baltic and the Rhine. Most Slav tribes fell under their domination by 451 AD, the year in which Attila was first defeated – by the Franks at Orléans.

500

Miles

0

WHITE HUNS

Oxus

PERSIAN EMPIRE

Caspian Sea

FINNS

Volga

SLAVS

Dvina

SLAVS

Don

Dnieper

EMPIRE OF THE HUNS

Pripet Marshes

SLAVS

Dniester

Caucasus

Phasis

Phanagoria

Heraclea

Black Sea

EASTERN ROMAN EMPIRE

FINNS

Baltic Sea

SCANDINAVIANS

Vistula

Carpathians

Byzantium

Aegean Sea

Oder

Danube

Elbe

Adriatic Sea

Rome

A l p s

WESTERN ROMAN EMPIRE

Rhine

FRANKS

6

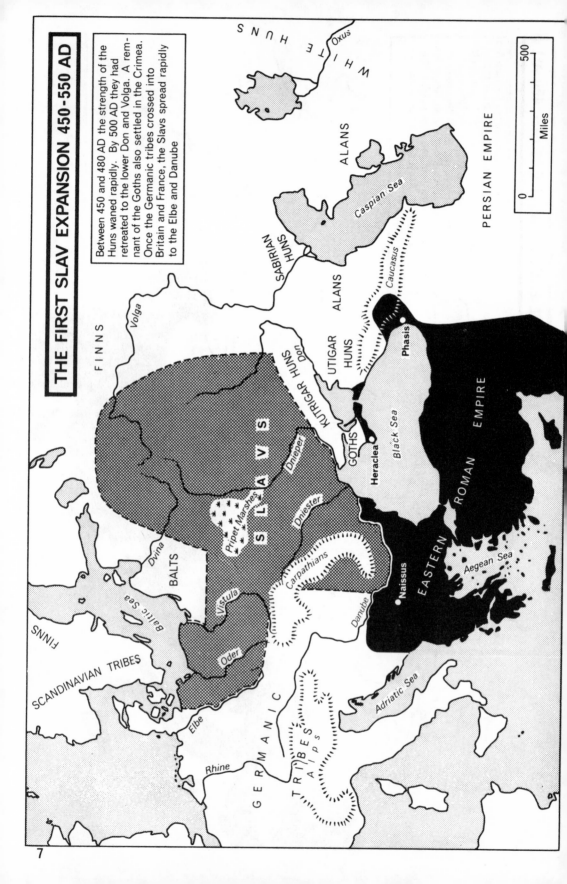

THE FIRST SLAV EXPANSION 450-550 AD

Between 450 and 480 AD the strength of the Huns waned rapidly. By 500 AD they had retreated to the lower Don and Volga. A remnant of the Germanic tribes also settled in the Crimea. Once the Germanic tribes crossed into Britain and France, the Slavs spread rapidly to the Elbe and Danube

WHITE HUNS

Oxus

ALANS

PERSIAN EMPIRE

500

Miles

0

Caspian Sea

SABIRIAN HUNS

ALANS

Caucasus

FINNS

Volga

UTIGAR HUNS

Phasis

KUTRIGAR HUNS

Don

GOTHS

Black Sea

Heraclea

S L A V S

Dnieper

Pripet Marshes

Dniester

EASTERN ROMAN EMPIRE

Aegean Sea

Naissus

Dvina

BALTS

Carpathians

Vistula

Danube

FINNS

Baltic Sea

Oder

G E R M A N I C

Adriatic Sea

SCANDINAVIAN TRIBES

Elbe

T R I B E S

Alps

Rhine

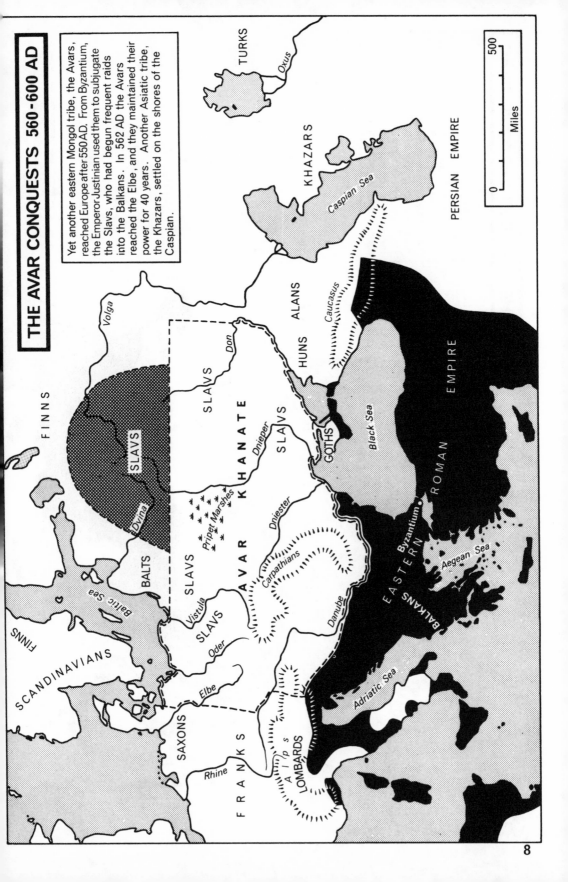

THE AVAR CONQUESTS 560-600 AD

Yet another eastern Mongol tribe, the Avars, reached Europe after 550AD. From Byzantium, the Emperor Justinian used them to subjugate the Slavs, who had begun frequent raids into the Balkans. In 562 AD the Avars reached the Elbe, and they maintained their power for 40 years. Another Asiatic tribe, the Khazars, settled on the shores of the Caspian.

TURKS

Oxus

KHAZARS

Caspian Sea

PERSIAN EMPIRE

0 — 500

Miles

Volga

Don

SLAVS

ALANS

HUNS

Caucasus

FINNS

SLAVS

Dvina

SLAVS

A V A R   K H A N A T E

Dnieper

SLAVS

GOTHS

Black Sea

Pripet Marshes

Dniester

BALTS

Baltic Sea

SLAVS

Carpathians

Byzantium

E A S T E R N   R O M A N   E M P I R E

Aegean Sea

SCANDINAVIANS

FINNS

Vistula

Oder

Danube

B A L K A N S

Elbe

SAXONS

A l p s

Adriatic Sea

F R A N K S

Rhine

LOMBARDS

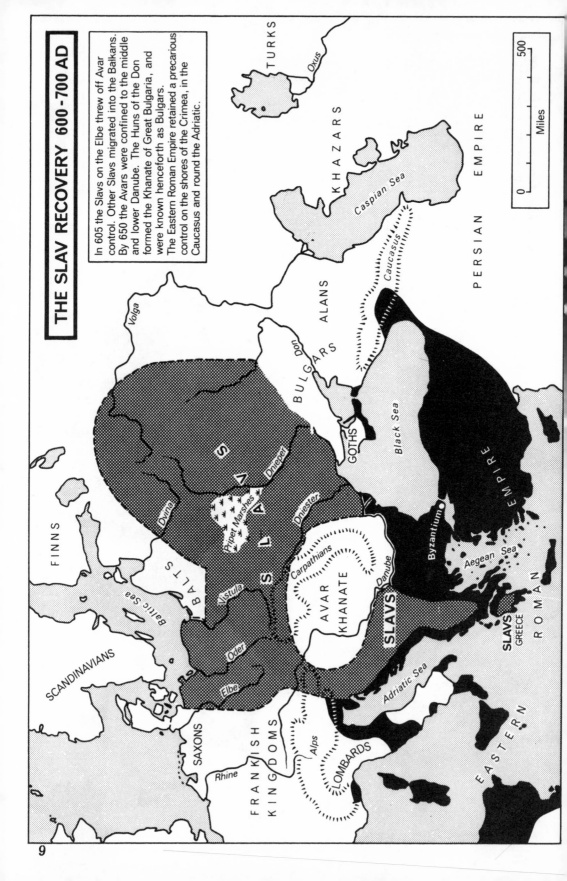

THE SLAV RECOVERY 600-700 AD

In 605 the Slavs on the Elbe threw off Avar control. Other Slavs migrated into the Balkans. By 650 the Avars were confined to the middle and lower Danube. The Huns of the Don formed the Khanate of Great Bulgaria, and were known henceforth as Bulgars. The Eastern Roman Empire retained a precarious control on the shores of the Crimea, in the Caucasus and round the Adriatic.

500

0

Miles

TURKS

Oxus

KHAZARS

Caspian Sea

PERSIAN EMPIRE

Volga

BULGARS

Don

ALANS

Caucasus

Caucasus

FINNS

Dvina

S L A V S

Dnieper

Pripet Marshes

Dniester

GOTHS

Black Sea

EMPIRE

BALTS

Baltic Sea

Vistula

Carpathians

AVAR KHANATE

Danube

Byzantium

Aegean Sea

ROMAN

SCANDINAVIANS

Oder

SLAVS

SLAVS

GREECE

SAXONS

Elbe

FRANKISH KINGDOMS

Alps

LOMBARDS

Adriatic Sea

EASTERN

Rhine

9

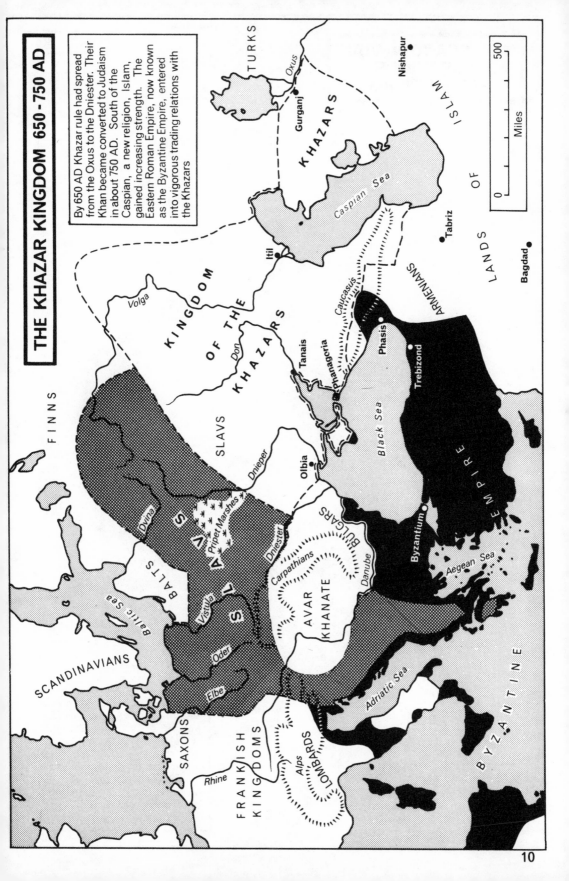

THE KHAZAR KINGDOM 650 - 750 AD

By 650 AD Khazar rule had spread from the Oxus to the Dniester. Their Khan became converted to Judaism in about 750 AD. South of the Caspian, a new religion, Islam, gained increasing strength. The Eastern Roman Empire, now known as the Byzantine Empire, entered into vigorous trading relations with the Khazars

TURKS

Oxus

Nishapur

KHAZARS

Gurganj

Caspian Sea

LANDS OF ISLAM

KINGDOM

Itil

Tabriz

Volga

OF THE

Bagdad

Don

KHAZARS

Phanagoria

Phasis

ARMENIANS

SLAVS

Tanais

Caucasus

Trebizond

FINNS

Dnieper

Olbia

Black Sea

Dvina

Pripet Marshes

S
L
A
V
S

Dniester

BULGARS

Byzantium

EMPIRE

BALTS

Vistula

Carpathians

Danube

Aegean Sea

SCANDINAVIANS

Baltic Sea

Oder

AVAR KHANATE

Elbe

Adriatic Sea

SAXONS

Alps

LOMBARDS

BYZANTINE

FRANKISH KINGDOMS

Rhine

Miles

0   500

THE SCANDINAVIAN MIGRATIONS 800 – 1000 AD

0   400
Miles

VINLAND
(Site unknown)

St. Lawrence

GREENLAND

NORTH
ATLANTIC
OCEAN

ICELAND

North
Pole

FAROE
ISLANDS

Iona

Lindisfarne
Jarrow
ENGLAND

Lisbon
SPAIN
Seville
FRANCE
Pamplona
Paris

Valence

Rome

Mediterranean Sea

Novgorod   Ladoga

Kiev   Dnieper

Olbia

KHAZARIA

Constantinople   Black Sea

Tanais   Volga

BYZANTIUM

Itil

ARMENIA   Semender

Antioch   Edessa   Baku
SYRIA

Caspian Sea

Red Sea

Gümüsh
Tepe

PERSIA

Persian Gulf

The Vikings, or Norsemen, sailed in
successive waves from Scandinavia
from 793 AD, when they landed at
Lindisfarne, to 1098 when they
reached Armenia. One line of Norse
penetration and settlement was
through the Slav lands, from
Novgorod to Kiev, along the river
trade routes which linked
Scandinavia with Constantinople

◼ The Scandinavian
homelands in 800 AD

← Principal Scandinavian
migrations 800-1000 AD

THE SLAVS AND
THE NORSEMEN
BY 880 AD

Slav settlement by 880 AD
SERB Principal Slav tribes
BALTS Other tribes
'Kievan Rus', ruled by the
Norsemen (Varangarians),
who took tribute from the
neighbouring Slavs, and
protected them against
Khazar and Pecheneg attacks

NORSE
SWEDES
DANES
FINNS
OBODRICH
BALTS
Visby
Baltic Sea
SLOVIANIANS
Novgorod
CHEREMESIANS
Volga
VIATCHIANS
MORDVINS
POLOCHANE
Smolensk
POLES
MAZOVIANS
KRIVICHIANS
GERMANS
Elbe
Pripett
Marshes
RADIMICHIANS
SILESIANS
DEREVLIANS
SEVERIANS
CZECHS
Don
MORAVIANS
Kiev
KHAZARS
SLOVAKS
VOLHYANIANS
POLANIANS
Danube
SLOVENES
MAGYARS
Venice
PECHENEGS
CROATS
VLACHS
Adriatic Sea
Tmutorokan
Caucasus
SERBS
Black Sea
Preslav
Constantinople
BULGARS
ARMENIANS
Ægean
Sea
Athens
GREEKS

The Norse settlers between Novgorod and Kiev quickly
dominated the local Slavs, over whom they established political
control. Known as "Varangarians", these Norse overlords moulded
the Slavs into a coherent federation, "Kievan Rus". Originally
Norse speaking, Kievan Rus, or Russia, saw a close mingling of
Scandinavian and Slav culture; and the emergence of a strong
Kievan, or Russian national consciousness. The first
Varangarian ruler, Rurik, led an expedition against
Constantinople in 860 AD. His successor Oleg established
his capital at Kiev in about 880 AD.

0   300
Miles

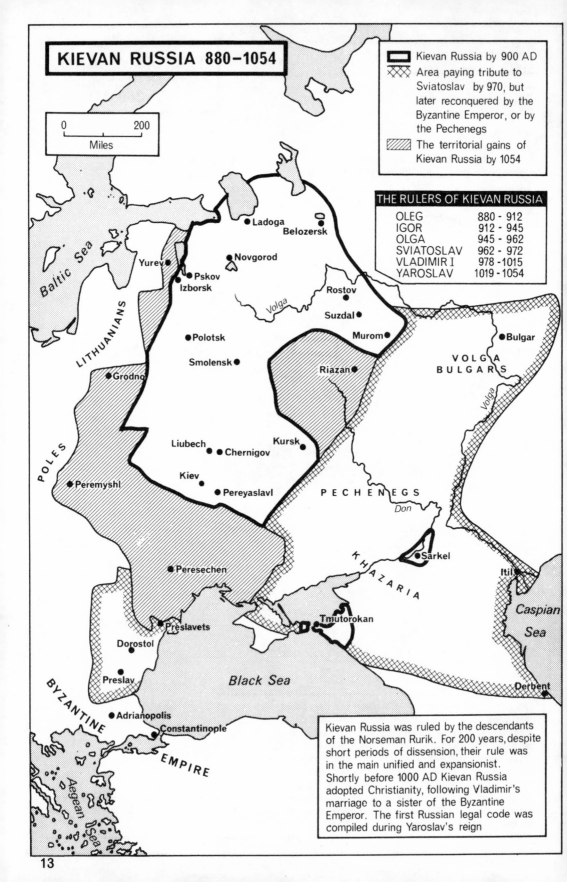

KIEVAN RUSSIA 880–1054

0   200
Miles

Kievan Russia by 900 AD

Area paying tribute to
Sviatoslav by 970, but
later reconquered by the
Byzantine Emperor, or by
the Pechenegs

The territorial gains of
Kievan Russia by 1054

THE RULERS OF KIEVAN RUSSIA

OLEG	880 - 912
IGOR	912 - 945
OLGA	945 - 962
SVIATOSLAV	962 - 972
VLADIMIR I	978 -1015
YAROSLAV	1019 - 1054

Baltic Sea

LITHUANIANS

POLES

BYZANTINE

EMPIRE

Aegean Sea

Ladoga
Belozersk
Yurev
Novgorod
Pskov
Izborsk
Rostov
Volga
Suzdal
Polotsk
Murom
Bulgar
Smolensk
Riazan
VOLGA
BULGARS
Volga
Liubech
Chernigov
Kursk
Kiev
Peremyshl
Pereyaslavl
PECHENEGS
Don
KHAZARIA
Sarkel
Itil
Peresechen
Caspian
Sea
Preslavets
Tmutorokan
Dorostol
Preslav
Black Sea
Derbent
Adrianopolis
Constantinople

Grodno

Kievan Russia was ruled by the descendants
of the Norseman Rurik. For 200 years, despite
short periods of dissension, their rule was
in the main unified and expansionist.
Shortly before 1000 AD Kievan Russia
adopted Christianity, following Vladimir's
marriage to a sister of the Byzantine
Emperor. The first Russian legal code was
compiled during Yaroslav's reign

13

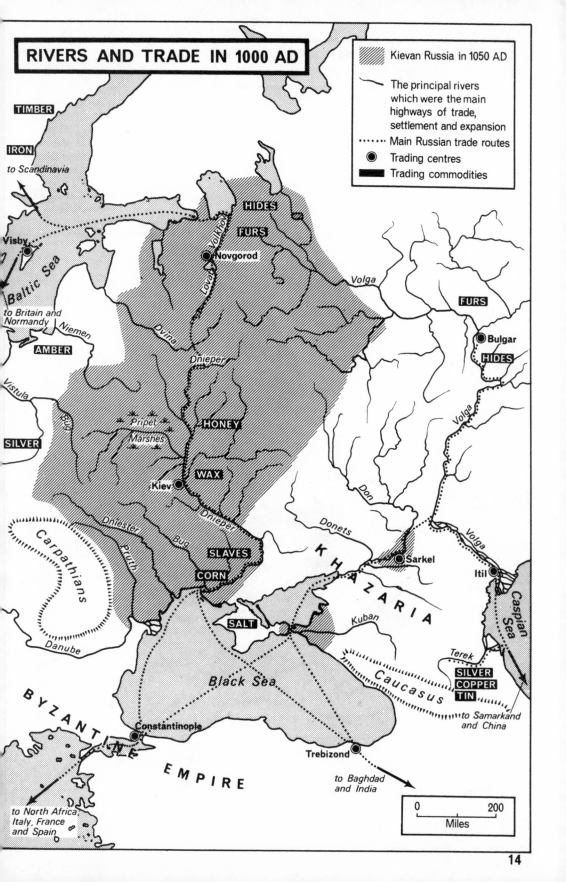

RIVERS AND TRADE IN 1000 AD

Kievan Russia in 1050 AD

The principal rivers which were the main highways of trade, settlement and expansion

Main Russian trade routes

Trading centres

Trading commodities

TIMBER

IRON

to Scandinavia

Visby

Baltic Sea

to Britain and Normandy

Niemen

AMBER

Vistula

Bug

SILVER

Dvina

Dnieper

Pripet Marshes

HONEY

WAX

Kiev

Dniester

Bug

Prut

Carpathians

Danube

SLAVES

CORN

SALT

Black Sea

Constantinople

BYZANTINE EMPIRE

to North Africa, Italy, France and Spain

HIDES

FURS

Novgorod

Lovat

Volkhov

Volga

FURS

Bulgar

HIDES

Volga

Don

Donets

KHAZARIA

Sarkel

Itil

Volga

Kuban

Caucasus

Terek

SILVER COPPER TIN

Caspian Sea

to Samarkand and China

Trebizond

to Baghdad and India

0   200
Miles

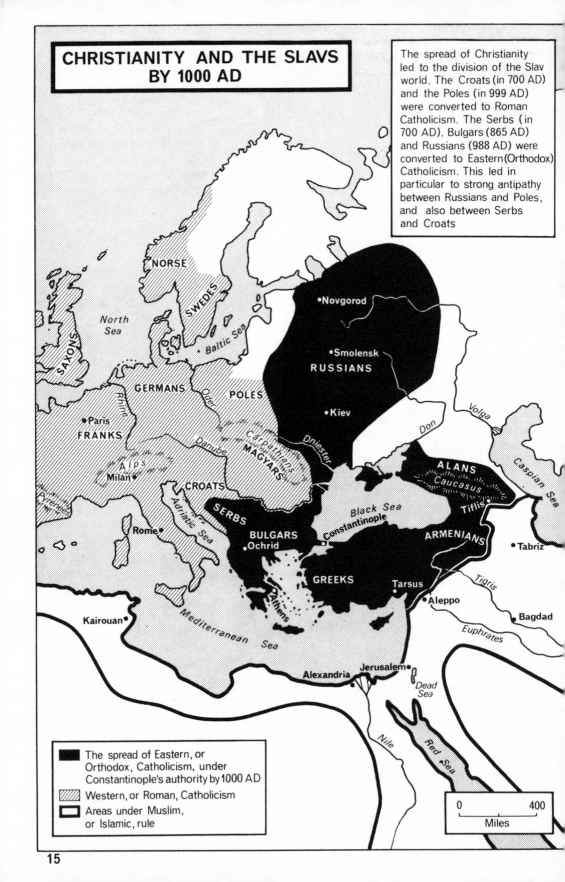

CHRISTIANITY AND THE SLAVS BY 1000 AD

The spread of Christianity led to the division of the Slav world. The Croats (in 700 AD) and the Poles (in 999 AD) were converted to Roman Catholicism. The Serbs (in 700 AD), Bulgars (865 AD) and Russians (988 AD) were converted to Eastern (Orthodox) Catholicism. This led in particular to strong antipathy between Russians and Poles, and also between Serbs and Croats

NORSE

SWEDES

SAXONS

North Sea

Baltic Sea

GERMANS

Oder

POLES

•Novgorod

•Smolensk

RUSSIANS

Rhine

•Paris

FRANKS

Danube

Carpathians

MAGYARS

•Kiev

Dniester

Don

Volga

Alps

Milan•

CROATS

ALANS

Caucasus

Caspian Sea

SERBS

Adriatic Sea

Black Sea

Tiflis

Rome•

BULGARS

•Ochrid

Constantinople

ARMENIANS

•Tabriz

Pyrenees

GREEKS

•Tarsus

Tigris

Kairouan•

Athens

•Aleppo

Bagdad•

Mediterranean Sea

Euphrates

Alexandria•

Jerusalem•

Dead Sea

Nile

Red Sea

■ The spread of Eastern, or Orthodox, Catholicism, under Constantinople's authority by 1000 AD

▨ Western, or Roman, Catholicism

▢ Areas under Muslim, or Islamic, rule

0   400
Miles

THE FLOURISHING OF RUSSIAN MONASTICISM 1200-1600

White Sea

Urals

Solovetski monastery

ZIRIANS

Siskoi monastery

Ustiug

PERMIAKS

KINGDOM OF SWEDEN

Valaam

Belozersk

Ladoga

Spaso-Kamenni monastery

Baltic Sea

Novgorod

Galich

Kostroma

TEUTONIC KNIGHTS

Pskov

Tver

Rostov
Pereyaslavl
Suzdal

Nizhni Novgorod

Volokolamsk

Troitski-Sergievski monastery

Vladimir

Polotsk

Moscow

Volga

Smolensk

GRAND DUCHY OF LITHUANIA

Chernigov

Kiev

MONGOL KHANATES

Volga

Caspian Sea

The foundation of urban monasteries was most intense between 1200 and 1350. By 1400 the majority of monasteries being founded were rural or "desert" monasteries. Between 1350 and 1450 over 150 new monasteries were established, and by 1500 many monastic colonies had been set up in the predominantly pagan areas between Galich and the Urals. In 1588 the English Ambassador to Moscow wrote of the monasteries owning all the best land in Russia and being among the principal landowners

- ◉ Principal Orthodox monasteries established by 1500
- ⫽⫽⫽ Area of most active monastic colonization before 1500
- ▆ Nomadic and heathen tribes among whom monastic missionary work was most active 1400-1500
- –·–·– National frontiers in 1500

0   200
Miles

THE FRAGMENTATION OF KIEVAN RUSSIA 1054-1238

0 200
Miles

DEPENDENCIES OF NOVGOROD

FINNS

Ustiug

Ladoga
Belozersk
REPUBLIC
OF NOVGOROD
VLADIMIR-SUZDAL

Reval
Novgorod
Kostroma
Yaroslavl
Rostov

VOLGA
BULGARS

Pskov
Torzhok
Suzdal

Riga
Izborsk
Tver
Vladimir
Murom

Dvina
Moscow

LITHUANIA
Polotsk
SMOLENSK
Riazan

Kovno
Vitebsk
Viazma
Smolensk
MUROM-
RIAZAN

POLOTSK
Minsk
CHERNIGOV

Bialystok
TUROV
NOVGOROD-
SEVERSK

Vistula
Pinsk

POLAND
Turov
Chernigov

VOLHYNIA
KIEV

Cracow
Kiev
PEREYASLAVL

Zhitomir
Pereyaslavl

GALICIA
Galich
Don

Carpathians
Dniester
CUMANS or POLOVTSI

HUNGARY

Black
Sea

Constantinople

On the death of Yaroslav in 1054, Kievan Russia
was divided among his sons. Their constant
feuds led to the fragmentation of the once
powerful kingdom. United briefly from 1113 to 1125
by Vladimir Monomakh, the Russian lands were again
divided and in conflict during the hundred years
before the Mongol invasion of 1238. In 1199 Galicia
and Volhynia were united, and in 1254 recognised
by the Pope as an independent kingdom. In
1307 Polotsk came under Lithuanian suzerainty

☐ The twelve Principalities
of Russia in 1100

17

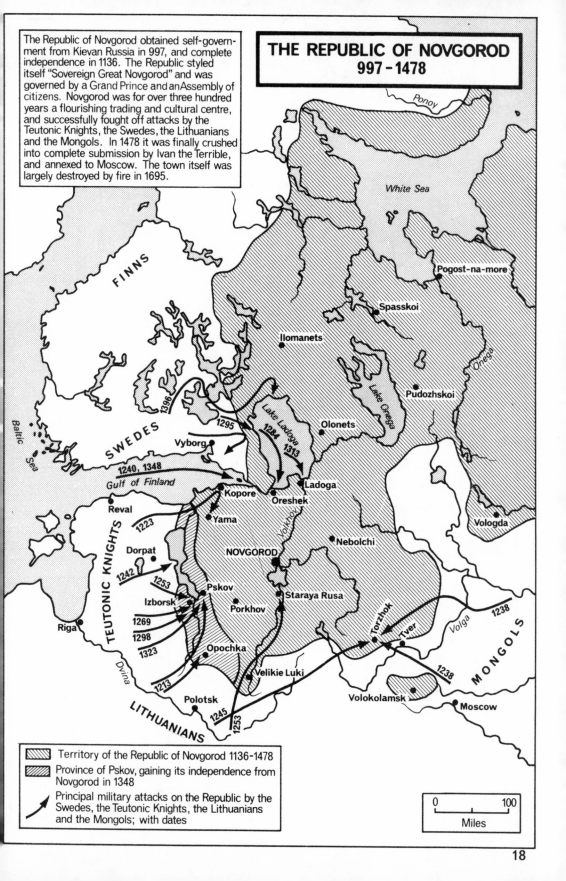

THE REPUBLIC OF NOVGOROD
997 – 1478

The Republic of Novgorod obtained self-government from Kievan Russia in 997, and complete independence in 1136. The Republic styled itself "Sovereign Great Novgorod" and was governed by a Grand Prince and an Assembly of citizens. Novgorod was for over three hundred years a flourishing trading and cultural centre, and successfully fought off attacks by the Teutonic Knights, the Swedes, the Lithuanians and the Mongols. In 1478 it was finally crushed into complete submission by Ivan the Terrible, and annexed to Moscow. The town itself was largely destroyed by fire in 1695.

Ponoy

White Sea

FINNS

Pogost-na-more

Spasskoi

Ilomanets

Lake Ladoga

Lake Onega

Onega

Pudozhskoi

Baltic Sea

SWEDES

1396

1295

1284

1313

Olonets

Vyborg

1240, 1348

Gulf of Finland

Reval

1223

Kopore

Oreshek

Ladoga

Volkhov

Yama

Vologda

Dorpat

NOVGOROD

Nebolchi

TEUTONIC KNIGHTS

1242

1253

Pskov

Staraya Rusa

Riga

Izborsk

1269

1298

1323

Porkhov

Torzhok

Tver

Volga

1238

M O N G O L S

Dvina

Opochka

Velikie Luki

1238

Polotsk

1213

1245

1253

Volokolamsk

Moscow

LITHUANIANS

▨ Territory of the Republic of Novgorod 1136-1478

▨ Province of Pskov, gaining its independence from Novgorod in 1348

↗ Principal military attacks on the Republic by the Swedes, the Teutonic Knights, the Lithuanians and the Mongols; with dates

0   100

Miles

18

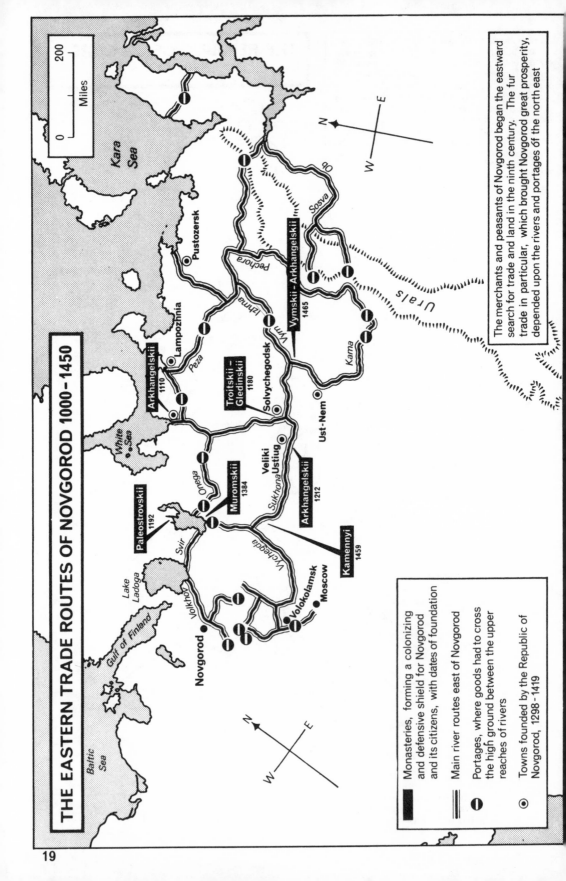

THE EASTERN TRADE ROUTES OF NOVGOROD 1000-1450

The merchants and peasants of Novgorod began the eastward search for trade and land in the ninth century. The fur trade in particular, which brought Novgorod great prosperity, depended upon the rivers and portages of the north east

Monasteries, forming a colonizing and defensive shield for Novgorod and its citizens, with dates of foundation

Main river routes east of Novgorod

Portages, where goods had to cross the high ground between the upper reaches of rivers

Towns founded by the Republic of Novgorod, 1298-1419

Kara Sea

Baltic Sea

White Sea

Gulf of Finland

Lake Ladoga

Pustozersk

Lampozhnia

Peza

Arkhangelskii
1110

Troitskii –
Gledinskii
1180

Solvychegodsk

 Izhma

Pechora

Vym

Vymskii – Arkhangelskii
1465

Sosva

Ob

Urals

Kama

Ust-Nem

Paleostrovskii
1192

Onega

Suir

Muromskii
1384

Veliki Ustiug

Sukhona

Arkhangelskii
1212

Vchegda

Kamennyi
1459

Volkhov

Volokolamsk

Moscow

Novgorod

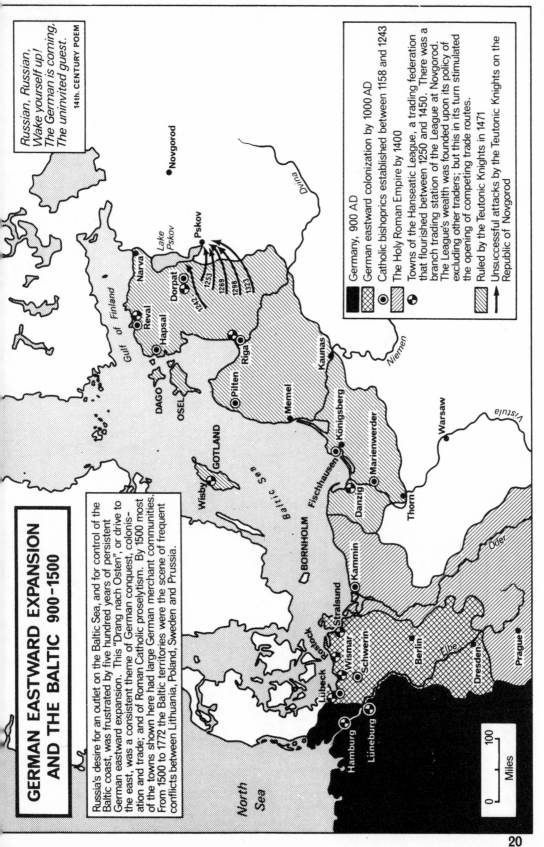

GERMAN EASTWARD EXPANSION AND THE BALTIC 900–1500

Russia's desire for an outlet on the Baltic Sea, and for control of the Baltic coast, was frustrated by five hundred years of persistent German eastward expansion. This "Drang nach Osten", or drive to the east, was a consistent theme of German conquest, colonisation and trade; and of Roman Catholic proselytism. By 1500 most of the towns shown here had large German merchant communities. From 1500 to 1772 the Baltic territories were the scene of frequent conflicts between Lithuania, Poland, Sweden and Prussia.

Russian, Russian,
Wake yourself up!
The German is coming.
The uninvited guest.

14th. CENTURY POEM

Germany, 900 AD

German eastward colonization by 1000 AD

Catholic bishoprics established between 1158 and 1243

The Holy Roman Empire by 1400

Towns of the Hanseatic League, a trading federation that flourished between 1250 and 1450. There was a branch trading station of the League at Novgorod. The League's wealth was founded upon its policy of excluding other traders; but this in its turn stimulated the opening of competing trade routes.

Ruled by the Teutonic Knights in 1471

Unsuccessful attacks by the Teutonic Knights on the Republic of Novgorod

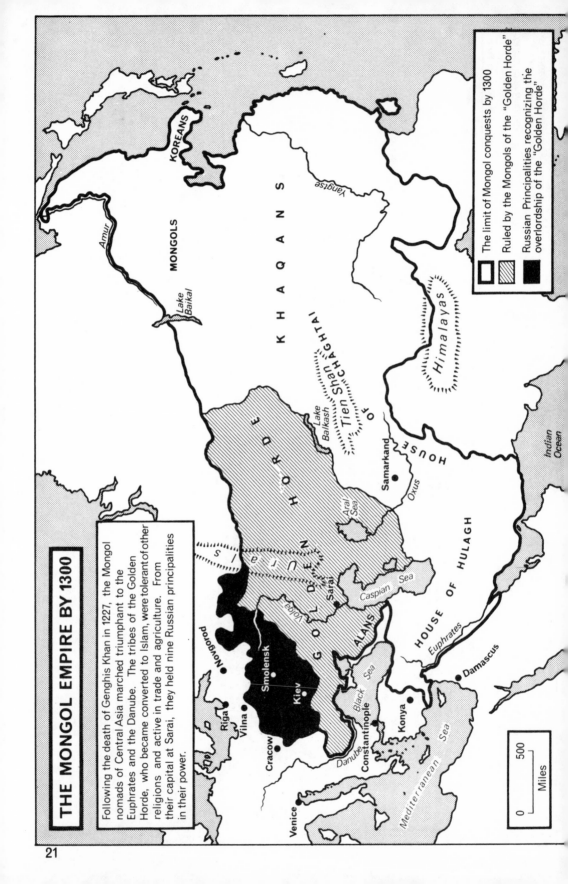

THE MONGOL EMPIRE BY 1300

Following the death of Genghis Khan in 1227, the Mongol nomads of Central Asia marched triumphant to the Euphrates and the Danube. The tribes of the Golden Horde, who became converted to Islam, were tolerant of other religions and active in trade and agriculture. From their capital at Sarai, they held nine Russian principalities in their power.

The limit of Mongol conquests by 1300

Ruled by the Mongols of the "Golden Horde"

Russian Principalities recognizing the overlordship of the "Golden Horde"

KOREANS

MONGOLS

Amur

Lake Baikal

Yangtse

KHAQANS

Tien Shan

CHAGHTAI

HOUSE OF

Himalayas

Indian Ocean

Lake Balkash

Samarkand

Oxus

Aral Sea

GOLDEN HORDE

SEIJURE

Sarai

Volga

Caspian Sea

HOUSE OF HULAGH

Euphrates

ALANS

Novgorod

Damascus

Smolensk

Riga

Kiev

Vilna

Black Sea

Konya

Cracow

Constantinople

Danube

Venice

Mediterranean Sea

0   500
Miles

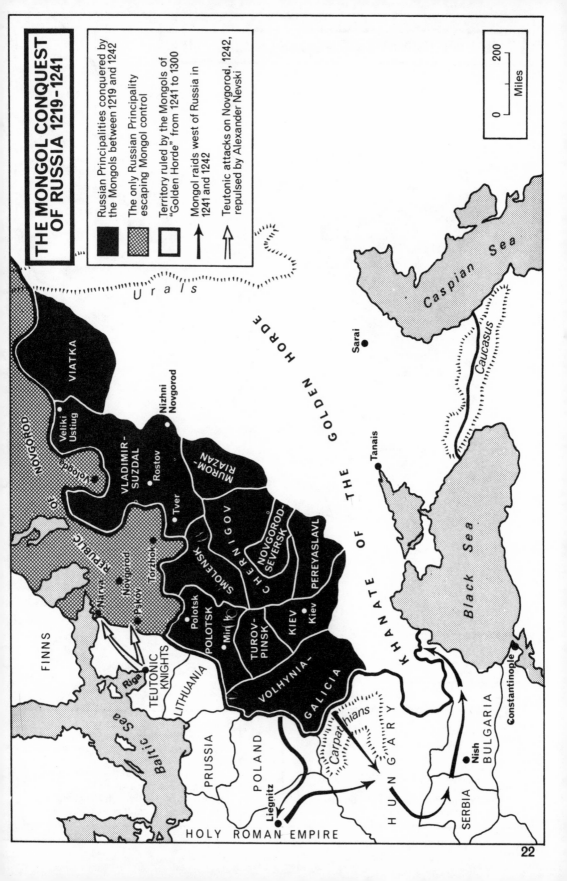

THE MONGOL CONQUEST OF RUSSIA 1219-1241

Russian Principalities conquered by the Mongols between 1219 and 1242

The only Russian Principality escaping Mongol control

Territory ruled by the Mongols of "Golden Horde" from 1241 to 1300

Mongol raids west of Russia in 1241 and 1242

Teutonic attacks on Novgorod, 1242, repulsed by Alexander Nevski

0 — 200 Miles

Urals

Caspian Sea

Caucasus

Sarai

Tanais

Black Sea

KHANATE OF THE GOLDEN HORDE

VIATKA

NOVGOROD

Veliki Ustiug

Vologda

Nizhni Novgorod

VLADIMIR-SUZDAL

Rostov

Tver

MUROM-RIAZAN

CHERNIGOV

NOVGOROD-SEVERSK

PEREYASLAVL

SMOLENSK

REPUBLIC

Narva

Novgorod

Pskov

Torzhok

Polotsk

POLOTSK

Minsk

TUROV-PINSK

KIEV

Kiev

VOLHYNIA-GALICIA

FINNS

TEUTONIC KNIGHTS

Riga

LITHUANIA

Baltic Sea

PRUSSIA

POLAND

Liegnitz

HOLY ROMAN EMPIRE

Carpathians

HUNGARY

SERBIA

Nish

BULGARIA

Constantinople

22

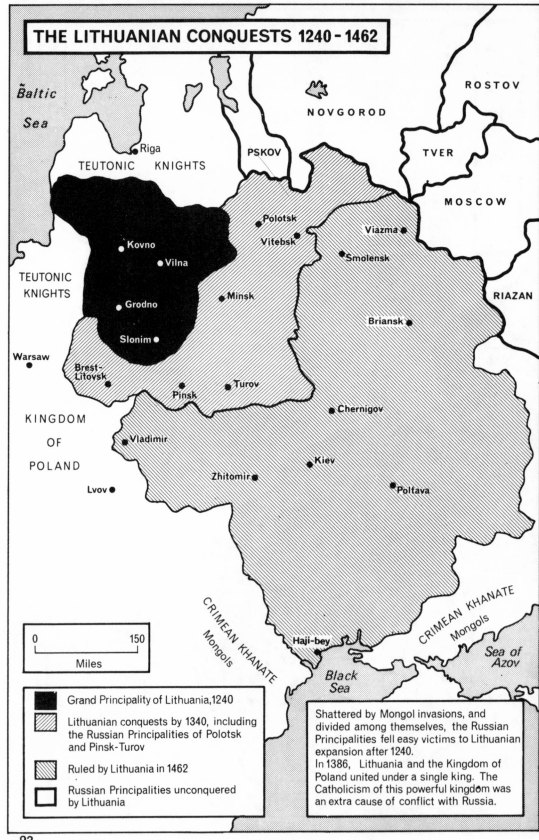

THE LITHUANIAN CONQUESTS 1240-1462

Baltic Sea

NOVGOROD

ROSTOV

PSKOV

TVER

Riga

TEUTONIC KNIGHTS

MOSCOW

Polotsk

Viazma

Vitebsk

Smolensk

Kovno

Vilna

TEUTONIC KNIGHTS

RIAZAN

Grodno

Minsk

Briansk

Slonim

Warsaw

Brest-Litovsk

Turov

Pinsk

Chernigov

KINGDOM

OF

POLAND

Vladimir

Kiev

Zhitomir

Poltava

Lvov

CRIMEAN KHANATE Mongols

CRIMEAN KHANATE Mongols

Haji-bey

Sea of Azov

| 0 | 150 |
Miles

Black Sea

Grand Principality of Lithuania, 1240

Lithuanian conquests by 1340, including the Russian Principalities of Polotsk and Pinsk-Turov

Ruled by Lithuania in 1462

Russian Principalities unconquered by Lithuania

Shattered by Mongol invasions, and divided among themselves, the Russian Principalities fell easy victims to Lithuanian expansion after 1240.

In 1386, Lithuania and the Kingdom of Poland united under a single king. The Catholicism of this powerful kingdom was an extra cause of conflict with Russia.

THE EASTWARD SPREAD OF CATHOLICISM BY 1462

Simultaneously with the Mongol invasions from the east, Russia was subjected to the continual westward movement of Roman Catholicism. Under Swedish and Lithuanian pressure, Russian Orthodoxy was pushed back almost to Moscow. Roman Catholicism also made advances against the Orthodox Bulgars in the Balkans, and against the Muslim lands in the eastern Mediterranean.

LAPLAND 1300

NORWAY

SWEDEN

DENMARK

Baltic Sea

Vyborg 1293

Reval 1219

RUSSIA

Novgorod

Pskov

Tver

Moscow

Mitava 1271

Kaluga

Danzig 1200

PRUSSIA

Vilna 1386

Smolensk 1450

Warsaw

LITHUANIA

POLAND

THE

Prague

HOLY

BOHEMIA

GALICIA

Kiev 1385

ROMAN

Vienna

Lvov 1340

UKRAINE

HUNGARY

EMPIRE

CROATIA

TRANSYLVANIA

Tana 1261

Kaffa 1261

Black Sea

Rome

BALKANS

Constantinople 1261

Amastris 1310

Samsun 1310

Athens 1305

Aegean Sea

Edessa 1098

Antioch 1098

The Roman Catholic world in 1000 AD

Conquered between 1000 and 1462 AD by Roman Catholic rulers, and forming part of Catholic kingdoms

0   300
Miles

24

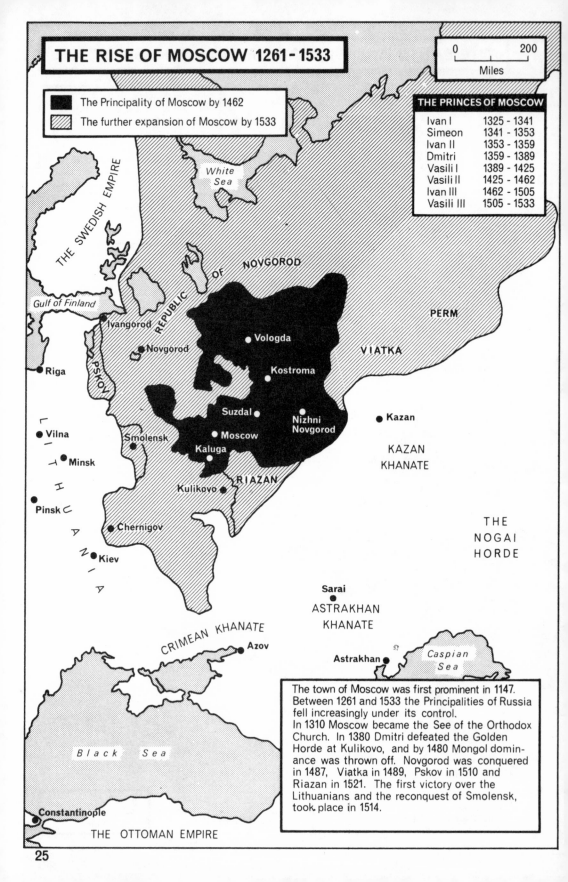

THE RISE OF MOSCOW 1261-1533

0   200
Miles

■ The Principality of Moscow by 1462

▨ The further expansion of Moscow by 1533

THE PRINCES OF MOSCOW

Ivan I	1325 - 1341
Simeon	1341 - 1353
Ivan II	1353 - 1359
Dmitri	1359 - 1389
Vasili I	1389 - 1425
Vasili II	1425 - 1462
Ivan III	1462 - 1505
Vasili III	1505 - 1533

THE SWEDISH EMPIRE

White Sea

REPUBLIC OF NOVGOROD

Gulf of Finland

PERM

Ivangorod

Vologda

VIATKA

Novgorod

● Riga

PSKOV

Kostroma

Suzdal

Nizhni Novgorod

● Kazan

● Vilna

Smolensk

Moscow

KAZAN KHANATE

● Minsk

Kaluga

L I T H U A N I A

Kulikovo

RIAZAN

THE NOGAI HORDE

Pinsk

● Chernigov

● Kiev

Sarai
●
ASTRAKHAN KHANATE

CRIMEAN KHANATE

● Azov

Astrakhan

Caspian Sea

Black Sea

The town of Moscow was first prominent in 1147. Between 1261 and 1533 the Principalities of Russia fell increasingly under its control.
In 1310 Moscow became the See of the Orthodox Church. In 1380 Dmitri defeated the Golden Horde at Kulikovo, and by 1480 Mongol dominance was thrown off. Novgorod was conquered in 1487, Viatka in 1489, Pskov in 1510 and Riazan in 1521. The first victory over the Lithuanians and the reconquest of Smolensk, took place in 1514.

Constantinople

THE OTTOMAN EMPIRE

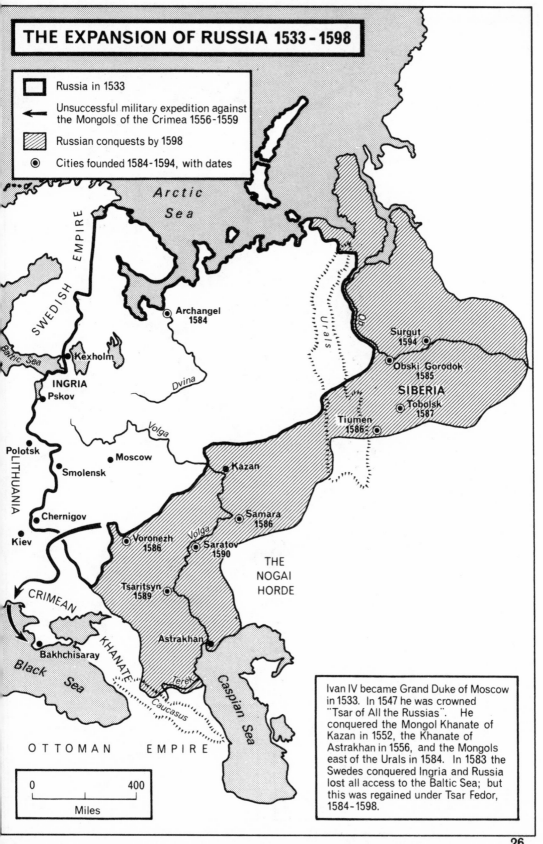

THE EXPANSION OF RUSSIA 1533-1598

Russia in 1533

← Unsuccessful military expedition against the Mongols of the Crimea 1556-1559

Russian conquests by 1598

⊙ Cities founded 1584-1594, with dates

Arctic Sea

SWEDISH EMPIRE

Baltic Sea

Urals

Ob

Archangel 1584

Kexholm

Surgut 1594

Obski Gorodok 1585

SIBERIA

INGRIA

Pskov

Dvina

Tobolsk 1587

Tiumen 1586

Polotsk

Moscow

Volga

Smolensk

Kazan

LITHUANIA

Chernigov

Samara 1586

Kiev

Voronezh 1586

Volga

Saratov 1590

THE NOGAI HORDE

CRIMEAN

Tsaritsyn 1589

KHANATE

Astrakhan

Bakhchisaray

Black Sea

Terek

Caucasus

Caspian Sea

OTTOMAN EMPIRE

Ivan IV became Grand Duke of Moscow in 1533. In 1547 he was crowned "Tsar of All the Russias". He conquered the Mongol Khanate of Kazan in 1552, the Khanate of Astrakhan in 1556, and the Mongols east of the Urals in 1584. In 1583 the Swedes conquered Ingria and Russia lost all access to the Baltic Sea; but this was regained under Tsar Fedor, 1584-1598.

0   400

Miles

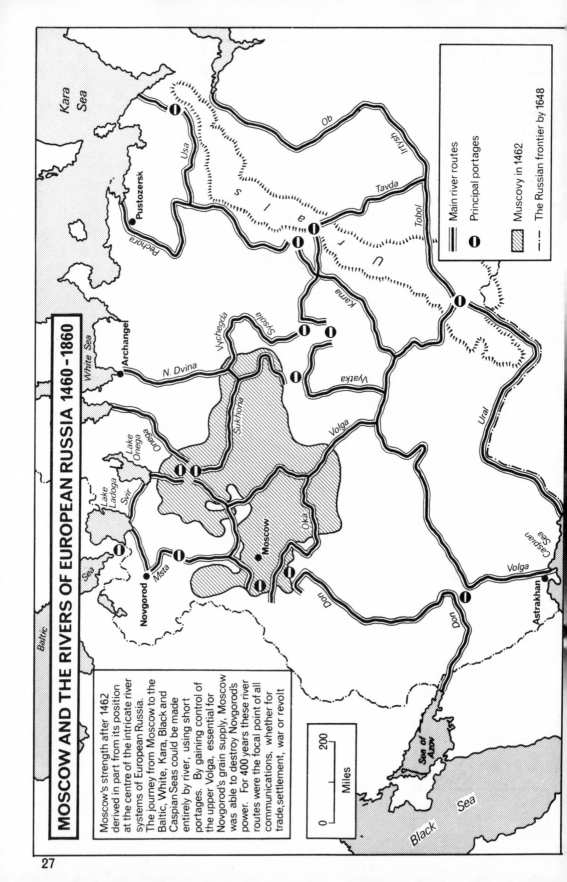

MOSCOW AND THE RIVERS OF EUROPEAN RUSSIA 1460–1860

Moscow's strength after 1462 derived in part from its position at the centre of the intricate river systems of European Russia. The journey from Moscow to the Baltic, White, Kara, Black and Caspian Seas could be made entirely by river, using short portages. By gaining control of the upper Volga, essential for Novgorod's grain supply, Moscow was able to destroy Novgorod's power. For 400 years these river routes were the focal point of all communications, whether for trade, settlement, war or revolt

Main river routes

Principal portages

Muscovy in 1462

The Russian frontier by 1648

0   200

Miles

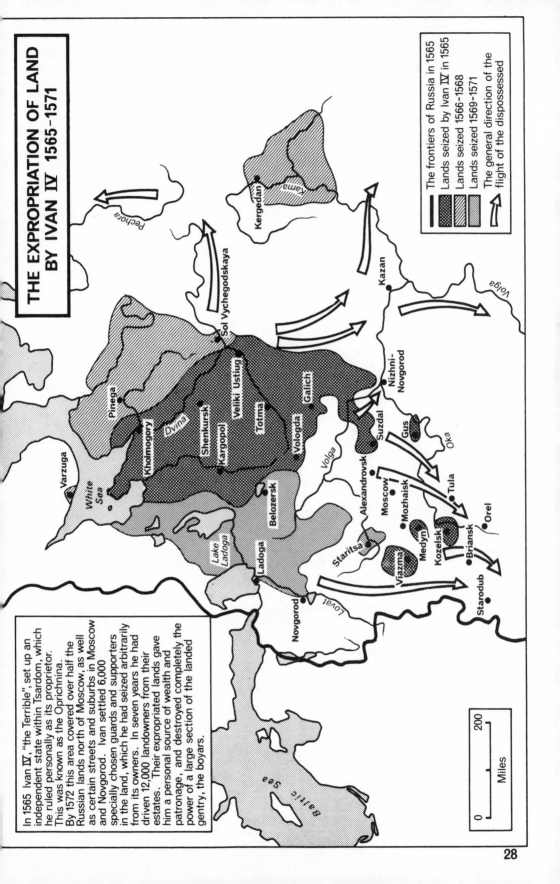

THE EXPROPRIATION OF LAND BY IVAN IV 1565-1571

In 1565 Ivan IV, "the Terrible", set up an independent state within Tsardom, which he ruled personally as its proprietor. This was known as the Oprichnina.
By 1572 this area covered over half the Russian lands north of Moscow, as well as certain streets and suburbs in Moscow and Novgorod. Ivan settled 6,000 specially chosen guards and supporters in the land, which he had seized arbitrarily from its owners. In seven years he had driven 12,000 landowners from their estates. Their expropriated lands gave him a personal source of wealth and patronage, and destroyed completely the power of a large section of the landed gentry, the boyars.

The frontiers of Russia in 1565
Lands seized by Ivan IV in 1565
Lands seized 1566-1568
Lands seized 1569-1571
The general direction of the flight of the dispossessed

Kergedan
Kama
Kazan
Volga
Sol Vychegodskaya
Pinega
Dvina
Varzuga
White Sea
Kholmogory
Shenkursk
Kargopol
Veliki Ustiug
Totma
Vologda
Galich
Nizhni-Novgorod
Suzdal
Gus
Oka
Volga
Belozersk
Lake Ladoga
Ladoga
Alexandrovsk
Moscow
Mozhaisk
Tula
Orel
Staritsa
Medyn
Kozelsk
Briansk
Viazma
Starodub
Novgorod
Lovat
Baltic Sea

0   200
Miles

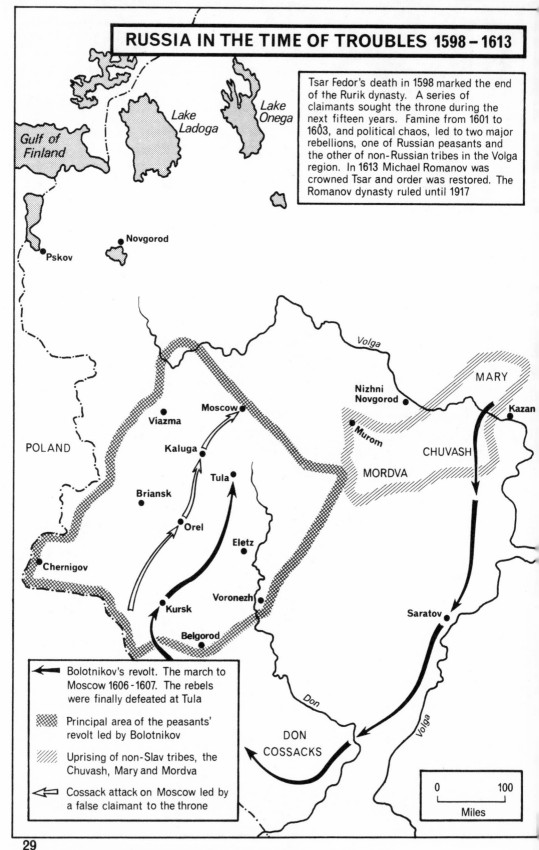

RUSSIA IN THE TIME OF TROUBLES 1598 – 1613

Tsar Fedor's death in 1598 marked the end of the Rurik dynasty. A series of claimants sought the throne during the next fifteen years. Famine from 1601 to 1603, and political chaos, led to two major rebellions, one of Russian peasants and the other of non-Russian tribes in the Volga region. In 1613 Michael Romanov was crowned Tsar and order was restored. The Romanov dynasty ruled until 1917

Gulf of Finland

Lake Ladoga

Lake Onega

Pskov

Novgorod

POLAND

Viazma

Moscow

Kaluga

Brisnk

Tula

Orel

Eletz

Chernigov

Kursk

Voronezh

Belgorod

Volga

Nizhni Novgorod

Murom

MARY

Kazan

CHUVASH

MORDVA

Saratov

Don

Volga

DON COSSACKS

← Bolotnikov's revolt. The march to Moscow 1606-1607. The rebels were finally defeated at Tula

▨ Principal area of the peasants' revolt led by Bolotnikov

▨ Uprising of non-Slav tribes, the Chuvash, Mary and Mordva

⇐ Cossack attack on Moscow led by a false claimant to the throne

0   100

Miles

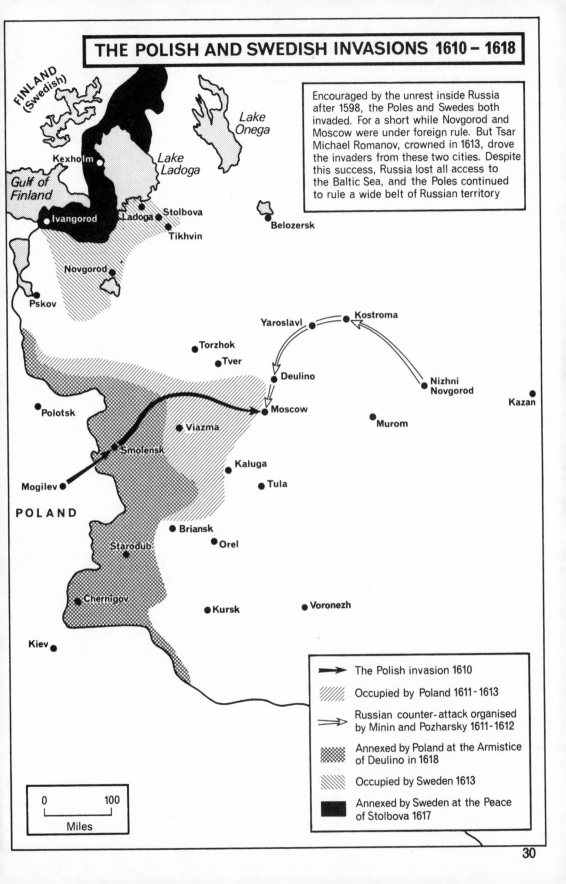

THE POLISH AND SWEDISH INVASIONS 1610 – 1618

FINLAND
(Swedish)

Lake
Onega

Lake
Ladoga

Gulf of
Finland

Kexholm

Ivangorod
Ladoga Stolbova
Tikhvin

Belozersk

Novgorod

Pskov

Encouraged by the unrest inside Russia
after 1598, the Poles and Swedes both
invaded. For a short while Novgorod and
Moscow were under foreign rule. But Tsar
Michael Romanov, crowned in 1613, drove
the invaders from these two cities. Despite
this success, Russia lost all access to
the Baltic Sea, and the Poles continued
to rule a wide belt of Russian territory

Yaroslavl   Kostroma

Torzhok
Tver

Deulino

Nizhni
Novgorod

Kazan

Polotsk

Viazma   Moscow

Murom

Smolensk

Kaluga

Mogilev

Tula

POLAND

Briansk

Starodub   Orel

Chernigov

Kursk   Voronezh

Kiev

	The Polish invasion 1610
	Occupied by Poland 1611 - 1613
	Russian counter-attack organised by Minin and Pozharsky 1611-1612
	Annexed by Poland at the Armistice of Deulino in 1618
	Occupied by Sweden 1613
	Annexed by Sweden at the Peace of Stolbova 1617

0   100

Miles

THE WESTWARD EXPANSION OF RUSSIA 1640–1667

Western Russia in 1640

Cossack revolt of 1648 against Polish landowners and gentry. The revolt was led by Bogdan Khmelnitski. After defeating the Polish army, the Cossacks joined with the Polish peasantry, murdering over 100,000 Jews

Towns in which Jews were murdered by Cossacks and Poles 1648–1652

Advance of Russian and Ukrainian forces against the Poles 1654–1655

Polish territory ceded to Russia at the Armistice of Andrusovo in 1667

Baltic Sea

PRUSSIA

LITHUANIA

Moscow

Nevel

Polotsk

Vitebsk

Viazma

Smolensk

Andrusovo

Königsberg

Kovno

Vilna

Orsha

Borisov

Grodno

Minsk

Mogilev

WHITE RUSSIA

Briansk

Orel

Wa saw

Gomel

Starodub

Kursk

PCLAND

Brest-Litovsk

Pinsk

Mozyr

Turov

Chernigov

Lublin

Pripet Marshes

WESTERN UKRAINE

EASTERN UKRAINE

Belgorod

Kovel

Zamosc

Berestechke

Lutsk

Rovno

Zhitomir

Kiev

Kharkov

Przemysl

Belz

Lvov

Pereyaslavl

Poltava

Carpathians

Zbarazh

Kamenets

Bar

Vinnitsa

Korsun

Kodak

HUNGARY

ZAPOROZHE

Sech

OTTOMAN EMPIRE

CRIMEAN KHANATE

Haji-bey

0   100
Miles

SOCIAL UNREST 1648 and 1670

In 1648 uprisings took place in many of the principal Russian towns. As a result, a new code of laws was drawn up, protecting the rights of traders and town-dwellers. In 1670 a Don Cossack, Stenka Razin, led a widespread revolt of Cossacks, peasants, small traders, minor officials and the dispossessed of the Volga, Don and Donets river valleys. The revolt was crushed in 1671 and Razin broken on the wheel in Moscow.

Kargopol

Solvychegodsk

Veliki Ustiug

Cherdin

Olonets

Solikamsk

Totma

Gdov

Novgorod

Pskov

Ostrov

Romanov

Volga

Vladimir

Ruza

Moscow

Yadrin

Koslov

Simbirsk

Penza

Donets

Tambov

Samara

Kursk

Voronezh

Saratov

Don

Tsaritsyn

DON COSSACKS

Gurev

Sea of Azov

Astrakhan

Caspian Sea

Terski Gorodok

Black Sea

⊙ Urban uprisings of 1648-1650

■ The peasants' revolt led by Stenka Razin 1670-1671

— The Russian frontier in 1670

| 0 | 500 |

Miles

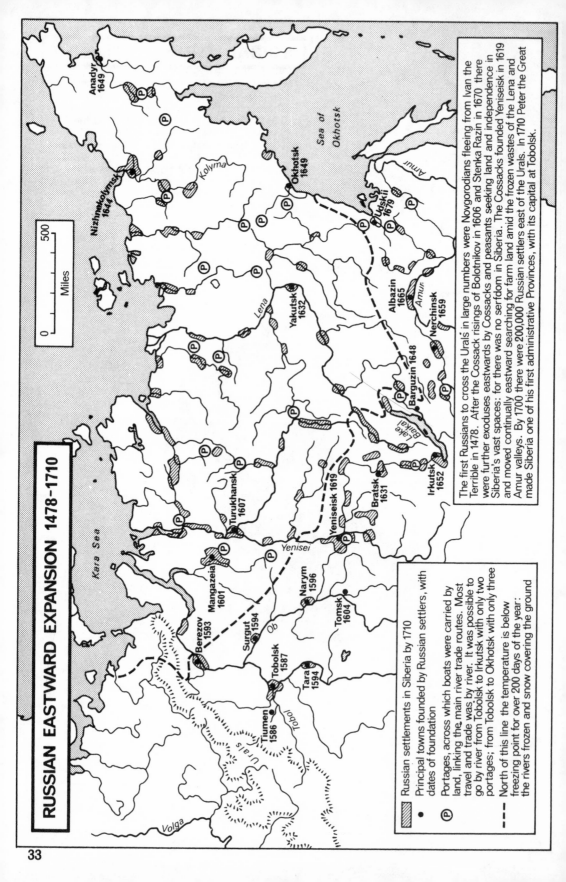

RUSSIAN EASTWARD EXPANSION 1478–1710

Sea of Okhotsk

Kara Sea

Lake Baikal

Kolyma

Lena

Amur

Yenisei

Ob

Tobol

Urals

Volga

Anadyr 1649

Nizhnekolymsk 1644

Okhotsk 1649

Udskii 1679

Albazin 1665

Nerchinsk 1659

Barguzin 1648

Irkutsk 1652

Bratsk 1631

Yakutsk 1632

Turukhansk 1607

Yeniseisk 1619

Mangazeia 1601

Narym 1596

Tomsk 1604

Berezov 1593

Surgut 1594

Tobolsk 1587

Tara 1594

Tyumen 1586

500

Miles

0

The first Russians to cross the Urals in large numbers were Novgorodians fleeing from Ivan the Terrible in 1478. After the Cossack risings of Bolotnikov in 1606 and Stenka Razin in 1670 there were further exoduses eastwards by Cossacks and peasants seeking land and independence in Siberia's vast spaces; for there was no serfdom in Siberia. The Cossacks founded Yeniseisk in 1619 and moved continually eastward searching for farm land amid the frozen wastes of the Lena and Amur valleys. By 1700 there were 200,000 Russian settlers east of the Urals. In 1710 Peter the Great made Siberia one of his first administrative Provinces, with its capital at Tobolsk.

Russian settlements in Siberia by 1710

● Principal towns founded by Russian settlers, with dates of foundation

Ⓟ Portages, across which boats were carried by land, linking the main river trade routes. Most travel and trade was by river. It was possible to go by river from Tobolsk to Irkutsk with only two portages; from Tobolsk to Okhotsk with only three

– – – North of this line the temperature is below freezing point for over 200 days of the year: the rivers frozen and snow covering the ground

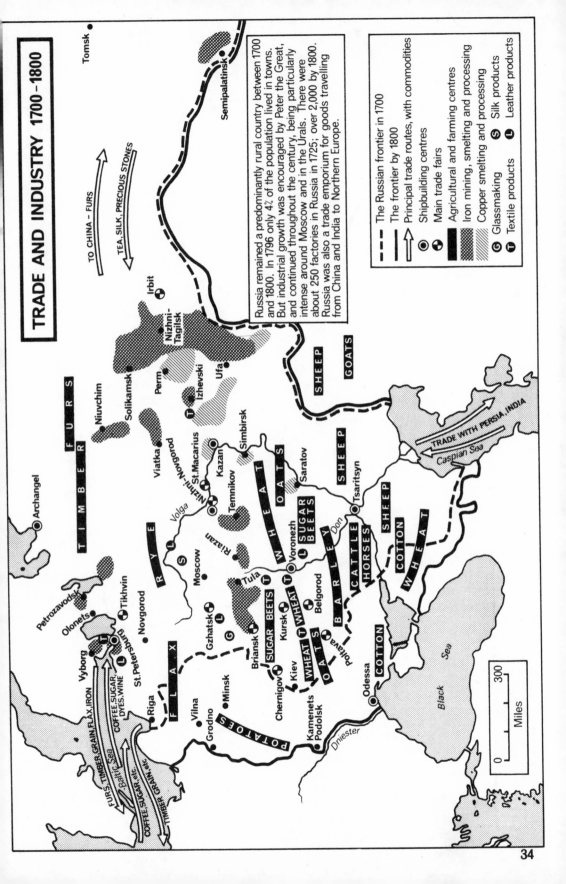

TRADE AND INDUSTRY 1700–1800

Russia remained a predominantly rural country between 1700 and 1800. In 1796 only 4% of the population lived in towns. But industrial growth was encouraged by Peter the Great, and continued throughout the century, being particularly intense around Moscow and in the Urals. There were about 250 factories in Russia in 1725; over 2,000 by 1800. Russia was also a trade emporium for goods travelling from China and India to Northern Europe.

Legend:
- The Russian frontier in 1700
- The frontier by 1800
- Principal trade routes, with commodities
- Shipbuilding centres
- Main trade fairs
- Agricultural and farming centres
- Iron mining, smelting and processing
- Copper smelting and processing
- Textile products
- Silk products
- Leather products
- G Glassmaking
- T Textile products
- S Silk products
- L Leather products

TO CHINA – FURS

TEA, SILK, PRECIOUS STONES

TRADE WITH PERSIA, INDIA

Caspian Sea

Black Sea

Baltic Sea

FURS, TIMBER, GRAIN, FLAX, IRON
COFFEE, SUGAR, DYES, WINE
COFFEE, SUGAR, etc.
TIMBER, GRAIN, etc.
COFFEE, SUGAR, etc.

Tomsk

Semipalatinsk

Irbit

Nizhni-Tagilsk

Niuvchim

Solikamsk

Perm

Izhevski

Ufa

Viatka

Simbirsk

Archangel

Kazan

St.Macarius

Nizhni-Novgorod

Temnikov

Saratov

Saratov

Tsaritsyn

Petrozavodsk

Olonets

Tikhvin

Novgorod

Vyborg

St.Petersburg

Riga

Vilna

Grodno

Minsk

Gzhatsk

Moscow

Riazan

Tula

Voronezh

Belgorod

Poltava

Brian sk

Kursk

Kiev

Chernigov

Kamenets Podolsk

Odessa

Volga

Don

Dniester

TIMBER

FURS

RYE

FLAX

POTATOES

WHEAT

OATS

SUGAR BEETS

WHEAT

BARLEY

CATTLE HORSES

SHEEP

SHEEP

SHEEP

GOATS

COTTON

COTTON

WHEAT

OATS

SUGAR BEETS

Miles
0   300

34

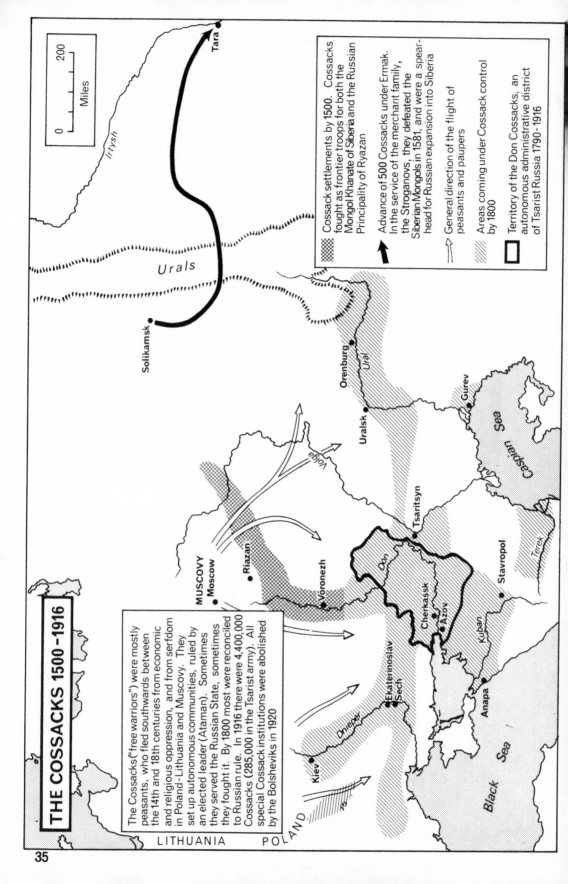

THE COSSACKS 1500–1916

The Cossacks ("free warriors") were mostly peasants, who fled southwards between the 14th and 18th centuries from economic and religious oppression, and from serfdom in Poland-Lithuania and Muscovy. They set up autonomous communities, ruled by an elected leader (Ataman). Sometimes they served the Russian State, sometimes they fought it. By 1800 most were reconciled to Russian rule. In 1916 there were 4,400,000 Cossacks (285,000 in the Tsarist army). All special Cossack institutions were abolished by the Bolsheviks in 1920

Cossack settlements by 1500. Cossacks fought as frontier troops for both the Mongol Khanate of Siberia and the Russian Principality of Ryazan

Advance of 500 Cossacks under Ermak. In the service of the merchant family, the Stroganovs, they defeated the Siberian Mongols in 1581, and were a spear-head for Russian expansion into Siberia

General direction of the flight of peasants and paupers

Areas coming under Cossack control by 1800

Territory of the Don Cossacks, an autonomous administrative district of Tsarist Russia 1790–1916

Miles
0   200

Tara
Irtysh
Urals
Solikamsk
Orenburg
Ural
Gurev
Caspian Sea
Uralsk
Tsaritsyn
Volga
MUSCOVY
Moscow
Riazan
Voronezh
Don
Cherkassk
Azov
Stavropol
Terek
Ekaterinoslav
Sech
Kuban
Anapa
Kiev
Dnieper
Black Sea
LITHUANIA
POLAND

35

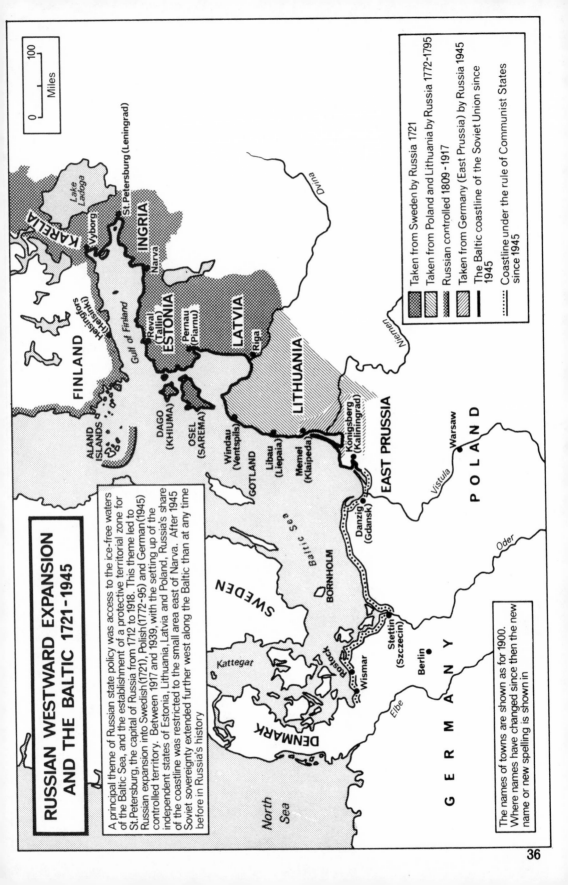

RUSSIAN WESTWARD EXPANSION AND THE BALTIC 1721-1945

A principal theme of Russian state policy was access to the ice-free waters of the Baltic Sea, and the establishment of a protective territorial zone for St.Petersburg, the capital of Russia from 1712 to 1918. This theme led to Russian expansion into Swedish (1721), Polish (1772-95) and German (1945) controlled territory. Between 1917 and 1939, with the setting up of the independent states of Estonia, Lithuania, Latvia and Poland, Russia's share of the coastline was restricted to the small area east of Narva. After 1945 Soviet sovereignty extended further west along the Baltic than at any time before in Russia's history

The names of towns are shown as for 1900. Where names have changed since then the new name or new spelling is shown in

Taken from Sweden by Russia 1721

Taken from Poland and Lithuania by Russia 1772-1795

Russian controlled 1809 - 1917

Taken from Germany (East Prussia) by Russia 1945

The Baltic coastline of the Soviet Union since 1945

Coastline under the rule of Communist States since 1945

North Sea

Kattegat

DENMARK

SWEDEN

FINLAND

Lake Ladoga

KARELIA

Helsingfors (Helsinki)

Vyborg

St. Petersburg (Leningrad)

INGRIA

Narva

Gulf of Finland

ALAND ISLANDS

Reval (Tallin)

ESTONIA

Pernau (Piarnu)

DAGO (KHIUMA)

OSEL (SAREMA)

LATVIA

Riga

Dvina

GOTLAND

Windau (Ventspils)

Libau (Liepaia)

LITHUANIA

Memel (Klaipeda)

Königsberg (Kaliningrad)

EAST PRUSSIA

Niemen

Baltic Sea

BORNHOLM

Danzig (Gdansk)

Vistula

Warsaw

POLAND

Rostock

Wismar

Stettin (Szczecin)

Oder

Berlin

G E R M A N Y

Elbe

Miles
0   100

36

Section Two

IMPERIAL RUSSIA

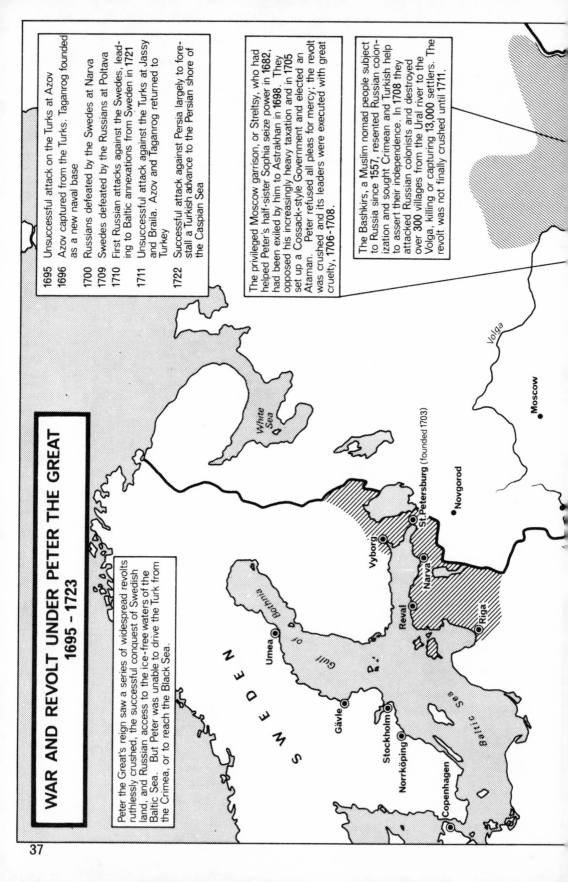

WAR AND REVOLT UNDER PETER THE GREAT
1695 – 1723

Peter the Great's reign saw a series of widespread revolts ruthlessly crushed, the successful conquest of Swedish land, and Russian access to the ice-free waters of the Baltic Sea. But Peter was unable to drive the Turk from the Crimea, or to reach the Black Sea.

1695   Unsuccessful attack on the Turks at Azov
1696   Azov captured from the Turks. Taganrog founded as a new naval base
1700   Russians defeated by the Swedes at Narva
1709   Swedes defeated by the Russians at Poltava
1710   First Russian attacks against the Swedes, leading to Baltic annexations from Sweden in 1721
1711   Unsuccessful attack against the Turks at Jassy and Braila. Azov and Taganrog returned to Turkey
1722   Successful attack against Persia largely to forestall a Turkish advance to the Persian shore of the Caspian Sea

The privileged Moscow garrison, or Streltsy, who had helped Peter's half-sister Sophia seize power in 1682, had been exiled by him to Astrakhan in 1698. They opposed his increasingly heavy taxation and in 1705 set up a Cossack-style Government and elected an Ataman. Peter refused all pleas for mercy; the revolt was crushed and its leaders were executed with great cruelty, 1706-1708.

The Bashkirs, a Muslim nomad people subject to Russia since 1557, resented Russian colonization and sought Crimean and Turkish help to assert their independence. In 1708 they attacked Russian colonists and destroyed over 300 villages from the Ural river to the Volga, killing or capturing 13,000 settlers. The revolt was not finally crushed until 1711.

White Sea

Volga

Moscow

St.Petersburg (founded 1703)

Novgorod

Vyborg

Narva

Reval

Riga

S W E D E N

Gulf of Bothnia

Baltic Sea

Umeå

Gävle

Stockholm

Norrköping

Copenhagen

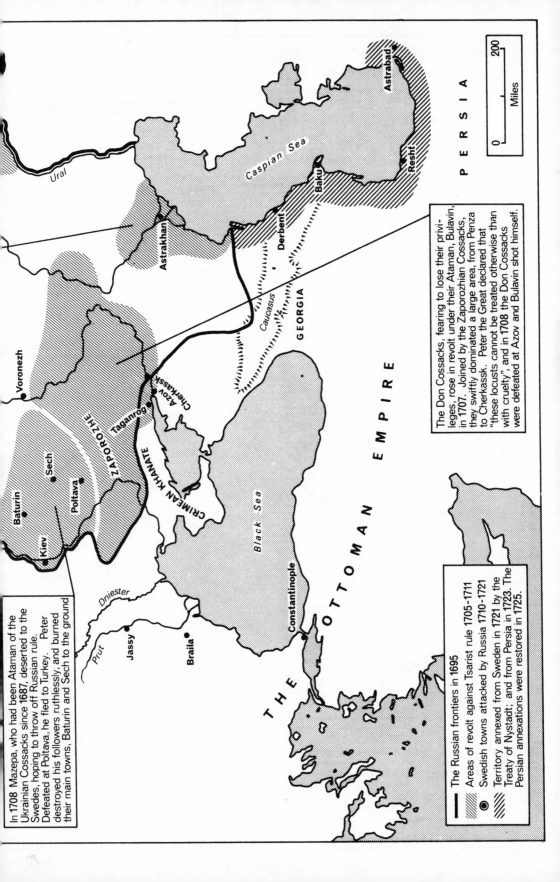

In 1708 Mazepa, who had been Ataman of the Ukrainian Cossacks since 1687, deserted to the Swedes, hoping to throw off Russian rule. Peter Defeated at Poltava, he fled to Turkey. Peter destroyed his followers ruthlessly, and burned their main towns, Baturin and Sech to the ground.

The Don Cossacks, fearing to lose their privileges, rose in revolt under their Ataman, Bulavin, in 1707. Joined by the Zaporozhian Cossacks, they swiftly dominated a large area, from Penza to Cherkassk. Peter the Great declared that "these locusts cannot be treated otherwise than with cruelty", and in 1708 the Don Cossacks were defeated at Azov and Bulavin shot himself.

The Russian frontiers in 1695

///// Areas of revolt against Tsarist rule 1705-1711

⊙ Swedish towns attacked by Russia 1710-1721

\\\\ Territory annexed from Sweden in 1721 by the Treaty of Nystadt; and from Persia in 1723. The Persian annexations were restored in 1725.

PERSIA

Caspian Sea

Astrabad
Resht
Baku
Derbent
GEORGIA
Caucasus
Astrakhan
Ural

Voronezh
Baturin
Sech
Kiev
Poltava
ZAPOROZHE
Taganrog
Azov
Cherkassk
CRIMEAN KHANATE

Black Sea

Constantinople

THE OTTOMAN EMPIRE

Jassy
Braila
Dniester
Prut

200
0   Miles

THE PROVINCES AND POPULATION OF RUSSIA IN 1724

0   300

Miles

St. Petersburg

Selected as the site of a new town by Peter the Great in 1703, and built at great cost in human life by serf labour, St. Petersburg became the seat of the Russian Government in 1712. Courtiers and noble families were compelled by law to live there from 1725. The city had a population of 200,000 by 1788.

White Sea

Archangel

A R C H A N G E L

Dvina

S I B E R I A

Gulf of Finland

St. Petersburg

Novgorod

Pskov

S T .   P E T E R S B U R G

Vologda

Viatka

Perm

Kostroma

Tver

Volga

Kazan

Moscow

Nizhni Novgorod

K A Z A N

Smolensk

M O S C O W

Simbirsk

Mogilev

Riazan

Samara

SMOLENSK

Tula

Orenburg

Dnieper

Orel

Tambov

Penza

Chernigov

Saratov

C O S S A C K S

Ural

K I E V

A Z O V

Voronezh

Kiev

Poltava

Kharkov

Don

Dniester

Volga

C O S S A C K S

Azov

Caspian Sea

Black Sea

COSSACKS

COSSACKS

It was Peter the Great who first divided Russia into Provinces (known as "Gubernii" or "Governments"). These administrative divisions served a military, financial and judicial purpose. They enabled Peter to supervise the whole kingdom by means of Governors responsible directly to himself. Catherine the Great later divided these Provinces into smaller units. The establishment of Provincial administrations led to a rapid growth of bureaucracy, and a complex hierarchy of local seniority. The population of Russia in 1724 was just over 15 million, of whom only ½ million lived in towns.

–·– Russia's frontiers by 1725

▬ Provinces established by Peter the Great

▨ Area with over 20 inhabitants in every square verst. (One verst=two-thirds of a mile)

▧ Area with between 10 and 20 inhabitants per square verst

Russian territory with less than 10 inhabitants per square verst is not shaded

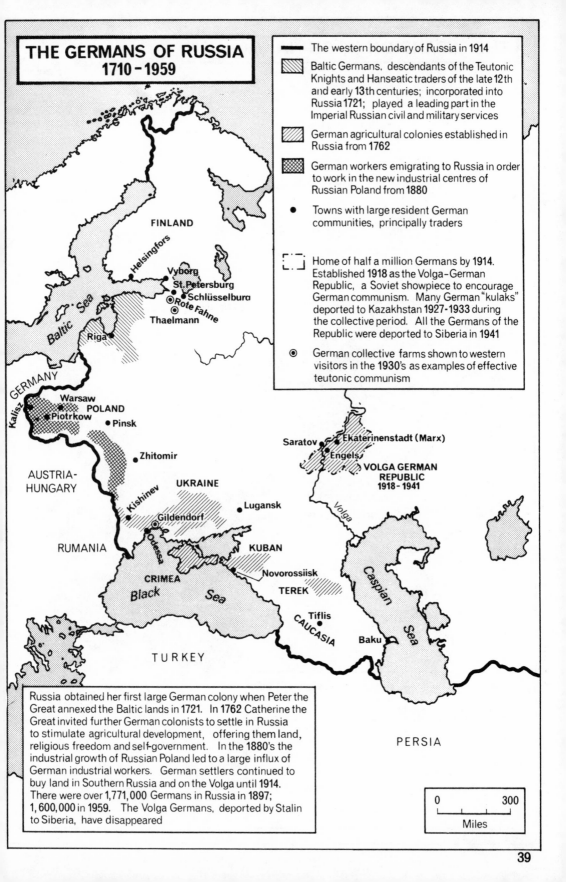

THE GERMANS OF RUSSIA
1710 - 1959

The western boundary of Russia in 1914

Baltic Germans, descendants of the Teutonic Knights and Hanseatic traders of the late 12th and early 13th centuries; incorporated into Russia 1721; played a leading part in the Imperial Russian civil and military services

German agricultural colonies established in Russia from 1762

German workers emigrating to Russia in order to work in the new industrial centres of Russian Poland from 1880

Towns with large resident German communities, principally traders

Home of half a million Germans by 1914. Established 1918 as the Volga-German Republic, a Soviet showpiece to encourage German communism. Many German "kulaks" deported to Kazakhstan 1927-1933 during the collective period. All the Germans of the Republic were deported to Siberia in 1941

German collective farms shown to western visitors in the 1930's as examples of effective teutonic communism

FINLAND

Helsingfors
Vyborg
St. Petersburg
Rote Fahne
Schlüsselburg
Thaelmann
Riga

Baltic Sea

GERMANY

Kalisz
Warsaw
POLAND
Piotrkow
Pinsk
Zhitomir

AUSTRIA-HUNGARY

Saratov
Ekaterinenstadt (Marx)
Engels
VOLGA GERMAN REPUBLIC
1918 - 1941

UKRAINE
Kishinev
Lugansk
Gildendorf
Odessa
KUBAN
Novorossiisk
TEREK

Volga

RUMANIA

CRIMEA
Black   Sea

Caspian Sea

Tiflis
CAUCASIA
Baku

TURKEY

PERSIA

Russia obtained her first large German colony when Peter the Great annexed the Baltic lands in 1721. In 1762 Catherine the Great invited further German colonists to settle in Russia to stimulate agricultural development, offering them land, religious freedom and self-government. In the 1880's the industrial growth of Russian Poland led to a large influx of German industrial workers. German settlers continued to buy land in Southern Russia and on the Volga until 1914. There were over 1,771,000 Germans in Russia in 1897; 1,600,000 in 1959. The Volga Germans, deported by Stalin to Siberia, have disappeared

0   300
Miles

THE EXPANSION OF CHINA 1720–1760

THE

RUSSIAN

EMPIRE

○ Okhotsk

○ Yakutsk

U r a l s

○ Tobolsk

○ Yeniseisk

Tomsk ○   ○ Krasnoyarsk   Nerchinsk ○   ● Albazin

Omsk ○   Irkutsk ○   *Lake Baikal*   ● Harbin

Amur

Semipalatinsk ○   ● Maimachin

Ustkamenogorsk ○

M O N G O L S

Lake Balkhash

Kulja ●   ● Hami   ● Peking

Urumchi

DOMINIONS OF THE   Nanking ○
ZUNGAR KALMUKS

Yarkand ●   Sian ○

Khotan ●   C H I N A

Chengtu ○

H i m a l a y a s   T I B E T   Canton ●

Lhasa ●   Yunnan ○

○ Cities founded by the Russians before 1720

■ The Chinese Empire in 1720, ruled by the Manchu Dynasty

▨ Under Chinese control by 1720, providing the Manchus with a reservoir of military power

▨ Conquered by China between 1724 and 1764

▨ Conquered by China in 1780

0   500
Miles

40

RUSSIAN EXPANSION UNDER CATHERINE THE GREAT 1762–1796

The Provinces of Russia in 1750

Territory annexed by Russia 1762-1796, giving Russia an outlet on the Black Sea, and a common frontier with Prussia and Austria

White Sea

Archangel

ARCHANGEL

FINLAND

Helsingfors

Baltic Sea

ESTONIA

LIVONIA

ST. PETERSBURG

Novgorod

NOVGOROD

Vologda

Viatka

Perm

Pskov

KURLAND

Tver

KAZAN

PRUSSIA

Vilna

LITHUANIA

Minsk

SMOLENSK

MOSCOW

Moscow

NIZHNI NOVGOROD

Kazan

Ufa

Niemen

WHITE RUSSIA

UFA

Warsaw

Pinsk

BELGOROD

Orel

Stavropol

Samara

AUSTRIA

PODLESIA

Lutsk

KIEV

Kiev

VORONEZH

Belgorod

Dniester

PODOLIA

Dnieper

ASTRAKHAN

Jassy

ZAPOROZHE

Odessa

Taganrog

Astrakhan

Kutchuk Kainardji

CRIMEA

KUBAN

Caspian Sea

Sebastopol

KABARDA

Tarki

Black Sea

THE

Constantinople

OTTOMAN

EMPIRE

Kars

0   200

Miles

PERSIA

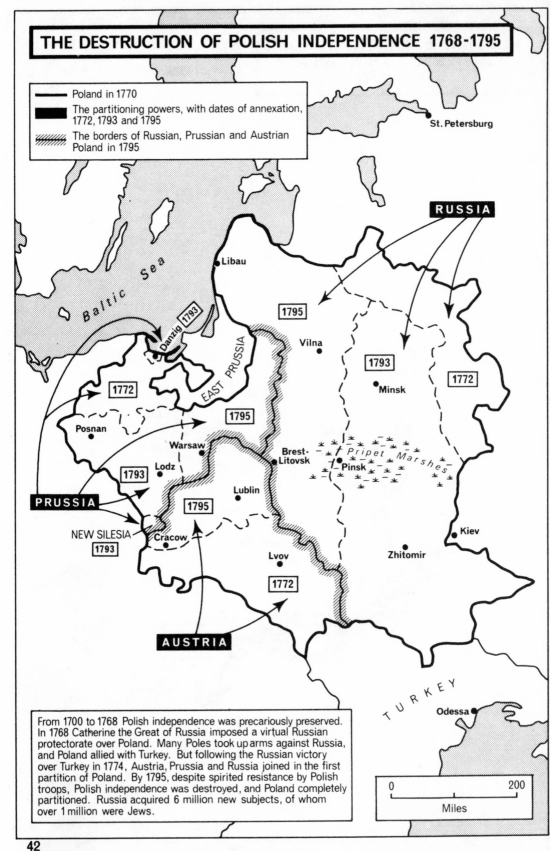

THE DESTRUCTION OF POLISH INDEPENDENCE 1768-1795

Poland in 1770

The partitioning powers, with dates of annexation, 1772, 1793 and 1795

The borders of Russian, Prussian and Austrian Poland in 1795

St. Petersburg

Baltic Sea

Libau

RUSSIA

1795

Danzig 1793

EAST PRUSSIA

1772

Vilna

1793

Minsk

1772

1795

Posnan

Warsaw

Brest-Litovsk

Pripet Marshes

Pinsk

1793

Lodz

Lublin

Kiev

PRUSSIA

1793

1795

Zhitomir

NEW SILESIA

1793

Cracow

Lvov

1772

AUSTRIA

TURKEY

Odessa

From 1700 to 1768 Polish independence was precariously preserved. In 1768 Catherine the Great of Russia imposed a virtual Russian protectorate over Poland. Many Poles took up arms against Russia, and Poland allied with Turkey. But following the Russian victory over Turkey in 1774, Austria, Prussia and Russia joined in the first partition of Poland. By 1795, despite spirited resistance by Polish troops, Polish independence was destroyed, and Poland completely partitioned. Russia acquired 6 million new subjects, of whom over 1 million were Jews.

0   200

Miles

THE RUSSIAN ANNEXATIONS OF POLAND 1772-1795

Baltic Sea

LATVIA

• Pskov

0   150
Miles

• Windau

Riga

• Libau
• Mitau

Dvinsk •

• Nevel

• Palanga

• Memel

• Polotsk

Dvina

LITHUANIA

Königsberg •

Kovno •

[1795]

⊙ Vilna

Vitebsk •

Smolensk •

EAST
PRUSSIA

Suvalki •

Troki •

[1793]

[1772]

Borisov •

Orsha •

Lida •

Mogilev •

• Mstislav

• Minsk

Grodno •
Novogrudok •

Mir ⊙

WHITE
RUSSIA

Dnieper

Vilkoviski ⊙

Baranovichi ⊙

Bobruisk •

Bialystok •

Slutsk •

PRUSSIAN-ANNEXED POLAND

Warsaw •

⊙⊙
Brest-Litovsk
⊙

Pinsk •

Pripet   Marshes

Gomel •

• Starodub

Pripet

Turov •

Mozyr •

Lublin •

⊙ Kovel

Olevsk •

• Chernigov

AUSTRIAN-ANNEXED
POLAND

VOLHYNIA
Lutsk •

WESTERN

UKRAINE

Lvov •

Rovno •

Zhitomir •

Kiev •

Dubno •

• Pereyaslavl

Przemysl •

GALICIA

Tarnopol •

⊙
Staro-
Konstantinov

⊙

Berdychev •

Boguslav •

Dnieper

Vinnitsa •

Stanislavov •

PODOLIA

Kamenets-
Podolsk

BESSARABIA

AUSTRIA

Dniester

Bug

Balta •

TURKEY

RUSSIAN-
ANNEXED

Kherson •

1791
Odessa

TURKEY

1774

Dnieper

*Black
Sea*

░░ The western part of Russia in 1770
--- Partition lines
⊙ Principal Polish military resistance
   to the Russians
━━ The western frontier of Russia 1795

43

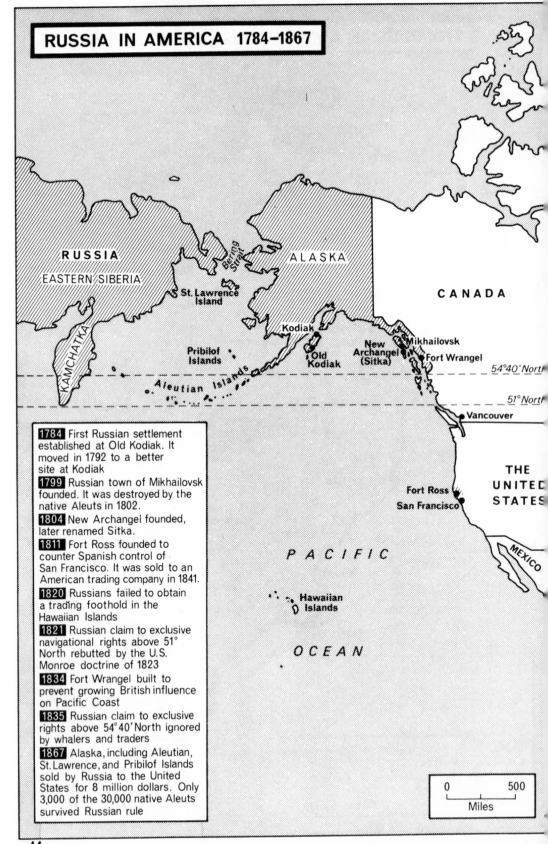

RUSSIA IN AMERICA 1784–1867

RUSSIA

EASTERN SIBERIA

KAMCHATKA

Bering Strait

St. Lawrence Island

ALASKA

CANADA

Kodiak

Pribilof Islands

Old Kodiak

New Archangel (Sitka)

Mikhailovsk

Fort Wrangel

54°40' North

Aleutian Islands

51° North

Vancouver

THE UNITED STATES

Fort Ross

San Francisco

PACIFIC

MEXICO

Hawaiian Islands

OCEAN

1784 First Russian settlement established at Old Kodiak. It moved in 1792 to a better site at Kodiak

1799 Russian town of Mikhailovsk founded. It was destroyed by the native Aleuts in 1802.

1804 New Archangel founded, later renamed Sitka.

1811 Fort Ross founded to counter Spanish control of San Francisco. It was sold to an American trading company in 1841.

1820 Russians failed to obtain a trading foothold in the Hawaiian Islands

1821 Russian claim to exclusive navigational rights above 51° North rebutted by the U.S. Monroe doctrine of 1823

1834 Fort Wrangel built to prevent growing British influence on Pacific Coast

1835 Russian claim to exclusive rights above 54°40'North ignored by whalers and traders

1867 Alaska, including Aleutian, St. Lawrence, and Pribilof Islands sold by Russia to the United States for 8 million dollars. Only 3,000 of the 30,000 native Aleuts survived Russian rule

0   500

Miles

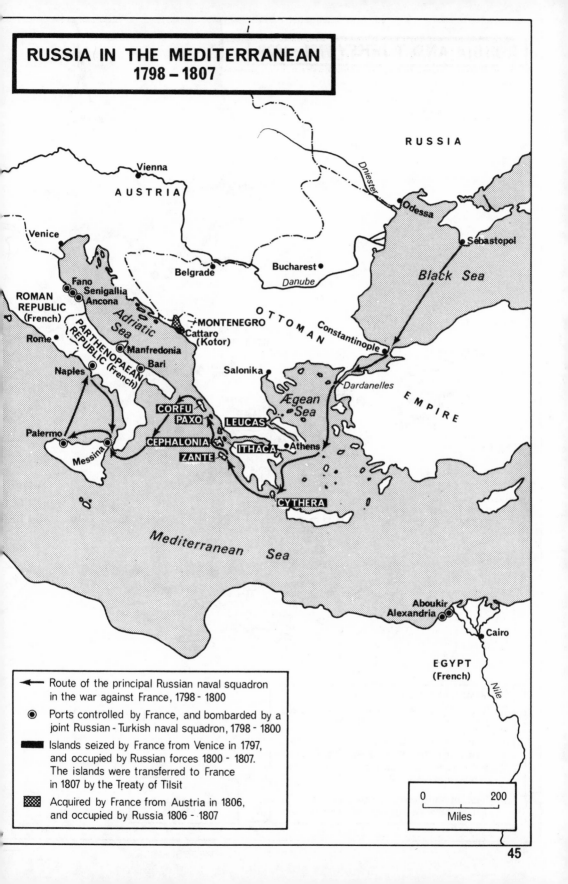

RUSSIA IN THE MEDITERRANEAN
1798 – 1807

RUSSIA

Vienna

AUSTRIA

Venice

Odessa

Sebastopol

Belgrade

Bucharest

Danube

Black Sea

ROMAN
REPUBLIC
(French)

Fano
Senigallia
Ancona

MONTENEGRO
Cattaro
(Kotor)

Rome

Manfredonia

Bari

Salonika

Constantinople

Naples

Dardanelles

EMPIRE

CORFU
PAXO

LEUCAS

Palermo

Messina

CEPHALONIA

ZANTE

ITHACA

Athens

Ægean
Sea

CYTHERA

Adriatic Sea

PARTHENOPAEAN REPUBLIC (French)

Mediterranean Sea

OTTOMAN

Dniester

Aboukir
Alexandria

Cairo

EGYPT
(French)

Nile

Route of the principal Russian naval squadron
in the war against France, 1798 - 1800

Ports controlled by France, and bombarded by a
joint Russian - Turkish naval squadron, 1798 - 1800

Islands seized by France from Venice in 1797,
and occupied by Russian forces 1800 - 1807.
The islands were transferred to France
in 1807 by the Treaty of Tilsit

Acquired by France from Austria in 1806,
and occupied by Russia 1806 - 1807

0   200
Miles

45

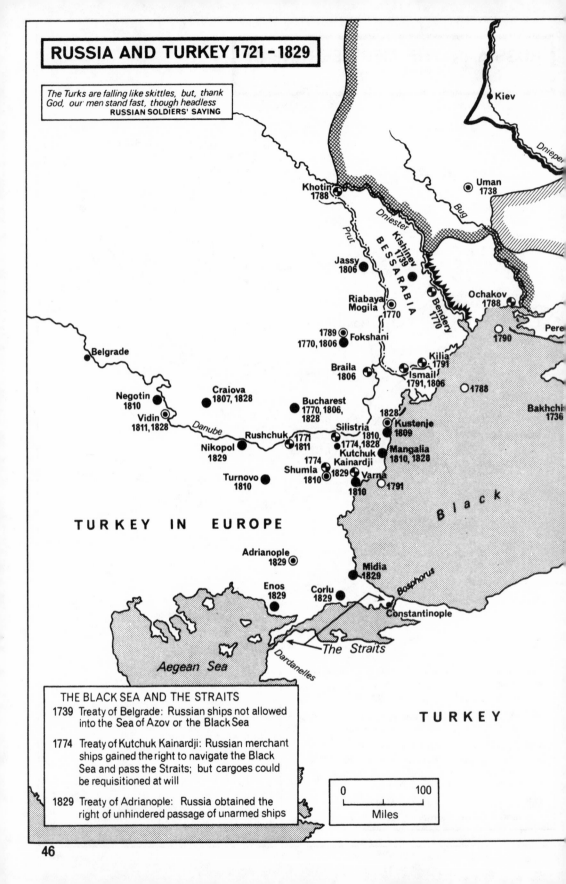

RUSSIA AND TURKEY 1721-1829

The Turks are falling like skittles, but, thank God, our men stand fast, though headless
RUSSIAN SOLDIERS' SAYING

Kiev

Dnieper

Khotin
1788

Dniester

Uman
1738

BESSARABIA

Kishinev
1739

Jassy
1806

Bug

Riabaya
Mogila
1770

Bendery
1770

Ochakov
1788

Pere

1790

1789 Fokshani
1770, 1806

Kilia
1791

Belgrade

Braila
1806

Ismail
1791, 1806

Bakhchi
1736

Negotin
1810

Craiova
1807, 1828

Bucharest
1770, 1806,
1828

1828

1788

Vidin
1811, 1828

Danube

Rushchuk
1771
1811

Silistria
1810,
1774, 1828

Kustenje
1809

Nikopol
1829

Kutchuk
Kainardji

Mangalia
1810, 1828

1774
Shumla
1810

1829 Varna
1810

1791

Turnovo
1810

TURKEY   IN   EUROPE

Black

Adrianople
1829

Midia
1829

Bosphorus

Enos
1829

Corlu
1829

Constantinople

Dardanelles

The Straits

Aegean Sea

TURKEY

THE BLACK SEA AND THE STRAITS

1739 Treaty of Belgrade: Russian ships not allowed
into the Sea of Azov or the Black Sea

1774 Treaty of Kutchuk Kainardji: Russian merchant
ships gained the right to navigate the Black
Sea and pass the Straits; but cargoes could
be requisitioned at will

1829 Treaty of Adrianople: Russia obtained the
right of unhindered passage of unarmed ships

0   100

Miles

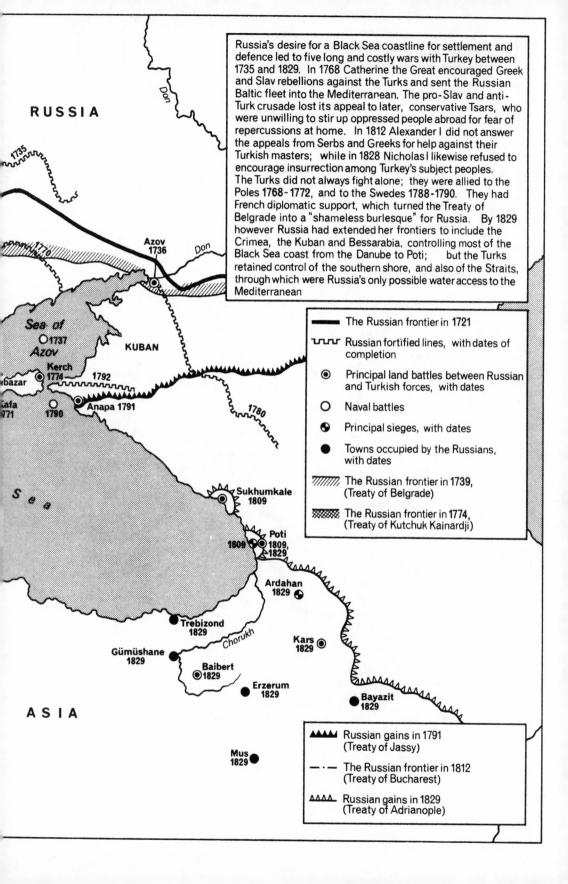

Russia's desire for a Black Sea coastline for settlement and defence led to five long and costly wars with Turkey between 1735 and 1829. In 1768 Catherine the Great encouraged Greek and Slav rebellions against the Turks and sent the Russian Baltic fleet into the Mediterranean. The pro-Slav and anti-Turk crusade lost its appeal to later, conservative Tsars, who were unwilling to stir up oppressed people abroad for fear of repercussions at home. In 1812 Alexander I did not answer the appeals from Serbs and Greeks for help against their Turkish masters; while in 1828 Nicholas I likewise refused to encourage insurrection among Turkey's subject peoples.
The Turks did not always fight alone; they were allied to the Poles 1768-1772, and to the Swedes 1788-1790. They had French diplomatic support, which turned the Treaty of Belgrade into a "shameless burlesque" for Russia. By 1829 however Russia had extended her frontiers to include the Crimea, the Kuban and Bessarabia, controlling most of the Black Sea coast from the Danube to Poti; but the Turks retained control of the southern shore, and also of the Straits, through which were Russia's only possible water access to the Mediterranean

RUSSIA

Don

1735

Azov 1736

Don

1770

Sea of Azov
1737

KUBAN

Kerch 1774

1792

bazar

afa 1771

1790

Anapa 1791

1780

Sea

Sukhumkale 1809

Poti
1809 1809, 1829

Ardahan 1829

Trebizond 1829

Chorukh

Kars 1829

Gümüshane 1829

Baibert 1829

Erzerum 1829

Bayazit 1829

ASIA

Mus 1829

Legend:

— The Russian frontier in 1721

ᴜᴜᴜ Russian fortified lines, with dates of completion

◉ Principal land battles between Russian and Turkish forces, with dates

○ Naval battles

✚ Principal sieges, with dates

● Towns occupied by the Russians, with dates

▨ The Russian frontier in 1739, (Treaty of Belgrade)

▨ The Russian frontier in 1774, (Treaty of Kutchuk Kainardji)

▲▲▲ Russian gains in 1791 (Treaty of Jassy)

—·— The Russian frontier in 1812 (Treaty of Bucharest)

△△△ Russian gains in 1829 (Treaty of Adrianople)

RUSSIA AND SWEDEN 1700-1809

0 — 300
Miles

From 1621 Sweden controlled the Baltic Sea and the Gulfs of Finland and Bothnia. In 1700 Peter the Great allied Russia with Poland and Denmark, in 1714 with Prussia and Hanover. His first conquest was Ingria, giving Russia a small but valued outlet on the Baltic. After several defeats, the Russians finally broke Sweden's dominance in 1721. Russia's annexation of Finland in 1809 further extended her control of the Baltic.

LAPLAND

Tornea

Uleaborg

Gulf of Bothnia

S W E D E N

Vasa

F I N L A N D

KARELIA

Kexholm

Helsingfors

Vyborg

Nystad
Abo

Noteborg
St.Petersburg

ALAND IS.

Gulf of Finland

Narva

INGRIA

DAGÖ

Reval

Ivangorod

Novgorod

ESTLAND

Stockholm

ÖSEL

Dorpat

Pskov

GOTLAND

LIVLAND

Riga

Baltic Sea

DENMARK

Copenhagen

POLAND

Stralsund

BORNHOLM

SWEDISH
POMERANIA

Stettin

HANOVER

PRUSSIA

Sweden in 1700

Swedish territory conquered by Peter the Great during the Great Northern War 1700-1721, and annexed to Russia at the Treaty of Nystad 1721

Conquered by Russia, 1743

Swedish territory conquered by Alexander I and annexed to Russia in 1809

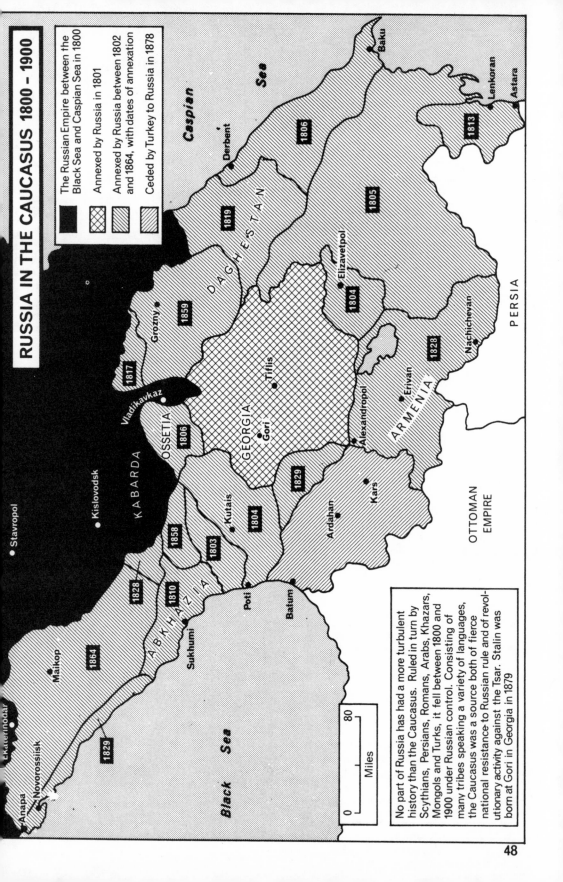

RUSSIA IN THE CAUCASUS 1800 – 1900

The Russian Empire between the Black Sea and Caspian Sea in 1800

Annexed by Russia in 1801

Annexed by Russia between 1802 and 1864, with dates of annexation

Ceded by Turkey to Russia in 1878

Caspian Sea

Baku

Lenkoran
Astara
1813

Derbent
1806

1805

1819

DAGHESTAN

Elizavetpol
1804

Grozny
1859

Nachichevan

1817

PERSIA

Vladikavkaz

OSSETIA
1806

ARMENIA
1828

Erivan

Tiflis

KABARDA

GEORGIA

Alexandropol

Kislovodsk

Gori

Kars

1829

Kutais

Ardahan

Stavropol

1804

OTTOMAN
EMPIRE

1858

1803

Poti

1828

ABKHAZIA

1810

Batum

Sukhumi

Maikop
1864

Ekaterinodar

1829

Novorossiisk

Anapa

Black Sea

0   80
Miles

No part of Russia has had a more turbulent history than the Caucasus. Ruled in turn by Scythians, Persians, Romans, Arabs, Khazars, Mongols and Turks, it fell between 1800 and 1900 under Russian control. Consisting of many tribes speaking a variety of languages, the Caucasus was a source both of fierce national resistance to Russian rule and of revolutionary activity against the Tsar. Stalin was born at Gori in Georgia in 1879

48

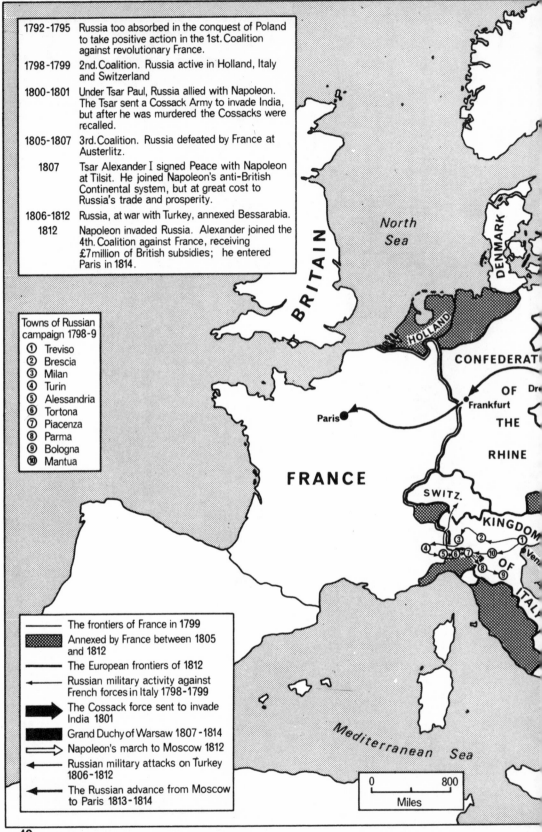

1792-1795   Russia too absorbed in the conquest of Poland to take positive action in the 1st. Coalition against revolutionary France.

1798-1799   2nd. Coalition. Russia active in Holland, Italy and Switzerland

1800-1801   Under Tsar Paul, Russia allied with Napoleon. The Tsar sent a Cossack Army to invade India, but after he was murdered the Cossacks were recalled.

1805-1807   3rd. Coalition. Russia defeated by France at Austerlitz.

1807   Tsar Alexander I signed Peace with Napoleon at Tilsit. He joined Napoleon's anti-British Continental system, but at great cost to Russia's trade and prosperity.

1806-1812   Russia, at war with Turkey, annexed Bessarabia.

1812   Napoleon invaded Russia. Alexander joined the 4th. Coalition against France, receiving £7 million of British subsidies; he entered Paris in 1814.

Towns of Russian campaign 1798-9
① Treviso
② Brescia
③ Milan
④ Turin
⑤ Alessandria
⑥ Tortona
⑦ Piacenza
⑧ Parma
⑨ Bologna
⑩ Mantua

North Sea

BRITAIN

DENMARK

HOLLAND

CONFEDERAT

OF   Dr

Frankfurt

THE

RHINE

Paris

FRANCE

SWITZ.

KINGDOM

Ven

OF

ITAL

Mediterranean Sea

—————— The frontiers of France in 1799

▓▓▓▓ Annexed by France between 1805 and 1812

—————— The European frontiers of 1812

◄————— Russian military activity against French forces in Italy 1798-1799

◀██████ The Cossack force sent to invade India 1801

███ Grand Duchy of Warsaw 1807-1814

▭▭▭▷ Napoleon's march to Moscow 1812

◄————— Russian military attacks on Turkey 1806-1812

◄————— The Russian advance from Moscow to Paris 1813-1814

0   800
Miles

RUSSIA AND EUROPE 1789-1815

R U S S I A

Tver

Moscow

Riga

Borodino

Viazma

Riazan

Smolensk

Tula

Tilsit

Borisov

Baltic Sea

SSIA

GRAND
DUCHY
OF WARSAW

Kalisz

Napoleon championed Polish independence, and many Polish emigres joined him after 1795. In 1807 he established a Grand Duchy of Warsaw, entirely out of Prussian and Austrian Poland. The Russians planned to crush this new state, but to forestall them Napoleon marched to Moscow in 1812. 85.000 Poles served in his army. After his defeat most of the Grand Duchy was transferred to Russia, giving Russia a further 3 million Polish and 300,000 Jewish citizens.

Austerlitz

enna

AUSTRIA

Jassy

BESS-
ARABIA

Ismail

RUMANIANS

Bucharest

Iasika

Black Sea

ROATS

SERBS

Tirnovo

Shumla

Varna

BULGARS

TURKEY IN EUROPE

GREEKS

TURKEY IN ASIA

Balkan peoples under Turkish rule, whom Alexander planned to enlist in an anti-French crusade in return for helping them obtain independence from Turkey. The plan failed.

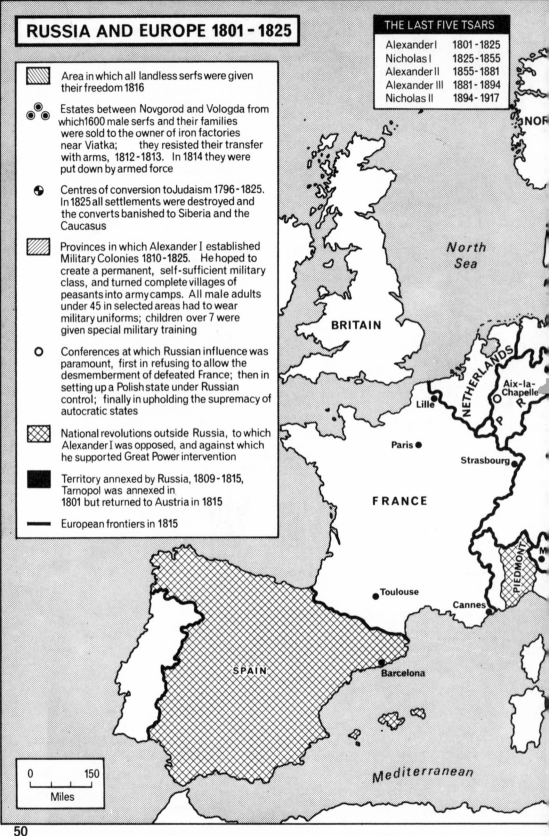

RUSSIA AND EUROPE 1801 - 1825

THE LAST FIVE TSARS

Alexander I	1801 - 1825
Nicholas I	1825 - 1855
Alexander II	1855 - 1881
Alexander III	1881 - 1894
Nicholas II	1894 - 1917

Area in which all landless serfs were given their freedom 1816

Estates between Novgorod and Vologda from which 1600 male serfs and their families were sold to the owner of iron factories near Viatka; they resisted their transfer with arms, 1812 - 1813. In 1814 they were put down by armed force

Centres of conversion to Judaism 1796 - 1825. In 1825 all settlements were destroyed and the converts banished to Siberia and the Caucasus

Provinces in which Alexander I established Military Colonies 1810 - 1825. He hoped to create a permanent, self-sufficient military class, and turned complete villages of peasants into army camps. All male adults under 45 in selected areas had to wear military uniforms; children over 7 were given special military training

Conferences at which Russian influence was paramount, first in refusing to allow the desmemberment of defeated France; then in setting up a Polish state under Russian control; finally in upholding the supremacy of autocratic states

National revolutions outside Russia, to which Alexander I was opposed, and against which he supported Great Power intervention

Territory annexed by Russia, 1809 - 1815, Tarnopol was annexed in 1801 but returned to Austria in 1815

European frontiers in 1815

NOR

North Sea

BRITAIN

NETHERLANDS

Aix-la-Chapelle

Lille

O
P
R
P

Paris

Strasbourg

FRANCE

PIEDMONT

M

Toulouse

Cannes

SPAIN

Barcelona

Mediterranean

0   150
Miles

FINLAND

ALAND
ISLANDS

SWEDEN

Viatka

Vologda

St.
Petersburg

Novgorod

Moscow

Baltic Sea

Tula

Saratov

R U S S I A

Mogilev

Bobrov

S I A

Pavlovsk

POLAND

Ekaterinoslav

Carlsbad

Lemberg

Prague

Troppau

Tarnopol

Nikolaev

BESSARABIA

Vienna

AUSTRIA-
HUNGARY

Laibach

Bucharest

Black Sea

Belgrade

T
U

NAPLES

Cattaro

R

aples

Constantinople

K

E

Y

GREECE

Like Catherine the Great on her accession,
Alexander I was looked to on his accession
(in 1801) as a potential source of liberal-
ization. In the war against Napoleon he acted
as the enemy of tyrants and friend of the
oppressed. But by 1820 he had become a
pillar of autocracy both in Russia and
abroad. Under Alexander, Russia's western
frontier reached its furthest western extent,
and from 1820 to 1917 it was unchanged

Athens

Sea

RUSSIA UNDER NICHOLAS I 1825-1855

Nicholas I, known as the Gendarme of Europe, was equally the gendarme of Russia. In 1827 he set up a special Corps of Gendarmes, as the main instrument of the political police. The country was divided into Gendarme Districts, each commanded by a General. There were an estimated total of at least 4,000 Gendarmes in 1837, when the Districts were reorganised; and at least 8,000 by 1855. A squadron was set up to patrol the Moscow - St. Petersburg railway in 1846

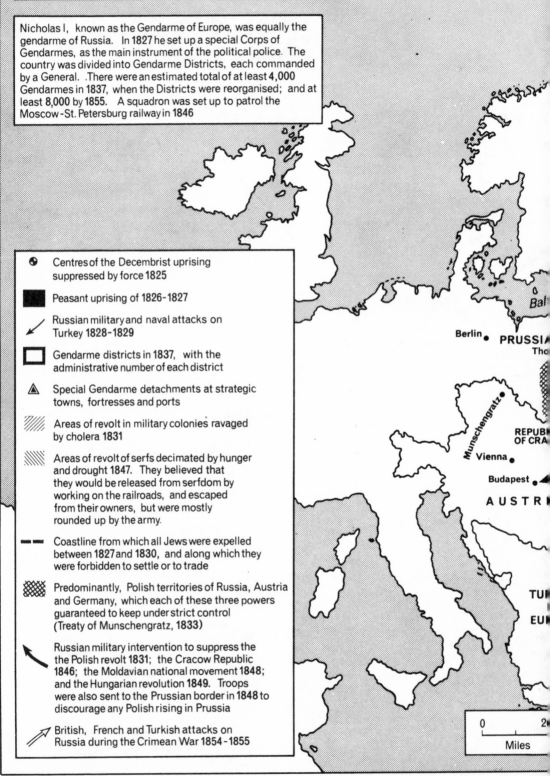

⊕ Centres of the Decembrist uprising suppressed by force 1825

◼ Peasant uprising of 1826-1827

↙ Russian military and naval attacks on Turkey 1828-1829

☐ Gendarme districts in 1837, with the administrative number of each district

▲ Special Gendarme detachments at strategic towns, fortresses and ports

▨ Areas of revolt in military colonies ravaged by cholera 1831

▧ Areas of revolt of serfs decimated by hunger and drought 1847. They believed that they would be released from serfdom by working on the railroads, and escaped from their owners, but were mostly rounded up by the army.

– – Coastline from which all Jews were expelled between 1827 and 1830, and along which they were forbidden to settle or to trade

▨ Predominantly, Polish territories of Russia, Austria and Germany, which each of these three powers guaranteed to keep under strict control (Treaty of Munschengratz, 1833)

↰ Russian military intervention to suppress the the Polish revolt 1831; the Cracow Republic 1846; the Moldavian national movement 1848; and the Hungarian revolution 1849. Troops were also sent to the Prussian border in 1848 to discourage any Polish rising in Prussia

↗ British, French and Turkish attacks on Russia during the Crimean War 1854-1855

Berlin ● PRUSSIA
Tho

Munschengratz ●

Vienna ●

REPUBI
OF CRA

Budapest ●

AUSTR

Bal

TU
EU

0 2
Miles

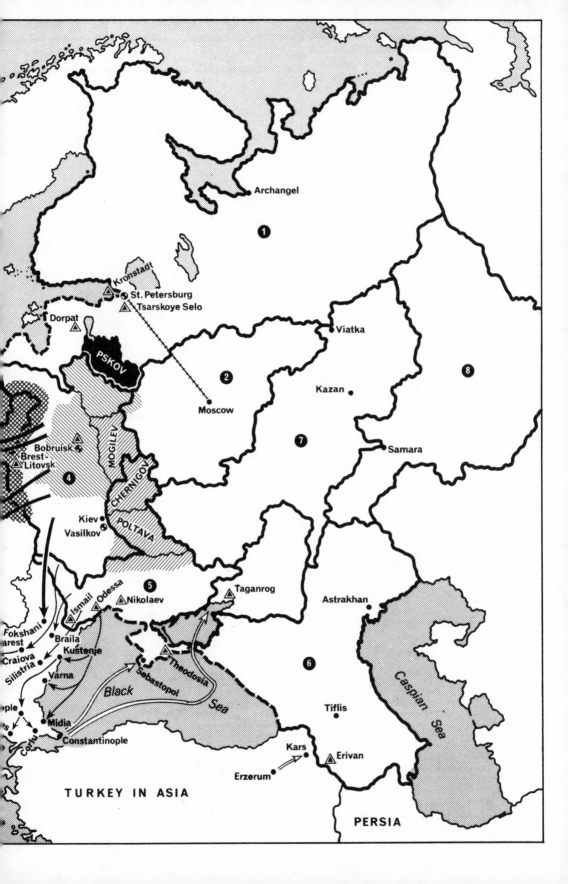

THE POLISH REVOLT IN 1831

After Napoleon's defeat in 1814, Russia set up its new Polish territory as a separate kingdom, CONGRESS POLAND, ruled directly by the Tsar. After 1814, Alexander I adopted a liberal, pro-Polish policy. But in 1825 his successor, Nicholas I, began to restrict Polish liberties. In 1830 the Poles rose in open war against Russian rule. They hoped for help from France, but it never came. The revolt was crushed by superior Russian force.

Palanga

Memel

Königsberg

Danzig

P R U S S I A

Masurian Lakes

0   50

Miles

Suvalki

Vilna

Grodno

Posen

Bialystok

R U S S I A

Kalisz

Warsaw

Pripet Marshes

Lodz

Brest-Litovsk

Pinsk

Piotrkow

Breslau

Czenstochowa

Kovel

S I L E S I A

Krasnik

REPUBLIC OF CRACOW

Cracow

Tarnow

GALICIA

Congress Poland, ruled by the Russian Tsar 1815-1914

Principal areas of Polish partisan activity in 1831 against the local Russian authorities

⊙   Battles between Russian and Polish troops in 1831

→   Polish troop movements. All these ended in exile across the Prussian, Austrian and Cracovian borders

Przemysl

Lvov

A U S T R I A

Tarnopol

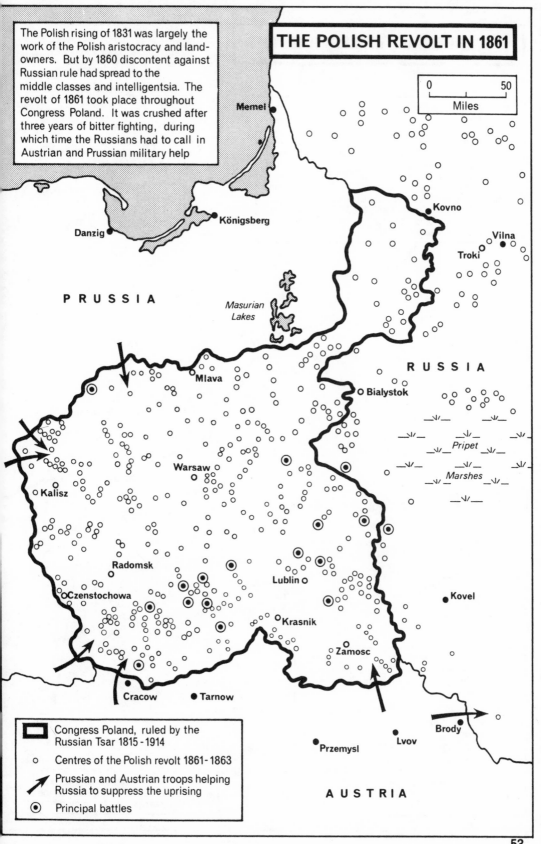

THE POLISH REVOLT IN 1861

The Polish rising of 1831 was largely the work of the Polish aristocracy and landowners. But by 1860 discontent against Russian rule had spread to the middle classes and intelligentsia. The revolt of 1861 took place throughout Congress Poland. It was crushed after three years of bitter fighting, during which time the Russians had to call in Austrian and Prussian military help

0   50
Miles

Memel

Königsberg

Danzig

PRUSSIA

Masurian Lakes

Kovno

Vilna
Troki

Mlava

Bialystok

RUSSIA

Pripet

Marshes

Warsaw

Kalisz

Radomsk

Czenstochowa

Lublin

Krasnik

Kovel

Zamosc

Cracow   Tarnow

Brody

Przemysl   Lvov

AUSTRIA

Congress Poland, ruled by the Russian Tsar 1815 - 1914

○ Centres of the Polish revolt 1861 - 1863

↗ Prussian and Austrian troops helping Russia to suppress the uprising

⊙ Principal battles

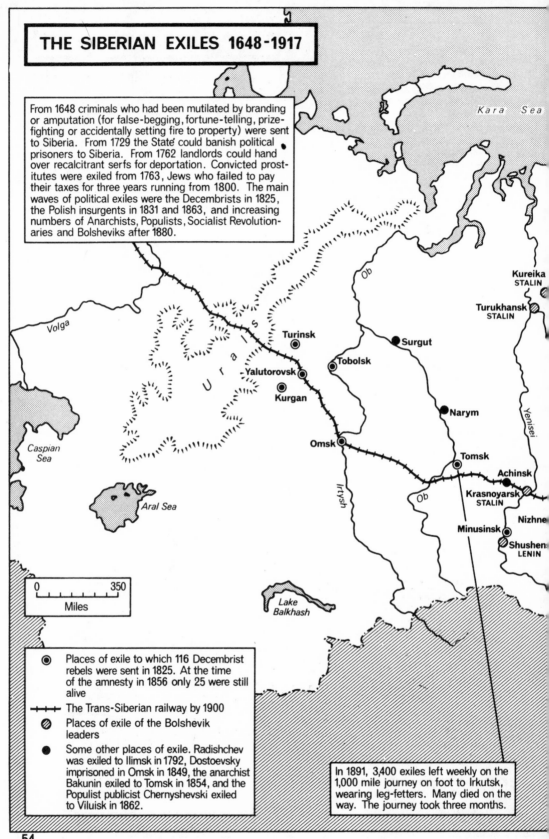

THE SIBERIAN EXILES 1648-1917

Kara Sea

From 1648 criminals who had been mutilated by branding or amputation (for false-begging, fortune-telling, prize-fighting or accidentally setting fire to property) were sent to Siberia. From 1729 the State could banish political prisoners to Siberia. From 1762 landlords could hand over recalcitrant serfs for deportation. Convicted prostitutes were exiled from 1763, Jews who failed to pay their taxes for three years running from 1800. The main waves of political exiles were the Decembrists in 1825, the Polish insurgents in 1831 and 1863, and increasing numbers of Anarchists, Populists, Socialist Revolutionaries and Bolsheviks after 1880.

Ob

Kureika
STALIN

Turukhansk
STALIN

Volga

Turinsk

Urals

Surgut

Yalutorovsk

Tobolsk

Kurgan

Narym

Yenisei

Caspian Sea

Omsk

Tomsk

Achinsk

Aral Sea

Irtysh

Ob

Krasnoyarsk
STALIN

Nizhne

Minusinsk

Shushen:
LENIN

0	350

Miles

Lake Balkhash

⊙ Places of exile to which 116 Decembrist rebels were sent in 1825. At the time of the amnesty in 1856 only 25 were still alive

┼┼┼ The Trans-Siberian railway by 1900

⊘ Places of exile of the Bolshevik leaders

● Some other places of exile. Radishchev was exiled to Ilimsk in 1792, Dostoevsky imprisoned in Omsk in 1849, the anarchist Bakunin exiled to Tomsk in 1854, and the Populist publicist Chernyshevski exiled to Viluisk in 1862.

In 1891, 3,400 exiles left weekly on the 1,000 mile journey on foot to Irkutsk, wearing leg-fetters. Many died on the way. The journey took three months.

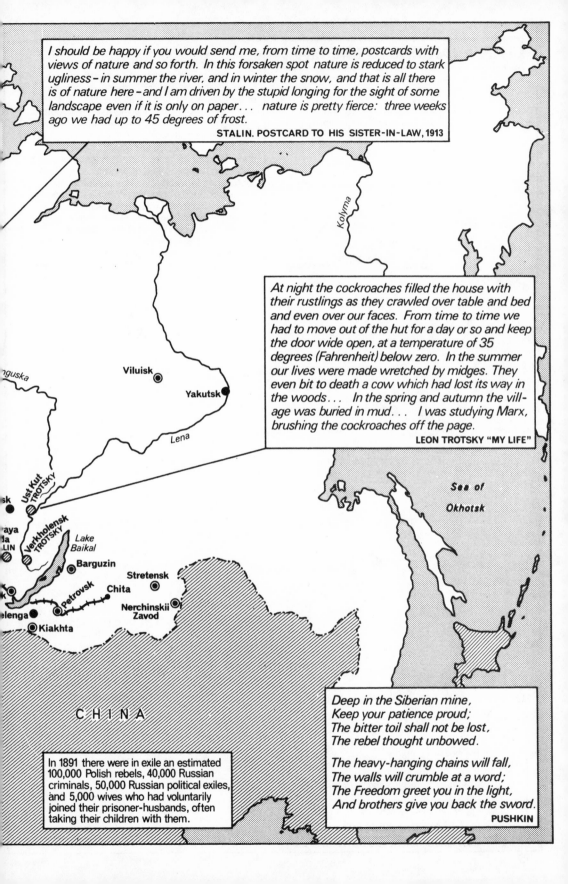

I should be happy if you would send me, from time to time, postcards with views of nature and so forth. In this forsaken spot nature is reduced to stark ugliness – in summer the river, and in winter the snow, and that is all there is of nature here – and I am driven by the stupid longing for the sight of some landscape even if it is only on paper... nature is pretty fierce: three weeks ago we had up to 45 degrees of frost.

STALIN. POSTCARD TO HIS SISTER-IN-LAW, 1913

At night the cockroaches filled the house with their rustlings as they crawled over table and bed and even over our faces. From time to time we had to move out of the hut for a day or so and keep the door wide open, at a temperature of 35 degrees (Fahrenheit) below zero. In the summer our lives were made wretched by midges. They even bit to death a cow which had lost its way in the woods... In the spring and autumn the village was buried in mud... I was studying Marx, brushing the cockroaches off the page.

LEON TROTSKY "MY LIFE"

Kolyma

Viluisk ⊙

Yakutsk ●

Lena

nguska

sk

Ust Kut
TROTSKY

aya
da
LIN

Verkholensk
TROTSKY

Lake
Baikal

Barguzin

Stretensk

Petrovsk **Chita**

Nerchinskii
Zavod

lenga

⊙ **Kiakhta**

*Sea of
Okhotsk*

C H I N A

In 1891 there were in exile an estimated 100,000 Polish rebels, 40,000 Russian criminals, 50,000 Russian political exiles, and 5,000 wives who had voluntarily joined their prisoner-husbands, often taking their children with them.

Deep in the Siberian mine,
Keep your patience proud;
The bitter toil shall not be lost,
The rebel thought unbowed.

The heavy-hanging chains will fall,
The walls will crumble at a word;
The Freedom greet you in the light,
And brothers give you back the sword.

PUSHKIN

THE ANARCHISTS 1840-1906

"What is property? Property is theft" wrote the French philosopher Proudhon, the father of anarchism, in 1840. He urged the destruction of officialdom, bureaucracy money and state organisation in order to make all men equal and free. But he shunned violent revolt, fearing that revolution might bring new tyranny. The Russian, Bakunin, bent anarchism to violence. *"The passion to destroy is at the same time a passion to create,"* he wrote in 1842. Bakunin believed that the Russian peasant would be the instrument of anarchic revolt, and encouraged terrorist acts. The murder of Tsar Alexander II at St. Petersburg in 1881 encouraged further assassinations, aimed at provoking revolution. The Russian anarchist, Prince Kropotkin, said after the execution of one of the 5 assassins: *"By her death she was dealing an even more terrible blow, from which the autocracy will never recover."*

St.Petersburg

Viatka

Baltic Sea

Riga

LITHUANIA

Kovno

Vilna

Grodno

Minsk

Bialystok

Warsaw

POLAND

Moscow

Nizhni Novgorod

Volga

Tula

Orel

Samara

Nezhin

Kiev

Kharkov

UKRAINE

Ekaterinoslav

Kishinev

Odessa

Volga

Sebastopol

Yalta

Black Sea

Batum

Tiflis

CAUCASIA

Baku

Caspian Sea

⊙	Anarchist groups meeting from the 1840's to 1880's
●	Revolutionary anarchist groups in existence from 1903 and "revolting" in 1905 - 1906
▨	The "Forest Brethren" carrying out terrorist activity in 1905 - 1906

0   300

Miles

RUSSIAN INDUSTRY BY 1860

0   200
Miles

Archangel

Urals

Vyborg

Schlüsselburg
St. Petersburg   540,000
LEATHER

Reval
Narva
Viatka
Kama
Perm
GOLD
COAL
COPPER

WOOL

Dorpat
Pskov
Yaroslavl
LINEN
Volga
COAL
COPPER
LEATHER
Ufa

Libau
Mitau
Riga
77,000
Tver
Vladimir
Vegorevsk
Nizhni
Novgorod
Kazan
63,000
COPPER

LEATHER
Dvinsk
Moscow
460,000
LEATHER
LINEN

Kovno
Kaluga
Riazan
LINEN

Vilna
69,000
Tula
LEATHER

Grodno
Orel
WOOL
Saratov
84,000

Warsaw
Bialystok
LINEN
LINEN
Voronezh

Lodz
LINEN
Chernigov

Kiev
68,000
LINEN
Kharkov
Donets
COAL
Don
Volga

Poltava

Kishinev
94,000
64,000
Nikolaev

Odessa

120,000
TOBACCO
Caucasus

Caspian
Sea

POPULATION
1811: 41,000,000
1863: 74,000,000
Black   Sea
Baku
OIL

The Russian frontier 1815-1914

● Principal cities, with their estimated
   population in 1860

━━━ Railways built by 1860

━━━ Railways under construction in 1860

⊙ Factory development before 1860

⊕ Towns with large factory growth
   from 1860

▬ Industries expanding rapidly from 1860

▓ Centres of the iron and steel production

▨ Sugar factories

PRINCIPAL IMPORTS: Cotton, machine tools, alcohol,
dyes, fruit and nuts, wool, tea, olive and vegetable oil, silk,
sugar, zinc, steel, iron, copper, horses, cattle, poultry,
salt. Over 80% of all imports and exports went through
the ports of St. Petersburg and Odessa

PRINCIPAL EXPORTS: Wheat, rye, cereals, flour, flax, hemp,
wool, animal fat, lard, seeds, wood, wood products, paper

Baltic
Sea

Dnieper

Ural

56

PEASANT DISCONTENT 1827–1860

White Sea

ARCHANGEL

FINLAND

OLONETS

VOLOGDA

PERM

Baltic Sea

ESTLAND

ST PETERSBURG

NOVGOROD

KOSTROMA

VIATKA

KURLAND

LIVLAND

PSKOV

YAROSLAV

UFA

KOVNO

VITEBSK

TVER

VLADIMIR

NIZHNI NOVGOROD

KAZAN

GERMANY

VILNA

MOSCOW

SIMBIRSK

ORENBURG

GRODNO

MOGILEV

SMOLENSK

KALUGA

RIAZAN

PENZA

SAMARA

POLAND

MINSK

TULA

CHERNIGOV

OREL

TAMBOV

SARATOV

VOLHYNIA

KIEV

KURSK

VORONEZH

POLTAVA

AUSTRIA-HUNGARY

PODOLIA

BESSARABIA

KHARKOV

DON

ASTRAKHAN

EKATERINOSLAV

RUMANIA

TAURIDA

KHERSON

KUBAN

STAVROPOL

Black Sea

TEREK

Caspian Sea

KUTAIS

TIFLIS

BAKU

KARS

ERIVAN

ELIZAVETPOL

■ Provinces in which the peasants rose most frequently against their landowners, murdered them, resisted arrest by force of arms, and were hunted down by troops and police

▨ Provinces where peasant discontent led to mass crop damage, illegal timber-cutting, and looting of estates

▨ Provinces where peasants damaged crops, cut timber and refused to pay dues owed to landlords. There were also some minor outbreaks of unrest in the unshaded Provinces

0   200
Miles

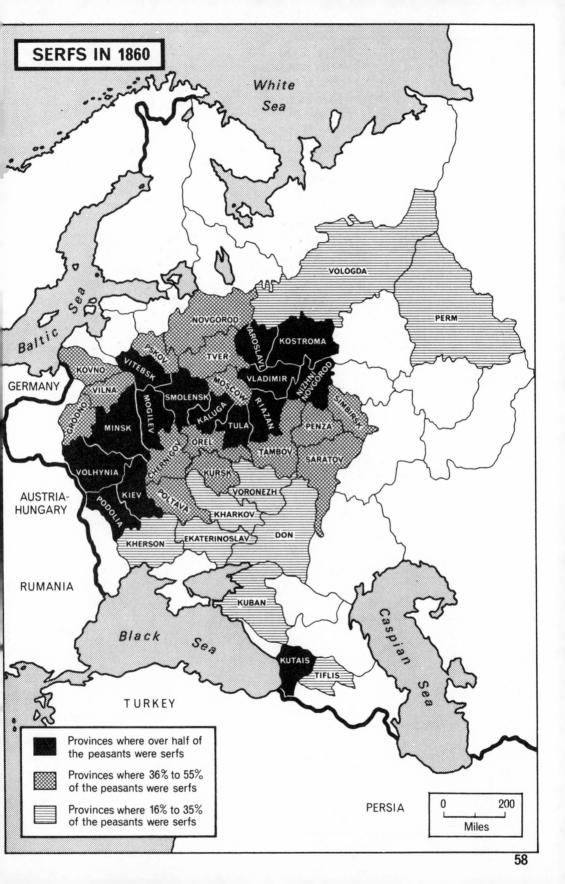

SERFS IN 1860

Provinces where over half of the peasants were serfs

Provinces where 36% to 55% of the peasants were serfs

Provinces where 16% to 35% of the peasants were serfs

White Sea

Baltic Sea

GERMANY

AUSTRIA-HUNGARY

RUMANIA

Black Sea

TURKEY

Caspian Sea

PERSIA

VOLOGDA

PERM

NOVGOROD

PSKOV

VITEBSK

KOVNO

VILNA

GRODNO

MINSK

MOGILEV

SMOLENSK

TVER

YAROSLAVL

KOSTROMA

VLADIMIR

MOSCOW

KALUGA

RIAZAN

NIZHNI NOVGOROD

SIMBIRSK

TULA

PENZA

OREL

TAMBOV

SARATOV

VOLHYNIA

KIEV

CHERNIGOV

POLTAVA

KURSK

VORONEZH

KHARKOV

DON

PODOLIA

KHERSON

EKATERINOSLAV

KUBAN

KUTAIS

TIFLIS

0   200
Miles

58

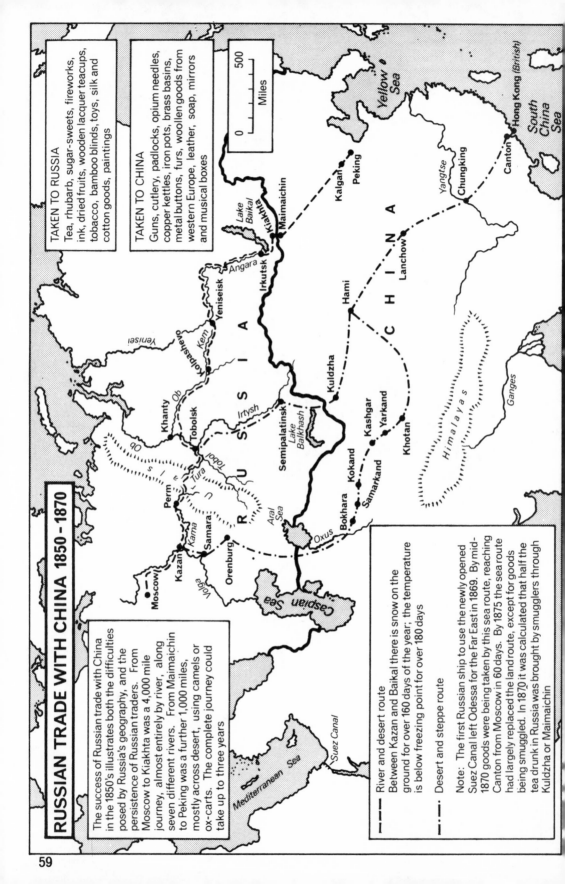

RUSSIAN TRADE WITH CHINA 1850 – 1870

The success of Russian trade with China in the 1850's illustrates both the difficulties posed by Russia's geography, and the persistence of Russian traders. From Moscow to Kiakhta was a 4,000 mile journey, almost entirely by river, along seven different rivers. From Maimaichin to Peking was a further 1,000 miles, mostly across desert, using camels or ox-carts. The complete journey could take up to three years

TAKEN TO RUSSIA

Tea, rhubarb, sugar-sweets, fireworks, ink, dried fruits, wooden lacquer teacups, tobacco, bamboo blinds, toys, silk and cotton goods, paintings

TAKEN TO CHINA

Guns, cutlery, padlocks, opium needles, copper kettles, iron pots, brass basins, metal buttons, furs, woollen goods from western Europe, leather, soap, mirrors and musical boxes

- – – – River and desert route
  Between Kazan and Baikal there is snow on the ground for over 160 days of the year; the temperature is below freezing point for over 180 days

- – · – Desert and steppe route

Note: The first Russian ship to use the newly opened Suez Canal left Odessa for the Far East in 1869. By mid-1870 goods were being taken by this sea route, reaching Canton from Moscow in 60 days. By 1875 the sea route had largely replaced the land route, except for goods being smuggled. In 1870 it was calculated that half the tea drunk in Russia was brought by smugglers through Kuldzha or Maimaichin

500

0   Miles

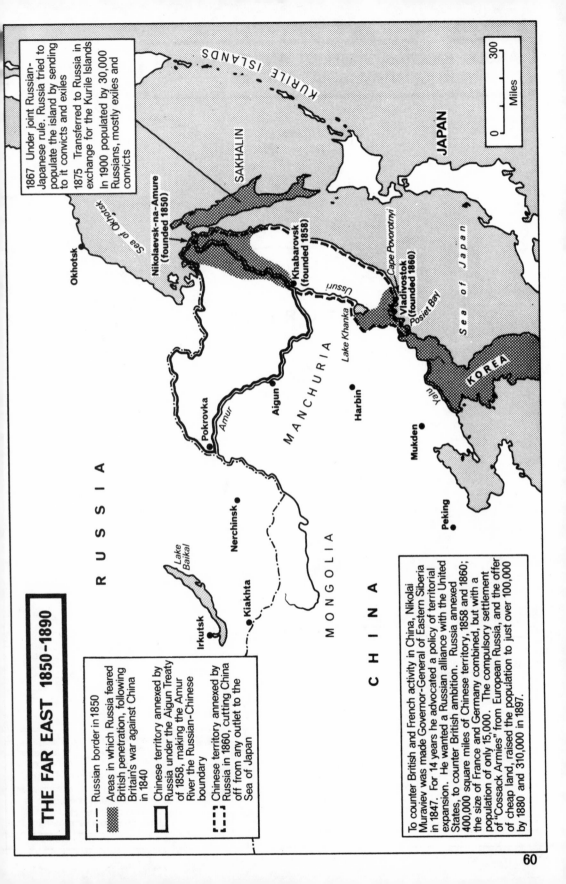

THE FAR EAST 1850-1890

Legend:

- –·– Russian border in 1850
- Areas in which Russia feared British penetration, following Britain's war against China in 1840
- ☐ Chinese territory annexed by Russia under the Aigun Treaty of 1858, making the Amur River the Russian-Chinese boundary
- ⌐ ⌐ Chinese territory annexed by Russia in 1860, cutting China off from any outlet to the Sea of Japan

1867 Under joint Russian-Japanese rule. Russia tried to populate the island by sending to it convicts and exiles

1875 Transferred to Russia in exchange for the Kurile Islands In 1900 populated by 30,000 Russians, mostly exiles and convicts

To counter British and French activity in China, Nikolai Muraviev was made Governor-General of Eastern Siberia in 1847. For 14 years he advocated a policy of territorial expansion. He wanted a Russian alliance with the United States, to counter British ambition. Russia annexed 400,000 square miles of Chinese territory, 1858 and 1860; the size of France and Germany combined, but with a population of only 15,000. The compulsory settlement of "Cossack Armies" from European Russia, and the offer of cheap land, raised the population to just over 100,000 by 1880 and 310,000 in 1897.

Place names and labels:
Irkutsk · Lake Baikal · Nerchinsk · Kiakhta · RUSSIA · Okhotsk · Sea of Okhotsk · Nikolaevsk-na-Amure (founded 1850) · SAKHALIN · KURILE ISLANDS · JAPAN · Khabarovsk (founded 1858) · Pokrovka · Amur · Aigun · MANCHURIA · Ussuri · Lake Khanka · Harbin · Cape Povorotnyi · Vladivostok (founded 1860) · Posiet Bay · Sea of Japan · MONGOLIA · Mukden · Yalu · KOREA · CHINA · Peking

Scale: 0 ——— 300 Miles

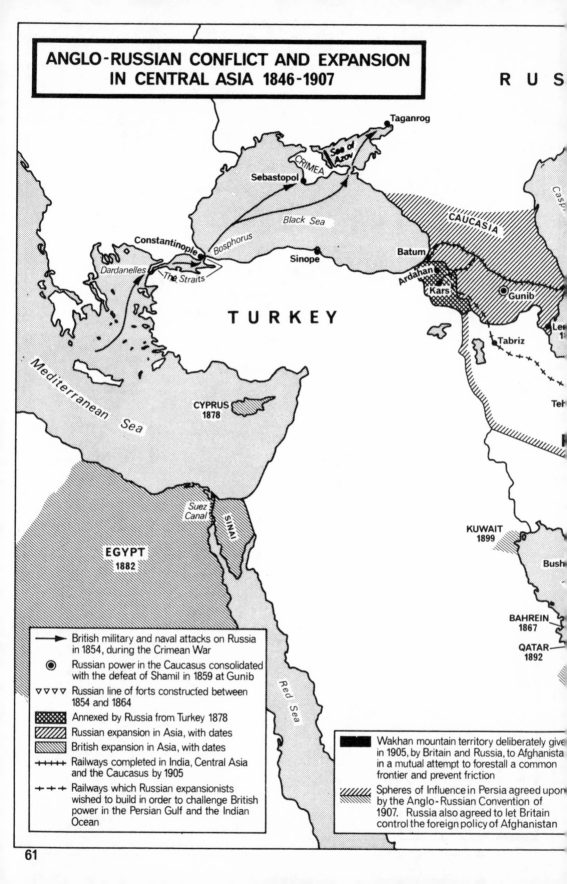

ANGLO-RUSSIAN CONFLICT AND EXPANSION IN CENTRAL ASIA 1846-1907

R U S

Taganrog

Sea of Azov

CRIMEA

Sebastopol

Black Sea

CAUCASIA

Constantinople

Bosphorus

Batum

Dardanelles

The Straits

Sinope

Ardahan

Kars

Gunib

TURKEY

Mediterranean Sea

Tabriz

Tel

CYPRUS 1878

Suez Canal

SINAI

KUWAIT 1899

EGYPT 1882

Bush

Red Sea

BAHREIN 1867

QATAR 1892

→ British military and naval attacks on Russia in 1854, during the Crimean War

◉ Russian power in the Caucasus consolidated with the defeat of Shamil in 1859 at Gunib

▽▽▽▽ Russian line of forts constructed between 1854 and 1864

▨ Annexed by Russia from Turkey 1878

▨ Russian expansion in Asia, with dates

▨ British expansion in Asia, with dates

+++++ Railways completed in India, Central Asia and the Caucasus by 1905

+ + + Railways which Russian expansionists wished to build in order to challenge British power in the Persian Gulf and the Indian Ocean

■ Wakhan mountain territory deliberately give in 1905, by Britain and Russia, to Afghanista in a mutual attempt to forestall a common frontier and prevent friction

▨ Spheres of Influence in Persia agreed upon by the Anglo-Russian Convention of 1907. Russia also agreed to let Britain control the foreign policy of Afghanistan

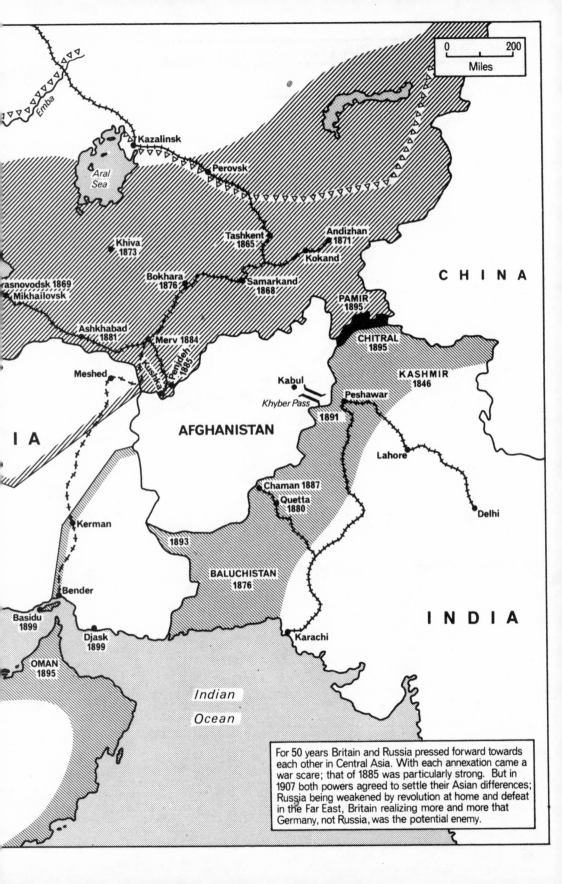

Emba

0 200 Miles

Kazalinsk

Aral Sea

Perovsk

CHINA

Khiva 1873

Tashkent 1865

Andizhan 1871

Kokand

asnovodsk 1869
Mikhailovsk

Bokhara 1876

Samarkand 1868

PAMIR 1895

Ashkhabad 1881

Merv 1884

Penjdeh 1885

CHITRAL 1895

Meshed

Kushka

KASHMIR 1846

Kabul

Khyber Pass

Peshawar

IA

AFGHANISTAN

1891

Lahore

Chaman 1887

Quetta 1880

Delhi

Kerman

1893

INDIA

BALUCHISTAN 1876

Bender

Basidu 1899

Djask 1899

Karachi

OMAN 1895

Indian

Ocean

For 50 years Britain and Russia pressed forward towards
each other in Central Asia. With each annexation came a
war scare; that of 1885 was particularly strong. But in
1907 both powers agreed to settle their Asian differences;
Russia being weakened by revolution at home and defeat
in the Far East, Britain realizing more and more that
Germany, not Russia, was the potential enemy.

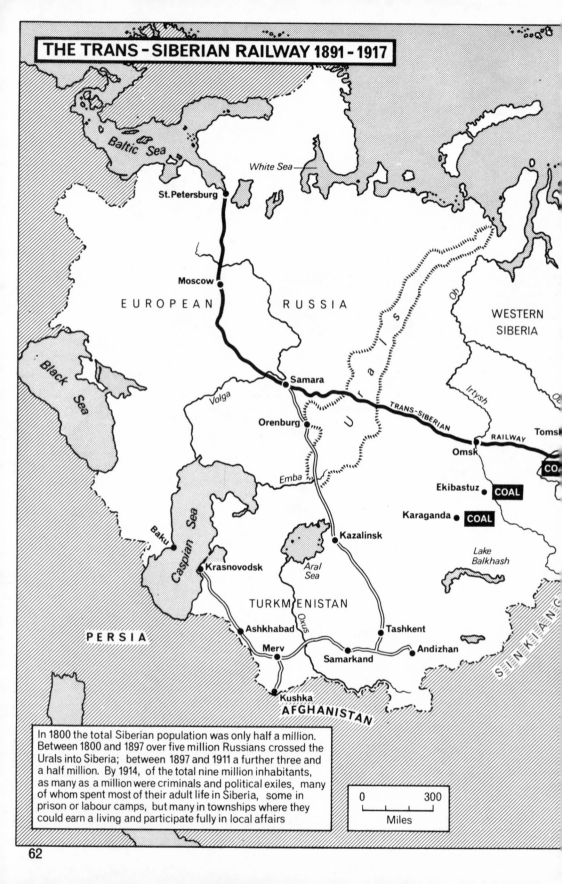

THE TRANS-SIBERIAN RAILWAY 1891-1917

Baltic Sea

White Sea

St.Petersburg

Moscow

E U R O P E A N   R U S S I A

Black Sea

Volga

Samara

Orenburg

Emba

Caspian Sea

Baku

U r a l s

TRANS-SIBERIAN

RAILWAY

Omsk

WESTERN SIBERIA

Ob

Irtysh

Toms

CO

Ekibastuz **COAL**

Karaganda **COAL**

Lake Balkhash

Kazalinsk

Krasnovodsk

Aral Sea

TURKMENISTAN

Oxus

Ashkhabad

P E R S I A

Merv

Samarkand

Tashkent

Andizhan

S I N K I A N G

Kushka

AFGHANISTAN

In 1800 the total Siberian population was only half a million.
Between 1800 and 1897 over five million Russians crossed the
Urals into Siberia; between 1897 and 1911 a further three and
a half million. By 1914, of the total nine million inhabitants,
as many as a million were criminals and political exiles, many
of whom spent most of their adult life in Siberia, some in
prison or labour camps, but many in townships where they
could earn a living and participate fully in local affairs

0   300

Miles

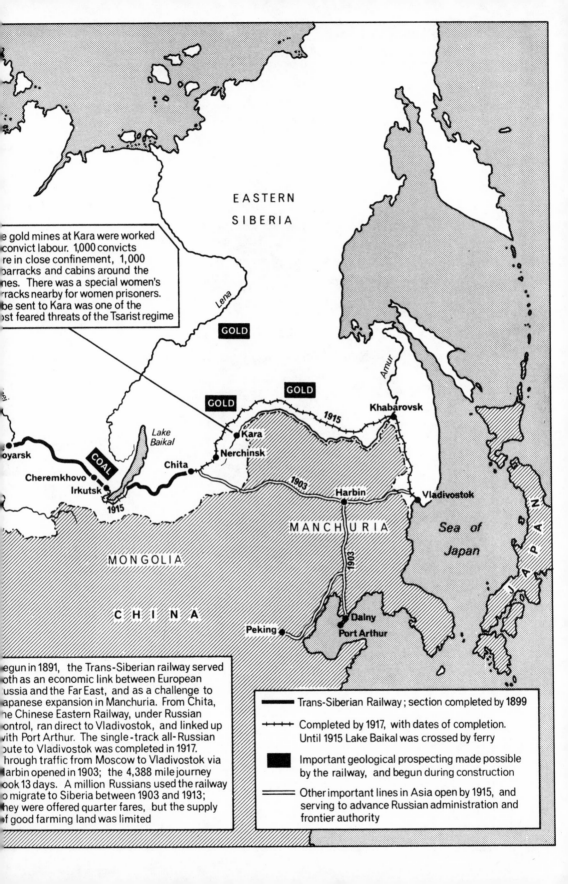

EASTERN
SIBERIA

e gold mines at Kara were worked
convict labour. 1,000 convicts
re in close confinement, 1,000
barracks and cabins around the
nes. There was a special women's
racks nearby for women prisoners.
be sent to Kara was one of the
st feared threats of the Tsarist regime

Lena

GOLD

Amur

GOLD

GOLD

1915

Khabarovsk

Lake
Baikal

COAL

Kara

Nerchinsk

oyarsk

Cheremkhovo

Chita

1903

Harbin

Vladivostok

Irkutsk

1915

MANCHURIA

Sea of
Japan

MONGOLIA

1903

JAPAN

C H I N A

Dalny

Peking

Port Arthur

egun in 1891, the Trans-Siberian railway served
oth as an economic link between European
ussia and the Far East, and as a challenge to
apanese expansion in Manchuria. From Chita,
ne Chinese Eastern Railway, under Russian
ontrol, ran direct to Vladivostok, and linked up
vith Port Arthur. The single-track all-Russian
oute to Vladivostok was completed in 1917.
hrough traffic from Moscow to Vladivostok via
larbin opened in 1903; the 4,388 mile journey
ook 13 days. A million Russians used the railway
o migrate to Siberia between 1903 and 1913;
hey were offered quarter fares, but the supply
f good farming land was limited

Trans-Siberian Railway; section completed by 1899

+++++ Completed by 1917, with dates of completion.
Until 1915 Lake Baikal was crossed by ferry

Important geological prospecting made possible
by the railway, and begun during construction

Other important lines in Asia open by 1915, and
serving to advance Russian administration and
frontier authority

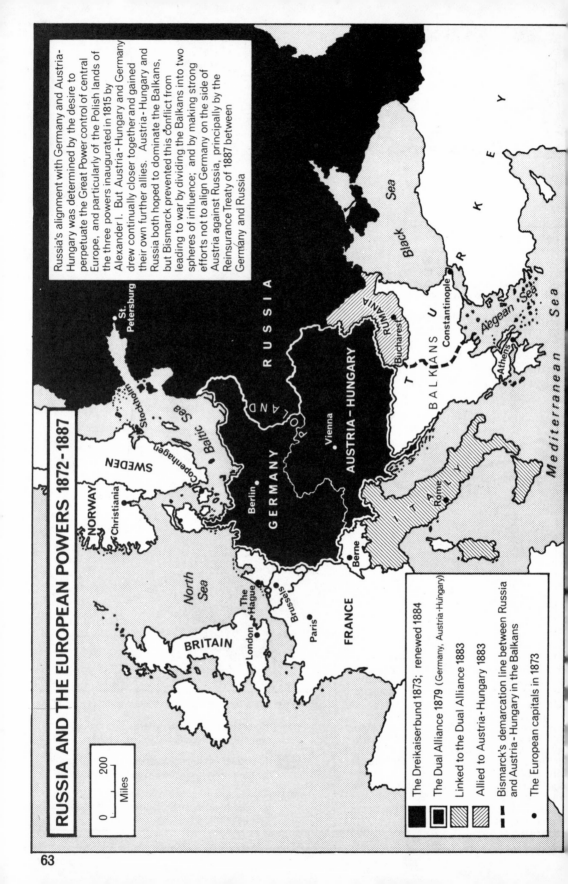

RUSSIA AND THE EUROPEAN POWERS 1872-1887

Russia's alignment with Germany and Austria-Hungary was determined by the desire to perpetuate the Great Power control of central Europe, and particularly of the Polish lands of the three powers inaugurated in 1815 by Alexander I. But Austria-Hungary and Germany drew continually closer together and gained their own further allies. Austria-Hungary and Russia both hoped to dominate the Balkans, but Bismarck prevented this conflict from leading to war by dividing the Balkans into two spheres of influence; and by making strong efforts not to align Germany on the side of Austria against Russia, principally by the Reinsurance Treaty of 1887 between Germany and Russia

The Dreikaiserbund 1873; renewed 1884

The Dual Alliance 1879 (Germany, Austria-Hungary)

Linked to the Dual Alliance 1883

Allied to Austria-Hungary 1883

Bismarck's demarcation line between Russia and Austria-Hungary in the Balkans

The European capitals in 1873

0   200
Miles

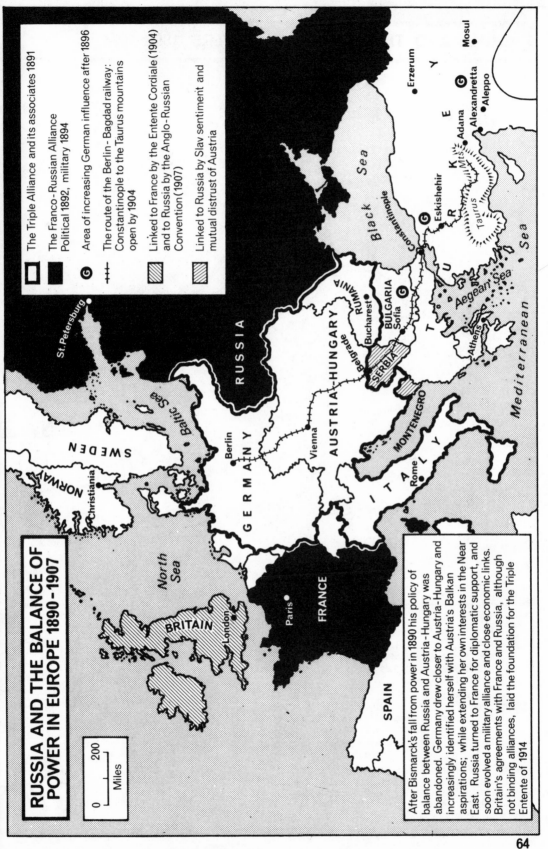

RUSSIA AND THE BALANCE OF POWER IN EUROPE 1890-1907

0   200
Miles

The Triple Alliance and its associates 1891

The Franco-Russian Alliance
Political 1892, military 1894

Ⓖ Area of increasing German influence after 1896

┼┼┼ The route of the Berlin-Bagdad railway:
Constantinople to the Taurus mountains
open by 1904

Linked to France by the Entente Cordiale (1904)
and to Russia by the Anglo-Russian
Convention (1907)

Linked to Russia by Slav sentiment and
mutual distrust of Austria

After Bismarck's fall from power in 1890 his policy of
balance between Russia and Austria-Hungary was
abandoned. Germany drew closer to Austria-Hungary and
increasingly identified herself with Austria's Balkan
aspirations; while extending her own interests in the Near
East. Russia turned to France for diplomatic support, and
soon evolved a military alliance and close economic links.
Britain's agreements with France and Russia, although
not binding alliances, laid the foundation for the Triple
Entente of 1914

64

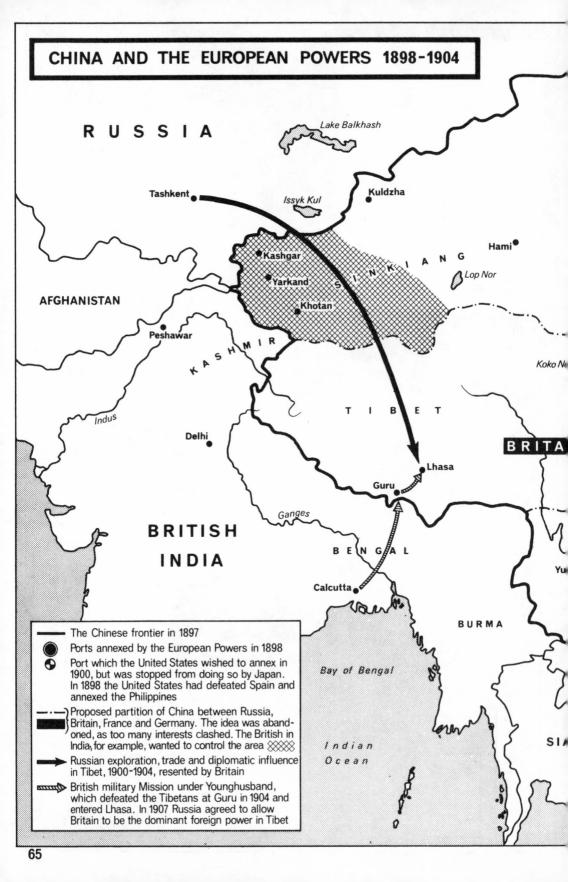

CHINA AND THE EUROPEAN POWERS 1898-1904

RUSSIA

Lake Balkhash

Tashkent

Issyk Kul

Kuldzha

Hami

Kashgar

S I N K I A N G

Lop Nor

Yarkand

AFGHANISTAN

Khotan

Koko No

Peshawar

K A S H M I R

Indus

T I B E T

BRITA

Delhi

Lhasa

Guru

Ganges

BRITISH

INDIA

B E N G A L

Yu

Calcutta

BURMA

Bay of Bengal

SI

The Chinese frontier in 1897

Ports annexed by the European Powers in 1898

Port which the United States wished to annex in 1900, but was stopped from doing so by Japan. In 1898 the United States had defeated Spain and annexed the Philippines

Proposed partition of China between Russia, Britain, France and Germany. The idea was abandoned, as too many interests clashed. The British in India, for example, wanted to control the area

Russian exploration, trade and diplomatic influence in Tibet, 1900-1904, resented by Britain

British military Mission under Younghusband, which defeated the Tibetans at Guru in 1904 and entered Lhasa. In 1907 Russia agreed to allow Britain to be the dominant foreign power in Tibet

Indian Ocean

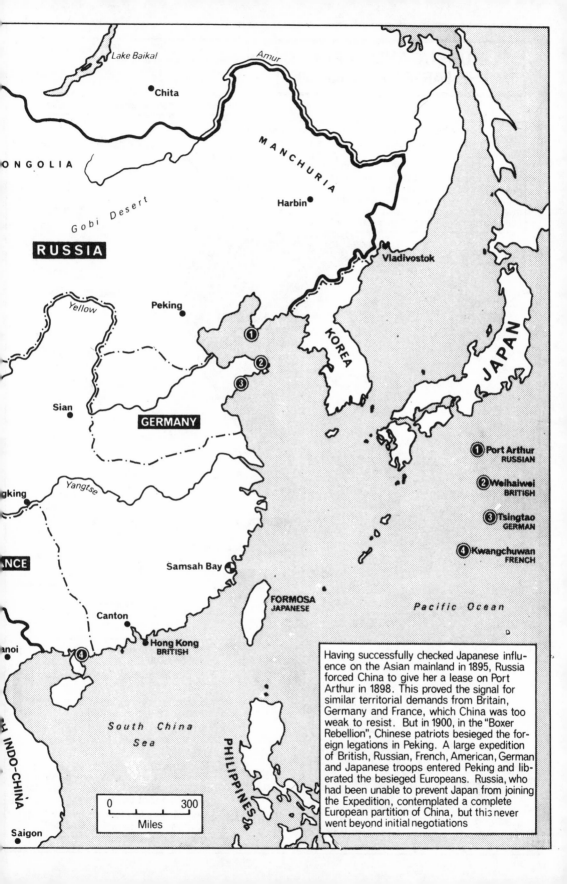

Lake Baikal

Amur

•Chita

MANCHURIA

ONGOLIA

Gobi Desert

Harbin•

RUSSIA

Vladivostok

Yellow

Peking•

①

②

KOREA

③

Sian•

GERMANY

JAPAN

① Port Arthur
RUSSIAN

② Weihaiwei
BRITISH

Yangtse

③ Tsingtao
GERMAN

gking•

④ Kwangchuwan
FRENCH

NCE

Samsah Bay

FORMOSA
JAPANESE

Pacific Ocean

Canton•

④

anoi

•Hong Kong
BRITISH

South China
Sea

PHILIPPINES

INDO-CHINA

Saigon•

0	300

Miles

Having successfully checked Japanese influence on the Asian mainland in 1895, Russia forced China to give her a lease on Port Arthur in 1898. This proved the signal for similar territorial demands from Britain, Germany and France, which China was too weak to resist. But in 1900, in the "Boxer Rebellion", Chinese patriots besieged the foreign legations in Peking. A large expedition of British, Russian, French, American, German and Japanese troops entered Peking and liberated the besieged Europeans. Russia, who had been unable to prevent Japan from joining the Expedition, contemplated a complete European partition of China, but this never went beyond initial negotiations

RUSSIA AND JAPAN IN THE FAR EAST 1860-1895

Kamchatka: part of Russia in 1650. Since 1750 used largely as a place of exile for criminals and political prisoners. Russian schoolboys were often threatened that slackers would be "sent to Kamchatka"–the furthest corner of the classroom. The peninsula has over 20 active volcanoes.

The struggle between Russia and Japan in the Far East was long and bitter. In 1860 Russia acquired an outlet on the Sea of Japan. The Japanese at once adopted a forward policy in China and Korea. When Japan defeated China in 1895 she expected to make wide territorial gains. But Russia, France, Britain and Germany combined to deprive Japan of the fruits of victory. This led to deep anti-Russian resentment throughout Japan. Throughout this period, European penetration in south China continued unabated.

RUSSIA

SIBERIA

KAMCHATKA

Petropavlovsk

Sea of Okhotsk

Amur

EASTERN

Nikolaevsk

SAKHALIN

MANCHURIA

Khabarovsk

KURILE ISLANDS

Uruppu

Harbin

Sungari

Ussuri

Etorofu

Changchun

Kirin

Mukden

Vladivostok

Peking

Yalu

Sea of Japan

JAPAN

Pacific

Tientsin

Wonsan

Weihaiwei

Port Arthur

Seoul

KOREA

Ocean

Inchon

Tsingtao

Yellow

Yellow Sea

Pusan

Nanking

Hankow

Shanghai

0   500

Miles

Yangtse

Oshima

Okinawa

RYUKYU ISLANDS

Macao (Portuguese 1557)

Kowloon (British 1861)

Hongkong (British 1841)

FORMOSA

South China Sea

PHILIPPINES (Spanish 1521)

■ Territory annexed by Russia from China in 1858-1860

┌─┐ Islands annexed by Japan from China in 1874

Islands annexed by Japan in return for Russian control of Sakhalin

⊙ Korean ports open, as the result of Japanese pressure, to Japanese trade 1876-1878

Occupied by Japan during the war with China, 1894-95. Russia, France, Britain and Germany combined to prevent Japan keeping any of this territory

Only Chinese territory actually annexed by Japan after the war of 1894-1895

THE RUSSIAN RESPONSE IN THE FAR EAST 1895-1905

0 — 300
Miles

WAR DEAD 1904-05	
Russian	120,000
Japanese	75,000

RUSSIA

Chita
Nerchinsk
Amur
Nikolaevsk
Argun
Hailar
MANCHURIA
Khabarovsk
Amur
SAKHALIN
Tsitsihar
Harbin
Sungari
CHINA
Mukden
Vladivostok
Yalu
Sea of Japan
Peking
Port Arthur
KOREA
Seoul
Yellow Sea
Tsushima Strait
Tokyo
JAPAN

The Trans-Siberian Railway by 1895
Under increasing Russian control after 1895
Leased by Russia from China in 1898, together with the right to build a railway to Harbin; (completed by 1904)
The Chinese Eastern Railway, controlled by Russia after its completion in 1903
Russian economic penetration. Russia refused to allow Japan a sphere of influence in Korea
Japanese naval and military attacks 1904–1905
Annexed by Japan in 1905

After successfully halting Japanese expansion in 1895, the Russians adopted an active expansionist policy. For 10 years they pressed forward in Manchuria, and discussed the partition of China with the British Government in 1900. But Japan sought revenge for the humiliation of 1895, and in 1902 neutralized Britain by the Anglo-Japanese Alliance. In February 1904, under Russian provocation, Japan attacked Port Arthur. Russia was defeated on land and sea, and a peace treaty was signed in the United States in Sept. 1905. The grave demoralization created by Russia's defeat led to a mass of revolutionary outbreaks in Russia, and to a serious weakening of the Tsarist mystique.

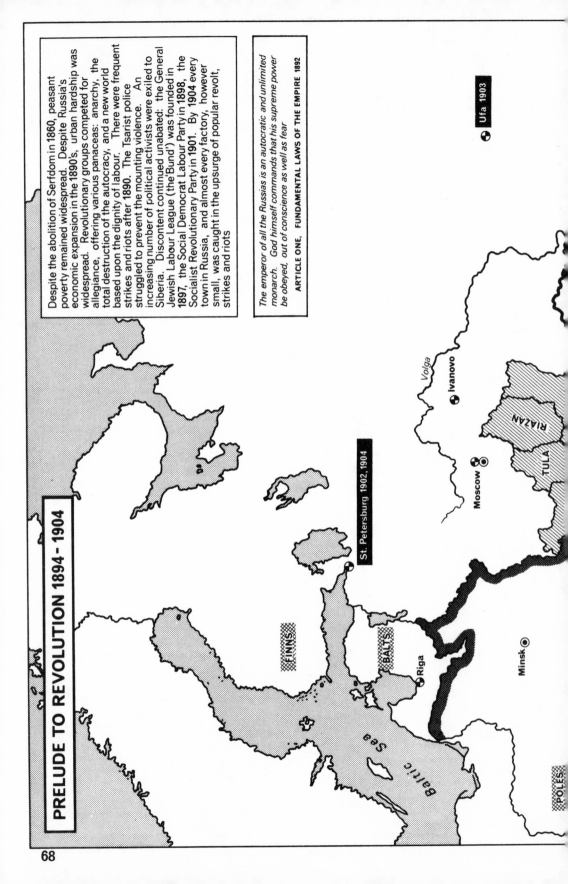

PRELUDE TO REVOLUTION 1894 - 1904

Despite the abolition of Serfdom in 1860, peasant poverty remained widespread. Despite Russia's economic expansion in the 1890's, urban hardship was widespread. Revolutionary groups competed for allegiance, offering various panaceas: anarchy, the total destruction of the autocracy, and a new world based upon the dignity of labour. There were frequent strikes and riots after 1890. The Tsarist police struggled to prevent the mounting violence. An increasing number of political activists were exiled to Siberia. Discontent continued unabated: the General Jewish Labour League (the 'Bund') was founded in 1897, the Social Democrat Labour Party in 1898, the Socialist Revolutionary Party in 1901. By 1904 every town in Russia, and almost every factory, however small, was caught in the upsurge of popular revolt, strikes and riots

The emperor of all the Russias is an autocratic and unlimited monarch. God himself commands that his supreme power be obeyed, out of conscience as well as fear

ARTICLE ONE, FUNDAMENTAL LAWS OF THE EMPIRE 1892

Ufa 1903

Volga

Ivanovo

St. Petersburg 1902, 1904

Moscow

RIAZAN

TULA

Baltic Sea

FINNS

BALTS

Riga

Minsk

POLES

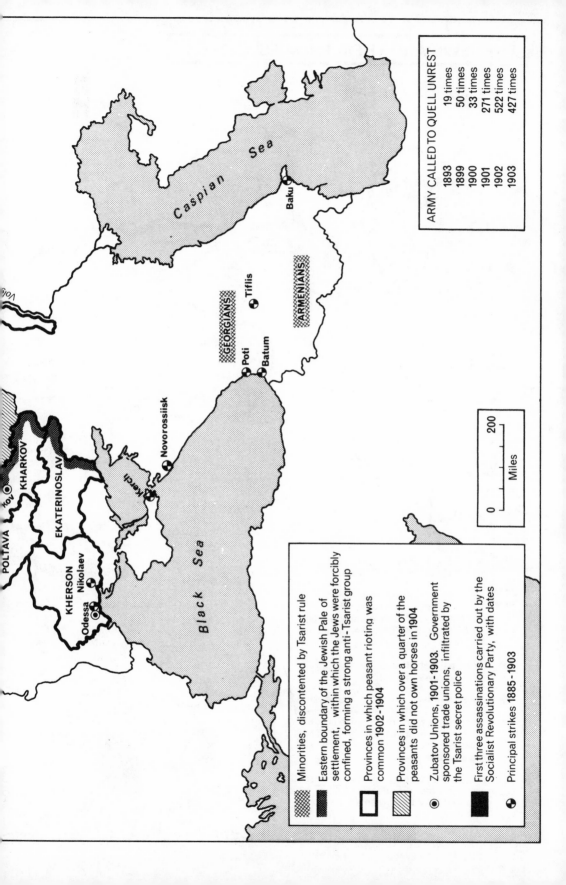

ARMY CALLED TO QUELL UNREST

1893	19 times
1899	50 times
1900	33 times
1901	271 times
1902	522 times
1903	427 times

Caspian Sea

Baku

GEORGIANS

Tiflis

ARMENIANS

Poti

Batum

Novorossiisk

Kerch

Black Sea

POLTAVA

KHARKOV

EKATERINOSLAV

KHERSON

Nikolaev

Odessa

Volga

Volga

0   200

Miles

Minorities, discontented by Tsarist rule

Eastern boundary of the Jewish Pale of settlement, within which the Jews were forcibly confined, forming a strong anti-Tsarist group

Provinces in which peasant rioting was common 1902-1904

Provinces in which over a quarter of the peasants did not own horses in 1904

Zubatov Unions, 1901-1903. Government sponsored trade unions, infiltrated by the Tsarist secret police

First three assassinations carried out by the Socialist Revolutionary Party, with dates

Principal strikes 1885-1903

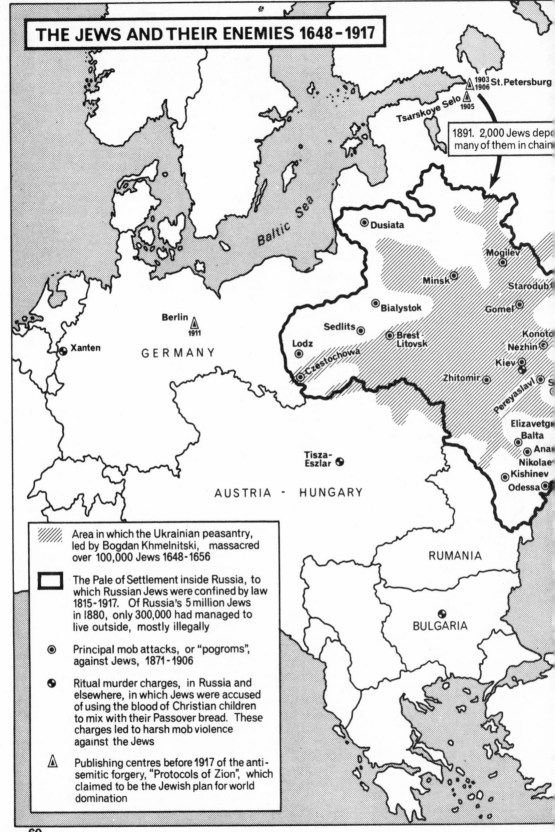

THE JEWS AND THEIR ENEMIES 1648-1917

1903
1906 St. Petersburg

Tsarskoye Selo 1905

1891. 2,000 Jews depo
many of them in chain

Dusiata

Mogilev

Minsk

Starodub

Berlin 1911

Bialystok

Gomel

Xanten

GERMANY

Sedlits

Brest-Litovsk

Konoto

Nezhin

Lodz

Kiev

Czestochowa

Zhitomir

Pereyaslavl

Elizavetg

Balta

Tisza-Eszlar

Ana

Nikolae

AUSTRIA - HUNGARY

Kishinev

Odessa

RUMANIA

BULGARIA

Baltic Sea

Area in which the Ukrainian peasantry, led by Bogdan Khmelnitski, massacred over 100,000 Jews 1648-1656

The Pale of Settlement inside Russia, to which Russian Jews were confined by law 1815-1917. Of Russia's 5 million Jews in 1880, only 300,000 had managed to live outside, mostly illegally

◎ Principal mob attacks, or "pogroms", against Jews, 1871-1906

✦ Ritual murder charges, in Russia and elsewhere, in which Jews were accused of using the blood of Christian children to mix with their Passover bread. These charges led to harsh mob violence against the Jews

△ Publishing centres before 1917 of the anti-semitic forgery, "Protocols of Zion", which claimed to be the Jewish plan for world domination

ogda

The three main anti-Jewish groups in Imperial Russia were the peasants and Cossacks of the Ukraine, the intellectual Slavophils, and the Tsarist Government and aristocracy. The peasants and Cossacks saw the rich Jew as an exploiter, the poor Jew as a rival, and the intellectual Jew as a dangerous revolutionary. The Slavophils believed in the sacred mission of the Slav peoples, under the guidance of their Orthodox Tsar; they wanted Russia to adopt a strong pro-Slav, and anti-Turk policy, and saw the Jew as anti-Christ, an alien on Russian soil, and a subversive influence acting against Russian interests. Both peasants and Slavophils were in many ways supported by the Government, whose laws discriminated against the Jews, and whose Pale of Settlement confined them

Nizhni
Novgorod ◉

◉ Murom   ◉ Simbirsk

scow

20,000 Jews expelled

⊕ Saratov

◉ Tsaritsyn

noslav

◉ Rostov

pol
◉

imferopol

⊕ Kutais

Caspian Sea

k   _Sea_

1882 500,000 Jews living in rural areas of the Pale were forced to leave their homes and live in towns or townlets (shtetls) in the Pale. 250,000 Jews living along the western frontier zone were also moved into the Pale. A further 700,000 Jews living east of the Pale were driven into the Pale by 1891

200

Miles

—— National boundaries of 1914

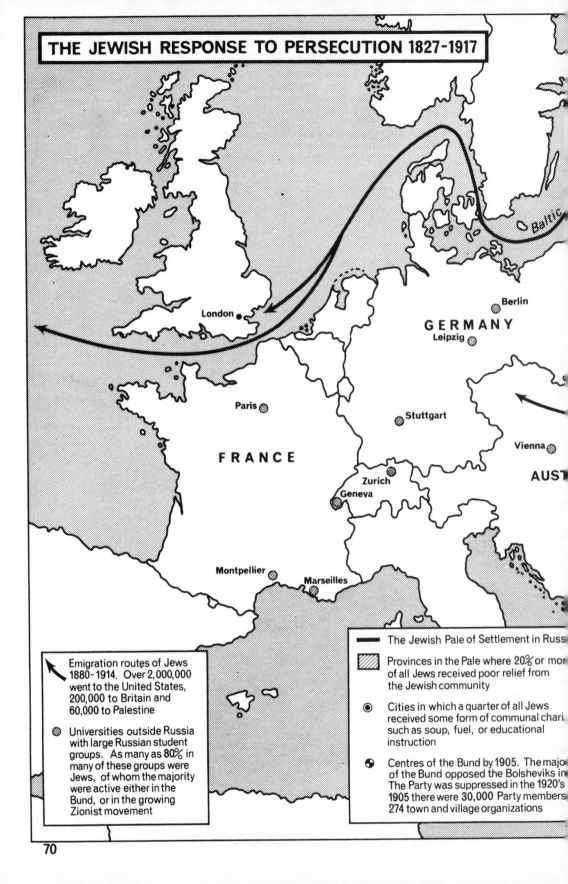

THE JEWISH RESPONSE TO PERSECUTION 1827-1917

Baltic

Berlin

GERMANY
Leipzig

London

Paris

Stuttgart

Vienna

FRANCE

AUST

Zurich
Geneva

Montpellier
Marseilles

The Jewish Pale of Settlement in Russ

Provinces in the Pale where 20% or mor
of all Jews received poor relief from
the Jewish community

Cities in which a quarter of all Jews
received some form of communal chari
such as soup, fuel, or educational
instruction

Centres of the Bund by 1905. The majo
of the Bund opposed the Bolsheviks in
The Party was suppressed in the 1920's
1905 there were 30,000 Party members
274 town and village organizations

Emigration routes of Jews
1880-1914. Over 2,000,000
went to the United States,
200,000 to Britain and
60,000 to Palestine

Universities outside Russia
with large Russian student
groups. As many as 80% in
many of these groups were
Jews, of whom the majority
were active either in the
Bund, or in the growing
Zionist movement

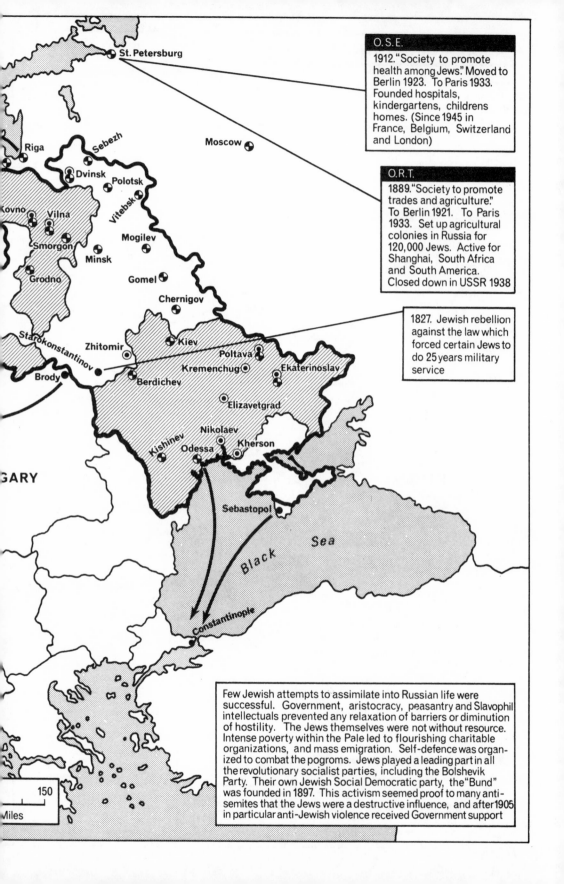

O.S.E.
1912. "Society to promote health among Jews." Moved to Berlin 1923. To Paris 1933. Founded hospitals, kindergartens, childrens homes. (Since 1945 in France, Belgium, Switzerland and London)

St. Petersburg

Moscow

O.R.T.
1889. "Society to promote trades and agriculture." To Berlin 1921. To Paris 1933. Set up agricultural colonies in Russia for 120,000 Jews. Active for Shanghai, South Africa and South America. Closed down in USSR 1938

Riga

Sebezh

Dvinsk

Polotsk

Kovno

Vilna

Vitebsk

Smorgon

Mogilev

Grodno

Minsk

Gomel

Chernigov

1827. Jewish rebellion against the law which forced certain Jews to do 25 years military service

Starokonstantinov

Zhitomir

Kiev

Poltava

Kremenchug

Ekaterinoslav

Brody

Berdichev

Elizavetgrad

Kishinev

Nikolaev

Odessa

Kherson

GARY

Sebastopol

Black Sea

Constantinople

150

Miles

Few Jewish attempts to assimilate into Russian life were successful. Government, aristocracy, peasantry and Slavophil intellectuals prevented any relaxation of barriers or diminution of hostility. The Jews themselves were not without resource. Intense poverty within the Pale led to flourishing charitable organizations, and mass emigration. Self-defence was organized to combat the pogroms. Jews played a leading part in all the revolutionary socialist parties, including the Bolshevik Party. Their own Jewish Social Democratic party, the "Bund" was founded in 1897. This activism seemed proof to many anti-semites that the Jews were a destructive influence, and after 1905 in particular anti-Jewish violence received Government support

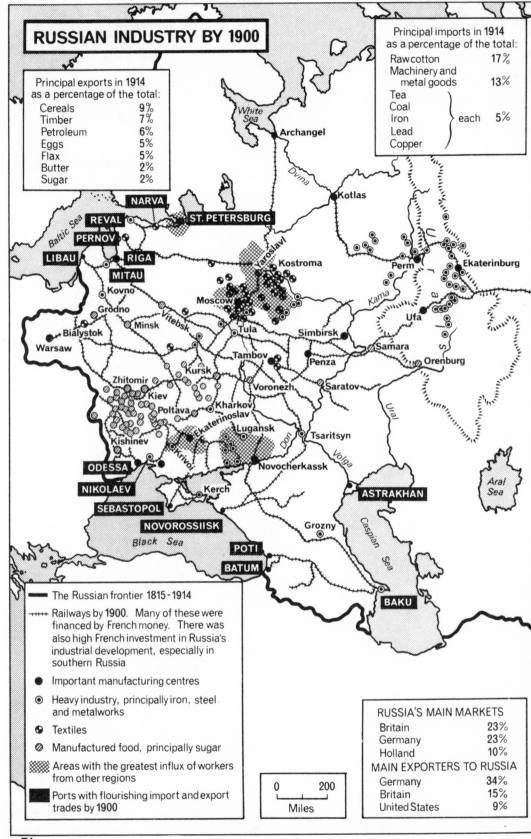

RUSSIAN INDUSTRY BY 1900

Principal exports in 1914 as a percentage of the total:

Cereals	9%
Timber	7%
Petroleum	6%
Eggs	5%
Flax	5%
Butter	2%
Sugar	2%

Principal imports in 1914 as a percentage of the total:

Raw cotton	17%
Machinery and metal goods	13%
Tea	
Coal	
Iron	each 5%
Lead	
Copper	

White Sea
Archangel
Dvina
Kotlas
NARVA
REVAL
PERNOV
ST. PETERSBURG
Baltic Sea
LIBAU
RIGA
MITAU
Kovno
Grodno
Vitebsk
Minsk
Bialystok
Warsaw
Zhitomir
Kiev
Poltava
Kishinev
Krivoi
ODESSA
NIKOLAEV
SEBASTOPOL
NOVOROSSIISK
Black Sea
POTI
BATUM
Kerch
Yaroslavl
Kostroma
Moscow
Tula
Kursk
Tambov
Voronezh
Kharkov
Ekaterinoslav
Lugansk
Novocherkassk
Don
Simbirsk
Penza
Saratov
Tsaritsyn
Volga
Perm
Kama
Ufa
Samara
Orenburg
Ekaterinburg
Ural
Grozny
Caspian Sea
ASTRAKHAN
Aral Sea
BAKU

— The Russian frontier 1815-1914

┼┼┼┼ Railways by 1900. Many of these were financed by French money. There was also high French investment in Russia's industrial development, especially in southern Russia

● Important manufacturing centres

◉ Heavy industry, principally iron, steel and metalworks

◉ Textiles

⊘ Manufactured food, principally sugar

▩ Areas with the greatest influx of workers from other regions

▬ Ports with flourishing import and export trades by 1900

0 200
Miles

RUSSIA'S MAIN MARKETS

Britain	23%
Germany	23%
Holland	10%

MAIN EXPORTERS TO RUSSIA

Germany	34%
Britain	15%
United States	9%

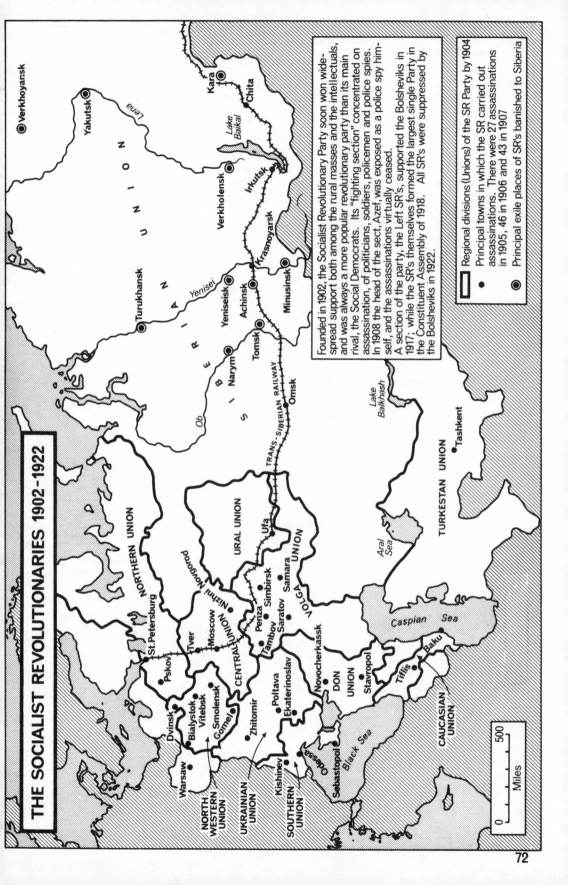

THE SOCIALIST REVOLUTIONARIES 1902–1922

Founded in 1902, the Socialist Revolutionary Party soon won wide-spread support both among the rural masses and the intellectuals, and was always a more popular revolutionary party than its main rival, the Social Democrats. Its "fighting section" concentrated on assassination, of politicians, soldiers, policemen and police spies. In 1908 the head of the sect, Azef, was exposed as a police spy him-self, and the assassinations virtually ceased.
A section of the party, the Left SR's, supported the Bolsheviks in 1917; while the SR's themselves formed the largest single Party in the Constituent Assembly of 1918.   All SR's were suppressed by the Bolsheviks in 1922.

▢   Regional divisions (Unions) of the SR Party by 1904

•   Principal towns in which the SR carried out assassinations.   There were 27 assassinations in 1905, 46 in 1906 and 43 in 1907

◉   Principal exile places of SR's banished to Siberia

72

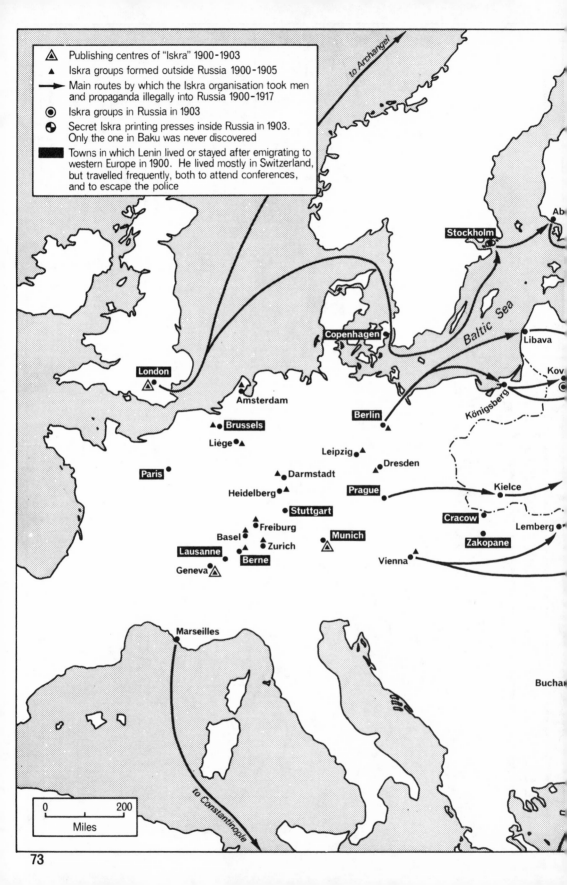

Publishing centres of "Iskra" 1900-1903

▲ Iskra groups formed outside Russia 1900-1905

→ Main routes by which the Iskra organisation took men and propaganda illegally into Russia 1900-1917

◉ Iskra groups in Russia in 1903

◕ Secret Iskra printing presses inside Russia in 1903. Only the one in Baku was never discovered

▬ Towns in which Lenin lived or stayed after emigrating to western Europe in 1900. He lived mostly in Switzerland, but travelled frequently, both to attend conferences, and to escape the police

to Archangel

Baltic Sea

Stockholm

Ab

Copenhagen

Libava

Kov

London

Königsberg

Amsterdam

Berlin

Brussels

Liége

Leipzig

Paris

Darmstadt

Dresden

Heidelberg

Prague

Kielce

Stuttgart

Cracow

Freiburg

Munich

Lemberg

Basel

Zurich

Zakopane

Lausanne

Berne

Vienna

Geneva

Marseilles

Bucha

to Constantinople

| 0 | 200 |
Miles

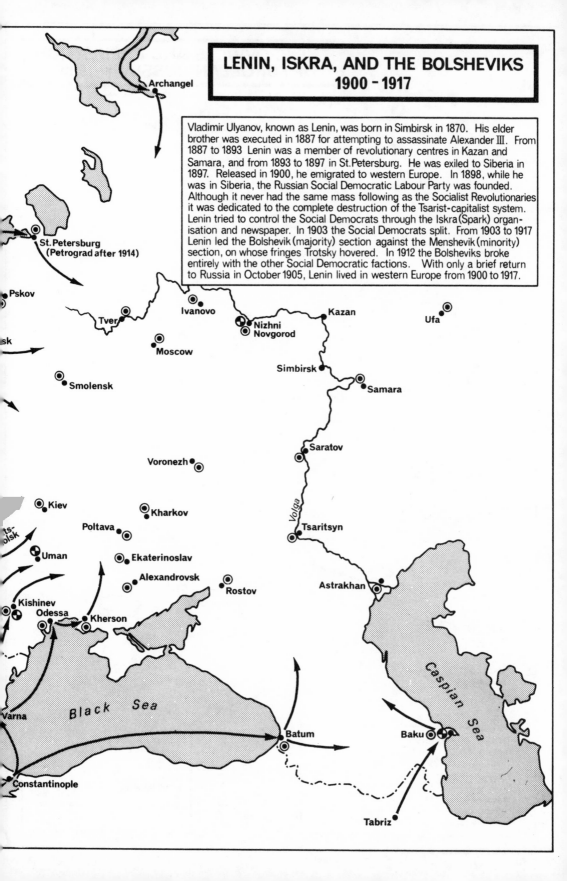

LENIN, ISKRA, AND THE BOLSHEVIKS
1900 - 1917

Vladimir Ulyanov, known as Lenin, was born in Simbirsk in 1870. His elder brother was executed in 1887 for attempting to assassinate Alexander III. From 1887 to 1893 Lenin was a member of revolutionary centres in Kazan and Samara, and from 1893 to 1897 in St.Petersburg. He was exiled to Siberia in 1897. Released in 1900, he emigrated to western Europe. In 1898, while he was in Siberia, the Russian Social Democratic Labour Party was founded. Although it never had the same mass following as the Socialist Revolutionaries it was dedicated to the complete destruction of the Tsarist-capitalist system. Lenin tried to control the Social Democrats through the Iskra(Spark) organisation and newspaper. In 1903 the Social Democrats split. From 1903 to 1917 Lenin led the Bolshevik (majority) section against the Menshevik (minority) section, on whose fringes Trotsky hovered. In 1912 the Bolsheviks broke entirely with the other Social Democratic factions.   With only a brief return to Russia in October 1905, Lenin lived in western Europe from 1900 to 1917.

Archangel

St.Petersburg
(Petrograd after 1914)

Pskov

Tver

Ivanovo

Nizhni
Novgorod

Kazan

Ufa

Moscow

Simbirsk

Smolensk

Samara

Voronezh

Saratov

Kiev

Kharkov

Poltava

Volga

Uman

Ekaterinoslav

Tsaritsyn

Alexandrovsk

Rostov

Astrakhan

Kishinev

Odessa

Kherson

Caspian Sea

Black Sea

Varna

Batum

Baku

Constantinople

Tabriz

THE PROVINCES AND POPULATION OF EUROPEAN RUSSIA IN 1900

White Sea

NORWAY

SWEDEN

ARCHANGEL

FINLAND

OLONETS

VOLOGDA

Baltic Sea

ESTLAND

ST PETERSBURG

NOVGOROD

PERM

VIATKA

KURLAND

LIVLAND

PSKOV

YAROSLAVL

KOSTROMA

KOVNO

VITEBSK

TVER

VLADIMIR

NIZHNI NOVGOROD

KAZAN

UFA

GERMANY

VILNA

MOSCOW

GRODNO

MOGILEV

SMOLENSK

KALUGA

RIAZAN

SIMBIRSK

POLISH PROVINCES

MINSK

TULA

PENZA

SAMARA

ORENBURG

OREL

TAMBOV

SARATOV

CHERNIGOV

KURSK

VOLHYNIA

KIEV

POLTAVA

VORONEZH

AUSTRIA-HUNGARY

PODOLIA

KHARKOV

BESSARABIA

KHERSON

EKATERINOSLAV

DON

ASTRAKHAN

RUMANIA

TAURIDA

KUBAN

STAVROPOL

Caspian Sea

Black Sea

TEREK

TRANS-CAUCASIAN PROVINCES

TURKEY

PERSIA

The first official Russian census was held in 1897. The total population was just over 129 million - nearly as large as the combined populations of Britain, France, and Germany. Over 80% of all Russians were peasants. Finland was an autonomous Duchy, and, like Poland, was subdivided into Provinces

MAIN NATIONAL & ETHNIC GROUPS IN EUROPEAN RUSSIA IN 1900	
Russians	55 million
Ukrainians	22 million
Poles	8 million
White Russians	6 million
Jews	5 million
Balts	4 million
Caucasians	3 million
Germans	2 million

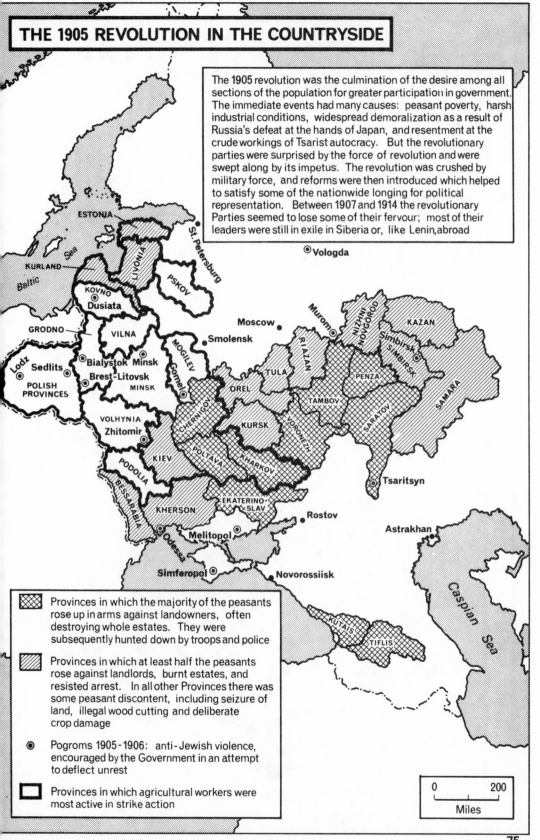

THE 1905 REVOLUTION IN THE COUNTRYSIDE

The 1905 revolution was the culmination of the desire among all sections of the population for greater participation in government. The immediate events had many causes: peasant poverty, harsh industrial conditions, widespread demoralization as a result of Russia's defeat at the hands of Japan, and resentment at the crude workings of Tsarist autocracy. But the revolutionary parties were surprised by the force of revolution and were swept along by its impetus. The revolution was crushed by military force, and reforms were then introduced which helped to satisfy some of the nationwide longing for political representation. Between 1907 and 1914 the revolutionary Parties seemed to lose some of their fervour; most of their leaders were still in exile in Siberia or, like Lenin, abroad

⊚ Vologda

ESTONIA

Baltic Sea

KURLAND

LIVONIA

St. Petersburg

PSKOV

KOVNO
● Dusiata

GRODNO

VILNA

Moscow ●
Smolensk ●

Murom ⊚

NIZHNI NOVGOROD

KAZAN

Simbirsk ⊚
S.MBIRSK

Lodz
Sedlits ●
POLISH PROVINCES

MOGILEV

● Bialystok Minsk ●
Brest-Litovsk
Gomel ⊚
MINSK

RIAZAN

TULA

OREL

PENZA

SAMARA

VOLHYNIA
Zhitomir ●

CHERNIGOV

KURSK

VORONEZH

TAMBOV

SARATOV

PODOLIA

KIEV

POLTAVA

KHARKOV

BESSARABIA

KHERSON

EKATERINO-SLAV

Tsaritsyn ⊚

Odessa ⊚
Melitopol ●

Rostov ●

Astrakhan ●

Simferopol ⊚

Novorossiisk ●

Caspian Sea

KUTAIS

TIFLIS

Provinces in which the majority of the peasants rose up in arms against landowners, often destroying whole estates. They were subsequently hunted down by troops and police

Provinces in which at least half the peasants rose against landlords, burnt estates, and resisted arrest. In all other Provinces there was some peasant discontent, including seizure of land, illegal wood cutting and deliberate crop damage

⊚ Pogroms 1905-1906: anti-Jewish violence, encouraged by the Government in an attempt to deflect unrest

Provinces in which agricultural workers were most active in strike action

0   200
Miles

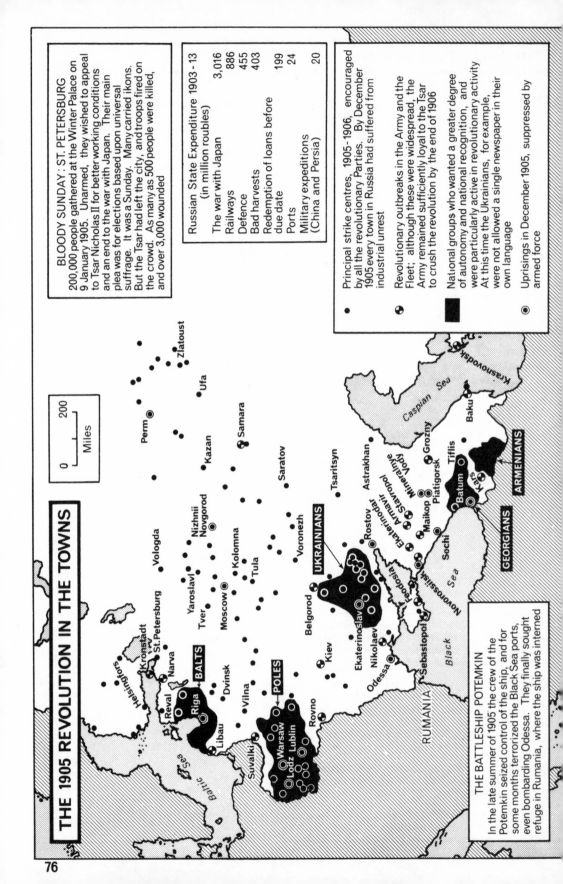

THE 1905 REVOLUTION IN THE TOWNS

BLOODY SUNDAY: ST. PETERSBURG
200,000 people gathered at the Winter Palace on 9 January 1905. Unarmed, they wished to appeal to Tsar Nicholas II for better working conditions and an end to the war with Japan. Their main plea was for elections based upon universal suffrage. It was a Sunday. Many carried ikons. But the Tsar had left the city, and troops fired on the crowd. As many as 500 people were killed, and over 3,000 wounded

Russian State Expenditure 1903 - 13 (in million roubles)	
The war with Japan	3,016
Railways	886
Defence	455
Bad harvests	403
Redemption of loans before due date	199
Ports	24
Military expeditions (China and Persia)	20

• Principal strike centres, 1905-1906, encouraged by all the revolutionary Parties. By December 1905 every town in Russia had suffered from industrial unrest

◐ Revolutionary outbreaks in the Army and the Fleet; although these were widespread, the Army remained sufficiently loyal to the Tsar to crush the revolution by the end of 1906

■ National groups who wanted a greater degree of autonomy and national recognition, and were particularly active in revolutionary activity. At this time the Ukrainians, for example, were not allowed a single newspaper in their own language

◉ Uprisings in December 1905, suppressed by armed force

THE BATTLESHIP POTEMKIN
In the late summer of 1905 the crew of the Potemkin seized control of the ship, and for some months terrorized the Black Sea ports, even bombarding Odessa. They finally sought refuge in Rumania, where the ship was interned

BALTS
POLES
UKRAINIANS
ARMENIANS
GEORGIANS

Zlatoust
Ufa
Perm
Samara
Kazan
Saratov
Nizhnii Novgorod
Vologda
Kolomna
Tula
Voronezh
Tsaritsyn
Astrakhan
Yaroslavl
Tver
Moscow
Belgorod
Rostov
Ekaterinodar
Mineralnye Vody
Grozny
Piatigorsk
Stavropol
Armavir
Maikop
Sochi
Batum
Tiflis
Kars
Baku
Krasnovodsk
Helsingfors
Kronstadt
St. Petersburg
Narva
Reval
Riga
Libau
Dvinsk
Vilna
Suvalki
Warsaw
Lodz
Lublin
Rovno
Kiev
Ekaterinoslav
Nikolaev
Odessa
Sebastopol
Feodosia
Novorossiisk
RUMANIA

Baltic Sea
Black Sea
Caspian Sea

0   200
Miles

76

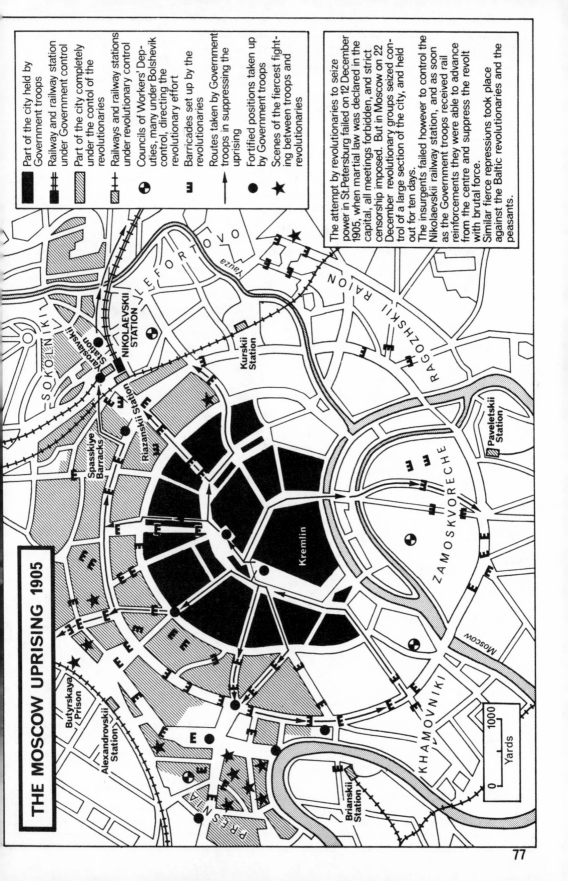

RUSSIA AND THE BALKANS 1876-1885

0   100

Miles

Russia wanted to drive the Turk from Europe and dominate the Balkans. Britain supported Russian protests against Turkish atrocities against the Bulgarians in 1875, which led Russia to attack Turkey. After defeating the Turks at Plevna in 1876 Russia tried to set up a large independent Bulgaria, but Britain and Austria-Hungary challenged Russia's aspirations, and under German mediation Russia agreed to the creation of a much smaller Bulgaria. Austria advanced her own Balkan interests by occupying the former Turkish province of Bosnia, which she formally annexed in 1908, and entering Novi Pazar.

RUSSIA

AUSTRIA-HUNGARY

RUMANIA

BOSNIA

Sarajevo

Belgrade

Bucharest

Constanza

SERBIA

Danube

Black Sea

NOVI PAZAR

Nish

Plevna

Silistria

BULGARIA

Varna

Tirnovo

Cattaro

Sofia

Burgas

EAST RUMELIA

MONTENEGRO

Adriatic Sea

Skopje

Midia

MACEDONIA

Kavalla

Adrianople

Constantinople

Rodosto

San Stephano

Dedeagatch

Chanak

TURKEY – IN – ASIA

Aegean Sea

G R E E C E

Athens

Legend:

- –·– The boundary of Turkey-in-Europe 1876
- ☐ Russian proposal for an independent "Big Bulgaria", agreed to by the Turks at the Treaty of San Stephano 1878
- ■ Bulgaria, autonomous, not independent, as allowed by Britain and Germany by the Treaty of Berlin 1878
- ▨ Turkish territory added to Serbia, Rumania and Montenegro (who each gained their independence from Turkey) by the Treaty of Berlin 1878; and to Greece in 1881
- ▦ Occupied by Austria-Hungary in 1878
- ▨ Added to Bulgaria in 1885, when Bulgaria became fully independent of Turkey

RUSSIA, THE BALKANS, AND THE COMING OF WAR 1912–1914

North Sea

BRITAIN

St. Petersburg

Reval

Riga

BALTIC PROVINCES

Moscow

RUSSIA

Danzig

Berlin

GERMANY

Warsaw

POLISH PROVINCES

Breslau

Pripet Marshes

Kiev

VOLHYNIA

Paris

FRANCE

Lemberg

Vienna

Budapest

AUSTRIA - HUNGARY

BOSNIA

Sarajevo

Belgrade

SERBIA

RUMANIA

Black Sea

BULGARIA

MONTENEGRO

ALBANIA

Skopje

GREECE

Constantinople

Bosphorus

Dardanelles

TURKEY

Adriatic Sea

0   500
Miles

Russia's mid-century alignment with Germany was changed during the 1880's to a new alignment with France, while at the same time Austria and Germany drew closer together. In the two Balkan Wars of 1912 and 1913 Turkey was driven almost entirely from Europe, but Russia's position did not improve; for as a result of Turkey's defeat Austrian influence increased even further. In June 1914 a Bosnian Serb murdered the Austrian heir to the throne, Archduke Franz-Ferdinand, at Sarajevo. Austria invaded Serbia on 28 July 1914. Russia then declared war on Austria. Germany supported her ally Austria and declared war on Russia. France and Britain joined Russia against Germany and Austria. Turkey attacked Russia in October 1914

Countries in which Austrian and German influence worked against Russia. Greece had a pro-German King; Turkey a pro-German Minister of War and virtual dictator; Bulgaria and Rumania had both accepted alliance with the Central Powers

Area of Russia in which Germany hoped to expand as a result of war

Russia's only two Balkan Allies, both threatened by Austria. Austria had created the state of Albania in 1912 in order to cut Serbia off from the sea.

Countries in western Europe sympathetic to Russia. France had a military alliance with Russia dating from 1894. Britain a convention dating from 1907

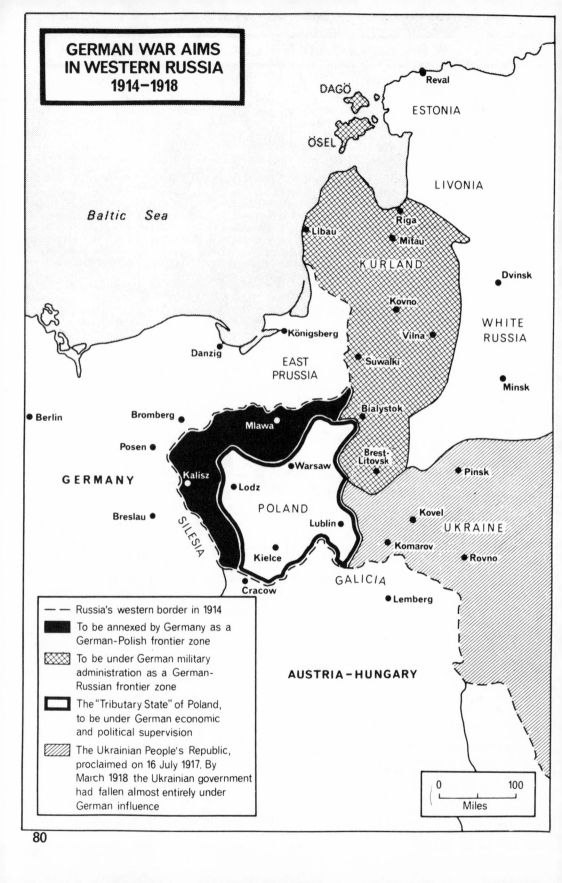

GERMAN WAR AIMS IN WESTERN RUSSIA 1914–1918

DAGÖ

Reval

ESTONIA

ÖSEL

LIVONIA

Baltic Sea

Riga

Libau

Mitau

KURLAND

Dvinsk

Kovno

Königsberg

Vilna

WHITE RUSSIA

Danzig

EAST PRUSSIA

Suwalki

Minsk

Berlin

Bromberg

Mlawa

Bialystok

Posen

Kalisz

Warsaw

Brest-Litovsk

Pinsk

GERMANY

Lodz

Kovel

UKRAINE

Breslau

POLAND

Lublin

Komarov

Rovno

SILESIA

Kielce

Cracow

GALICIA

Lemberg

AUSTRIA–HUNGARY

— — Russia's western border in 1914

To be annexed by Germany as a German-Polish frontier zone

To be under German military administration as a German-Russian frontier zone

The "Tributary State" of Poland, to be under German economic and political supervision

The Ukrainian People's Republic, proclaimed on 16 July 1917. By March 1918 the Ukrainian government had fallen almost entirely under German influence

0   100

Miles

THE EASTERN FRONT 1914

Baltic Sea

GERMANY

EAST PRUSSIA

Danzig

Elbing

Königsberg

Gumbinnen

Vilkoviski

Masurian Lakes

Suvalki

Augustow

Tannenberg

Mlawa

Bialystok

Vistula

RUSSIA

Plotsk

Bug

Kutno

Warsaw

Brest–Litovsk

Kalisz

Lodz

Vistula

Piotrkow

Kielce

Lublin

SILESIA

Novo Radomsk

Krasnik

Komarov

Czestochowa

Cracow

Tarnow

GALICIA

Przemysl

Lemberg

Gorlice

Carpathians

AUSTRIA-HUNGARY

Russian advance into East Prussia 4-23 August. Between August 26 and September 13 they were defeated at Tannenberg and the Masurian Lakes, and driven back into Russia

Russian territory conquered by Germany September 28 - December 31. At the Battle of Lodz, in November, the Germans prevented a Russian advance into Silesia

Austrian advances into Russia

Russian counter-attacks into Austria

Conquered by Russia from Austria

The front line on 31 December 1914

0   50
Miles

Russian victories

German victories

81

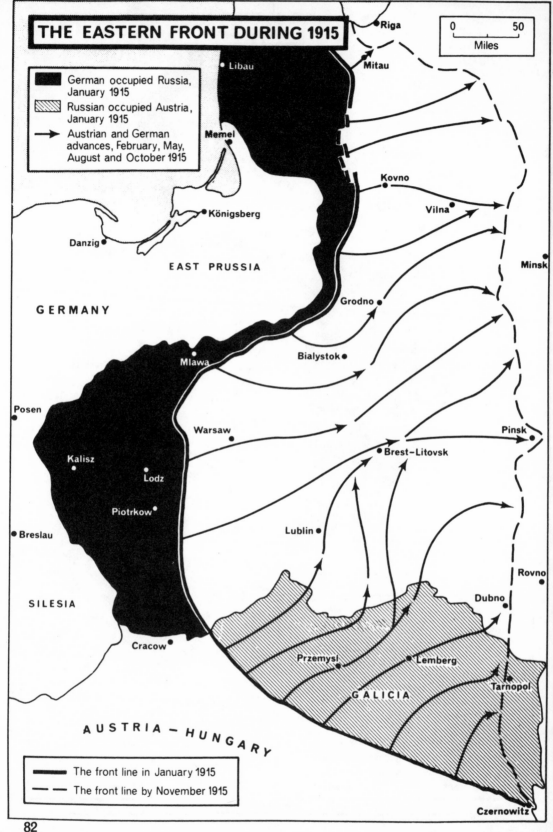

THE EASTERN FRONT DURING 1915

■	German occupied Russia, January 1915
▨	Russian occupied Austria, January 1915
→	Austrian and German advances, February, May, August and October 1915

0   50
Miles

Riga

Libau

Mitau

Memel

Kovno

Königsberg

Vilna

Danzig

EAST PRUSSIA

Minsk

GERMANY

Grodno

Mlawa

Bialystok

Posen

Warsaw

Pinsk

Kalisz

Brest–Litovsk

Lodz

Piotrkow

Lublin

Breslau

Rovno

SILESIA

Dubno

Cracow

Przemysl

Lemberg

Tarnopol

G A L I C I A

A U S T R I A – H U N G A R Y

▬▬▬	The front line in January 1915
┄┄┄	The front line by November 1915

Czernowitz

82

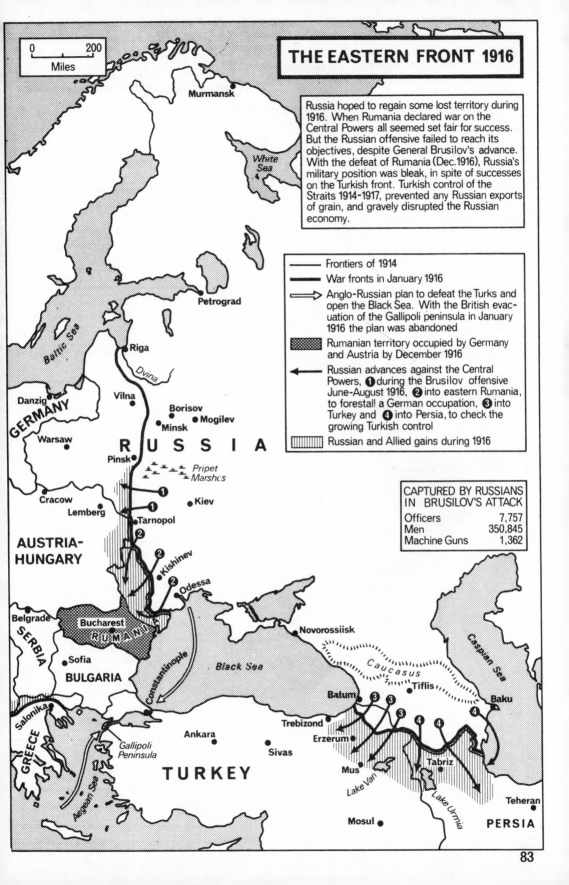

THE EASTERN FRONT 1916

Russia hoped to regain some lost territory during 1916. When Rumania declared war on the Central Powers all seemed set fair for success. But the Russian offensive failed to reach its objectives, despite General Brusilov's advance. With the defeat of Rumania (Dec.1916), Russia's military position was bleak, in spite of successes on the Turkish front. Turkish control of the Straits 1914-1917, prevented any Russian exports of grain, and gravely disrupted the Russian economy.

Frontiers of 1914

War fronts in January 1916

Anglo-Russian plan to defeat the Turks and open the Black Sea. With the British evacuation of the Gallipoli peninsula in January 1916 the plan was abandoned

Rumanian territory occupied by Germany and Austria by December 1916

Russian advances against the Central Powers, ❶ during the Brusilov offensive June-August 1916, ❷ into eastern Rumania, to forestall a German occupation, ❸ into Turkey and ❹ into Persia, to check the growing Turkish control

Russian and Allied gains during 1916

CAPTURED BY RUSSIANS IN BRUSILOV'S ATTACK	
Officers	7,757
Men	350,845
Machine Guns	1,362

Scale: 0 — 200 Miles

Murmansk

White Sea

Petrograd

Baltic Sea

Riga
Dvina

Danzig
Vilna

GERMANY
Borisov
Mogilev
Minsk

Warsaw
RUSSIA

Pinsk

Pripet Marshes

Cracow
Kiev
Lemberg
Tarnopol

AUSTRIA-HUNGARY

Kishinev
Odessa

Belgrade
Bucharest
RUMANIA

SERBIA
Sofia
BULGARIA

Constantinople

Novorossiisk

Black Sea

Caucasus
Tiflis
Caspian Sea
Baku

Batum
Trebizond
Erzerum

Salonika

GREECE

Ankara
Sivas

Gallipoli Peninsula

Mus
Tabriz
Lake Van
Lake Urmia

Aegean Sea

TURKEY

Mosul

Teheran

PERSIA

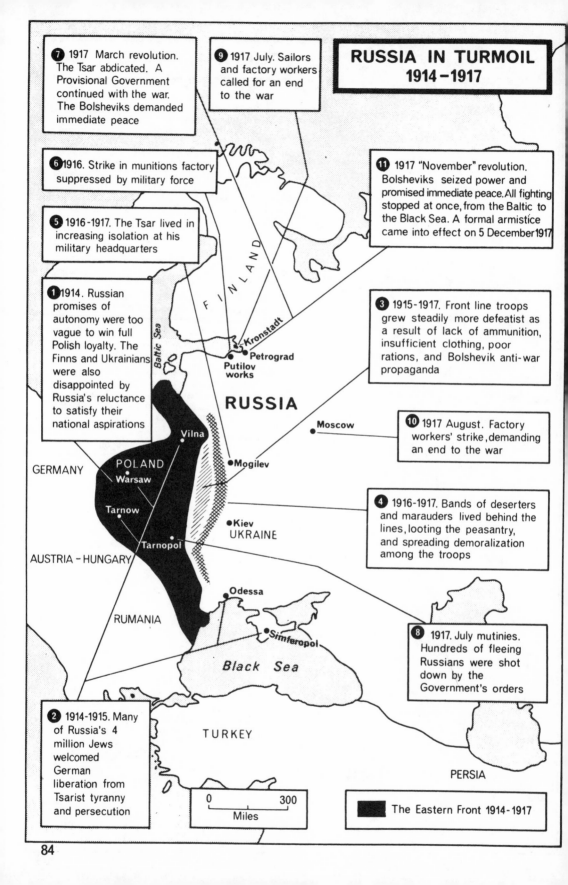

RUSSIA IN TURMOIL 1914–1917

7 1917 March revolution. The Tsar abdicated. A Provisional Government continued with the war. The Bolsheviks demanded immediate peace

9 1917 July. Sailors and factory workers called for an end to the war

6 1916. Strike in munitions factory suppressed by military force

5 1916-1917. The Tsar lived in increasing isolation at his military headquarters

1 1914. Russian promises of autonomy were too vague to win full Polish loyalty. The Finns and Ukrainians were also disappointed by Russia's reluctance to satisfy their national aspirations

11 1917 "November" revolution. Bolsheviks seized power and promised immediate peace. All fighting stopped at once, from the Baltic to the Black Sea. A formal armistice came into effect on 5 December 1917

3 1915-1917. Front line troops grew steadily more defeatist as a result of lack of ammunition, insufficient clothing, poor rations, and Bolshevik anti-war propaganda

10 1917 August. Factory workers' strike, demanding an end to the war

4 1916-1917. Bands of deserters and marauders lived behind the lines, looting the peasantry, and spreading demoralization among the troops

8 1917. July mutinies. Hundreds of fleeing Russians were shot down by the Government's orders

2 1914-1915. Many of Russia's 4 million Jews welcomed German liberation from Tsarist tyranny and persecution

FINLAND

Baltic Sea

Kronstadt

Petrograd
Putilov works

RUSSIA

Moscow

Vilna

Mogilev

GERMANY

POLAND
Warsaw

Tarnow

Kiev
UKRAINE

Tarnopol

AUSTRIA – HUNGARY

RUMANIA

Odessa

Simferopol

Black Sea

TURKEY

PERSIA

0   300
Miles

■ The Eastern Front 1914-1917

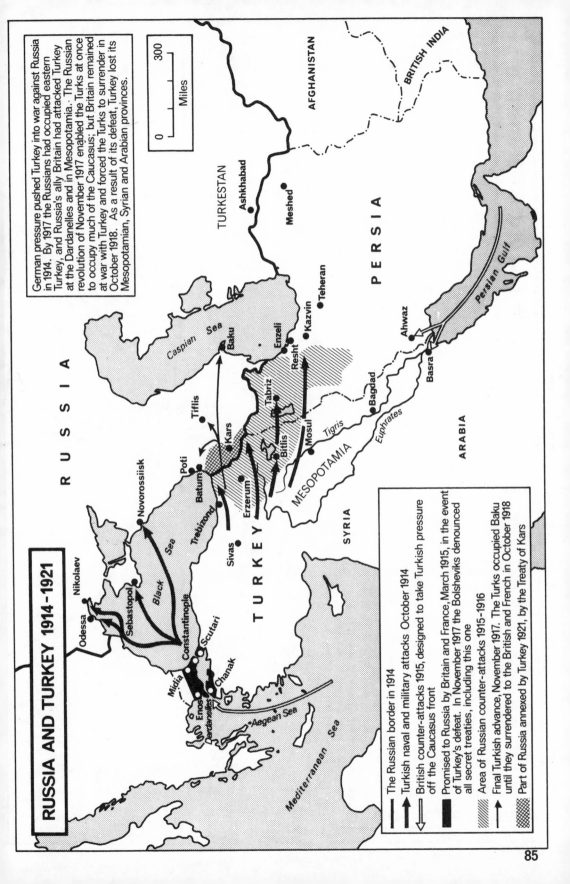

RUSSIA AND TURKEY 1914–1921

German pressure pushed Turkey into war against Russia in 1914. By 1917 the Russians had occupied eastern Turkey, and Russia's ally Britain had attacked Turkey at the Dardanelles and in Mesopotamia. The Russian revolution of November 1917 enabled the Turks at once to occupy much of the Caucasus; but Britain remained at war with Turkey and forced the Turks to surrender in October 1918. As a result of its defeat, Turkey lost its Mesopotamian, Syrian and Arabian provinces.

0 — 300

Miles

AFGHANISTAN

BRITISH INDIA

TURKESTAN

Ashkhabad

Meshed

PERSIA

Teheran

Kazvin

Ahwaz

Persian Gulf

Basra

Bagdad

Euphrates

ARABIA

Tigris

Mosul

MESOPOTAMIA

SYRIA

Enzeli

Resht

Tabriz

Bitlis

Erzerum

Kars

Tiflis

Baku

Caspian Sea

R U S S I A

Novorossiisk

Poti

Batum

Trebizond

Sivas

T U R K E Y

Black Sea

Sebastopol

Nikolaev

Odessa

Constantinople

Scutari

Midia

Enos

Chanak

Dardanelles

Aegean Sea

Mediterranean Sea

— The Russian border in 1914

↑ Turkish naval and military attacks October 1914

⇧ British counter-attacks 1915, designed to take Turkish pressure off the Caucasus front

▮ Promised to Russia by Britain and France, March 1915, in the event of Turkey's defeat. In November 1917 the Bolsheviks denounced all secret treaties, including this one

▨ Area of Russian counter-attacks 1915–1916

↑ Final Turkish advance, November 1917. The Turks occupied Baku until they surrendered to the British and French in October 1918

▧ Part of Russia annexed by Turkey 1921, by the Treaty of Kars

85

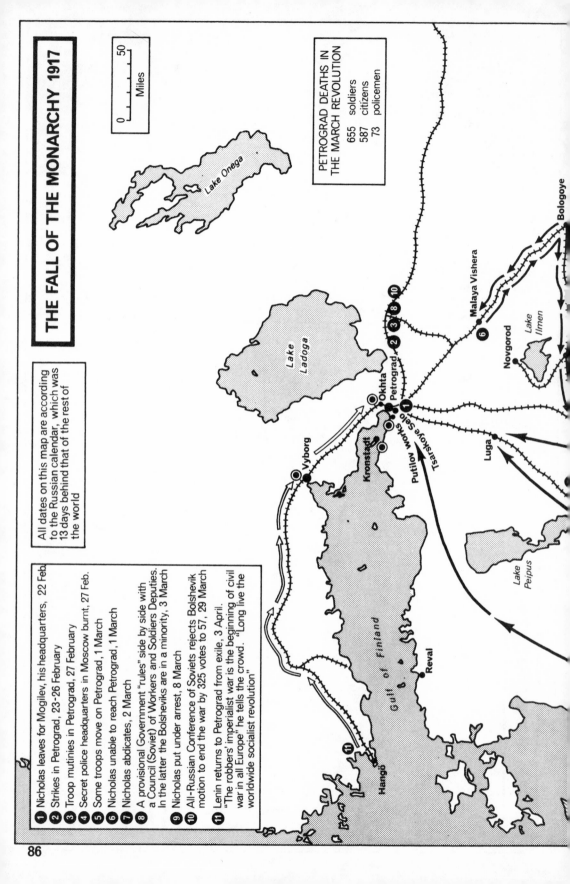

THE FALL OF THE MONARCHY 1917

0 50
Miles

PETROGRAD DEATHS IN
THE MARCH REVOLUTION

655	soldiers
587	citizens
73	policemen

All dates on this map are according
to the Russian calendar, which was
13 days behind that of the rest of
the world

1. Nicholas leaves for Mogilev, his headquarters, 22 Feb.
2. Strikes in Petrograd, 23-26 February
3. Troop mutinies in Petrograd, 27 February
4. Secret police headquarters in Moscow burnt, 27 Feb.
5. Some troops move on Petrograd, 1 March
6. Nicholas unable to reach Petrograd, 1 March
7. Nicholas abdicates, 2 March
8. A provisional Government "rules" side by side with
   a Council (Soviet) of Workers and Soldiers Deputies.
   In the latter the Bolsheviks are in a minority, 3 March
9. Nicholas put under arrest, 8 March
10. All-Russian Conference of Soviets rejects Bolshevik
    motion to end the war by 325 votes to 57, 29 March
11. Lenin returns to Petrograd from exile, 3 April.
    "The robbers' imperialist war is the beginning of civil
    war in all Europe" he tells the crowd. "Long live the
    worldwide socialist revolution"

Lake Onega

Lake Ladoga

Lake Ilmen

Lake Peipus

Gulf of Finland

Bologoye

Malaya Vishera

Novgorod

Luga

Reval

Hangö

Vyborg

Kronstadt

Okhta

Petrograd

Putilov
works

Tsarskoye Selo

86

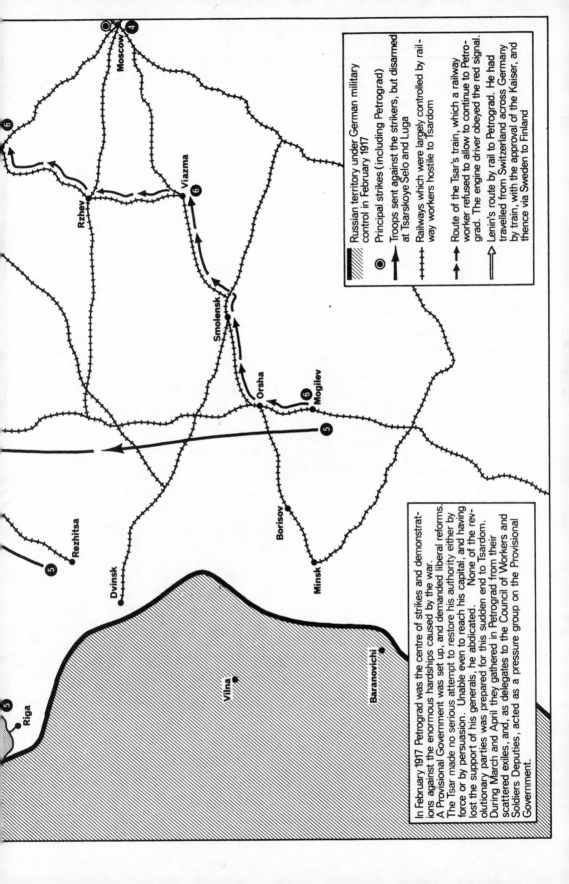

In February 1917 Petrograd was the centre of strikes and demonstrations against the enormous hardships caused by the war. A Provisional Government was set up, and demanded liberal reforms. The Tsar made no serious attempt to restore his authority either by force or by persuasion. Unable even to reach his capital, and having lost the support of his generals, he abdicated. None of the revolutionary parties was prepared for this sudden end to Tsardom. During March and April they gathered in Petrograd from their scattered exiles, and, as delegates to the Council of Workers and Soldiers Deputies, acted as a pressure group on the Provisional Government.

Russian territory under German military control in February 1917

Principal strikes (including Petrograd)

Troops sent against the strikers, but disarmed at Tsarskoye Selo and Luga

Railways which were largely controlled by railway workers hostile to Tsardom

Route of the Tsar's train, which a railway worker refused to allow to continue to Petrograd. The engine driver obeyed the red signal.

Lenin's route by rail to Petrograd. He had travelled from Switzerland across Germany by train, with the approval of the Kaiser, and thence via Sweden to Finland

Riga
Rezhitsa
Dvinsk
Vilna
Baranovichi
Minsk
Borisov
Mogilev
Orsha
Smolensk
Viazma
Rzhev
Moscow

LENIN'S RETURN TO RUSSIA 1917

Our tactics: absolute distrust; no support of new Government; Kerensky particularly suspect; to arm proletariat only guarantee; no rapprochement with other parties. This last is conditio sine qua non
**LENIN TO BOLSHEVIKS IN SWEDEN
TELEGRAM FROM BERN 26 MARCH 1917**

0   250
Miles

On 7 August 1914 Lenin was arrested in Cracow by the Austrians as an enemy alien and spy. He was released on 23 Aug., the Austrian Government having been persuaded that he was even more an enemy of Tsardom, and could "render great services" to Austria by fomenting anti-Tsarist troubles

The Central Powers and their conquests in February 1917

– ← – **Lenin's route from Austria to Switzerland, 1914**

•••→••• **Lenin's first proposed route back to Russia, which proved impossible for fear of arrest by the British**

→ **Lenin's actual route 9-16 April 1917**

▨ **Sea routes to Russia closed by Central Power minefields**

When revolution broke out in Petrograd in February 1917, Lenin, the Bolshevik leader, was in Switzerland. Wartime was not conducive to travel, nor did his plan to go through Britain prove possible. Instead, the German Government, eager to see dissension and chaos in Russia, agreed with alacrity to his request to travel across "enemy" territory, and provided him with facilities. Thus Imperial Germany served as a hand-maiden to the Russian revolution of October 1917

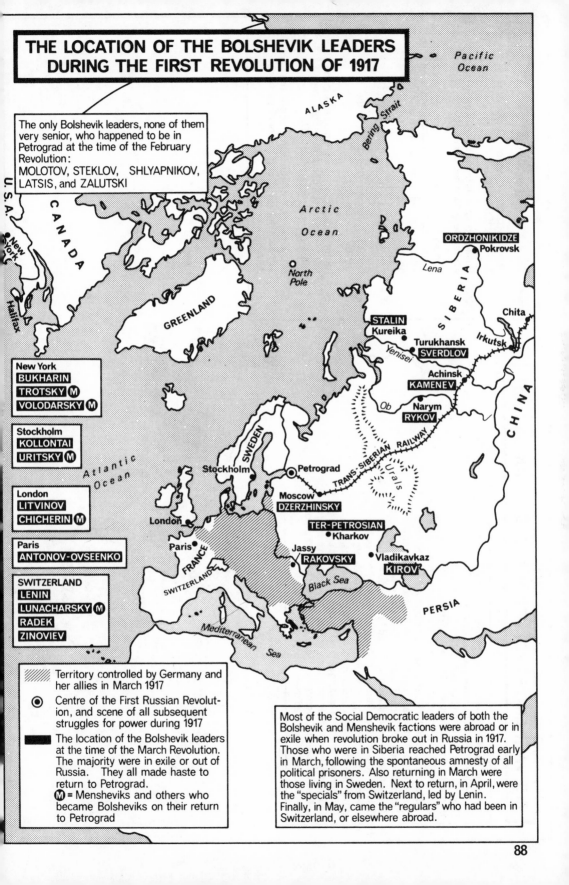

THE LOCATION OF THE BOLSHEVIK LEADERS DURING THE FIRST REVOLUTION OF 1917

The only Bolshevik leaders, none of them very senior, who happened to be in Petrograd at the time of the February Revolution:
MOLOTOV, STEKLOV, SHLYAPNIKOV, LATSIS, and ZALUTSKI

New York
BUKHARIN
TROTSKY Ⓜ
VOLODARSKY Ⓜ

Stockholm
KOLLONTAI
URITSKY Ⓜ

London
LITVINOV
CHICHERIN Ⓜ

Paris
ANTONOV-OVSEENKO

SWITZERLAND
LENIN
LUNACHARSKY Ⓜ
RADEK
ZINOVIEV

Pacific Ocean

ALASKA

Bering Strait

Arctic Ocean

North Pole

CANADA

U.S.A.

New York

Halifax

GREENLAND

Atlantic Ocean

SWEDEN

Stockholm

London

Paris

FRANCE

SWITZERLAND

Mediterranean Sea

Lena

SIBERIA

ORDZHONIKIDZE
● Pokrovsk

● Chita

STALIN
Kureika

Turukhansk
SVERDLOV

Irkutsk

Yenisei

Achinsk
KAMENEV

Ob

● Narym
RYKOV

TRANS-SIBERIAN RAILWAY

Urals

CHINA

Petrograd

Moscow
DZERZHINSKY

TER-PETROSIAN
● Kharkov

Jassy
RAKOVSKY

● Vladikavkaz
KIROV

Black Sea

PERSIA

///// Territory controlled by Germany and her allies in March 1917

◉ Centre of the First Russian Revolution, and scene of all subsequent struggles for power during 1917

▬ The location of the Bolshevik leaders at the time of the March Revolution. The majority were in exile or out of Russia. They all made haste to return to Petrograd.
Ⓜ = Mensheviks and others who became Bolsheviks on their return to Petrograd

Most of the Social Democratic leaders of both the Bolshevik and Menshevik factions were abroad or in exile when revolution broke out in Russia in 1917. Those who were in Siberia reached Petrograd early in March, following the spontaneous amnesty of all political prisoners. Also returning in March were those living in Sweden. Next to return, in April, were the "specials" from Switzerland, led by Lenin. Finally, in May, came the "regulars" who had been in Switzerland, or elsewhere abroad.

88

THE WAR AND REVOLUTION JULY AND AUGUST 1917

In March 1917 the Provisional Government assured Britain and France that it would continue the war against the Central Powers. But the offensive launched on 1 July ended two weeks later in mutiny and failure. Mass demonstrations in Petrograd on 16 and 17 July, though leaderless, showed how hated the war had become, and the Bolsheviks soon dominated the Soviets by their cry of "Bread and Peace". The Provisional Government then published evidence of financial dealings between the Bolsheviks and German agents, forced Lenin to go into hiding in Finland, and arrested Trotsky. In August General Kornilov led an army against Petrograd, intending to crush the Soviets and stiffen the Provisional Government against concessions. The Bolsheviks took a leading part in the defence of the city, and greatly increased their military power, having been armed by the Provisional Government. They also gained support among the masses, who feared the return of autocracy

The eastern front on 1 July 1917

Austrian territory conquered by Russia 1-16 July 1917

Russian proposals for further offensive action during the second two weeks of July

Subject peoples insisting on independence from Russian rule, and gravely hampering the war effort when their demands were rejected or disregarded

Principal areas of mutiny 17-30 July 1917

Kornilov's unsuccessful attack on the capital August 1917

Factory groups between Petrograd and the front with increasingly strong Bolshevik influence July-September 1917

Military units between Petrograd and the front with increasingly strong Bolshevik sections July-September 1917

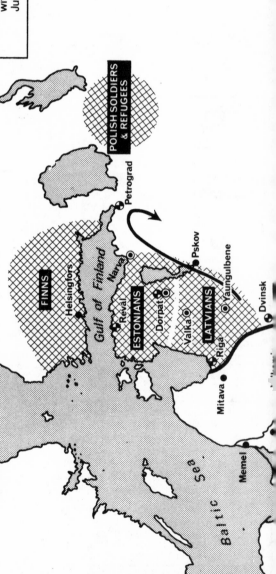

POLISH SOLDIERS & REFUGEES

Petrograd

FINNS

Gulf of Finland

Helsingfors

Pskov

Taungulbene

Reval

ESTONIANS

Dorpat

Narva

Valka

LATVIANS

Riga

Dvinsk

Mitava

Memel

Baltic Sea

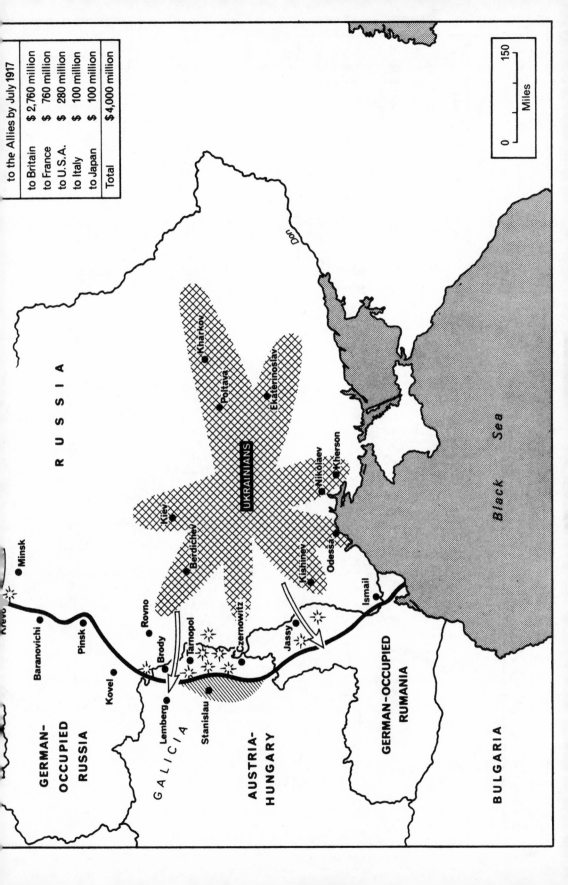

	to the Allies by July 1917	
to Britain	$	2,760 million
to France	$	760 million
to U.S.A.	$	280 million
to Italy	$	100 million
to Japan	$	100 million
Total		$4,000 million

RUSSIA

GERMAN-OCCUPIED RUSSIA

GALICIA

AUSTRIA-HUNGARY

GERMAN-OCCUPIED RUMANIA

BULGARIA

Black Sea

UKRAINIANS

Don

Minsk

Baranovichi

Pinsk

Kovel

Rovno

Brody

Lemberg

Stanislau

Tarnopol

Czernowitz

Jassy

Kishinev

Ismail

Odessa

Kherson

Nikolaev

Berdichev

Kiev

Poltava

Kharkov

Ekaterinoslav

Krevo

0   150

Miles

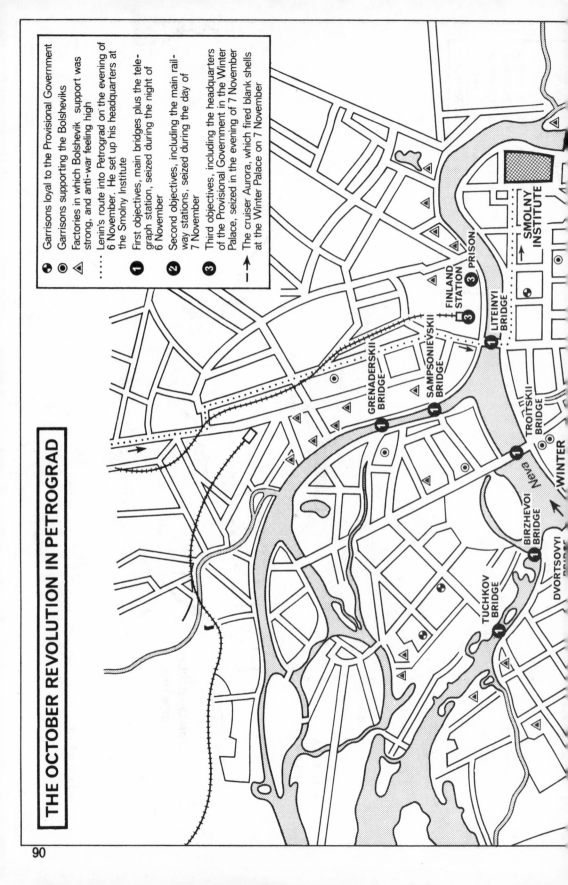

THE OCTOBER REVOLUTION IN PETROGRAD

Garrisons loyal to the Provisional Government

Garrisons supporting the Bolsheviks

Factories in which Bolshevik support was strong, and anti-war feeling high

Lenin's route into Petrograd on the evening of 6 November. He set up his headquarters at the Smolny Institute

1 First objectives, main bridges plus the telegraph station, seized during the night of 6 November

2 Second objectives, including the main railway stations, seized during the day of 7 November

3 Third objectives, including the headquarters of the Provisional Government in the Winter Palace, seized in the evening of 7 November

The cruiser Aurora, which fired blank shells at the Winter Palace on 7 November

SMOLNY INSTITUTE

FINLAND STATION

PRISON

LITEINYI BRIDGE

GRENADERSKII BRIDGE

SAMPSONIEVSKII BRIDGE

TROITSKII BRIDGE

Neva

WINTER

BIRZHEVOI BRIDGE

DVORTSOVYI

TUCHKOV BRIDGE

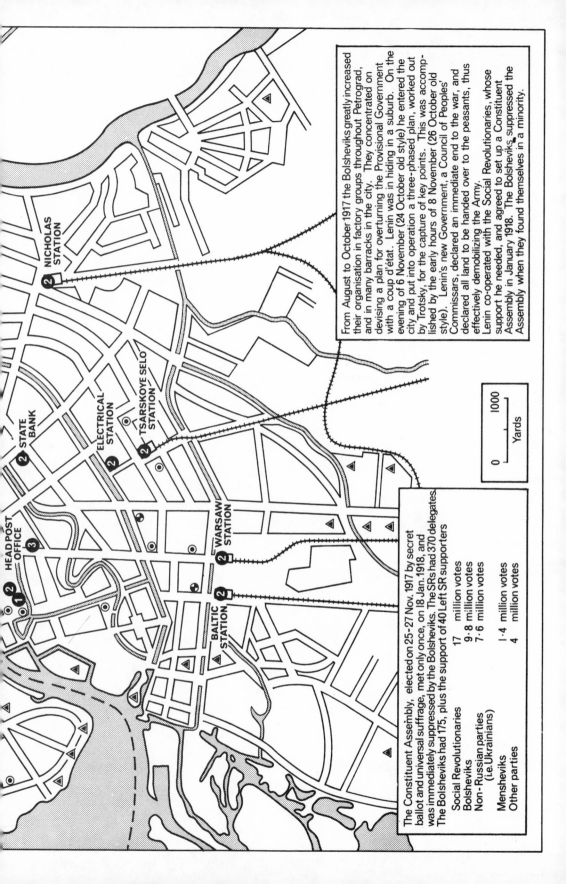

NICHOLAS STATION ②

HEAD POST OFFICE

② ②

STATE ② BANK

③

① ②

ELECTRICAL STATION ②

TSARSKOYE SELO STATION ②

WARSAW STATION ②

BALTIC STATION ②

From August to October 1917 the Bolsheviks greatly increased their organisation in factory groups throughout Petrograd, and in many barracks in the city. They concentrated on devising a plan for overturning the Provisional Government with a coup d'état. Lenin was in hiding in a suburb. On the evening of 6 November (24 October old style) he entered the city and put into operation a three-phased plan, worked out by Trotsky, for the capture of key points. This was accomplished by the early hours of 8 November (26 October old style). Lenin's new Government, a Council of Peoples' Commissars, declared an immediate end to the war, and declared all land to be handed over to the peasants, thus effectively demobilizing the Army.

Lenin co-operated with the Social Revolutionaries, whose support he needed, and agreed to set up a Constituent Assembly in January 1918. The Bolsheviks suppressed the Assembly when they found themselves in a minority.

0   1000
        Yards

The Constituent Assembly, elected on 25-27 Nov. 1917 by secret ballot and universal suffrage, met only once, on 18 Jan. 1918, and was immediately suppressed by the Bolsheviks. The SRs had 370 delegates. The Bolsheviks had 175, plus the support of 40 Left SR supporters

Social Revolutionaries	17	million votes
Bolsheviks	9·8	million votes
Non-Russian parties (i.e. Ukrainians)	7·6	million votes
Mensheviks	1·4	million votes
Other parties	4	million votes

Section Three

THE SOVIET UNION

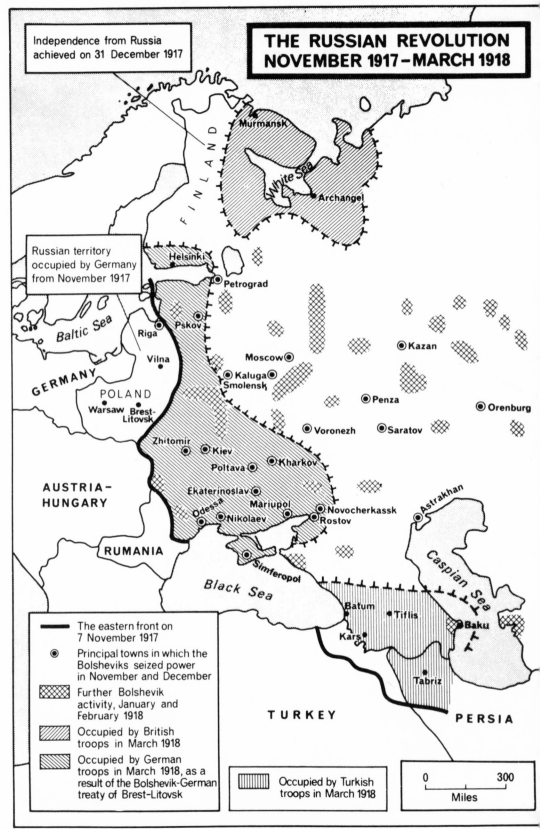

Independence from Russia
achieved on 31 December 1917

THE RUSSIAN REVOLUTION
NOVEMBER 1917–MARCH 1918

Murmansk

White Sea

Archangel

Russian territory
occupied by Germany
from November 1917

Helsinki

Petrograd

FINLAND

Baltic Sea

Pskov

Riga

Moscow

Kazan

Vilna

GERMANY

POLAND

Kaluga
Smolensk

Penza

Orenburg

Warsaw

Brest-
Litovsk

Voronezh

Saratov

Zhitomir

Kiev

AUSTRIA–
HUNGARY

Poltava

Kharkov

Ekaterinoslav

Odessa

Mariupol

Astrakhan

Nikolaev

Novocherkassk

RUMANIA

Rostov

Caspian Sea

Simferopol

Black Sea

Batum

Tiflis

Baku

Kars

The eastern front on
7 November 1917

Principal towns in which the
Bolsheviks seized power
in November and December

Tabriz

Further Bolshevik
activity, January and
February 1918

TURKEY

PERSIA

Occupied by British
troops in March 1918

Occupied by German
troops in March 1918, as a
result of the Bolshevik-German
treaty of Brest-Litovsk

Occupied by Turkish
troops in March 1918

0   300
Miles

91

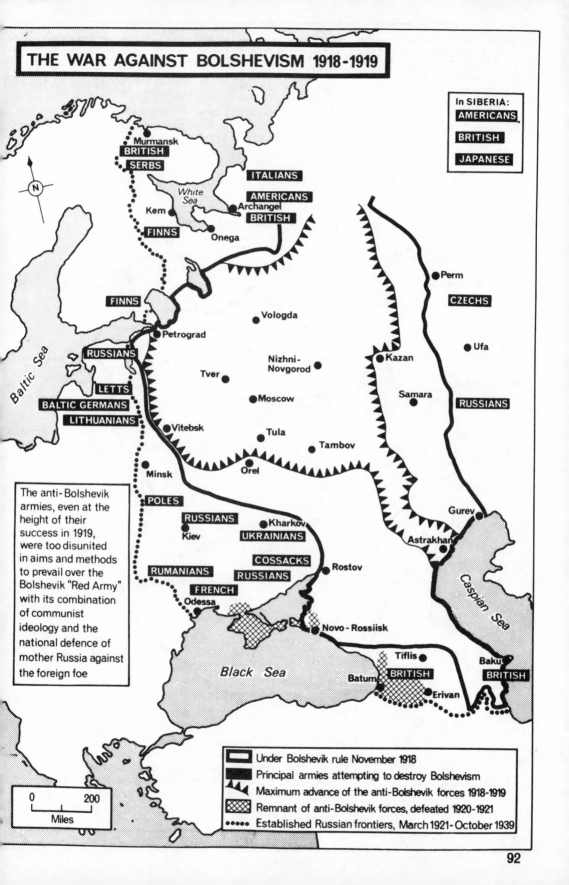

THE WAR AGAINST BOLSHEVISM 1918-1919

In SIBERIA:
AMERICANS
BRITISH
JAPANESE

Murmansk
BRITISH
SERBS

ITALIANS

White Sea

AMERICANS
Archangel
BRITISH

Kem

FINNS
Onega

Perm

CZECHS

FINNS

Vologda

Petrograd

Ufa

RUSSIANS

Nizhni-Novgorod

Kazan

Tver

Samara

Moscow

RUSSIANS

LETTS
BALTIC GERMANS
LITHUANIANS

Vitebsk

Tula

Tambov

Minsk

Orel

POLES

RUSSIANS
Kiev

Kharkov

Gurev

UKRAINIANS

Astrakhan

The anti-Bolshevik armies, even at the height of their success in 1919, were too disunited in aims and methods to prevail over the Bolshevik "Red Army" with its combination of communist ideology and the national defence of mother Russia against the foreign foe

COSSACKS

Rostov

RUMANIANS
RUSSIANS

FRENCH
Odessa

Novo - Rossiisk

Caspian Sea

Tiflis

Baku

Black Sea

Batum
BRITISH

BRITISH

Erivan

Baltic Sea

0   200
Miles

☐ Under Bolshevik rule November 1918

◼ Principal armies attempting to destroy Bolshevism

◣ Maximum advance of the anti-Bolshevik forces 1918-1919

▨ Remnant of anti-Bolshevik forces, defeated 1920-1921

•••• Established Russian frontiers, March 1921-October 1939

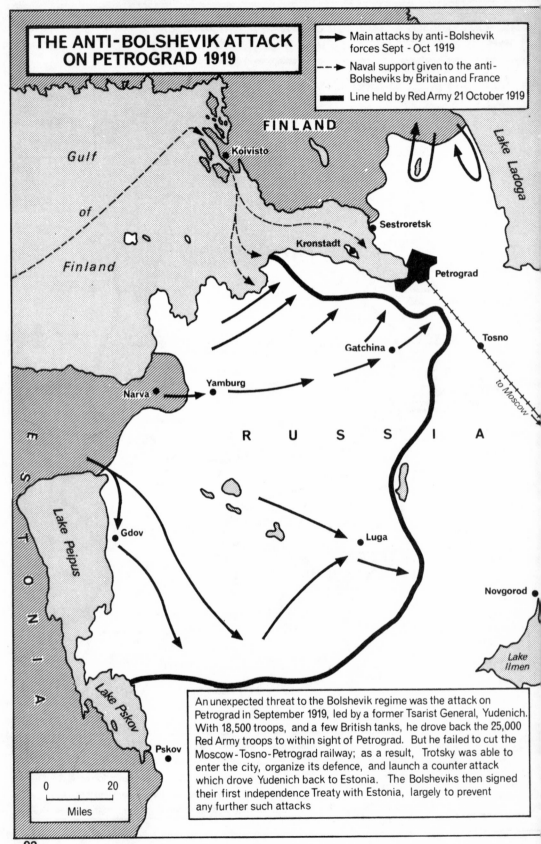

THE ANTI-BOLSHEVIK ATTACK ON PETROGRAD 1919

→ Main attacks by anti-Bolshevik forces Sept - Oct 1919

⇢ Naval support given to the anti-Bolsheviks by Britain and France

▬ Line held by Red Army 21 October 1919

FINLAND

Gulf

of

Finland

Lake Ladoga

Koivisto

Sestroretsk

Kronstadt

Petrograd

Tosno

to Moscow

Gatchina

Yamburg

Narva

R U S S I A

E S T O N I A

Lake Peipus

Gdov

Luga

Novgorod

Lake Ilmen

Lake Pskov

Pskov

An unexpected threat to the Bolshevik regime was the attack on Petrograd in September 1919, led by a former Tsarist General, Yudenich. With 18,500 troops, and a few British tanks, he drove back the 25,000 Red Army troops to within sight of Petrograd. But he failed to cut the Moscow-Tosno-Petrograd railway; as a result, Trotsky was able to enter the city, organize its defence, and launch a counter attack which drove Yudenich back to Estonia. The Bolsheviks then signed their first independence Treaty with Estonia, largely to prevent any further such attacks

0 20

Miles

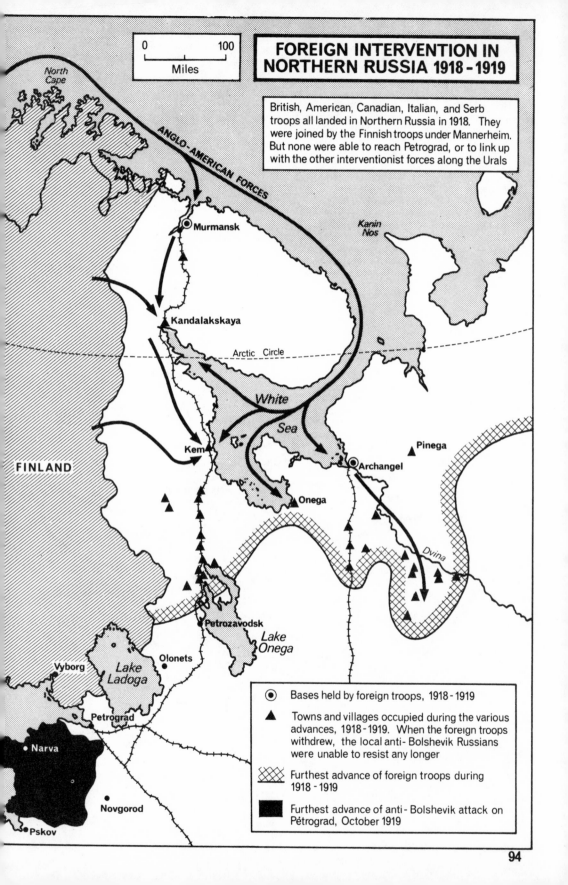

FOREIGN INTERVENTION IN NORTHERN RUSSIA 1918-1919

British, American, Canadian, Italian, and Serb troops all landed in Northern Russia in 1918. They were joined by the Finnish troops under Mannerheim. But none were able to reach Petrograd, or to link up with the other interventionist forces along the Urals

0   100
Miles

North Cape

ANGLO-AMERICAN FORCES

Murmansk

Kanin Nos

Kandalakskaya

Arctic Circle

White

Sea

Kem

Onega

Pinega

Archangel

FINLAND

Dvina

Petrozavodsk

Lake Onega

Olonets

Vyborg

Lake Ladoga

Petrograd

Narva

Novgorod

Pskov

⊙ Bases held by foreign troops, 1918-1919

▲ Towns and villages occupied during the various advances, 1918-1919. When the foreign troops withdrew, the local anti-Bolshevik Russians were unable to resist any longer

Furthest advance of foreign troops during 1918-1919

Furthest advance of anti-Bolshevik attack on Pétrograd, October 1919

MAKHNO AND THE ANARCHISTS 1917-1920

Nestor Makhno, the Ukrainian anarchist, was imprisoned for terrorism in 1907, at the age of eighteen. Released in February 1917, he organized a peasant army, and established control over a large area of southern Russia. He defeated the Austrians at Dibrivki (Sept 1918) and the Ukrainian nationalists at Ekaterinoslav (Nov 1918). In 1919 he allied with the Bolsheviks, defeating two anti-Bolshevik armies, Denikin's at Peregonovka (Sept 1919) and Wrangel's in the Crimea (June 1920). Makhno himself was then attacked continuously by the Bolsheviks and fled (November 1920) via Rumania to France, where he died in 1935

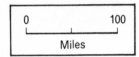

- ⊙ Centres of the Confederation of Anarchist Organizations (Nabat), 1918
- ▨ Anarchist conferences, with dates
- ◓ Makhno's Headquarters 1918-1920
- → Makhno's principal military activities

0   100
Miles

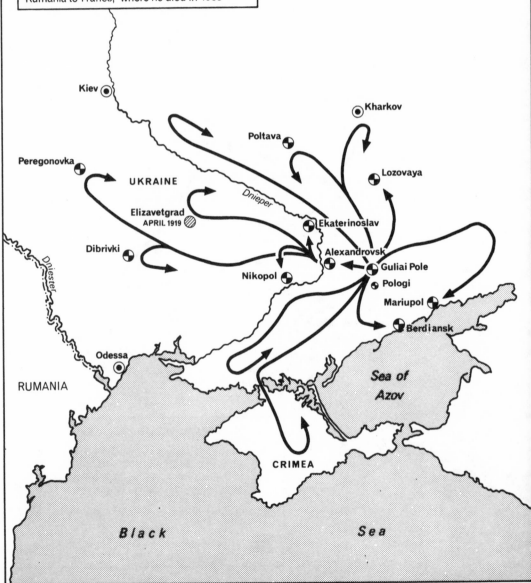

Kursk
NOV. 1918

Kiev

Kharkov

Poltava

Peregonovka

Lozovaya

UKRAINE

Dnieper

Elizavetgrad
APRIL 1919

Ekaterinoslav

Dibrivki

Alexandrovsk

Guliai Pole

Nikopol

Pologi

Mariupol

Dniester

Berdiansk

Odessa

RUMANIA

Sea of
Azov

CRIMEA

Black   Sea

95

THE RUSSO-POLISH WAR 1920

Legend:

— Poland's established frontiers, June 1920

•••• The eastern extent of Polish conquests, April, May and June 1920

← Russian attacks following the Polish occupation of Kiev in June 1920

▨ Polish lines of defence, August 1920

◉ The 'Miracle of the Vistula'. Russian armies were defeated; they retreated to Russia

▨ Seized by Poland from Lithuania, October 1920

▨ Annexed by Poland from Russia, Treaty of Riga, March 1921

— — Poland's eastern frontier from 1921 to 1939

Baltic Sea

ESTONIA

LATVIA

LITHUANIA

Vilna

RUSSIA

Minsk

DANZIG

EAST PRUSSIA

Grodno

GERMANY

Vistula

Bialystok

Plotsk

Poznan

Warsaw

Pinsk

POLAND

Radom

Lublin

Kholm

Kiev

Vistula

Lvov

Cracow

GERMANY

Kamenets Podolsk

CZECHOSLOVAKIA

0   100
Miles

HUNGARY

RUMANIA

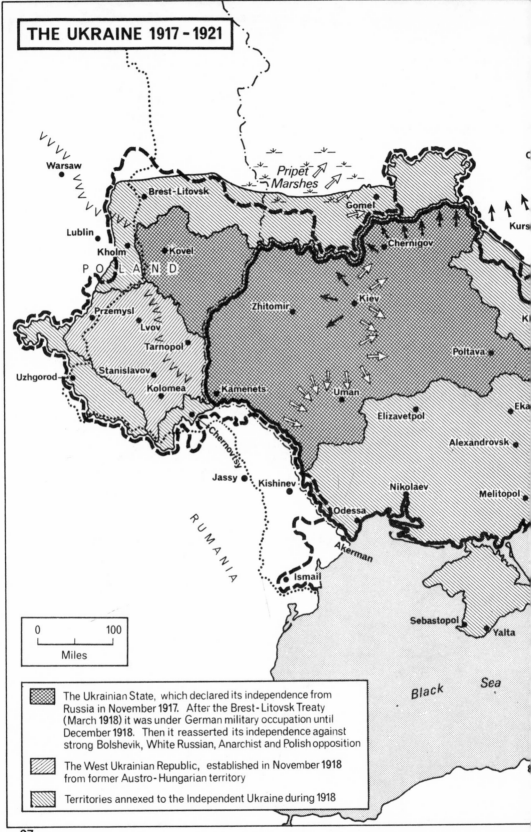

THE UKRAINE 1917-1921

Warsaw

Brest-Litovsk

Lublin

Kholm

Kovel

P O L A N D

Przemysl

Lvov

Tarnopol

Stanislavov

Uzhgorod

Kolomea

Kamenets

Chernovtsy

Jassy

Kishinev

R U M A N I A

Ismail

Pripet Marshes

Gomel

Chernigov

Zhitomir

Kiev

Uman

Elizavetpol

Nikolaev

Odessa

Akerman

Kurs

Poltava

K

Alexandrovsk

Eka

Melitopol

Sebastopol

Yalta

Black   Sea

0   100

Miles

The Ukrainian State, which declared its independence from Russia in November 1917. After the Brest-Litovsk Treaty (March 1918) it was under German military occupation until December 1918. Then it reasserted its independence against strong Bolshevik, White Russian, Anarchist and Polish opposition

The West Ukrainian Republic, established in November 1918 from former Austro-Hungarian territory

Territories annexed to the Independent Ukraine during 1918

Territory claimed by the Ukrainian nationalists as part of the "ethnographic" Ukraine

Boundary of the Ukrainian Soviet Socialist Republic 1921

Western boundary of the Soviet Union 1921-1939

Western boundary of the Soviet Union since 1945

Furthest northern advance of Denikin's anti-Bolshevik armies, November 1919. Denikin's Great Russian policies failed to gain him much Ukrainian support

Furthest eastern advance of the Polish Army in June 1920

Furthest western advance of the Red Army by August 1920

Voronezh

Buturlinovka

ugansk

Taganrog

Rostov

upol

Astrakhan

Ekaterinodar

Stavropol

Armavir

Novorossiisk

Mineralnye
Vody

Mozdok

Tuapse

Sochi

Caucasus

Caspian Sea

Batum

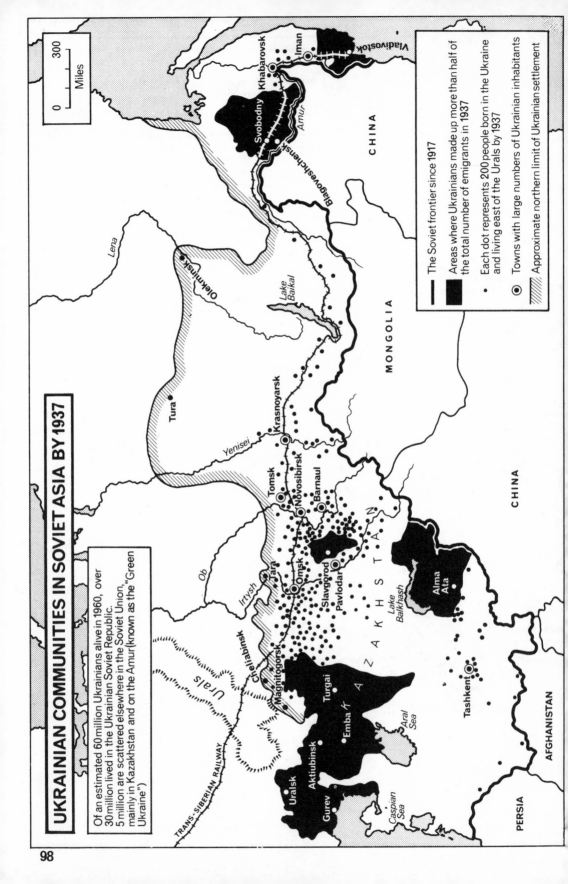

UKRAINIAN COMMUNITIES IN SOVIET ASIA BY 1937

Of an estimated 60 million Ukrainians alive in 1960, over 30 million lived in the Ukrainian Soviet Republic. 5 million are scattered elsewhere in the Soviet Union, mainly in Kazakhstan and on the Amur (known as the "Green Ukraine")

Legend:

— The Soviet frontier since 1917

▧ Areas where Ukrainians made up more than half of the total number of emigrants in 1937

• Each dot represents 200 people born in the Ukraine and living east of the Urals by 1937

◉ Towns with large numbers of Ukrainian inhabitants

▨ Approximate northern limit of Ukrainian settlement

Scale: 0 — 300 Miles

Labels: Vladivostok, Iman, Khabarovsk, Svobodny, Blagoveshchensk, Amur, CHINA, Lena, Olekminsk, Lake Baikal, Tura, Yenisei, Krasnoyarsk, Tomsk, Novosibirsk, Barnaul, MONGOLIA, Ob, Irtysh, Tara, Omsk, Slavgorod, Pavlodar, Lake Balkhash, Alma Ata, KAZAKHSTAN, Cheliabinsk, Magnitogorsk, Urals, Turgai, Emba R., Aral Sea, Tashkent, Uralsk, Gurev, Aktiubinsk, Caspian Sea, PERSIA, AFGHANISTAN, CHINA, TRANS-SIBERIAN RAILWAY

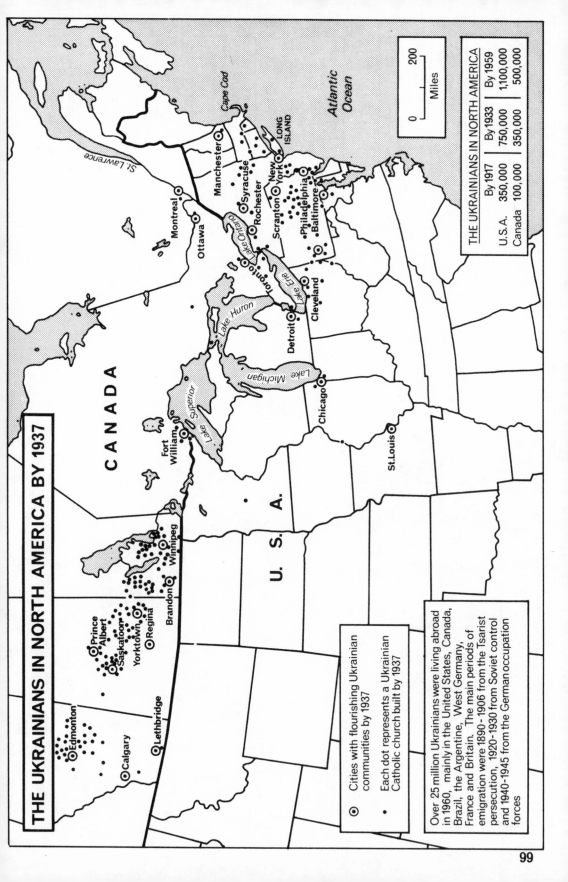

THE UKRAINIANS IN NORTH AMERICA BY 1937

THE UKRAINIANS IN NORTH AMERICA

	By 1917	By 1933	By 1959
U.S.A.	350,000	750,000	1,100,000
Canada	100,000	350,000	500,000

⊙   Cities with flourishing Ukrainian communities by 1937

•   Each dot represents a Ukrainian Catholic church built by 1937

Over 25 million Ukrainians were living abroad in 1960, mainly in the United States, Canada, Brazil, the Argentine, West Germany, France and Britain. The main periods of emigration were 1890-1906 from the Tsarist persecution, 1920-1930 from Soviet control and 1940-1945 from the German occupation forces

Atlantic Ocean

CANADA

U. S. A.

St. Lawrence

Lake Ontario
Lake Erie
Lake Huron
Lake Michigan
Lake Superior

Cape Cod
LONG ISLAND
Manchester
Syracuse
New York
Rochester
Scranton
Philadelphia
Baltimore
Montreal
Ottawa
Toronto
Cleveland
Detroit
Chicago
St. Louis
Fort William
Winnipeg
Brandon
Prince Albert
Saskatoon
Yorkton
Regina
Edmonton
Calgary
Lethbridge

200 Miles

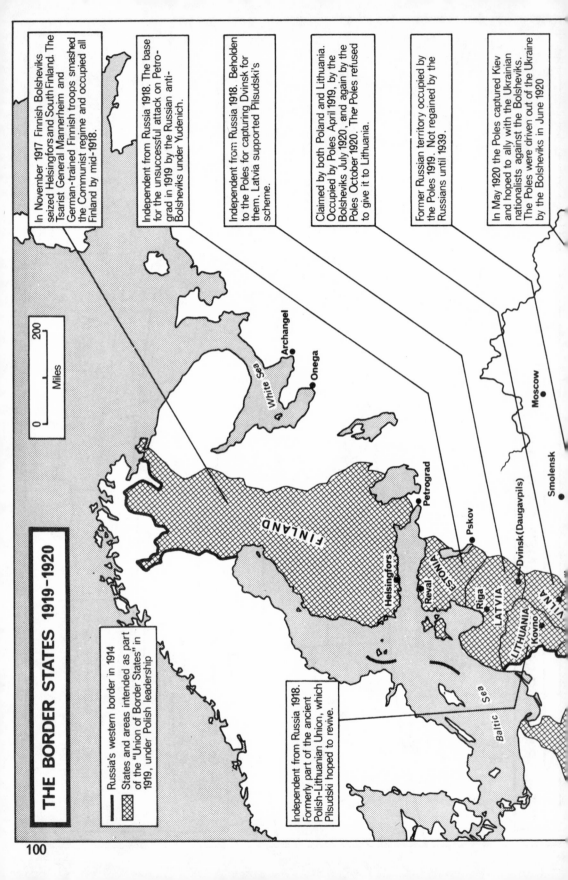

THE BORDER STATES 1919–1920

Russia's western border in 1914

States and areas intended as part of the "Union of Border States" in 1919, under Polish leadership

200 Miles

In November 1917 Finnish Bolsheviks seized Helsingfors and South Finland. The Tsarist General Mannerheim and German-trained Finnish troops smashed the Communist regime and occupied all Finland by mid-1918.

Independent from Russia 1918. The base for the unsuccessful attack on Petrograd in 1919 by the Russian anti-Bolsheviks under Yudenich.

Independent from Russia 1918. Beholden to the Poles for capturing Dvinsk for them. Latvia supported Pilsudski's scheme.

Claimed by both Poland and Lithuania. Occupied by Poles April 1919, by the Bolsheviks July 1920, and again by the Poles October 1920. The Poles refused to give it to Lithuania.

Former Russian territory occupied by the Poles 1919. Not regained by the Russians until 1939.

In May 1920 the Poles captured Kiev and hoped to ally with the Ukrainian nationalists against the Bolsheviks. The Poles were driven out of the Ukraine by the Bolsheviks in June 1920

Independent from Russia 1918. Formerly part of the ancient Polish-Lithuanian Union, which Pilsudski hoped to revive.

White Sea

Archangel

Onega

Petrograd

Pskov

FINLAND

Helsingfors

Reval

ESTONIA

Riga

LATVIA

Dvinsk (Daugavpils)

VILNA

LITHUANIA

Kovno

Baltic Sea

Moscow

Smolensk

100

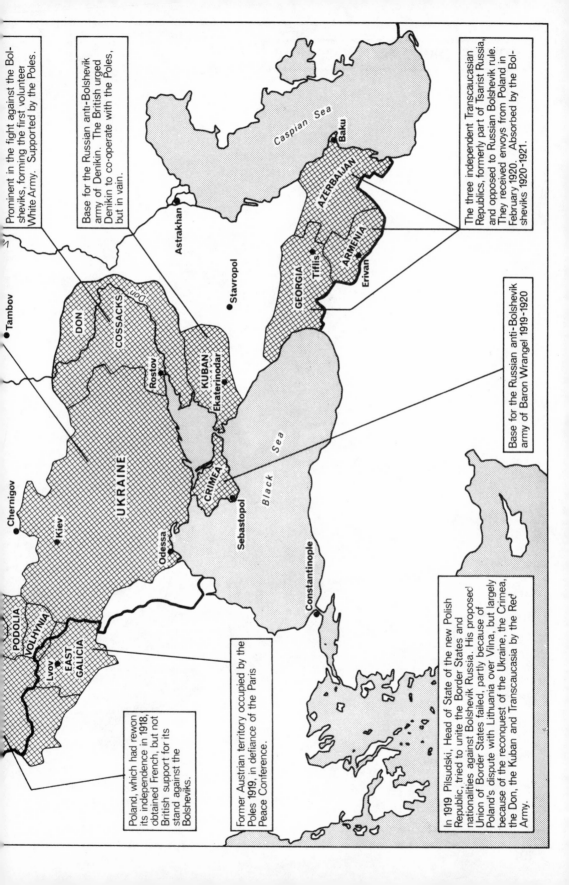

Prominent in the fight against the Bolsheviks, forming the first volunteer White Army. Supported by the Poles.

Base for the Russian anti-Bolshevik army of Denikin. The British urged Denikin to co-operate with the Poles, but in vain.

The three independent Transcaucasian Republics, formerly part of Tsarist Russia, and opposed to Russian Bolshevik rule. They received envoys from Poland in February 1920. Absorbed by the Bolsheviks 1920-1921.

Base for the Russian anti-Bolshevik army of Baron Wrangel 1919-1920

Poland, which had rewon its independence in 1918, obtained French, but not British support for its stand against the Bolsheviks.

Former Austrian territory occupied by the Poles 1919, in defiance of the Paris Peace Conference.

In 1919 Pilsudski, Head of State of the new Polish Republic, tried to unite the Border States and nationalities against Bolshevik Russia. His proposed Union of Border States failed, partly because of Poland's dispute with Lithuania over Vilna, but largely because of the reconquest of the Ukraine, the Crimea, the Don, the Kuban and Transcaucasia by the Red Army.

Caspian Sea
Baku
Astrakhan
AZERBAIJAN
ARMENIA
Stavropol
GEORGIA
Tiflis
Erivan
Tambov
DON
Don
COSSACKS
Rostov
KUBAN
Ekaterinodar
Black Sea
Chernigov
UKRAINE
Kiev
CRIMEA
Sebastopol
Odessa
Constantinople
PODOLIA
VOLHYNIA
Lvov
EAST
GALICIA

SOVIET DIPLOMACY 1920-1940

North Sea

Bay of Biscay

London

Paris

FRANCE

San Sebastian

Madrid

Barcelona

SPAIN

BRITAIN

10,000 VEHICLES
4,500 TONS MUNITIONS
1,000 OFFICERS & MEN

Berlin

GERMANY

AUSTRIA

ITALY

Baltic Sea

200 TANKS
3,390 MACHINE GUNS

Leningrad

ESTONIA

LATVIA

Warsaw

POLAND

CZECHO
SLOVAKIA

RUMANIA

NORWAY

FINLAND

Sr

FL
SC

1,000 OFFICERS & MEN
1,300 TRUCKS
1,300 RIFLES & GUNS
242 AEROPLANES

Mediterranean Sea

0   400
Miles

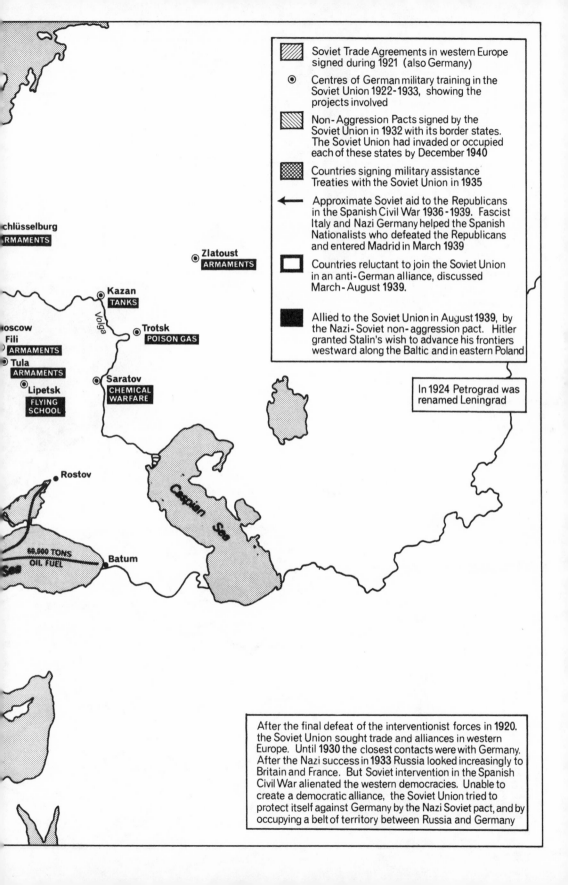

Legend:

- Soviet Trade Agreements in western Europe signed during 1921 (also Germany)
- ⊙ Centres of German military training in the Soviet Union 1922-1933, showing the projects involved
- Non-Aggression Pacts signed by the Soviet Union in 1932 with its border states. The Soviet Union had invaded or occupied each of these states by December 1940
- Countries signing military assistance Treaties with the Soviet Union in 1935
- ← Approximate Soviet aid to the Republicans in the Spanish Civil War 1936-1939. Fascist Italy and Nazi Germany helped the Spanish Nationalists who defeated the Republicans and entered Madrid in March 1939
- Countries reluctant to join the Soviet Union in an anti-German alliance, discussed March-August 1939.
- Allied to the Soviet Union in August 1939, by the Nazi-Soviet non-aggression pact. Hitler granted Stalin's wish to advance his frontiers westward along the Baltic and in eastern Poland

In 1924 Petrograd was renamed Leningrad

chlüsselburg
RMAMENTS

Zlatoust
ARMAMENTS

Kazan
TANKS

Volga

oscow
Fili
ARMAMENTS

Trotsk
POISON GAS

Tula
ARMAMENTS

Lipetsk
FLYING
SCHOOL

Saratov
CHEMICAL
WARFARE

Caspian Sea

Rostov

68,000 TONS
OIL FUEL

Batum

After the final defeat of the interventionist forces in 1920. the Soviet Union sought trade and alliances in western Europe. Until 1930 the closest contacts were with Germany. After the Nazi success in 1933 Russia looked increasingly to Britain and France. But Soviet intervention in the Spanish Civil War alienated the western democracies. Unable to create a democratic alliance, the Soviet Union tried to protect itself against Germany by the Nazi Soviet pact, and by occupying a belt of territory between Russia and Germany

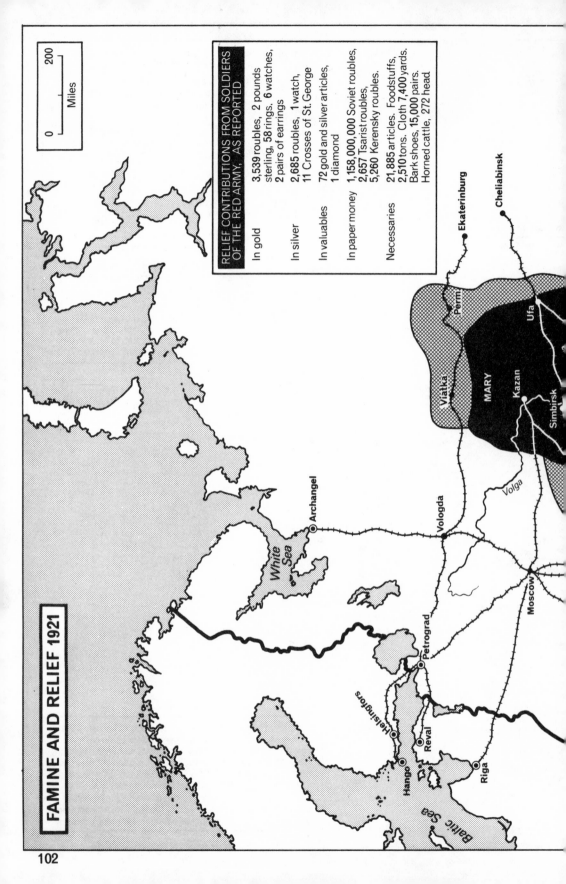

FAMINE AND RELIEF 1921

RELIEF CONTRIBUTIONS FROM SOLDIERS
OF THE RED ARMY, AS REPORTED

In gold	3,539 roubles, 2 pounds sterling, 58 rings, 6 watches, 2 pairs of earrings
In silver	2,685 roubles, 1 watch, 11 Crosses of St. George
In valuables	72 gold and silver articles, 1 diamond
In paper money	1,158,000,000 Soviet roubles, 2,657 Tsarist roubles, 5,260 Kerensky roubles.
Necessaries	21,885 articles. Foodstuffs, 2,510 tons. Cloth 7,400 yards. Bark shoes, 15,000 pairs. Horned cattle, 272 head

Miles

0   200

White Sea

Archangel

Vologda

Volga

Viatka

Perm

Ekaterinburg

MARY

Kazan

Ufa

Cheliabinsk

Simbirsk

Moscow

Petrograd

Helsingfors

Reval

Riga

Hango

Baltic Sea

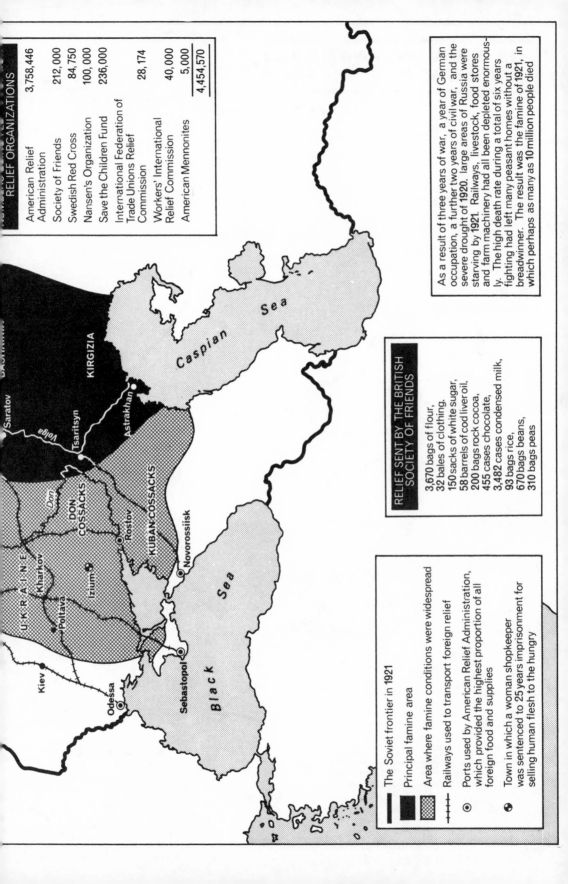

RELIEF ORGANIZATIONS

American Relief Administration	3,758,446
Society of Friends	212,000
Swedish Red Cross	84,750
Nansen's Organization	100,000
Save the Children Fund	236,000
International Federation of Trade Unions Relief Commission	28,174
Workers' International Relief Commission	40,000
American Mennonites	5,000
	4,454,570

As a result of three years of war, a year of German occupation, a further two years of civil war, and the severe drought of 1920. large areas of Russia were starving by 1921. Railways, livestock, food stores and farm machinery had all been depleted enormously. The high death rate during a total of six years fighting had left many peasant homes without a breadwinner. The result was the famine of 1921, in which perhaps as many as 10 million people died

RELIEF SENT BY THE BRITISH SOCIETY OF FRIENDS

3,670 bags of flour,
32 bales of clothing.
150 sacks of white sugar,
58 barrels of cod liver oil,
200 bags rock cocoa,
455 cases chocolate,
3,482 cases condensed milk,
93 bags rice,
670 bags beans,
310 bags peas

KIRGIZIA

Caspian Sea

Saratov

Tsaritsyn

Astrakhan

Volga

Don

DON COSSACKS

KUBAN-COSSACKS

Rostov

Novorossiisk

U K R A I N E

Kharkov

Izium

Poltava

Kiev

Odessa

Sebastopol

Black Sea

The Soviet frontier in 1921

Principal famine area

Area where famine conditions were widespread

Railways used to transport foreign relief

⊙ Ports used by American Relief Administration, which provided the highest proportion of all foreign food and supplies

● Town in which a woman shopkeeper was sentenced to 25 years imprisonment for selling human flesh to the hungry

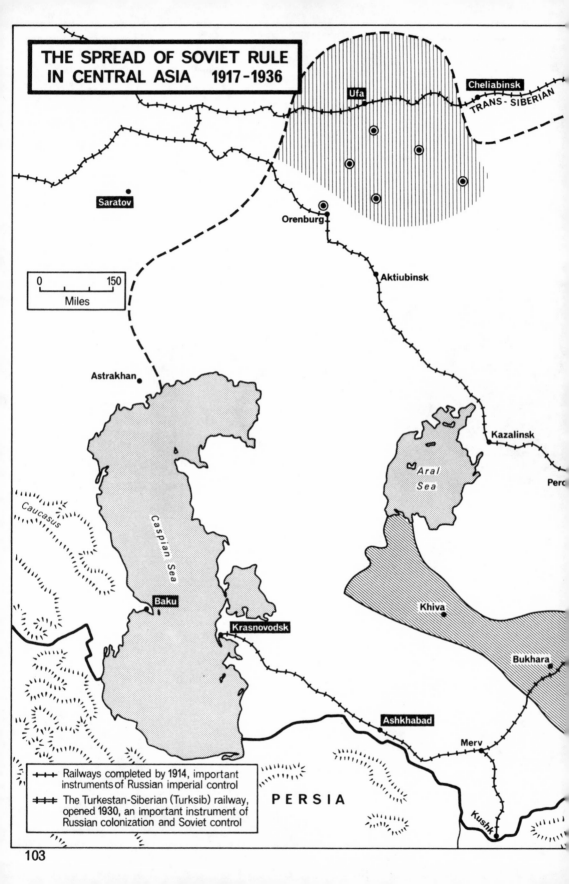

THE SPREAD OF SOVIET RULE
IN CENTRAL ASIA   1917-1936

Cheliabinsk

Ufa

TRANS - SIBERIAN

Saratov

Orenburg

Aktiubinsk

0   150
Miles

Astrakhan

Kazalinsk

Aral Sea

Perc

Caucasus

Caspian Sea

Khiva

Baku

Krasnovodsk

Bukhara

Ashkhabad

Merv

╈╈╈ Railways completed by 1914, important
    instruments of Russian imperial control

╈╈╈ The Turkestan-Siberian (Turksib) railway,
    opened 1930, an important instrument of
    Russian colonization and Soviet control

PERSIA

Kushk

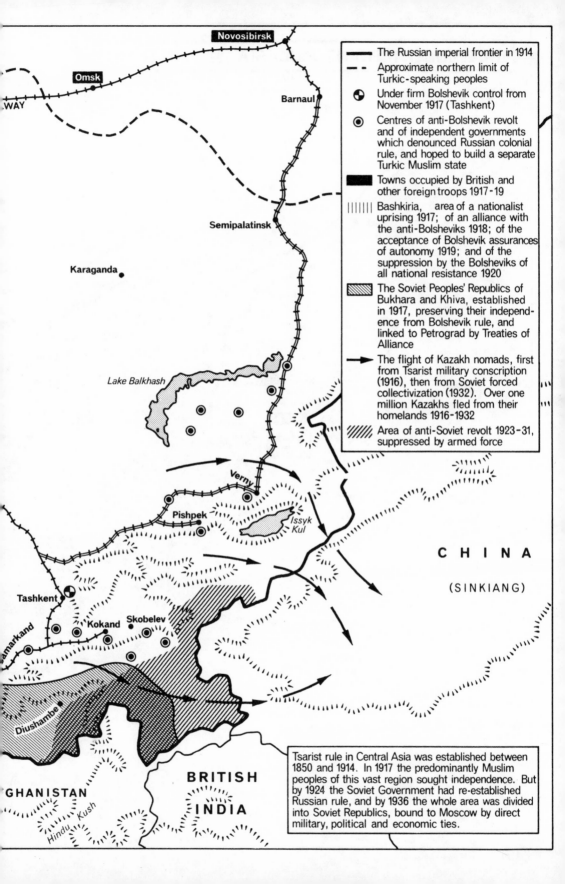

Novosibirsk

Omsk

...WAY

Barnaul

The Russian imperial frontier in 1914

Approximate northern limit of Turkic-speaking peoples

Under firm Bolshevik control from November 1917 (Tashkent)

Centres of anti-Bolshevik revolt and of independent governments which denounced Russian colonial rule, and hoped to build a separate Turkic Muslim state

Towns occupied by British and other foreign troops 1917-19

Bashkiria, area of a nationalist uprising 1917; of an alliance with the anti-Bolsheviks 1918; of the acceptance of Bolshevik assurances of autonomy 1919; and of the suppression by the Bolsheviks of all national resistance 1920

The Soviet Peoples' Republics of Bukhara and Khiva, established in 1917, preserving their independence from Bolshevik rule, and linked to Petrograd by Treaties of Alliance

The flight of Kazakh nomads, first from Tsarist military conscription (1916), then from Soviet forced collectivization (1932). Over one million Kazakhs fled from their homelands 1916-1932

Area of anti-Soviet revolt 1923-31, suppressed by armed force

Semipalatinsk

Karaganda

Lake Balkhash

Verny

Pishpek

Issyk Kul

CHINA

(SINKIANG)

Tashkent

Kokand   Skobelev

...amarkand

Diushambe

BRITISH

...GHANISTAN

INDIA

Hindu Kush

Tsarist rule in Central Asia was established between 1850 and 1914. In 1917 the predominantly Muslim peoples of this vast region sought independence. But by 1924 the Soviet Government had re-established Russian rule, and by 1936 the whole area was divided into Soviet Republics, bound to Moscow by direct military, political and economic ties.

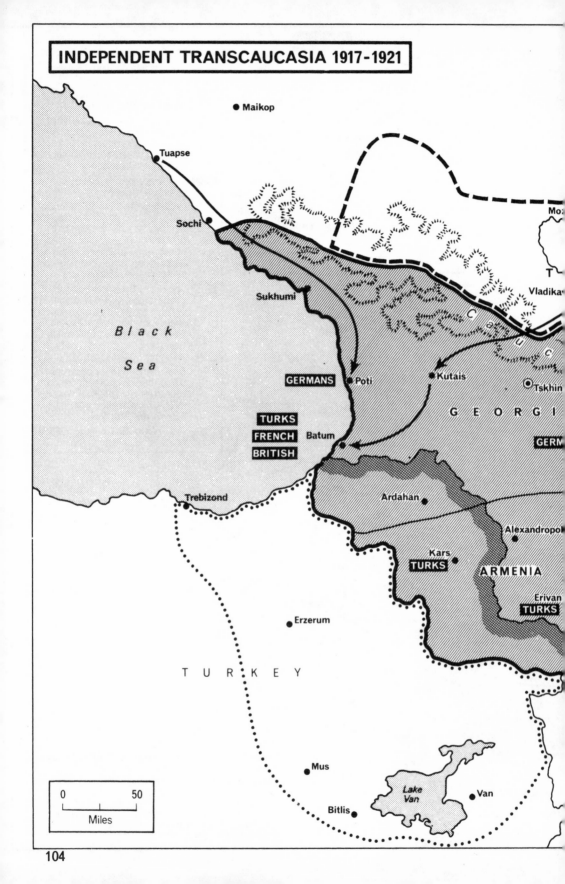

INDEPENDENT TRANSCAUCASIA 1917-1921

Maikop

Tuapse

Sochi

Black

Sea

Sukhumi

Mo

T

Vladika

GERMANS Poti

Kutais Tskhin

GEORGI

TURKS
FRENCH Batum GERM
BRITISH

Trebizond

Ardahan

Alexandropol

Kars ARMENIA
TURKS

Erivan
TURKS

Erzerum

TURKEY

0   50

Miles

Mus

Lake
Van Van

Bitlis

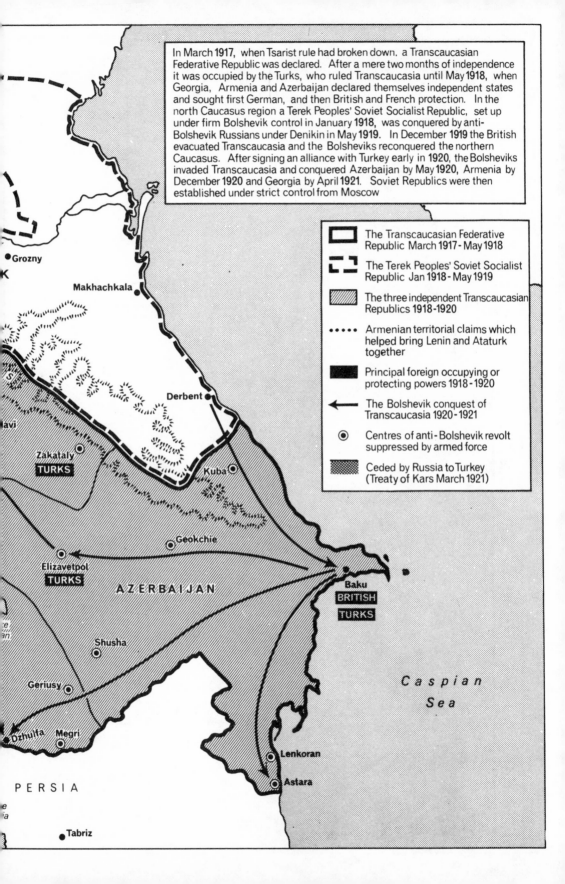

In March 1917, when Tsarist rule had broken down, a Transcaucasian
Federative Republic was declared. After a mere two months of independence
it was occupied by the Turks, who ruled Transcaucasia until May 1918, when
Georgia, Armenia and Azerbaijan declared themselves independent states
and sought first German, and then British and French protection. In the
north Caucasus region a Terek Peoples' Soviet Socialist Republic, set up
under firm Bolshevik control in January 1918, was conquered by anti-
Bolshevik Russians under Denikin in May 1919. In December 1919 the British
evacuated Transcaucasia and the Bolsheviks reconquered the northern
Caucasus. After signing an alliance with Turkey early in 1920, the Bolsheviks
invaded Transcaucasia and conquered Azerbaijan by May 1920, Armenia by
December 1920 and Georgia by April 1921. Soviet Republics were then
established under strict control from Moscow

The Transcaucasian Federative
Republic March 1917 - May 1918

The Terek Peoples' Soviet Socialist
Republic Jan 1918 - May 1919

The three independent Transcaucasian
Republics 1918-1920

Armenian territorial claims which
helped bring Lenin and Ataturk
together

Principal foreign occupying or
protecting powers 1918-1920

The Bolshevik conquest of
Transcaucasia 1920-1921

Centres of anti-Bolshevik revolt
suppressed by armed force

Ceded by Russia to Turkey
(Treaty of Kars March 1921)

Grozny

Makhachkala

K

Derbent

avi

Zakataly
TURKS

Kuba

Geokchie

Elizavetpol
TURKS

AZERBAIJAN

Baku
BRITISH
TURKS

Shusha

Caspian
Sea

Geriusy

Dzhulfa Megri

Lenkoran

PERSIA

Astara

e
ia

Tabriz

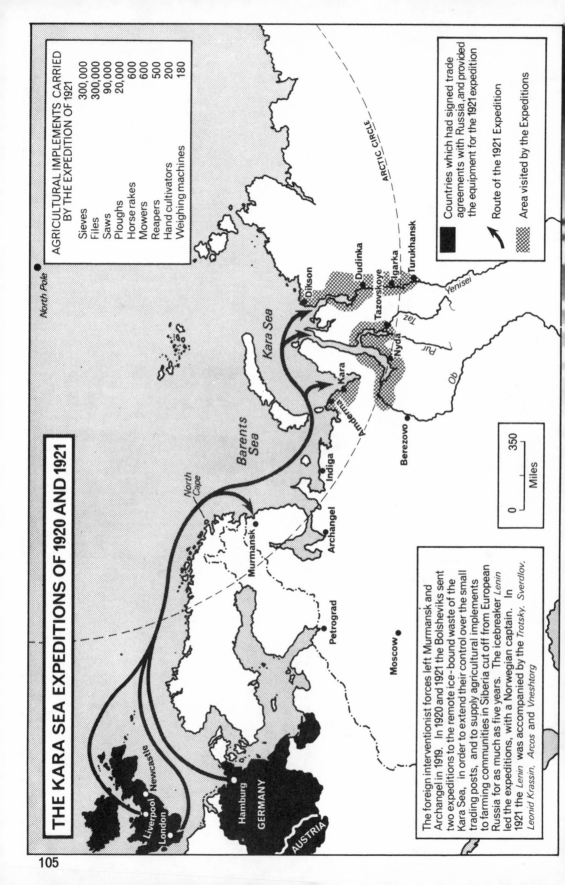

THE KARA SEA EXPEDITIONS OF 1920 AND 1921

AGRICULTURAL IMPLEMENTS CARRIED
BY THE EXPEDITION OF 1921

Sieves	300,000
Files	300,000
Saws	90,000
Ploughs	20,000
Horse rakes	600
Mowers	600
Reapers	500
Hand cultivators	200
Weighing machines	180

Countries which had signed trade
agreements with Russia, and provided
the equipment for the 1921 expedition

Route of the 1921 Expedition

Area visited by the Expeditions

North Pole

ARCTIC CIRCLE

Kara Sea

Barents
Sea

North
Cape

Dikson
Dudinka
Tazovskoye
Igarka
Turukhansk
Yenisei

Kara
Amderma
Nyda
Taz
Pur
Ob
Berezovo

Indiga

Archangel

Murmansk

Petrograd

Moscow

0   350
Miles

Liverpool Newcastle
London
Hamburg
GERMANY
AUSTRIA

The foreign interventionist forces left Murmansk and
Archangel in 1919. In 1920 and 1921 the Bolsheviks sent
two expeditions to the remote ice-bound waste of the
Kara Sea, in order to extend their control over the small
trading posts, and to supply agricultural implements
to farming communities in Siberia cut off from European
Russia for as much as five years. The icebreaker *Lenin*
led the expeditions, with a Norwegian captain.   In
1921 the *Lenin* was accompanied by the *Trotsky*, *Sverdlov*,
Leonid Krassin, *Arcos* and *Vneshtorg*

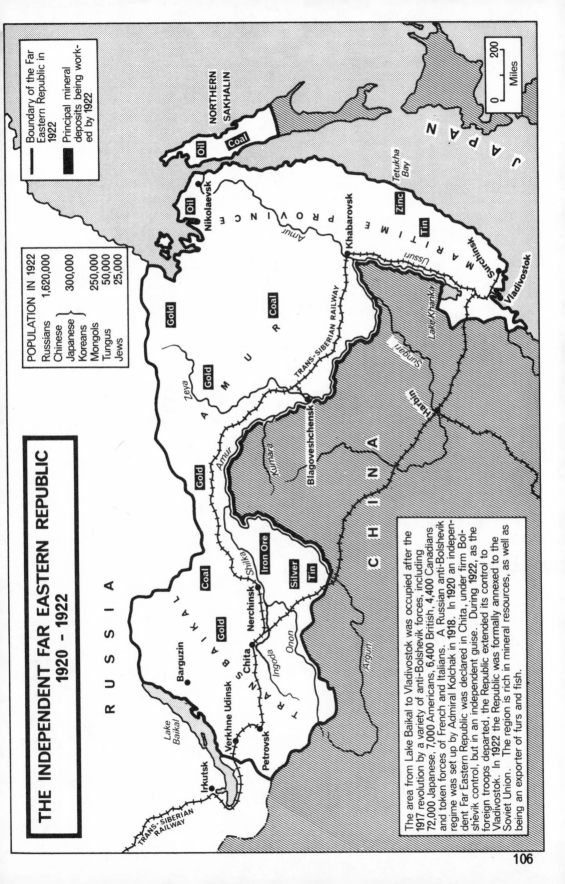

THE INDEPENDENT FAR EASTERN REPUBLIC
1920 – 1922

Boundary of the Far Eastern Republic in 1922

Principal mineral deposits being worked by 1922

POPULATION IN 1922
Russians 1,620,000
Chinese 300,000
Japanese }
Koreans } 250,000
Mongols 50,000
Tungus 25,000
Jews

Miles
0   200

RUSSIA

Lake Baikal

Irkutsk

TRANS-SIBERIAN RAILWAY

Barguzin

Verkhne Udinsk

Petrovsk

Gold

Coal

BAIKAL

Chita

Nerchinsk

Iron Ore

Silver

Tin

Coal

Gold

Gold

Gold

Zeya

Amur

Shilka

Ingoda

Onon

Argun

Kuriará

AMUR

Coal

TRANS-SIBERIAN RAILWAY

Blagoveshchensk

Amur

Ussuri

Khabarovsk

MARITIME PROVINCE

PROVINCE

NORTHERN SAKHALIN

Oil

Coal

Oil

Nikolaevsk

Tetukha Bay

Zinc

Tin

Suchisk

Vladivostok

Lake Khanka

Sungari

Harbin

CHINA

JAPAN

The area from Lake Baikal to Vladivostok was occupied after the 1917 revolution by a variety of anti-Bolshevik forces, including 72,000 Japanese, 7,000 Americans, 6,400 British, 4,400 Canadians and token forces of French and Italians. A Russian anti-Bolshevik regime was set up by Admiral Kolchak in 1918. In 1920 an independent Far Eastern Republic was declared in Chita, under firm Bolshevik control, but in an independent guise. During 1922, as the foreign troops departed, the Republic extended its control to Vladivostok. In 1922 the Republic was formally annexed to the Soviet Union. The region is rich in mineral resources, as well as being an exporter of furs and fish.

106

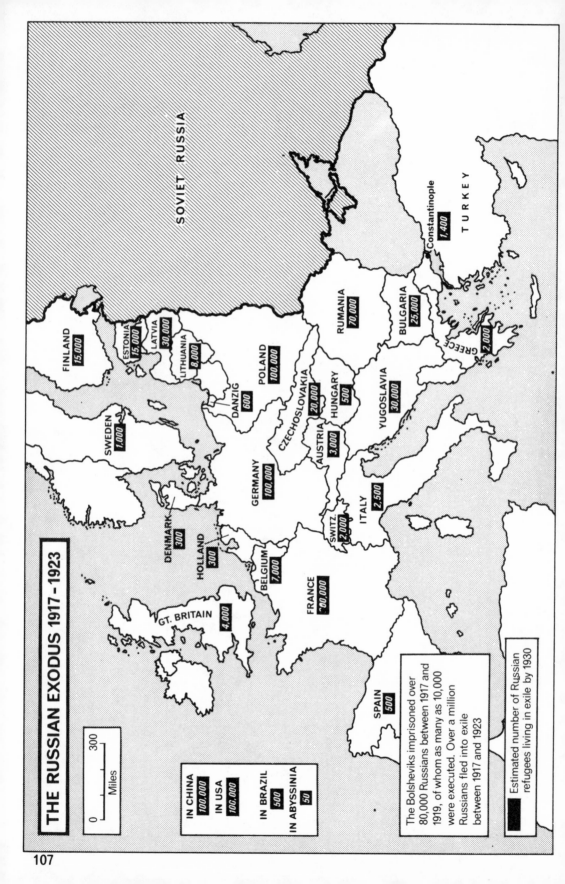

THE RUSSIAN EXODUS 1917–1923

SOVIET RUSSIA

TURKEY

Constantinople
1,400

FINLAND
15,000

ESTONIA
15,000

LATVIA
30,000

LITHUANIA
8,000

SWEDEN
1,000

DANZIG
600

POLAND
100,000

RUMANIA
70,000

BULGARIA
25,000

GREECE
2,000

CZECHOSLOVAKIA
20,000

HUNGARY
500

AUSTRIA
3,000

YUGOSLAVIA
30,000

GERMANY
100,000

SWITZ.
2,000

ITALY
2,500

DENMARK
300

HOLLAND
300

BELGIUM
7,000

FRANCE
400,000

GT. BRITAIN
4,000

SPAIN
500

The Bolsheviks imprisoned over
80,000 Russians between 1917 and
1919, of whom as many as 10,000
were executed. Over a million
Russians fled into exile
between 1917 and 1923

300
Miles
0

IN CHINA   100,000
IN USA   106,000
IN BRAZIL   500
IN ABYSSINIA   50

■ Estimated number of Russian
refugees living in exile by 1930

THE FAILURE OF WORLD REVOLUTION 1917–1927

SOVIET UNION

| 0 | 250 |
Miles

Samara · HUNGARY

Moscow · GERMANY ITALY

Smolensk · POLAND

Kharkov · TURKEY

Kronstadt
Petrograd · FRANCE
BRITAIN

Stockholm ◁
SWEDEN

Hamburg ◉
Bremen ◉
Berlin ◉ ◁
Essen ◉
GERMANY

Brussels ◁
Paris ◁
FRANCE
Geneva ◁

BRITAIN

SPAIN

Prague ◁
Vienna ◁
AUSTRIA
BAVARIA
SLOVAKIA
HUNGARY

POLAND

RUMANIA

YUGOSLAVIA

Sofia · BULGARIA

I T A L Y

TURKEY

Legend

Revolutionary attempts by non-Russian communists to seize power 1918–1923. All were suppressed by armed force

◉ Centres inside Russia which western intelligence believed were training non-Russian communists for revolutionary activity in their own countries, with countries in

◁ Russian communist propaganda centres outside Russia, receiving money from Petrograd to encourage communist activity

Countries of the Moscow Comintern Congress of 1920 whose delegates first demanded freedom of action for their own communist parties. By 1939 all communist parties had turned against Soviet control. The whole Polish Central Committee was summoned to Moscow in 1939 by Stalin, and then disappeared

Countries whose strong anti-communist policies after 1926 served as a barrier between Soviet communism and western Europe

Many Bolsheviks expected that their success in Russia would lead to a rapid seizure of power by communists throughout western Europe. But all later revolutionary attempts were crushed. Despite the propaganda and intrigue of the Third Communist International (Comintern) established by Lenin in 1919, no other communist regime held power successfully in western Europe between the First and Second World Wars

108

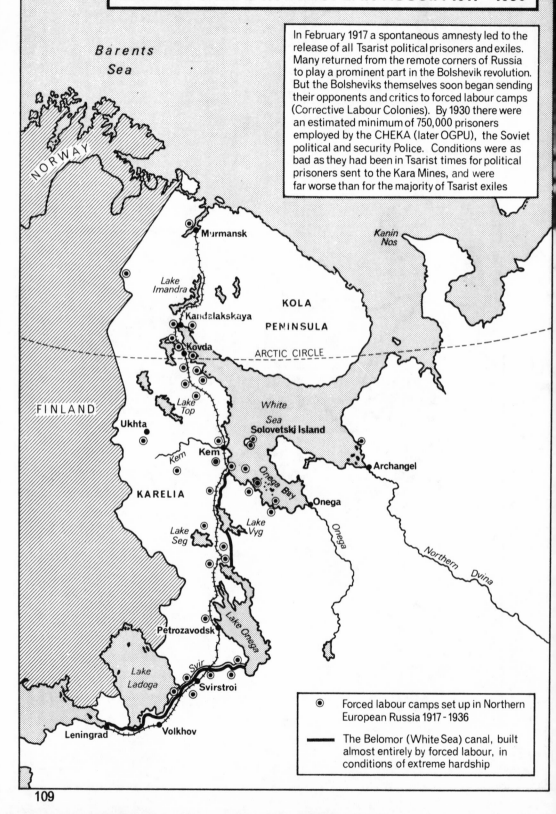

LABOUR CAMPS IN EUROPEAN RUSSIA 1917 - 1936

In February 1917 a spontaneous amnesty led to the release of all Tsarist political prisoners and exiles. Many returned from the remote corners of Russia to play a prominent part in the Bolshevik revolution. But the Bolsheviks themselves soon began sending their opponents and critics to forced labour camps (Corrective Labour Colonies). By 1930 there were an estimated minimum of 750,000 prisoners employed by the CHEKA (later OGPU), the Soviet political and security Police. Conditions were as bad as they had been in Tsarist times for political prisoners sent to the Kara Mines, and were far worse than for the majority of Tsarist exiles

Barents Sea

NORWAY

Murmansk

Kanin Nos

Lake Imandra

KOLA

Kandalakskaya

PENINSULA

Kovda

ARCTIC CIRCLE

FINLAND

Lake Top

White Sea

Solovetski Island

Ukhta

Kem

Kem

Archangel

Onega Bay

KARELIA

Onega

Onega

Lake Vyg

Lake Seg

Northern Dvina

Petrozavodsk

Lake Onega

Svir

Lake Ladoga

Svirstroi

Leningrad

Volkhov

◉　Forced labour camps set up in Northern European Russia 1917 - 1936

━━━　The Belomor (White Sea) canal, built almost entirely by forced labour, in conditions of extreme hardship

109

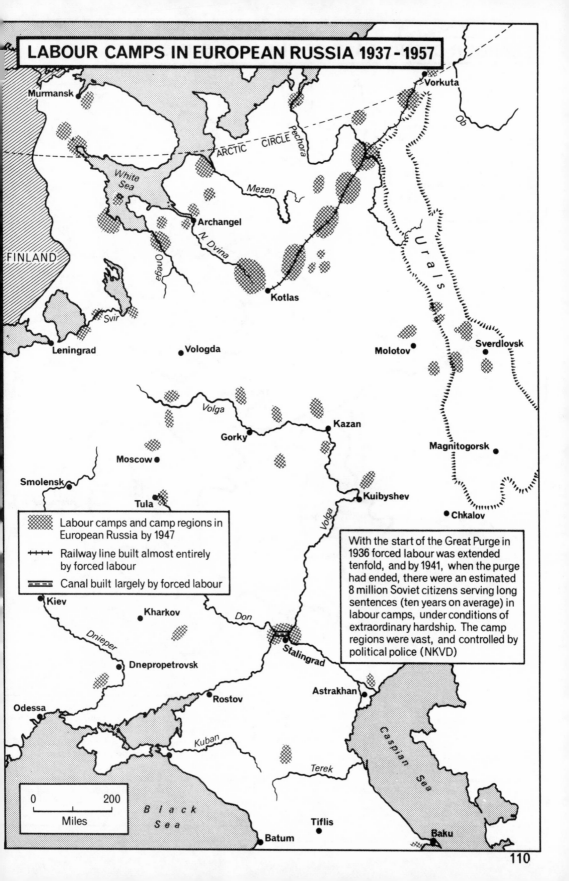

LABOUR CAMPS IN EUROPEAN RUSSIA 1937-1957

Murmansk

Vorkuta

ARCTIC CIRCLE

Pechora

Ob

White
Sea

Mezen

Urals

Archangel

N Dvina

Onega

FINLAND

Svir

Kotlas

Leningrad

Vologda

Molotov

Sverdlovsk

Volga

Gorky

Kazan

Magnitogorsk

Moscow

Smolensk

Kuibyshev

Tula

Chkalov

Labour camps and camp regions in
European Russia by 1947

Railway line built almost entirely
by forced labour

Canal built largely by forced labour

Kiev

Kharkov

Don

With the start of the Great Purge in
1936 forced labour was extended
tenfold, and by 1941, when the purge
had ended, there were an estimated
8 million Soviet citizens serving long
sentences (ten years on average) in
labour camps, under conditions of
extraordinary hardship. The camp
regions were vast, and controlled by
political police (NKVD)

Dnieper

Dnepropetrovsk

Stalingrad

Odessa

Rostov

Astrakhan

Kuban

Caspian
Sea

Terek

0   200

Miles

Black
Sea

Tiflis

Baku

Batum

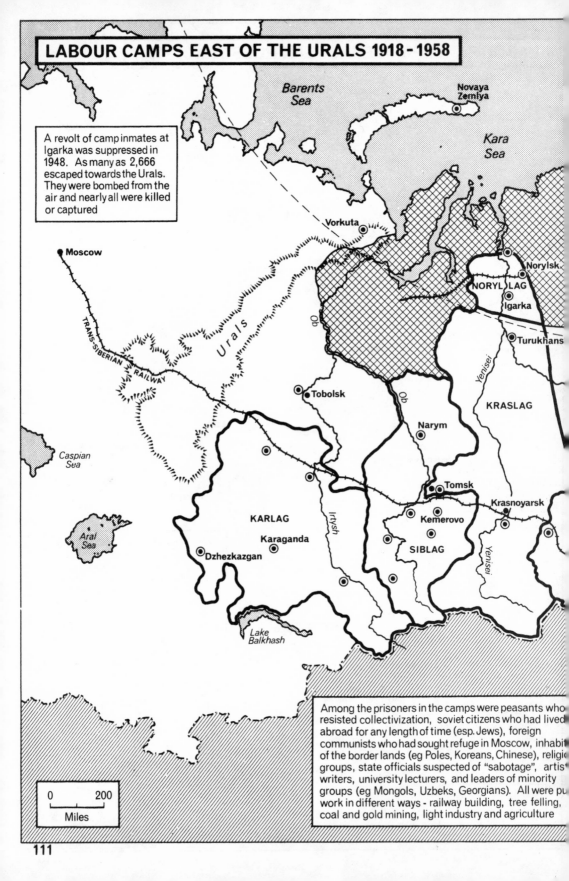

LABOUR CAMPS EAST OF THE URALS 1918-1958

Barents Sea

Novaya Zemlya

Kara Sea

A revolt of camp inmates at Igarka was suppressed in 1948. As many as 2,666 escaped towards the Urals. They were bombed from the air and nearly all were killed or captured

● Vorkuta

● Moscow

● Norylsk

NORYL LAG

● Igarka

Ob

U r a l s

● Turukhans

TRANS-SIBERIAN RAILWAY

Yenisei

● Tobolsk

Ob

KRASLAG

Narym

Caspian Sea

● Tomsk

● Krasnoyarsk

Irtysh

KARLAG

● Kemerovo

Aral Sea

Karaganda

● **SIBLAG**

● Dzhezkazgan

Yenisei

Lake Balkhash

Among the prisoners in the camps were peasants who resisted collectivization, soviet citizens who had lived abroad for any length of time (esp. Jews), foreign communists who had sought refuge in Moscow, inhabit of the border lands (eg Poles, Koreans, Chinese), religio groups, state officials suspected of "sabotage", artist writers, university lecturers, and leaders of minority groups (eg Mongols, Uzbeks, Georgians). All were pu work in different ways - railway building, tree felling, coal and gold mining, light industry and agriculture

0   200
Miles

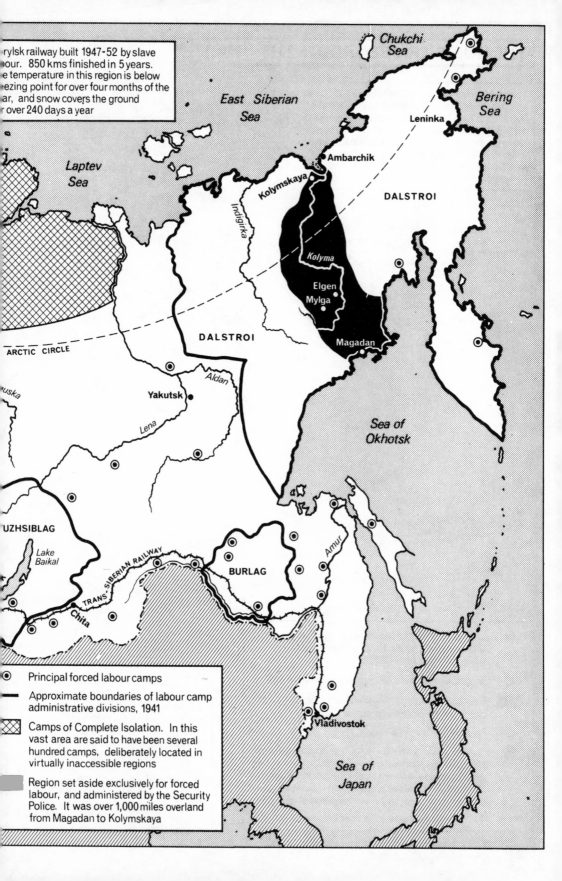

...rylsk railway built 1947-52 by slave
...our. 850 kms finished in 5 years.
...e temperature in this region is below
...eezing point for over four months of the
...ar, and snow covers the ground
...r over 240 days a year

Chukchi
Sea

East Siberian
Sea

Bering
Sea

Leninka

Laptev
Sea

Ambarchik

Kolymskaya

DALSTROI

Indigirka

Kolyma

Elgen

Mylga

DALSTROI

ARCTIC CIRCLE

Magadan

Aldan

Yakutsk

Lena

...uska

Sea of
Okhotsk

...UZHSIBLAG

Lake
Baikal

TRANS-SIBERIAN RAILWAY

BURLAG

Amur

Chita

Vladivostok

Sea of
Japan

⊙ Principal forced labour camps

── Approximate boundaries of labour camp
     administrative divisions, 1941

▨ Camps of Complete Isolation. In this
     vast area are said to have been several
     hundred camps, deliberately located in
     virtually inaccessible regions

▨ Region set aside exclusively for forced
     labour, and administered by the Security
     Police. It was over 1,000 miles overland
     from Magadan to Kolymskaya

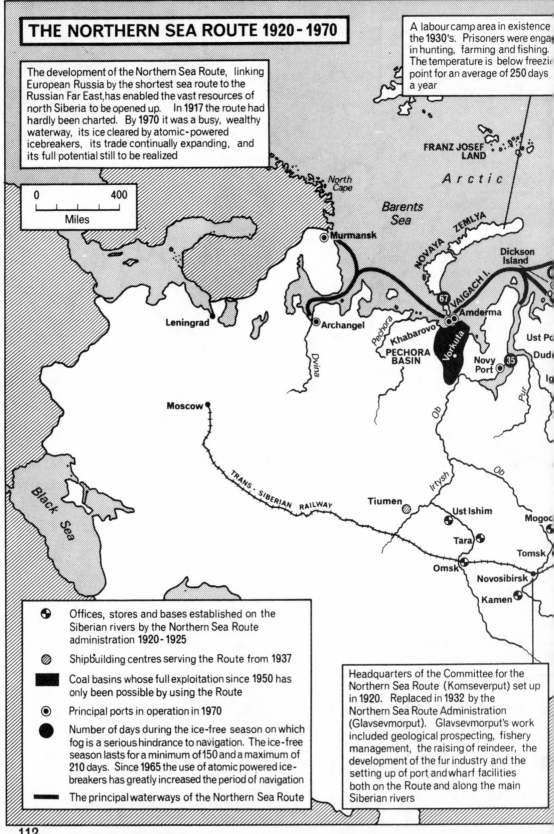

THE NORTHERN SEA ROUTE 1920-1970

The development of the Northern Sea Route, linking European Russia by the shortest sea route to the Russian Far East, has enabled the vast resources of north Siberia to be opened up. In 1917 the route had hardly been charted. By 1970 it was a busy, wealthy waterway, its ice cleared by atomic-powered icebreakers, its trade continually expanding, and its full potential still to be realized

A labour camp area in existence the 1930's. Prisoners were enga[g] in hunting, farming and fishing. The temperature is below freezi[ng] point for an average of 250 days a year

0   400
Miles

FRANZ JOSEF LAND

Arctic

North Cape

Barents Sea

NOVAYA ZEMLYA

Dickson Island

Murmansk

VAIGACH I.

67

Amderma

Archangel

Pechora

Khabarovo

Vorkuta

Ust Po[...]

PECHORA BASIN

Dvina

Novy Port

35

Dud[...]

Ig[...]

Ob

Pur

Moscow

Irtysh

Ob

TRANS-SIBERIAN RAILWAY

Tiumen

Ust Ishim

Mogoc[...]

Tara

Tomsk

Leningrad

Black Sea

Omsk

Novosibirsk

Kamen

Legend

✚	Offices, stores and bases established on the Siberian rivers by the Northern Sea Route administration 1920-1925
⊘	Shipbuilding centres serving the Route from 1937
■	Coal basins whose full exploitation since 1950 has only been possible by using the Route
◉	Principal ports in operation in 1970
●	Number of days during the ice-free season on which fog is a serious hindrance to navigation. The ice-free season lasts for a minimum of 150 and a maximum of 210 days. Since 1965 the use of atomic powered ice-breakers has greatly increased the period of navigation
▬	The principal waterways of the Northern Sea Route

Headquarters of the Committee for the Northern Sea Route (Komseverput) set up in 1920. Replaced in 1932 by the Northern Sea Route Administration (Glavsevmorput). Glavsevmorput's work included geological prospecting, fishery management, the raising of reindeer, the development of the fur industry and the setting up of port and wharf facilities both on the Route and along the main Siberian rivers

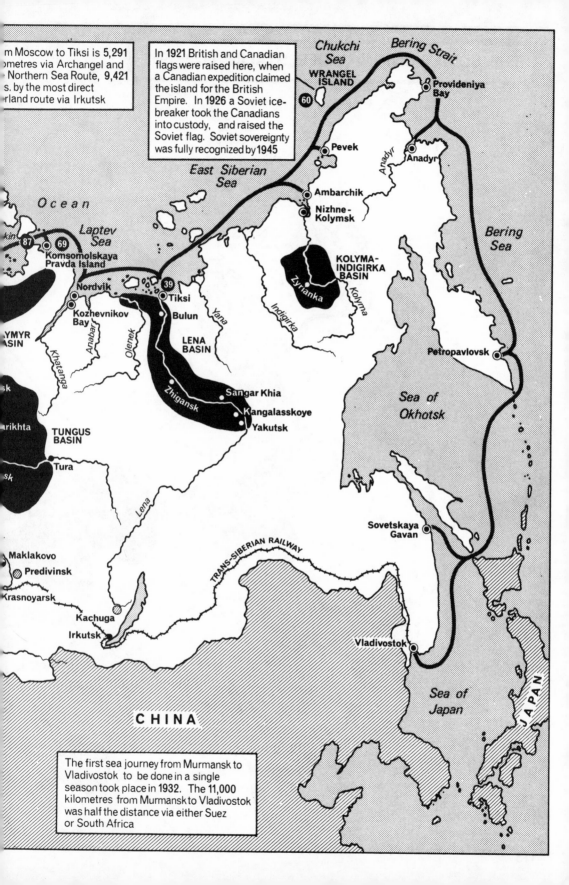

From Moscow to Tiksi is **5,291** kilometres via Archangel and the Northern Sea Route, **9,421** kms. by the most direct overland route via Irkutsk

In 1921 British and Canadian flags were raised here, when a Canadian expedition claimed the island for the British Empire. In **1926** a Soviet ice-breaker took the Canadians into custody, and raised the Soviet flag. Soviet sovereignty was fully recognized by **1945**

Chukchi Sea

Bering Strait

WRANGEL ISLAND

60

Provid
Bay

Pevek

Anadyr

East Siberian Sea

Ambarchik

Nizhne-Kolymsk

Bering Sea

Ocean

Laptev Sea

87

69

Komsomolskaya Pravda Island

KOLYMA-INDIGIRKA BASIN

Zyrianka

Kolyma

Nordvik

39

Tiksi

Bulun

Yana

Indigirka

Petropavlovsk

Kozhevnikov Bay

Olenek

LENA BASIN

YMYR ASIN

Anabar

Khatanga

Sea of Okhotsk

sk

Zhigansk

Sangar Khia

Kangalasskoye

rikhta

TUNGUS BASIN

Yakutsk

Tura

Lena

Sovetskaya Gavan

sk

Maklakovo

Predivinsk

TRANS-SIBERIAN RAILWAY

Krasnoyarsk

Kachuga

Irkutsk

Vladivostok

C H I N A

Sea of Japan

J A P A N

The first sea journey from Murmansk to Vladivostok to be done in a single season took place in 1932. The 11,000 kilometres from Murmansk to Vladivostok was half the distance via either Suez or South Africa

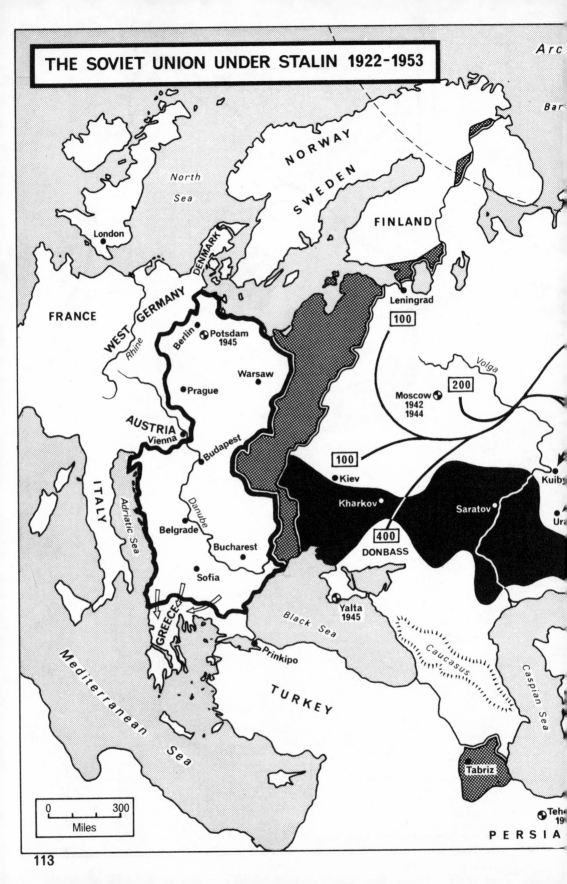

THE SOVIET UNION UNDER STALIN 1922-1953

Arc

Bar

NORWAY

SWEDEN

North Sea

FINLAND

London

Leningrad

100

FRANCE

WEST GERMANY

Rhine

Berlin

⊕ Potsdam 1945

Warsaw

Prague

DENMARK

Volga

Moscow 1942 1944

200

AUSTRIA

Vienna

Budapest

100

● Kiev

Kuiby

Danube

Kharkov ●

Saratov ●

Ura

ITALY

Belgrade

Bucharest

400

DONBASS

Adriatic Sea

Sofia

Yalta 1945

GREECE

Black Sea

Caucasus

Caspian Sea

Prinkipo

TURKEY

Mediterranean Sea

Tabriz

Teh

19

PERSIA

0 ——— 300

Miles

113

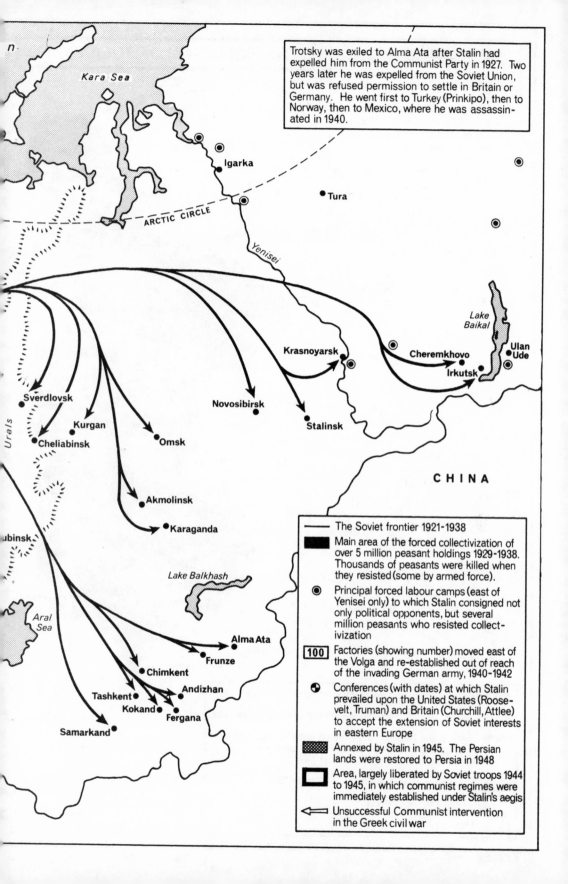

n.

Kara Sea

Igarka

Tura

ARCTIC CIRCLE

Yenisei

Trotsky was exiled to Alma Ata after Stalin had
expelled him from the Communist Party in 1927. Two
years later he was expelled from the Soviet Union,
but was refused permission to settle in Britain or
Germany. He went first to Turkey (Prinkipo), then to
Norway, then to Mexico, where he was assassinated in 1940.

Lake
Baikal

Krasnoyarsk

Cheremkhovo

Ulan
Ude

Irkutsk

Urals

Sverdlovsk

Kurgan

Cheliabinsk

Omsk

Novosibirsk

Stalinsk

CHINA

Akmolinsk

Karaganda

ubinsk

Lake Balkhash

Aral
Sea

Alma Ata

Frunze

Chimkent

Andizhan

Tashkent

Kokand

Fergana

Samarkand

The Soviet frontier 1921-1938

Main area of the forced collectivization of
over 5 million peasant holdings 1929-1938.
Thousands of peasants were killed when
they resisted (some by armed force).

Principal forced labour camps (east of
Yenisei only) to which Stalin consigned not
only political opponents, but several
million peasants who resisted collectivization

100 Factories (showing number) moved east of
the Volga and re-established out of reach
of the invading German army, 1940-1942

Conferences (with dates) at which Stalin
prevailed upon the United States (Roose-
velt, Truman) and Britain (Churchill, Attlee)
to accept the extension of Soviet interests
in eastern Europe

Annexed by Stalin in 1945. The Persian
lands were restored to Persia in 1948

Area, largely liberated by Soviet troops 1944
to 1945, in which communist regimes were
immediately established under Stalin's aegis

Unsuccessful Communist intervention
in the Greek civil war

The destruction of Poland was principally a German action. 1,700,000 German troops soon defeated the 600,000 Polish soldiers. German air attack destroyed the centres of the main Polish cities. The Poles hoped to make a final stand in the Pripet marsh area, but the Russian advance destroyed all chance of further Polish resistance

THE PARTITION OF POLAND 1939

Baltic Sea

LITHUANIA

Vilna

Königsberg

EAST

PRUSSIA

Suvalki

Minsk

Augustov

Grodno

Lomza

Bialystok

RUSSIA

Posnan

Warsaw

Brest-Litovsk

Pinsk

Pripet

Marshes

Lodz

Lublin

SOVIET

Lutsk

Sokal

Rovno

GERMANY

Tarnov

Cracow

Yaroslav

Lvov

Tarnopol

Przemysl

Stanislavov

Kamenets Podolsk

P O L A N D

SLOVAKIA

HUNGARY

RUMANIA

German advance against Poland from 3 September 1939

Russian advance against Poland from 17 September 1939

Dividing line between the German and Russian zones of occupation, agreed upon in advance by the Russo-German Pact of 23 August 1939

Annexed by the Soviet Union in October 1939

Annexed by Germany

Annexed by Lithuania

0   100

Miles

114

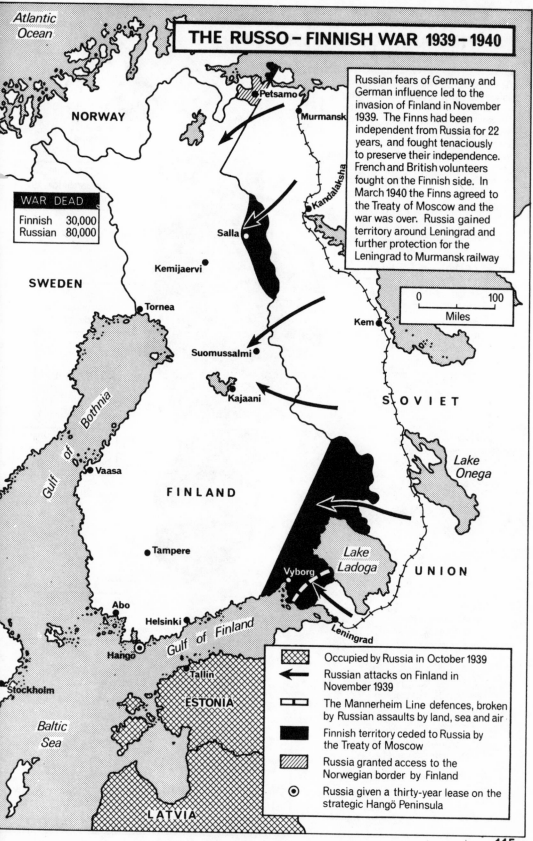

THE RUSSO – FINNISH WAR 1939 – 1940

Russian fears of Germany and German influence led to the invasion of Finland in November 1939. The Finns had been independent from Russia for 22 years, and fought tenaciously to preserve their independence. French and British volunteers fought on the Finnish side. In March 1940 the Finns agreed to the Treaty of Moscow and the war was over. Russia gained territory around Leningrad and further protection for the Leningrad to Murmansk railway

WAR DEAD	
Finnish	30,000
Russian	80,000

0   100
Miles

Atlantic Ocean

NORWAY

Petsamo

Murmansk

Kandalaksha

Salla

Kemijaervi

SWEDEN

Tornea

Kem

SOVIET

Gulf of Bothnia

Suomussalmi

Kajaani

Lake Onega

Vaasa

FINLAND

Lake Ladoga

Tampere

UNION

Vyborg

Abo

Helsinki

Leningrad

Hango

Gulf of Finland

Stockholm

Tallin

ESTONIA

Baltic Sea

LATVIA

Legend	
Occupied by Russia in October 1939	
Russian attacks on Finland in November 1939	
The Mannerheim Line defences, broken by Russian assaults by land, sea and air	
Finnish territory ceded to Russia by the Treaty of Moscow	
Russia granted access to the Norwegian border by Finland	
Russia given a thirty-year lease on the strategic Hangö Peninsula	

115

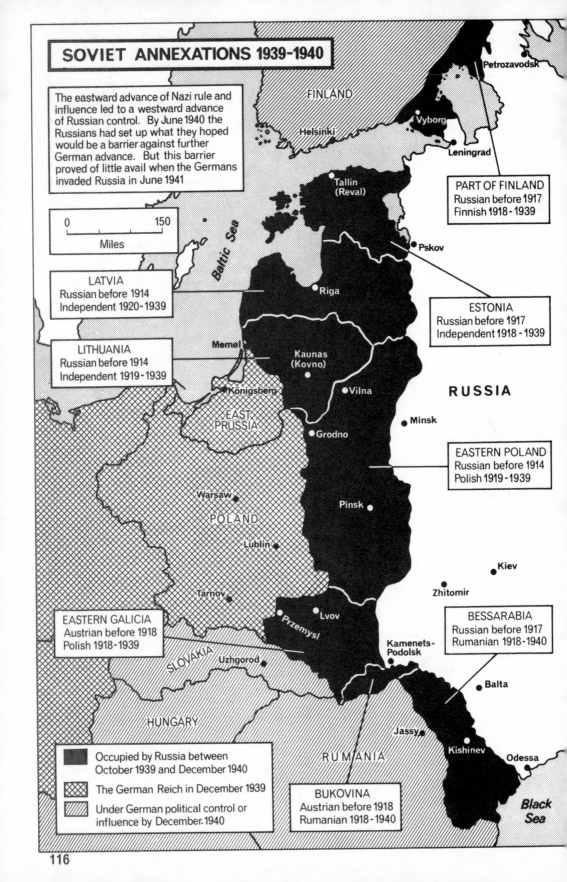

SOVIET ANNEXATIONS 1939-1940

The eastward advance of Nazi rule and influence led to a westward advance of Russian control. By June 1940 the Russians had set up what they hoped would be a barrier against further German advance. But this barrier proved of little avail when the Germans invaded Russia in June 1941

0 — 150
Miles

PART OF FINLAND
Russian before 1917
Finnish 1918 - 1939

LATVIA
Russian before 1914
Independent 1920 - 1939

LITHUANIA
Russian before 1914
Independent 1919 - 1939

ESTONIA
Russian before 1917
Independent 1918 - 1939

EASTERN POLAND
Russian before 1914
Polish 1919 - 1939

EASTERN GALICIA
Austrian before 1918
Polish 1918 - 1939

BESSARABIA
Russian before 1917
Rumanian 1918 - 1940

BUKOVINA
Austrian before 1918
Rumanian 1918 - 1940

FINLAND
Petrozavodsk
Vyborg
Helsinki
Leningrad
Tallin (Reval)
Baltic Sea
Pskov
Riga
Memel
Kaunas (Kovno)
Königsberg
EAST PRUSSIA
Vilna
RUSSIA
Grodno
Minsk
Warsaw
POLAND
Pinsk
Lublin
Kiev
Tarnov
Zhitomir
Lvov
Przemysl
Kamenets-Podolsk
Balta
SLOVAKIA
Uzhgorod
HUNGARY
Jassy
RUMANIA
Kishinev
Odessa
Black Sea

Occupied by Russia between October 1939 and December 1940

The German Reich in December 1939

Under German political control or influence by December 1940

EUROPE ON 22 JUNE 1941

Archangel

FINLAND

NORWAY

SWEDEN

Hango

Leningrad

BRITAIN

EIRE

Riga

Kovno

Moscow

Vilna

DENMARK

Danzig

SOVIET UNION

HOLLAND

London

Berlin

Brest-Litovsk

GREATER GERMANY

Warsaw

BELGIUM

Cologne

Cracow

Lvov

FRANCE

Prague

Munich

SLOVAKIA

Kishinev

Vienna

SWITZ.

HUNGARY

Odessa

RUMANIA

SPAIN

YUGOSLAVIA

BULGARIA

ITALY

ALBANIA

GREECE

TURKEY

The German Reich on 22 June 1941, the day of the German invasion of Russia

Countries under German rule or influence by June 1941

Neutral countries

Great Britain, the only state at war with Germany on 21 June 1941; and the Soviet Union, to whom Britain immediately offered all possible help and alliance in the fight against Nazism

0   300

Miles

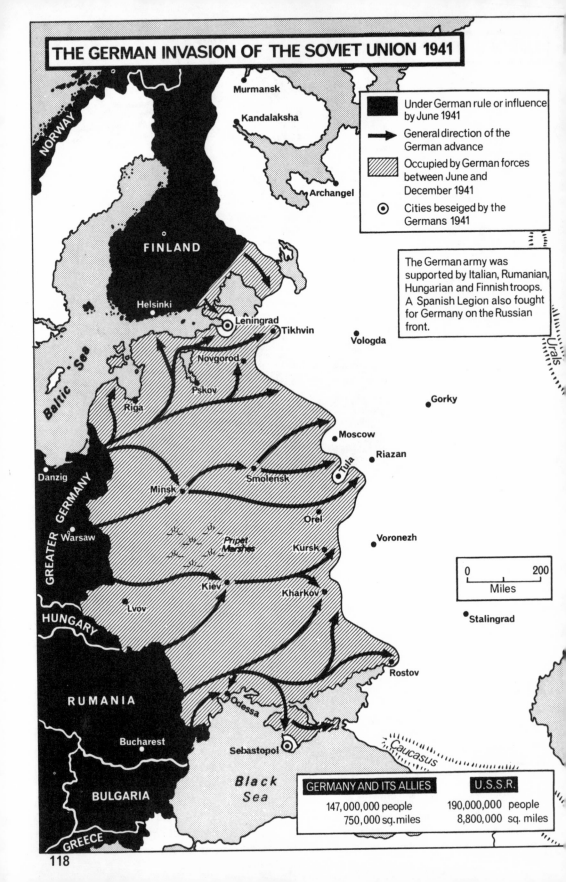

THE GERMAN INVASION OF THE SOVIET UNION 1941

Legend:

- ■ Under German rule or influence by June 1941
- → General direction of the German advance
- ▨ Occupied by German forces between June and December 1941
- ⊙ Cities beseiged by the Germans 1941

The German army was supported by Italian, Rumanian, Hungarian and Finnish troops. A Spanish Legion also fought for Germany on the Russian front.

NORWAY

Murmansk

Kandalaksha

Archangel

FINLAND

Helsinki

Baltic Sea

Leningrad

Tikhvin

Vologda

Novgorod

Pskov

Riga

Gorky

Urals

Danzig

Moscow

Riazan

GREATER GERMANY

Minsk

Smolensk

Tula

Warsaw

Pripet Marshes

Orel

Voronezh

Kursk

Kiev

Lvov

Kharkov

HUNGARY

Stalingrad

0   200
Miles

Rostov

RUMANIA

Odessa

Bucharest

Sebastopol

Caucasus

BULGARIA

Black Sea

GERMANY AND ITS ALLIES	U.S.S.R.
147,000,000 people	190,000,000 people
750,000 sq. miles	8,800,000 sq. miles

GREECE

118

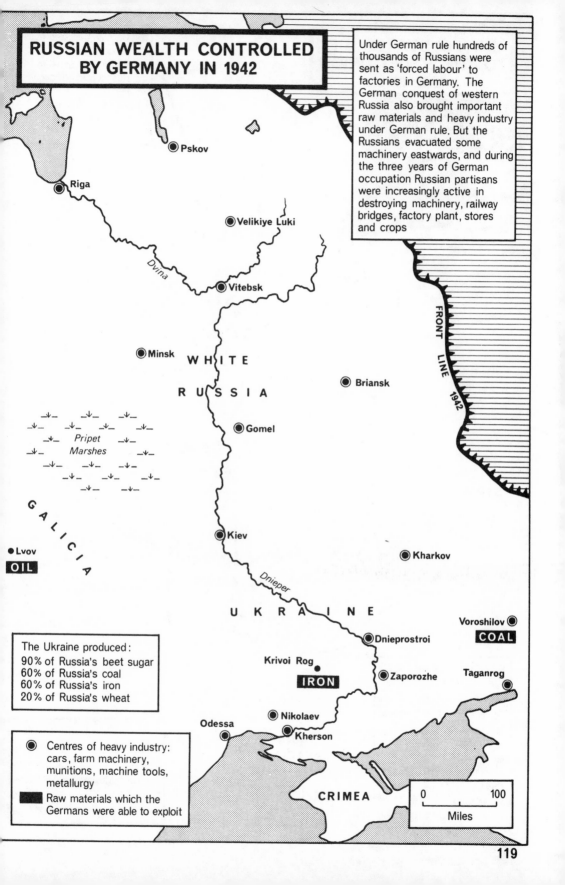

RUSSIAN WEALTH CONTROLLED BY GERMANY IN 1942

Under German rule hundreds of thousands of Russians were sent as 'forced labour' to factories in Germany. The German conquest of western Russia also brought important raw materials and heavy industry under German rule. But the Russians evacuated some machinery eastwards, and during the three years of German occupation Russian partisans were increasingly active in destroying machinery, railway bridges, factory plant, stores and crops

Pskov

Riga

Velikiye Luki

Dvina

Vitebsk

FRONT LINE 1942

Minsk

W H I T E

R U S S I A

Briansk

Gomel

Pripet
Marshes

G A L I C I A

Lvov
OIL

Kiev

Kharkov

Dnieper

U K R A I N E

Voroshilov
COAL

Dnieprostroi

Krivoi Rog
IRON

Zaporozhe

Taganrog

The Ukraine produced:
90% of Russia's beet sugar
60% of Russia's coal
60% of Russia's iron
20% of Russia's wheat

Nikolaev

Odessa

Kherson

◉ Centres of heavy industry:
cars, farm machinery,
munitions, machine tools,
metallurgy

■ Raw materials which the
Germans were able to exploit

CRIMEA

0   100
Miles

119

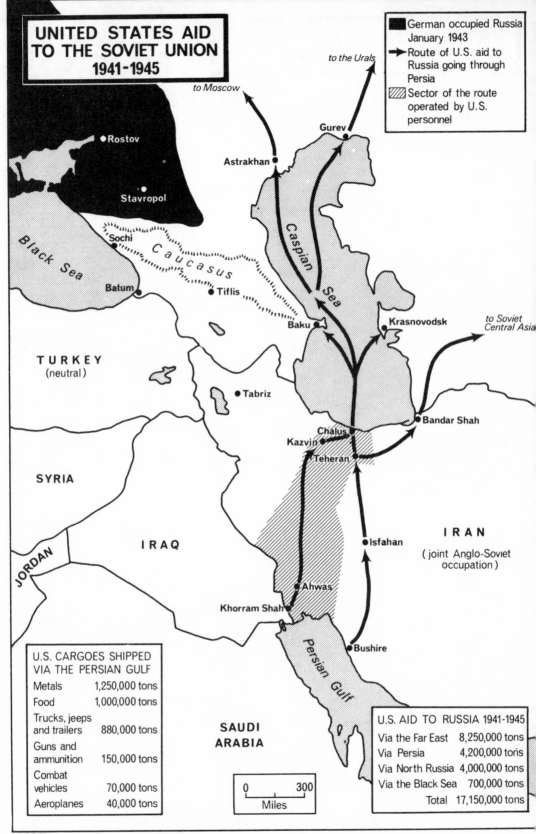

UNITED STATES AID TO THE SOVIET UNION 1941-1945

German occupied Russia January 1943

Route of U.S. aid to Russia going through Persia

Sector of the route operated by U.S. personnel

to Moscow

to the Urals

Rostov

Gurev

Astrakhan

Stavropol

Sochi

Caucasus

Black Sea

Batum

Tiflis

Caspian Sea

Baku

Krasnovodsk

to Soviet Central Asia

TURKEY
(neutral)

Tabriz

Bandar Shah

Chalus

Kazvin

Teheran

SYRIA

IRAN
(joint Anglo-Soviet occupation)

JORDAN

IRAQ

Isfahan

Ahwas

Khorram Shah

Bushire

Persian Gulf

SAUDI
ARABIA

U.S. CARGOES SHIPPED VIA THE PERSIAN GULF

Metals	1,250,000 tons
Food	1,000,000 tons
Trucks, jeeps and trailers	880,000 tons
Guns and ammunition	150,000 tons
Combat vehicles	70,000 tons
Aeroplanes	40,000 tons

0   300
Miles

U.S. AID TO RUSSIA 1941-1945

Via the Far East	8,250,000 tons
Via Persia	4,200,000 tons
Via North Russia	4,000,000 tons
Via the Black Sea	700,000 tons
Total	17,150,000 tons

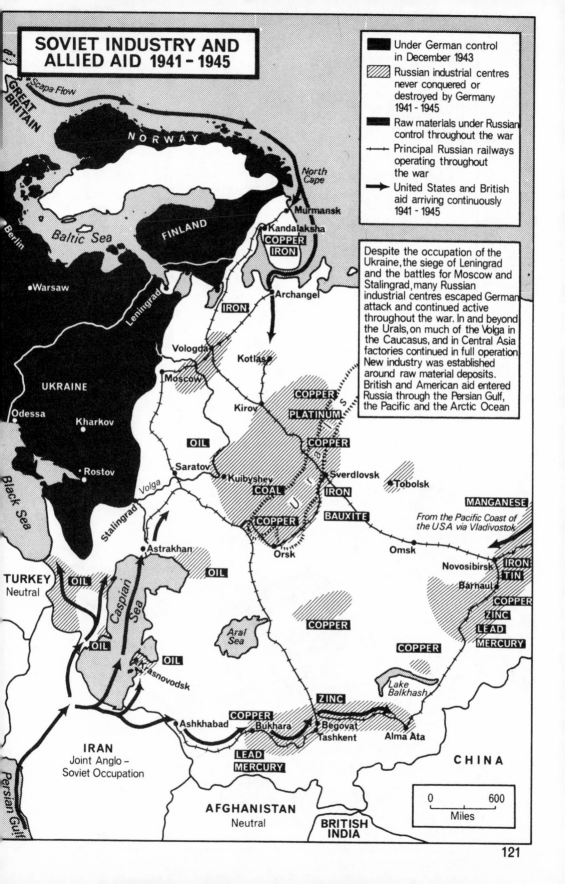

SOVIET INDUSTRY AND ALLIED AID 1941-1945

Legend:
- Under German control in December 1943
- Russian industrial centres never conquered or destroyed by Germany 1941-1945
- Raw materials under Russian control throughout the war
- Principal Russian railways operating throughout the war
- United States and British aid arriving continuously 1941-1945

Despite the occupation of the Ukraine, the siege of Leningrad and the battles for Moscow and Stalingrad, many Russian industrial centres escaped German attack and continued active throughout the war. In and beyond the Urals, on much of the Volga in the Caucasus, and in Central Asia factories continued in full operation. New industry was established around raw material deposits. British and American aid entered Russia through the Persian Gulf, the Pacific and the Arctic Ocean

GREAT BRITAIN

Scapa Flow

NORWAY

North Cape

Murmansk

Baltic Sea

FINLAND

Kandalaksha
COPPER
IRON

Berlin

•Warsaw

Leningrad

Archangel

IRON

Vologda

Kotlas

UKRAINE

Moscow

Kirov

COPPER

PLATINUM

COPPER

Odessa

Kharkov

OIL

•Rostov

Saratov

Volga

Kuibyshev
COAL

Sverdlovsk

•Tobolsk

IRON

MANGANESE

From the Pacific Coast of the USA via Vladivostok

Stalingrad

Astrakhan

COPPER

BAUXITE

Orsk

Omsk

Novosibirsk

IRON
TIN

TURKEY
Neutral

OIL

Caspian Sea

OIL

Barnaul

COPPER

ZINC
LEAD
MERCURY

OIL

Aral Sea

COPPER

COPPER

Krasnovodsk

OIL

Lake Balkhash

ZINC

Ashkhabad

COPPER
Bukhara

Begovat
Tashkent

Alma Ata

IRAN
Joint Anglo–
Soviet Occupation

LEAD
MERCURY

CHINA

Black Sea

Persian Gulf

AFGHANISTAN
Neutral

BRITISH INDIA

0   600
Miles

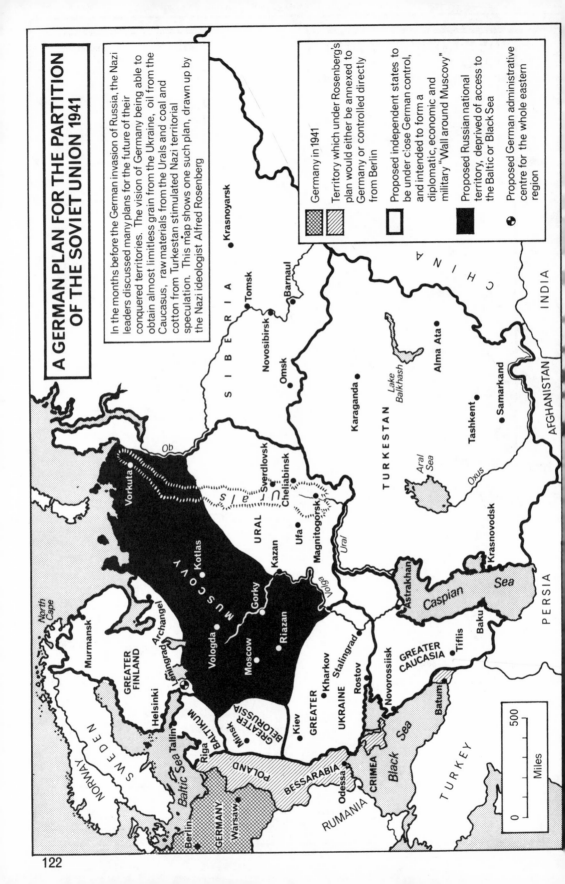

A GERMAN PLAN FOR THE PARTITION OF THE SOVIET UNION 1941

In the months before the German invasion of Russia, the Nazi leaders discussed many plans for the future of their conquered territories. The vision of Germany being able to obtain almost limitless grain from the Ukraine, oil from the Caucasus, raw materials from the Urals and coal and cotton from Turkestan stimulated Nazi territorial speculation. This map shows one such plan, drawn up by the Nazi ideologist Alfred Rosenberg

Legend:

- Germany in 1941
- Territory which under Rosenberg's plan would either be annexed to Germany or controlled directly from Berlin
- Proposed independent states to be under close German control, and intended to form a diplomatic, economic and military "Wall around Muscovy"
- Proposed Russian national territory, deprived of access to the Baltic or Black Sea
- Proposed German administrative centre for the whole eastern region

0   500
Miles

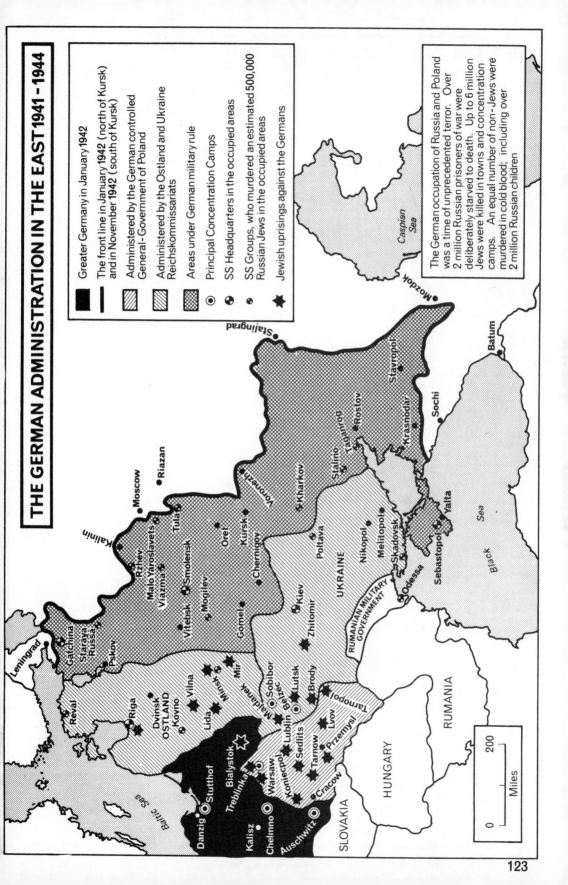

THE GERMAN ADMINISTRATION IN THE EAST 1941-1944

Greater Germany in January 1942

The front line in January 1942 (north of Kursk) and in November 1942 (south of Kursk)

Administered by the German controlled General-Government of Poland

Administered by the Ostland and Ukraine Reichskommissariats

Areas under German military rule

Principal Concentration Camps

SS Headquarters in the occupied areas

SS Groups, who murdered an estimated 500,000 Russian Jews in the occupied areas

Jewish uprisings against the Germans

The German occupation of Russia and Poland was a time of unprecedented terror. Over 2 million Russian prisoners of war were deliberately starved to death. Up to 6 million Jews were killed in towns and concentration camps. An equal number of non-Jews were murdered in cold blood; including over 2 million Russian children

123

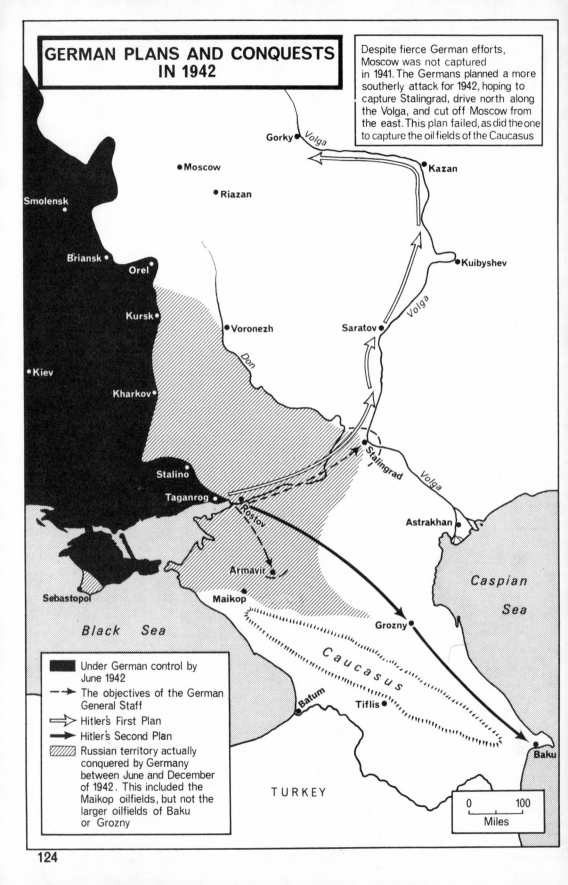

GERMAN PLANS AND CONQUESTS IN 1942

Despite fierce German efforts, Moscow was not captured in 1941. The Germans planned a more southerly attack for 1942, hoping to capture Stalingrad, drive north along the Volga, and cut off Moscow from the east. This plan failed, as did the one to capture the oil fields of the Caucasus

Gorky

Volga

•Moscow

• Kazan

• Riazan

Smolensk

• Kuibyshev

Briansk

Orel

Kursk

• Voronezh

Saratov

Volga

• Kiev

Don

Kharkov

Stalino

Stalingrad

Volga

Taganrog

Rostov

Astrakhan

Armavir

Caspian

Sebastopol

Maikop

Sea

Black Sea

Grozny

C a u c a s u s

Batum

Tiflis

Baku

TURKEY

Legend

- ■ Under German control by June 1942
- –‑► The objectives of the German General Staff
- ⇨ Hitler's First Plan
- ➡ Hitler's Second Plan
- ▨ Russian territory actually conquered by Germany between June and December of 1942. This included the Maikop oilfields, but not the larger oilfields of Baku or Grozny

0   100
Miles

124

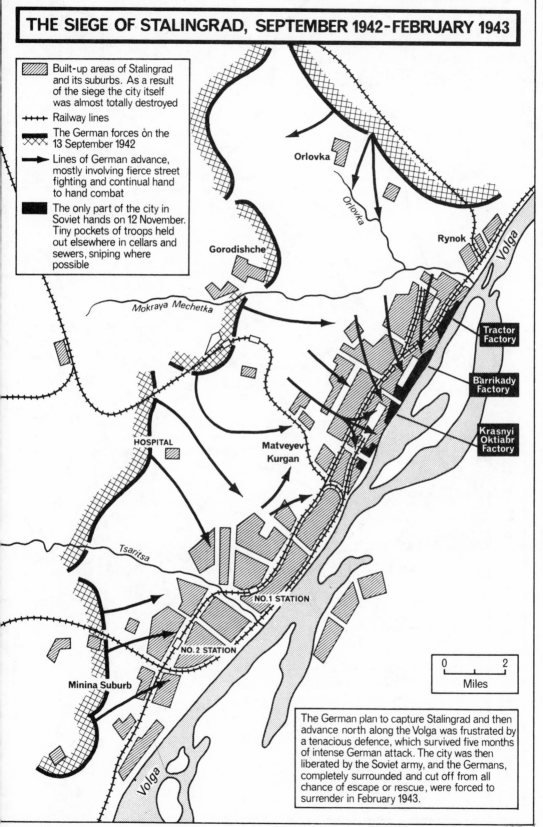

THE SIEGE OF STALINGRAD, SEPTEMBER 1942-FEBRUARY 1943

Legend:

- Built-up areas of Stalingrad and its suburbs. As a result of the siege the city itself was almost totally destroyed
- ┽┽┽┼ Railway lines
- The German forces on the 13 September 1942
- Lines of German advance, mostly involving fierce street fighting and continual hand to hand combat
- The only part of the city in Soviet hands on 12 November. Tiny pockets of troops held out elsewhere in cellars and sewers, sniping where possible

Orlovka

Orlovka

Rynok

Gorodishche

Volga

Mokraya Mechetka

Tractor Factory

Barrikady Factory

HOSPITAL

Matveyev Kurgan

Krasnyi Oktiabr Factory

Tsaritsa

NO.1 STATION

NO.2 STATION

Minina Suburb

Volga

0 — 2
Miles

The German plan to capture Stalingrad and then advance north along the Volga was frustrated by a tenacious defence, which survived five months of intense German attack. The city was then liberated by the Soviet army, and the Germans, completely surrounded and cut off from all chance of escape or rescue, were forced to surrender in February 1943.

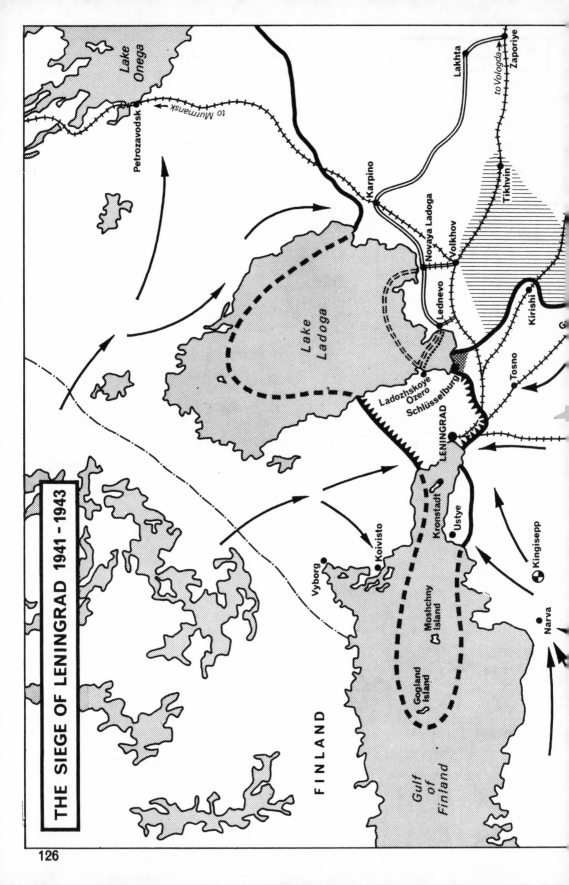

THE SIEGE OF LENINGRAD 1941 – 1943

Lake Onega

Petrozavodsk

to Murmansk

Karpino

Novaya Ladoga

Volkhov

Lednevo

Lahkta

to Vologda

Zaporiye

Tikhvin

Kirishi

Lake Ladoga

Ladozhskoye Ozero

Schlüsselburg

LENINGRAD

Tosno

G

FINLAND

Vyborg

Koivisto

Kronstadt

Ustye

Kingisepp

Moshchny Island

Gogland Island

Narva

Gulf of Finland

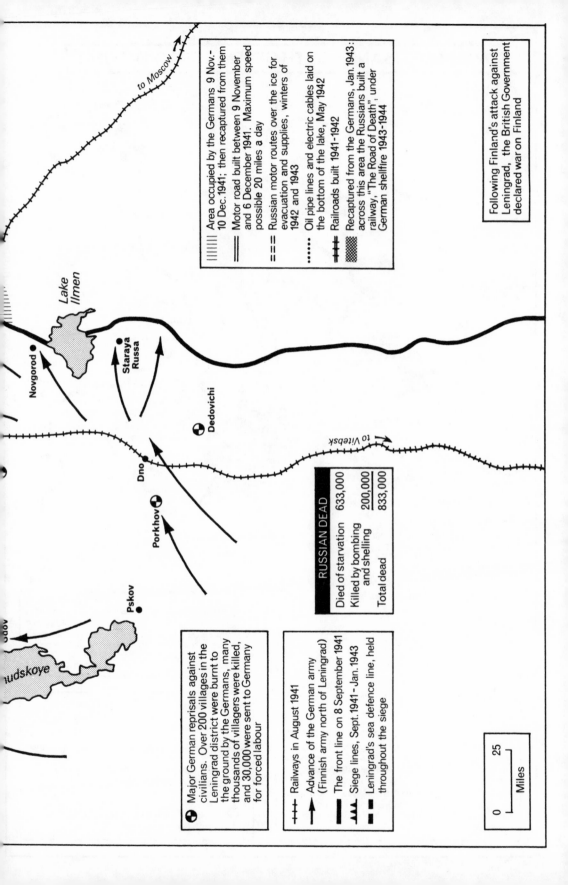

to Moscow

Lake Ilmen

Novgorod

Staraya Russa

Dedovichi

Dno

to Vitebsk

Porkhov

Pskov

|||||| Area occupied by the Germans 9 Nov.-10 Dec. 1941; then recaptured from them

═══ Motor road built between 9 November and 6 December 1941. Maximum speed possible 20 miles a day

═ ═ Russian motor routes over the ice for evacuation and supplies, winters of 1942 and 1943

····· Oil pipe lines and electric cables laid on the bottom of the lake, May 1942

┿┿┿ Railroads built 1941-1942

▦ Recaptured from the Germans, Jan.1943: across this area the Russians built a railway, "The Road of Death", under German shellfire 1943-1944

Following Finland's attack against Leningrad, the British Government declared war on Finland

RUSSIAN DEAD	
Died of starvation	633,000
Killed by bombing and shelling	200,000
Total dead	833,000

⊕ Major German reprisals against civilians. Over 200 villages in the Leningrad district were burnt to the ground by the Germans, many thousands of villagers were killed, and 30,000 were sent to Germany for forced labour

┿┿┿ Railways in August 1941

↑ Advance of the German army (Finnish army north of Leningrad)

▮ The front line on 8 September 1941

▮▲▲ Siege lines, Sept. 1941 - Jan. 1943

▮ ▮ Leningrad's sea defence line, held throughout the siege

0   25
Miles

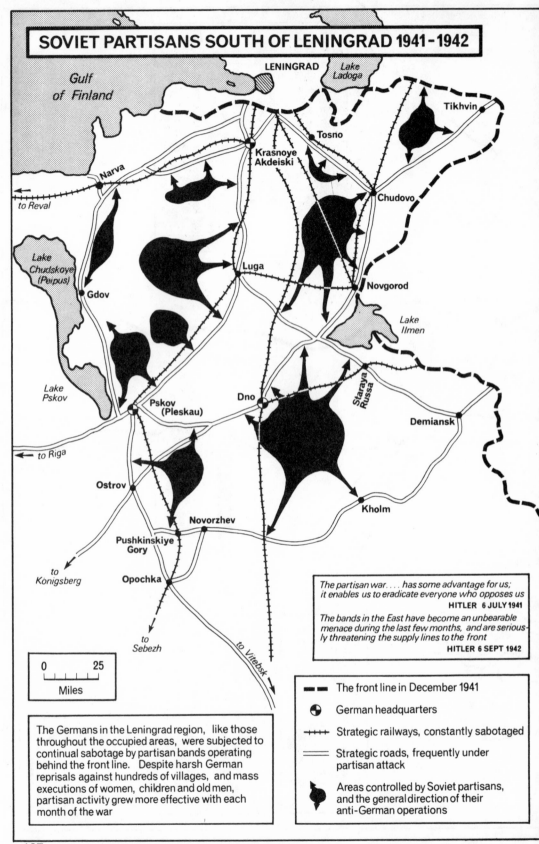

SOVIET PARTISANS SOUTH OF LENINGRAD 1941-1942

LENINGRAD

Lake Ladoga

Gulf of Finland

Tikhvin

Tosno

Narva

Krasnoye Akdeiski

Chudovo

to Reval

Lake Chudskoye (Peipus)

Luga

Novgorod

Gdov

Lake Ilmen

Lake Pskov

Staraya Russa

Pskov (Pleskau)

Dno

Demiansk

to Riga

Ostrov

Kholm

Novorzhev

Pushkinskiye Gory

to Königsberg

Opochka

The partisan war.... has some advantage for us; it enables us to eradicate everyone who opposes us
HITLER 6 JULY 1941

The bands in the East have become an unbearable menace during the last few months, and are seriously threatening the supply lines to the front
HITLER 6 SEPT 1942

to Sebezh

to Vitebsk

```
0        25
|__|__|__|
    Miles
```

– – – The front line in December 1941

🌓 German headquarters

+++++ Strategic railways, constantly sabotaged

═══ Strategic roads, frequently under partisan attack

Areas controlled by Soviet partisans, and the general direction of their anti-German operations

The Germans in the Leningrad region, like those throughout the occupied areas, were subjected to continual sabotage by partisan bands operating behind the front line. Despite harsh German reprisals against hundreds of villages, and mass executions of women, children and old men, partisan activity grew more effective with each month of the war

127

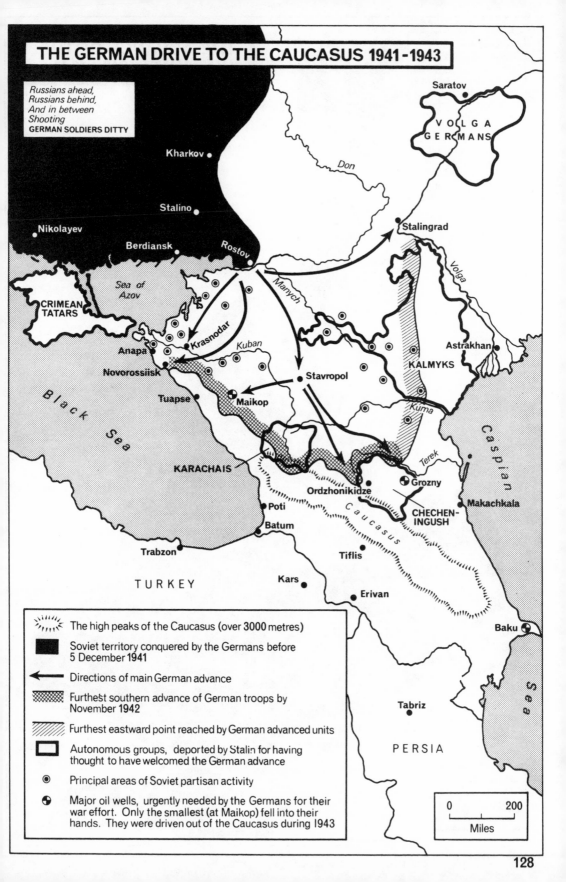

THE GERMAN DRIVE TO THE CAUCASUS 1941-1943

Russians ahead,
Russians behind,
And in between
Shooting
GERMAN SOLDIERS DITTY

Saratov

V O L G A
G E R M A N S

Kharkov

Don

Stalino

Nikolayev

Stalingrad

Berdiansk

Rostov

Volga

Sea of Azov

Manych

CRIMEAN TATARS

Krasnodar

Kuban

Astrakhan

Anapa

KALMYKS

Novorossiisk

Stavropol

Tuapse

Maikop

Kuma

Black Sea

KARACHAIS

Terek

Grozny

Caucasus

Ordzhonikidze

CHECHEN-INGUSH

Makachkala

Poti

Batum

Caspian Sea

Trabzon

Tiflis

T U R K E Y

Kars

Erivan

Baku

Legend:

- The high peaks of the Caucasus (over 3000 metres)
- Soviet territory conquered by the Germans before 5 December 1941
- ← Directions of main German advance
- Furthest southern advance of German troops by November 1942
- Furthest eastward point reached by German advanced units
- Autonomous groups, deported by Stalin for having thought to have welcomed the German advance
- ◉ Principal areas of Soviet partisan activity
- ✪ Major oil wells, urgently needed by the Germans for their war effort. Only the smallest (at Maikop) fell into their hands. They were driven out of the Caucasus during 1943

Tabriz

P E R S I A

0 — 200
Miles

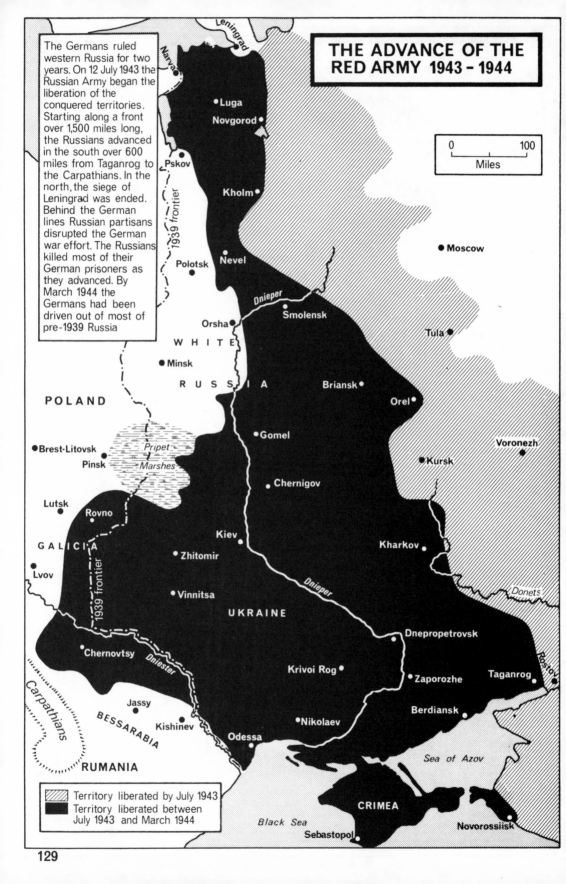

THE ADVANCE OF THE RED ARMY 1943 - 1944

The Germans ruled western Russia for two years. On 12 July 1943 the Russian Army began the liberation of the conquered territories. Starting along a front over 1,500 miles long, the Russians advanced in the south over 600 miles from Taganrog to the Carpathians. In the north, the siege of Leningrad was ended. Behind the German lines Russian partisans disrupted the German war effort. The Russians killed most of their German prisoners as they advanced. By March 1944 the Germans had been driven out of most of pre-1939 Russia

0   100
Miles

Leningrad

Narva

Luga
Novgorod

Pskov

Kholm

Moscow

1939 frontier

Polotsk   Nevel

Dnieper
Orsha   Smolensk   Tula

W H I T E

Minsk

R U S S I A   Briansk

POLAND   Orel

Brest-Litovsk   Gomel   Voronezh

Pinsk   Pripet   Kursk
Marshes

Chernigov

Lutsk

Rovno

G A L I C I A   Kiev
Zhitomir   Kharkov

1939 frontier

Lvov   Vinnitsa   Dnieper

U K R A I N E   Donets

Chernovtsy   Dnepropetrovsk

Dniester   Rostov

Krivoi Rog   Zaporozhe   Taganrog

Jassy   Berdiansk
BESSARABIA   Nikolaev
Kishinev
Odessa   Sea of Azov

Carpathians

RUMANIA

▨ Territory liberated by July 1943
■ Territory liberated between
   July 1943 and March 1944

CRIMEA   Novorossiisk
Black Sea
Sebastopol

THE DEFEAT OF GERMANY 1944 – 1945

EUROPEAN WAR DEAD 1939-1945

CIVILIANS

	approx.
Jews	6,000,000
Russians	3,000,000
Yugoslavs	1,280,000
Poles	1,000,000
Germans	800,000
Hungarians	280,000
Rumanians	260,000
Dutch	200,000
Greeks	140,000
French	107,000
Austrians	104,000
British	62,000
Belgians	16,000

Total civilian dead over 13 million

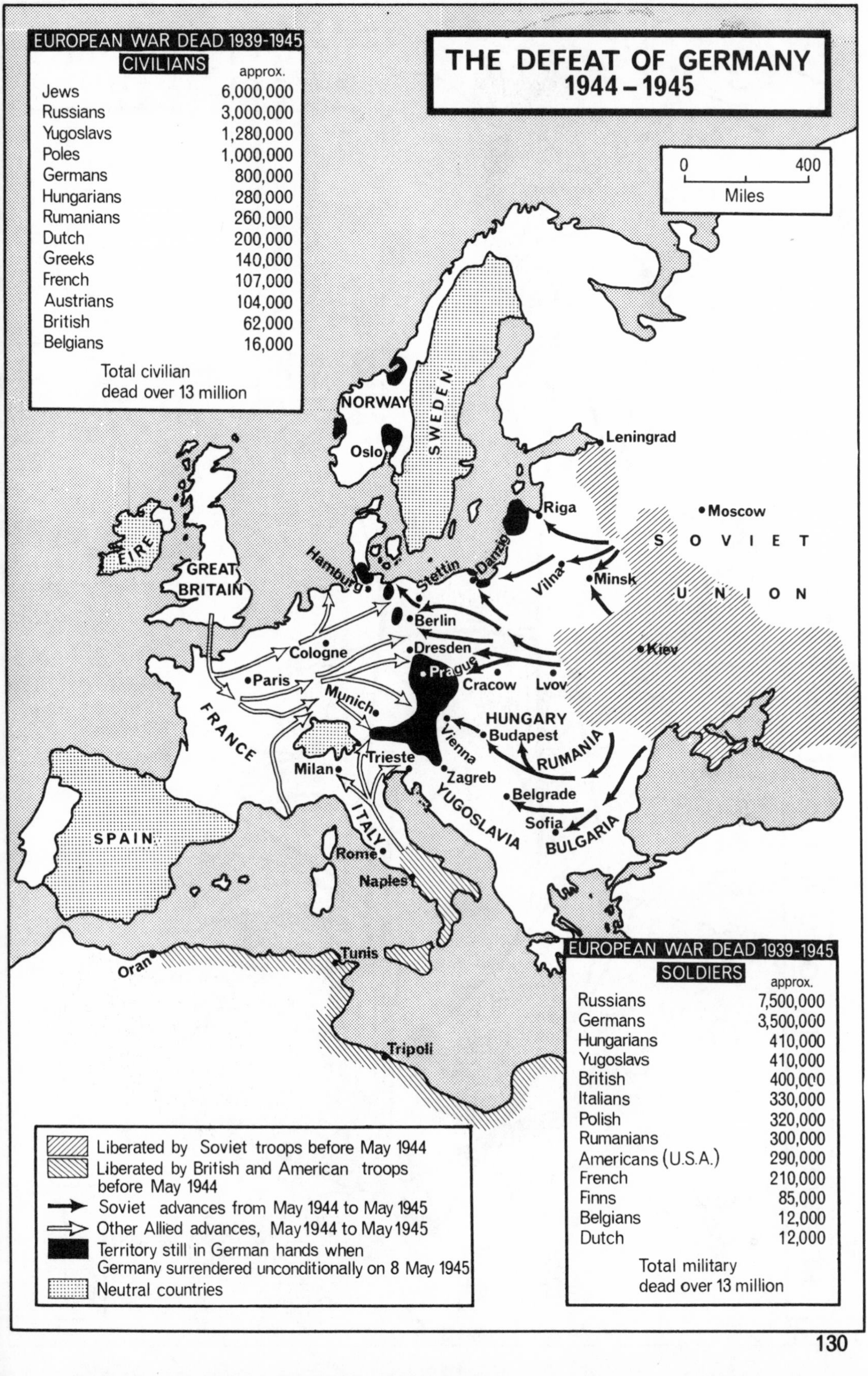
0
400
Miles
NORWAY
SWEDEN
Oslo
Leningrad
Riga
Moscow
SOVIET UNION
EIRE
GREAT BRITAIN
Hamburg
Stettin
Danzig
Vilna
Minsk
Berlin
Cologne
Dresden
Kiev
Paris
Prague
Cracow
Lvov
Munich
HUNGARY
Budapest
FRANCE
Vienna
RUMANIA
Trieste
Milan
Zagreb
Belgrade
ITALY
YUGOSLAVIA
Sofia
BULGARIA
SPAIN
Rome
Naples
Tunis
Oran
Tripoli

- Liberated by Soviet troops before May 1944
- Liberated by British and American troops before May 1944
- Soviet advances from May 1944 to May 1945
- Other Allied advances, May 1944 to May 1945
- Territory still in German hands when Germany surrendered unconditionally on 8 May 1945
- Neutral countries

EUROPEAN WAR DEAD 1939-1945

SOLDIERS

	approx.
Russians	7,500,000
Germans	3,500,000
Hungarians	410,000
Yugoslavs	410,000
British	400,000
Italians	330,000
Polish	320,000
Rumanians	300,000
Americans (U.S.A.)	290,000
French	210,000
Finns	85,000
Belgians	12,000
Dutch	12,000

Total military dead over 13 million

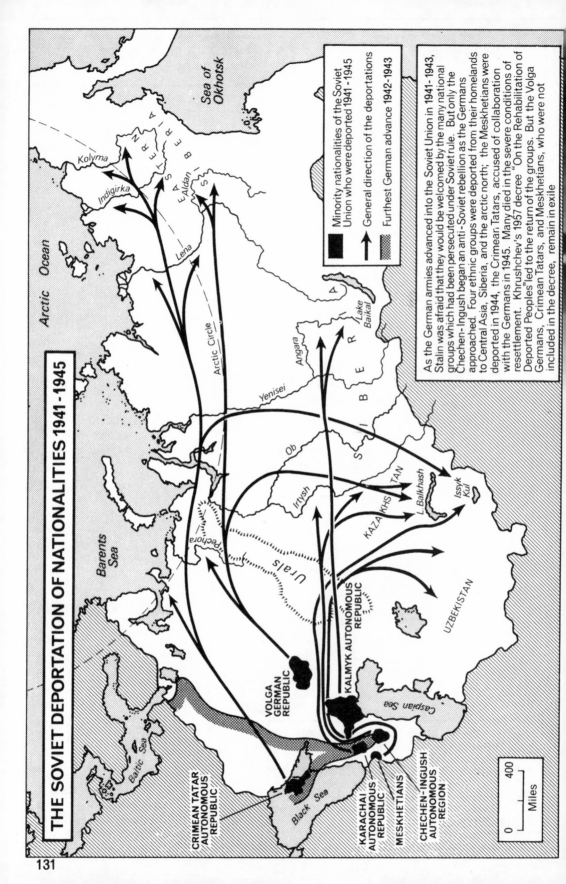

THE SOVIET DEPORTATION OF NATIONALITIES 1941-1945

Minority nationalities of the Soviet Union who were deported 1941-1945

General direction of the deportations

Furthest German advance 1942-1943

As the German armies advanced into the Soviet Union in 1941-1943, Stalin was afraid that they would be welcomed by the many national groups which had been persecuted under Soviet rule. But only the Chechen-Ingush began an anti-Soviet rebellion as the Germans approached. Four ethnic groups were deported from their homelands to Central Asia, Siberia, and the arctic north; the Meskhetians were deported in 1944, the Crimean Tatars, accused of collaboration with the Germans in 1945. Many died in the severe conditions of resettlement. Khrushchev's 1957 decree "On the Rehabilitation of Deported Peoples" led to the return of the groups. But the Volga Germans, Crimean Tatars, and Meskhetians, who were not included in the decree, remain in exile

Sea of Okhotsk

Kolyma

Indigirka

Arctic Ocean

E.Aldan

Lena

Arctic Circle

Angara

Lake Baikal

Yenisei

S I B E R I A

Ob

Irtysh

Urals

Pechora

KAZAKHSTAN

L.Balkhash

Issyk Kul

UZBEKISTAN

Barents Sea

Baltic Sea

VOLGA GERMAN REPUBLIC

KALMYK AUTONOMOUS REPUBLIC

Caspian Sea

CRIMEAN TATAR AUTONOMOUS REPUBLIC

KARACHAI AUTONOMOUS REPUBLIC

MESKHETIANS

CHECHEN-INGUSH AUTONOMOUS REGION

Black Sea

0   400
Miles

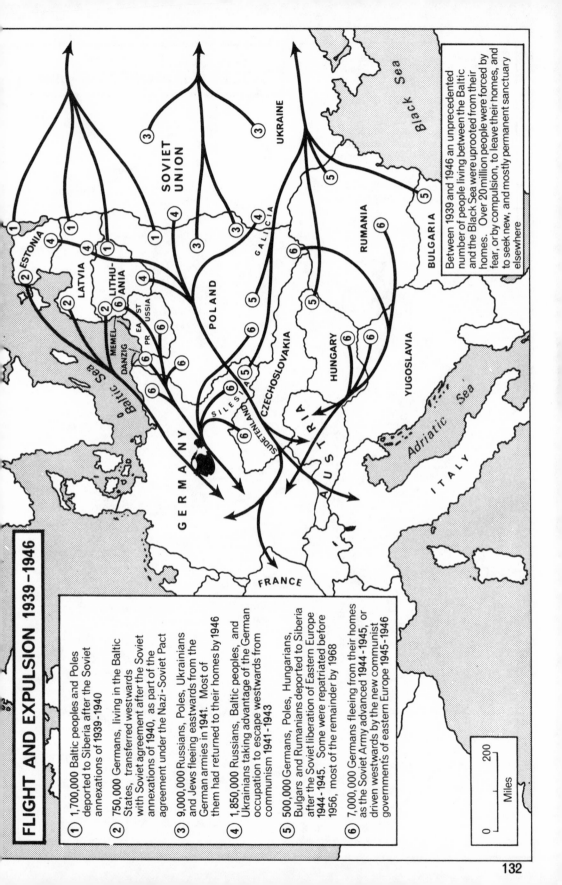

FLIGHT AND EXPULSION 1939-1946

Between 1939 and 1946 an unprecedented number of people living between the Baltic and the Black Sea were uprooted from their homes. Over 20 million people were forced by fear, or by compulsion, to leave their homes, and to seek new, and mostly permanent sanctuary elsewhere

① 1,700,000 Baltic peoples and Poles deported to Siberia after the Soviet annexations of 1939-1940

② 750,000 Germans, living in the Baltic States, transferred westwards with Soviet agreement after the Soviet annexations of 1940, as part of the agreement under the Nazi-Soviet Pact

③ 9,000,000 Russians, Poles, Ukrainians and Jews fleeing eastwards from the German armies in 1941. Most of them had returned to their homes by 1946

④ 1,850,000 Russians, Baltic peoples, and Ukrainians taking advantage of the German occupation to escape westwards from communism 1941-1943

⑤ 500,000 Germans, Poles, Hungarians, Bulgars and Rumanians deported to Siberia after the Soviet liberation of Eastern Europe 1944-1945. Some were repatriated before 1956, most of the remainder by 1968

⑥ 7,000,000 Germans fleeing from their homes as the Soviet Army advanced 1944-1945, or driven westwards by the new communist governments of eastern Europe 1945-1946

Miles 0 — 200

132

THE SOVIET UNION IN EASTERN EUROPE 1945 – 1948

Legend:

- Territory annexed by Russia 1939-1940, and re-incorporated in Russia in 1945
- Former German and Czechoslovak territory annexed by Russia in 1945
- States liberated by the Soviet army, and in which Communist regimes came to power between 1945 and 1948
- Russian occupation zones in Austria (evacuated 1950) and Germany
- British, French and American occupation zones
- The 'Iron Curtain' in 1948

North Sea

FINLAND

SWEDEN

Vyborg

Leningrad

Reval

Baltic Sea

ESTONIA

Pskov

Memel

Riga

LATVIA

Königsberg

LITHUANIA

Kovno

Vilna

EAST PRUSSIA

Minsk

Bremen

Stettin

annexed by Poland from Germany

Bialystok

S O V I E T

Berlin

Posnan

Warsaw

Pinsk

G E R M A N Y

Erfurt

POLAND

U N I O N

Bonn

Dresden

Breslau

SILESIA

Cracow

GALICIA

Lvov

Prague

Przemysl

Chernovtsy

Nuremburg

CZECHOSLOVAKIA

FRANCE

Munich

Vienna

AUSTRIA

Uzhgorod

Jassy

BESSARABIA

Kishinev

SWITZ.

Budapest

HUNGARY

RUMANIA

Trieste

Belgrade

Bucharest

ITALY

YUGOSLAVIA

Adriatic Sea

Sofia

BULGARIA

Black Sea

ALBANIA

Tirana

GREECE

Ægean Sea

TURKEY

The Russian liberation of Eastern Europe was quickly followed by the establishment of communist regimes, and an 'Iron Curtain' from the Baltic to the Adriatic. Communist rule brought national subservience to Russian policy, and the subordination of personal liberty. The cities of Berlin and Vienna were divided into Russian, British, French and American sectors

0 — 200 Miles

THE SOVIET UNION IN EASTERN EUROPE 1949 - 1968

0 — 200
Miles

Frontiers of communist states since 1945

Only European communist state entirely free from Soviet direction of foreign, economic and domestic policy since 1949

Only communist state within the Soviet bloc pursuing a relatively independent foreign policy since 1968

Only communist state in Europe aligned with China and refusing all contact with the Soviet Union since 1961

Only European communist state to accept Soviet guidance with equanimity

Principal areas of anti-Soviet protest and revolt 1953-1968, crushed by Soviet military intervention (East Germany, Hungary, Czechoslovakia) and by strong political pressure (Poland)

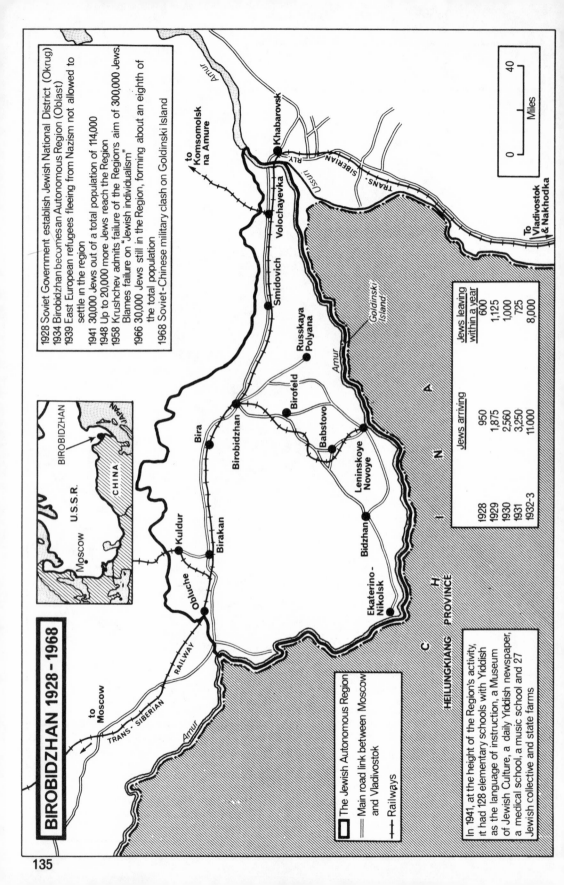

BIROBIDZHAN 1928–1968

1928 Soviet Government establish Jewish National District (Okrug)
1934 Birobidzhan becomes an Autonomous Region (Oblast)
1939 East European refugees fleeing from Nazism not allowed to
     settle in the region
1941 30,000 Jews out of a total population of 114,000
1948 Up to 20,000 more Jews reach the Region
1958 Krushchev admits failure of the Region's aim of 300,000 Jews.
     Blames failure on "Jewish individualism"
1966 30,000 Jews still in the Region, forming about an eighth of
     the total population
1968 Soviet-Chinese military clash on Goldinski Island

to Moscow

TRANS-SIBERIAN RAILWAY

Amur

Obluche

Kuldur

Birakan

Bira

Birobidzhan

Birofeld

Babstovo

Russkaya Polyana

Leninskoye Novoye

Bidzhan

Ekaterino-Nikolsk

HEILUNGKIANG PROVINCE

C H I N A

Amur

Goldinski Island

Smidovich

Volochayevka

Ussuri

TRANS-SIBERIAN RLY.

Khabarovsk

to Komsomolsk na Amure

To Vladivostok & Nakhodka

Amur

	Jews arriving	Jews leaving within a year
1928	950	600
1929	1,875	1,125
1930	2,560	1,000
1931	3,250	725
1932-3	11,000	8,000

BIROBIDZHAN

U.S.S.R.

Moscow

CHINA

JAPAN

▢	The Jewish Autonomous Region
═	Main road link between Moscow and Vladivostok
┼┼┼	Railways

In 1941, at the height of the Region's activity,
it had 128 elementary schools with Yiddish
as the language of instruction, a Museum
of Jewish Culture, a daily Yiddish newspaper,
a medical school, a music school and 27
Jewish collective and state farms

0   40
Miles

135

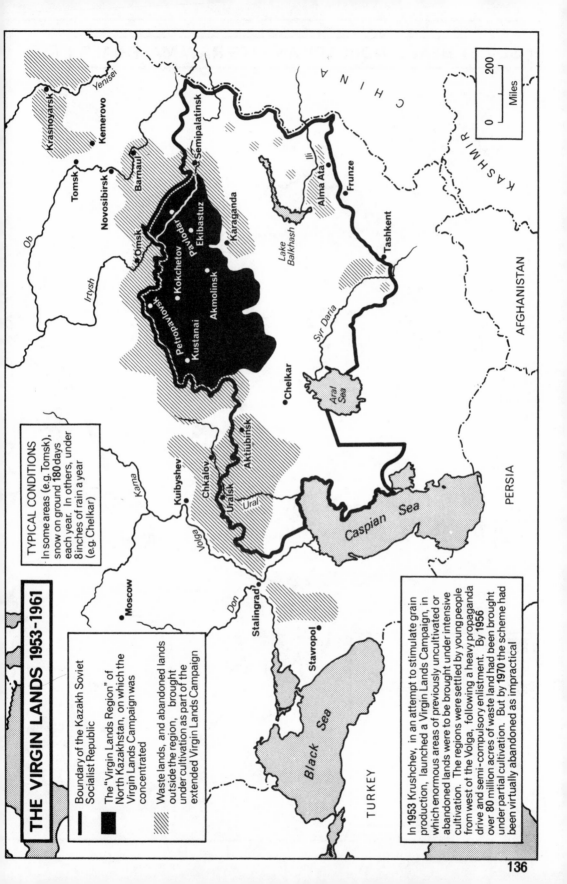

THE VIRGIN LANDS 1953–1961

Boundary of the Kazakh Soviet
Socialist Republic

The "Virgin Lands Region" of
North Kazakhstan, on which the
Virgin Lands Campaign was
concentrated

Waste lands, and abandoned lands
outside the region, brought
under cultivation as part of the
extended Virgin Lands Campaign

TYPICAL CONDITIONS
In some areas (e.g. Tomsk),
snow on ground 180 days
each year. In others, under
8 inches of rain a year
(e.g. Chelkar)

In 1953 Krushchev, in an attempt to stimulate grain
production, launched a Virgin Lands Campaign, in
which enormous areas of previously uncultivated or
abandoned lands were to be brought under intensive
cultivation. The regions were settled by young people
from west of the Volga, following a heavy propaganda
drive and semi-compulsory enlistment. By 1956
over 80 million acres of waste land had been brought
under partial cultivation. But by 1970 the scheme had
been virtually abandoned as impractical

Krasnoyarsk
Kemerovo
Tomsk
Novosibirsk
Barnaul
Semipalatinsk
Ekibastuz
Kokchetov
Pavlodar
Karaganda
Omsk
Akmolinsk
Petropavlovsk
Kustanai
Alma Ata
Frunze
Tashkent
Lake
Balkhash
Syr Daria
Chelkar
Aral
Sea
Aktiubinsk
Chkalov
Uralsk
Ural
Kuibyshev
Kama
Volga
Don
Moscow
Stalingrad
Stavropol
Caspian Sea
Black Sea
TURKEY
PERSIA
AFGHANISTAN
KASHMIR
CHINA
Yenisei
Ob
Irtysh
Ili

0   200
Miles

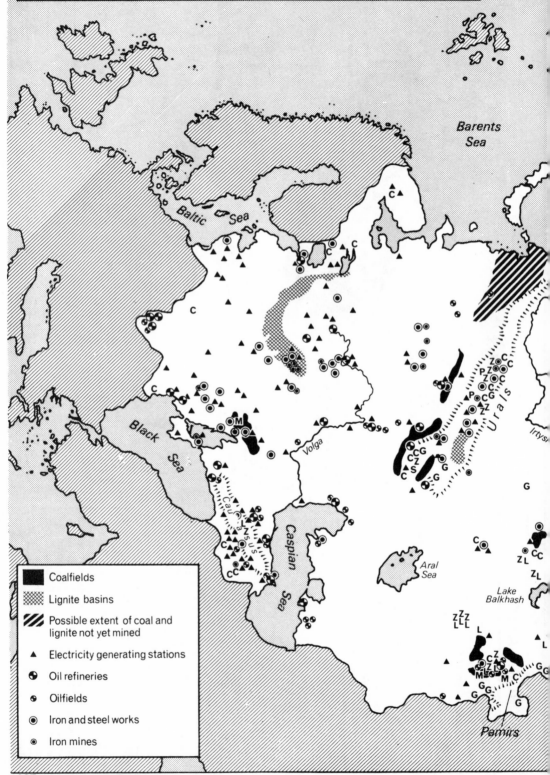

SOVIET HEAVY INDUSTRY AND ITS RAW MATERIALS

Barents Sea

Baltic Sea

Urals

Irtysh

Black Sea

Volga

Caucasus

Caspian Sea

Aral Sea

Lake Balkhash

Pamirs

Coalfields

Lignite basins

Possible extent of coal and lignite not yet mined

▲ **Electricity generating stations**

⊕ **Oil refineries**

⊛ **Oilfields**

◉ **Iron and steel works**

⊙ **Iron mines**

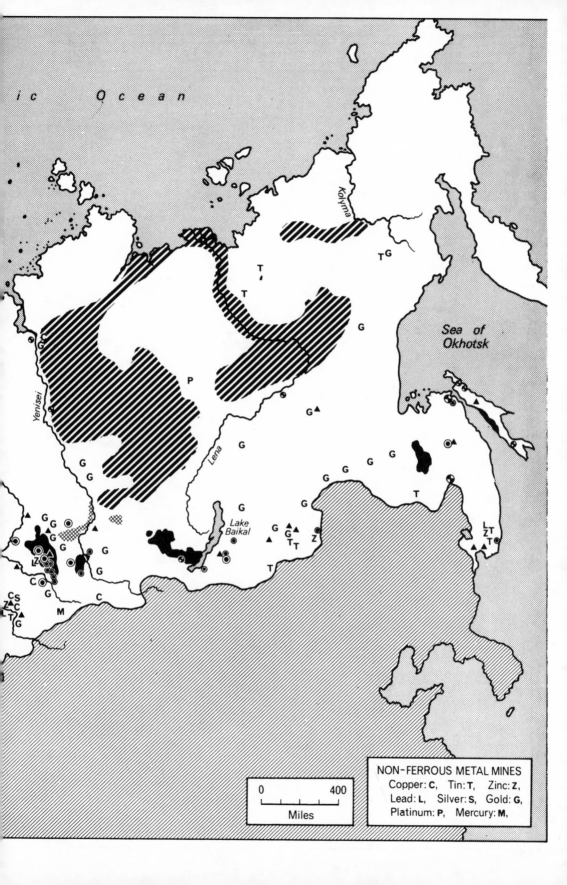

ic   O c e a n

Kolyma

Sea of
Okhotsk

Yenisei

Lena

T   G

T

T

G

G

G   G   G   G

G

G

G   G

G   G

G

G

Lake
Baikal

G   G

G   T   T   Z

T

G

G

Z

T

G

G

T

G

T

Z

L   Z   T

Z   T

G

C

M

C   S

Z   C

L   T

G

0   400

Miles

NON-FERROUS METAL MINES
Copper: **C**, Tin: **T**,   Zinc: **Z**,
Lead: **L**, Silver: **S**, Gold: **G**,
Platinum: **P**, Mercury: **M**,

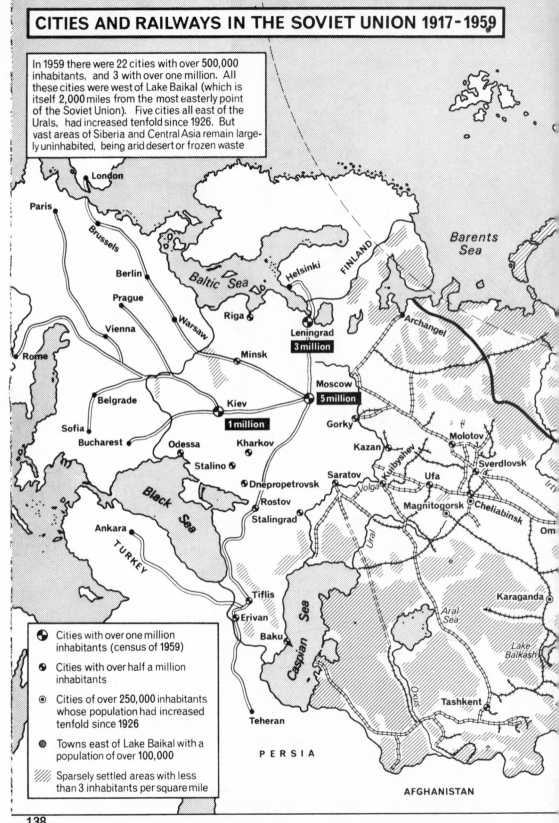

CITIES AND RAILWAYS IN THE SOVIET UNION 1917-1959

In 1959 there were 22 cities with over 500,000 inhabitants, and 3 with over one million. All these cities were west of Lake Baikal (which is itself 2,000 miles from the most easterly point of the Soviet Union). Five cities all east of the Urals, had increased tenfold since 1926. But vast areas of Siberia and Central Asia remain largely uninhabited, being arid desert or frozen waste

London

Paris

Brussels

Berlin

Prague

Vienna

Rome

Belgrade

Sofia

Bucharest

Helsinki

FINLAND

Barents Sea

Baltic Sea

Riga

Warsaw

Minsk

Kiev

1 million

Odessa

Kharkov

Stalino

Dnepropetrovsk

Rostov

Stalingrad

Ankara

TURKEY

Black Sea

Tiflis

Erivan

Baku

Caspian Sea

Teheran

PERSIA

Leningrad

3 million

Archangel

Moscow

5 million

Gorky

Kazan

Saratov

Volga

Kuibyshev

Ufa

Magnitogorsk

Molotov

Sverdlovsk

Irty

Cheliabinsk

Om

Ural

Aral Sea

Karaganda

Lake Balkash

Tashkent

Oxus

AFGHANISTAN

Cities with over one million inhabitants (census of 1959)

Cities with over half a million inhabitants

Cities of over 250,000 inhabitants whose population had increased tenfold since 1926

Towns east of Lake Baikal with a population of over 100,000

Sparsely settled areas with less than 3 inhabitants per square mile

138

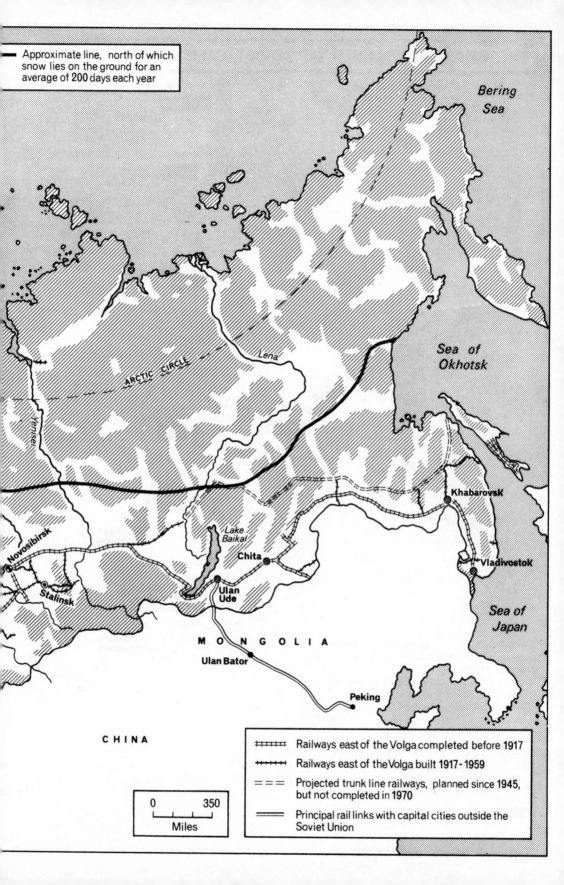

Approximate line, north of which
snow lies on the ground for an
average of 200 days each year

*Bering
Sea*

*Sea of
Okhotsk*

ARCTIC CIRCLE

Lena

Yenisei

Khabarovsk

*Lake
Baikal*

Chita

Vladivostok

Novosibirsk

Ulan
Ude

Stalinsk

*Sea of
Japan*

M O N G O L I A

Ulan Bator

Peking

CHINA

┼┼┼┼┼┼	Railways east of the Volga completed before 1917
┼━┼━┼━┼	Railways east of the Volga built 1917-1959
= = =	Projected trunk line railways, planned since 1945, but not completed in 1970
────	Principal rail links with capital cities outside the Soviet Union

0   350

Miles

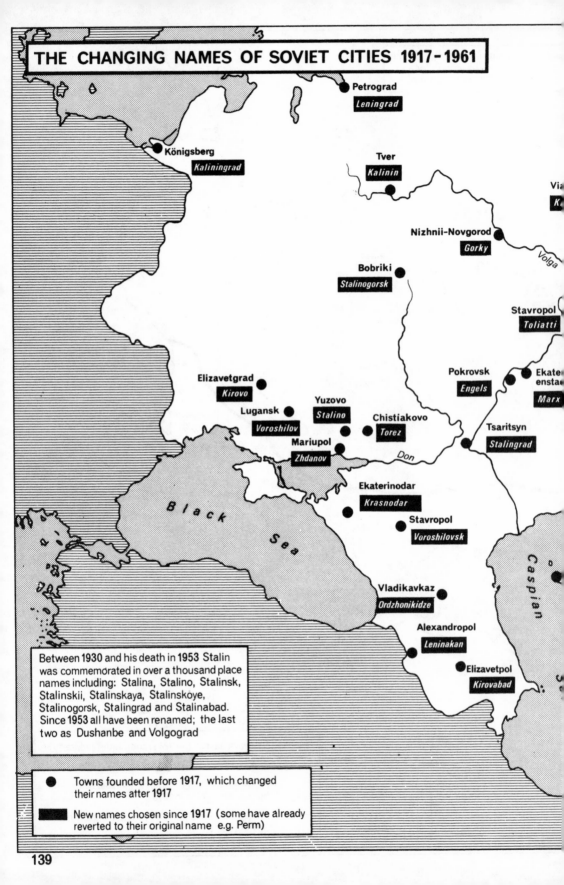

THE CHANGING NAMES OF SOVIET CITIES 1917-1961

Petrograd
Leningrad

Königsberg
Kaliningrad

Tver
Kalinin

Vi...
K...

Nizhnii-Novgorod
Gorky

Volga

Bobriki
Stalinogorsk

Stavropol
Toliatti

Elizavetgrad
Kirovo

Pokrovsk
Engels

Ekater
enstae
Marx

Lugansk
Voroshilov

Yuzovo
Stalino

Chistiakovo
Torez

Mariupol
Zhdanov

Don

Tsaritsyn
Stalingrad

Black   Sea

Ekaterinodar
Krasnodar

Stavropol
Voroshilovsk

Caspian

Vladikavkaz
Ordzhonikidze

Alexandropol
Leninakan

Elizavetpol
Kirovabad

Between 1930 and his death in 1953 Stalin
was commemorated in over a thousand place
names including: Stalina, Stalino, Stalinsk,
Stalinskii, Stalinskaya, Stalinskoye,
Stalinogorsk, Stalingrad and Stalinabad.
Since 1953 all have been renamed; the last
two as Dushanbe and Volgograd

●   Towns founded before 1917, which changed
their names after 1917

▬   New names chosen since 1917 (some have already
reverted to their original name e.g. Perm)

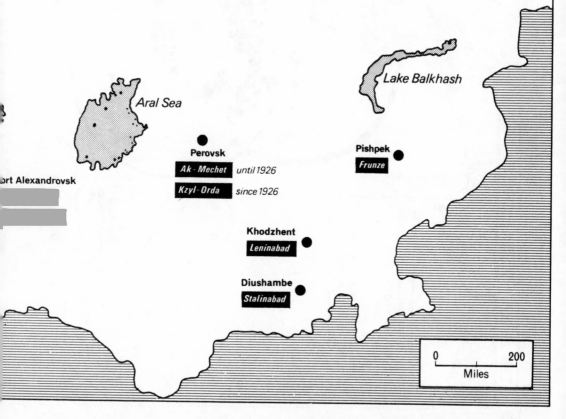

Since 1917 many Soviet cities have changed their names, choosing new names connected with the revolution and its leaders. Many hundred villages and small towns adopted such names as Oktiabrskii (after the October revolution of 1917), Komsomolsk (after the Young Communist League), Pervomaiskoie (the first of May), Krasnoarmeisk (the Red Army), Krasnogvardeisk (the Red Guard), Krasnyi Oktyabr (Red October), Krasnye Barrikady (the Red barricades) and Komintern (the Communist International)

Among the towns and villages named after Lenin are;
Lenina, Leninabad, Leninakan, Leningori, Leninka,
Lenino, Leninogorsk, Leninskii and Leninizm

Perm
Molotov

Ekaterinburg
Sverdlovsk

Kuznetsk
Stalinsk

ra
yshev

Orenburg
Chkalov

Aral Sea

Lake Balkhash

Perovsk
Ak - Mechet until 1926

Kzyl- Orda since 1926

Pishpek
Frunze

rt Alexandrovsk

Khodzhent
Leninabad

Diushambe
Stalinabad

0   200
Miles

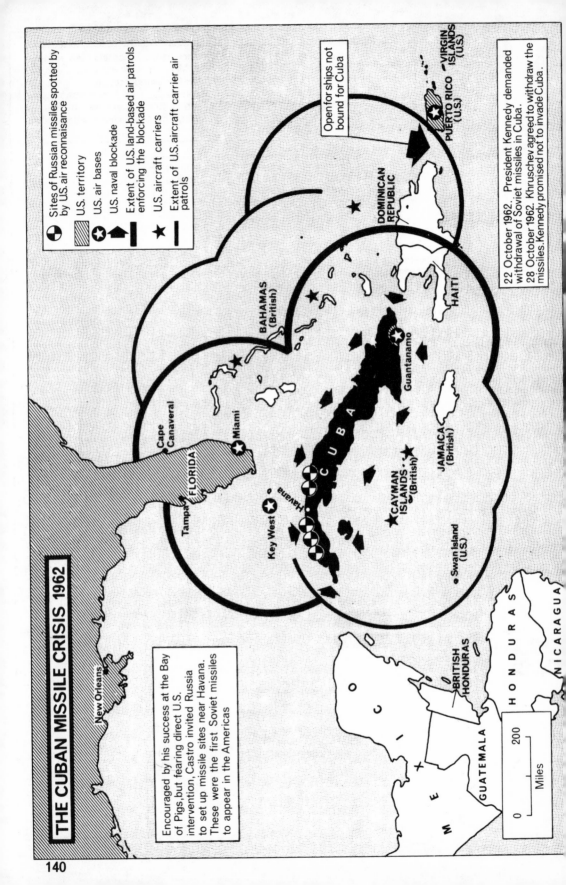

THE CUBAN MISSILE CRISIS 1962

Legend:
- ◒ Sites of Russian missiles spotted by by U.S. air reconnaisance
- ▨ U.S. territory
- ✪ U.S. air bases
- ▲ U.S. naval blockade
- ▬ Extent of U.S. land-based air patrols enforcing the blockade
- ★ U.S. aircraft carriers
- ▬ Extent of U.S. aircraft carrier air patrols

Open for ships not bound for Cuba

22 October 1962. President Kennedy demanded withdrawal of Soviet missiles in Cuba.
28 October 1962. Khruschev agreed to withdraw the missiles. Kennedy promised not to invade Cuba.

Encouraged by his success at the Bay of Pigs, but fearing direct U.S. intervention, Castro invited Russia to set up missile sites near Havana. These were the first Soviet missiles to appear in the Americas

New Orleans

FLORIDA

Tampa

Cape Canaveral

Miami

Key West

Havana

CUBA

Guantanamo

BAHAMAS (British)

DOMINICAN REPUBLIC

HAITI

PUERTO RICO (U.S.)

VIRGIN ISLANDS (U.S.)

JAMAICA (British)

CAYMAN ISLANDS (British)

Swan Island (U.S.)

BRITISH HONDURAS

GUATEMALA

HONDURAS

NICARAGUA

MEXICO

0   200
Miles

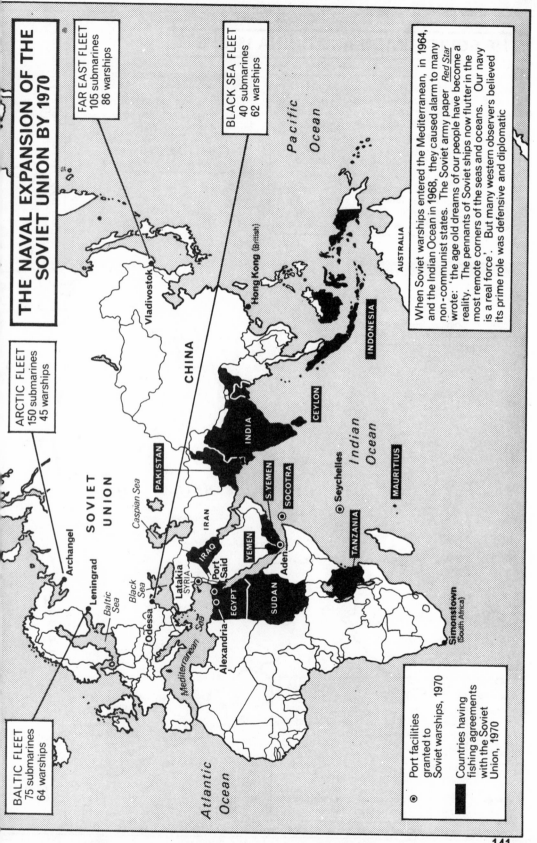

THE NAVAL EXPANSION OF THE SOVIET UNION BY 1970

ARCTIC FLEET
150 submarines
45 warships

BALTIC FLEET
75 submarines
64 warships

FAR EAST FLEET
105 submarines
86 warships

BLACK SEA FLEET
40 submarines
62 warships

Archangel

SOVIET UNION

Leningrad

Baltic Sea

Odessa

Black Sea

Caspian Sea

Vladivostok

CHINA

Mediterranean Sea

Latakia
SYRIA
Port Said
Alexandria
EGYPT

IRAQ
IRAN
YEMEN
Aden
S.YEMEN
SOCOTRA

PAKISTAN

INDIA

CEYLON

Seychelles

Indian Ocean

MAURITIUS

TANZANIA

SUDAN

Simonstown
(South Africa)

Atlantic Ocean

Hong Kong (British)

INDONESIA

Pacific Ocean

AUSTRALIA

When Soviet warships entered the Mediterranean, in 1964, and the Indian Ocean in 1968, they caused alarm to many non-communist states. The Soviet army paper *Red Star* wrote: 'the age old dreams of our people have become a reality. The pennants of Soviet ships now flutter in the most remote corners of the seas and oceans. Our navy is a real force'. But many western observers believed its prime role was defensive and diplomatic

⊙   Port facilities
  granted to
  Soviet warships, 1970

■   Countries having
  fishing agreements
  with the Soviet
  Union, 1970

THE SOVIET UNION AND CHINA 1860-1970

The Chinese Communist Party was founded in 1921.
But the Soviet Union preferred to support the
Kuomintang under Chiang Kai Shek, to which it gave
substantial military aid to establish its power 1923-
1927, and to fight the Japanese 1937-1941 (when
Stalin formed a Non-Aggression pact with Japan).
In 1945 Soviet troops drove the Japanese from
Northern China. In 1949 the Chinese Communists
came to power. From a policy of considerable
Soviet aid to China in the 1950's, the two nations
became increasingly hostile. By 1960 the rift was
open, and soon led to armed skirmishes on the frontier

TANNU TUVA

1914 Russian protectorate
1921 Independent "Peoples'
      Republic" allied with
      the Soviet Union
1944 Annexed by the Soviet
      Union

SINKIANG

1760-1920	Chinese
1921-1949	Under Soviet influence and partial occupation
Since 1949	Chinese. Heavily colonized by Chinese settlers

SOVIET UNIO

TANNU TUVA

MONG

Lake Balkhash

Alma Ata

Urumchi

Hami

Tashkent

Kashgar

SINKIANG

Lop Nor

Yarkand

AFGHANISTAN

Khotan

Kabul

Gilgit

KASHMIR

C H

Lahore

PAKISTAN

INDIA

TIBET

NEPAL

Lhasa

SIKKIM

BHUTAN

INDIA

INDIA

EAST
PAKISTAN

BUR

Irk

Territory annexed by Russia 1858-1860

Communist Party cells established under
Moscow's instructions 1920-1924 and
urged to collaborate with the
Kuomintang (nationalists)

Soviet air units defending Kuomintang
strongholds against Japan 1941

Soviet military advances across China
in the war against Japan 1945

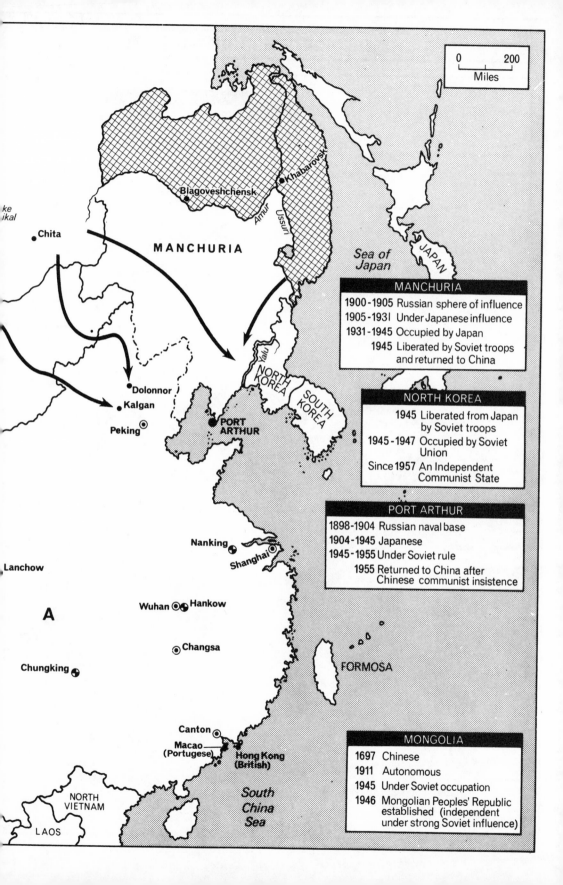

MANCHURIA

MANCHURIA	
1900-1905	Russian sphere of influence
1905-1931	Under Japanese influence
1931-1945	Occupied by Japan
1945	Liberated by Soviet troops and returned to China

NORTH KOREA	
1945	Liberated from Japan by Soviet troops
1945-1947	Occupied by Soviet Union
Since 1957	An Independent Communist State

PORT ARTHUR	
1898-1904	Russian naval base
1904-1945	Japanese
1945-1955	Under Soviet rule
1955	Returned to China after Chinese communist insistence

MONGOLIA	
1697	Chinese
1911	Autonomous
1945	Under Soviet occupation
1946	Mongolian Peoples' Republic established (independent under strong Soviet influence)

Khabarovsk

Blagoveshchensk

Chita

Sea of Japan

JAPAN

Amur

Ussuri

Lake Baikal

Dolonnor

Kalgan

Peking

Yalu

NORTH KOREA

SOUTH KOREA

PORT ARTHUR

Nanking

Shanghai

Lanchow

A

Wuhan Hankow

Changsa

Chungking

FORMOSA

Canton

Macao (Portugese)

Hong Kong (British)

South China Sea

NORTH VIETNAM

LAOS

THE SOVIET-CHINESE BORDERLANDS 1970

Legend:

— The Soviet-Chinese border

–·–·– Other international borders

+++++ Soviet, Mongolian and Chinese railways in the border area

▨ Land over 2000 metres (6562 feet)

⊕ Main airfields

Caspian Sea

Aral Sea

S O V I E

to Moscow

Omsk

TRANS - SIBERIAN RAILWAY

Novosibirsk

Achins

Krasnoyarsk

Karaganda

Barnaul

Rubtsovsk

Biisk

Semipalatinsk

Leninogorsk

Abakan

Lake Balkash

Aktogai

Urdzhar

Lake Zaisan

Lake Markakol

PERSIA

Tashkent

Lugovoi

Panfilov

L. Alakol

Zaisan

Tahcheng

Ulyungur Nor

Samarkand

Frunze

Alma Ata

Ebi Nor

Diushambe

Dzhalal Abad

R. bachiye

Issyk Kul

Kuldja

Osh

AFGHANISTAN

Kashgar

Aksu

Urumchi

M

PAKISTAN

Lop Nor

KASHMIR

C H I

INDIA

Lan

```
0        250
|_____|
   Miles
```

143

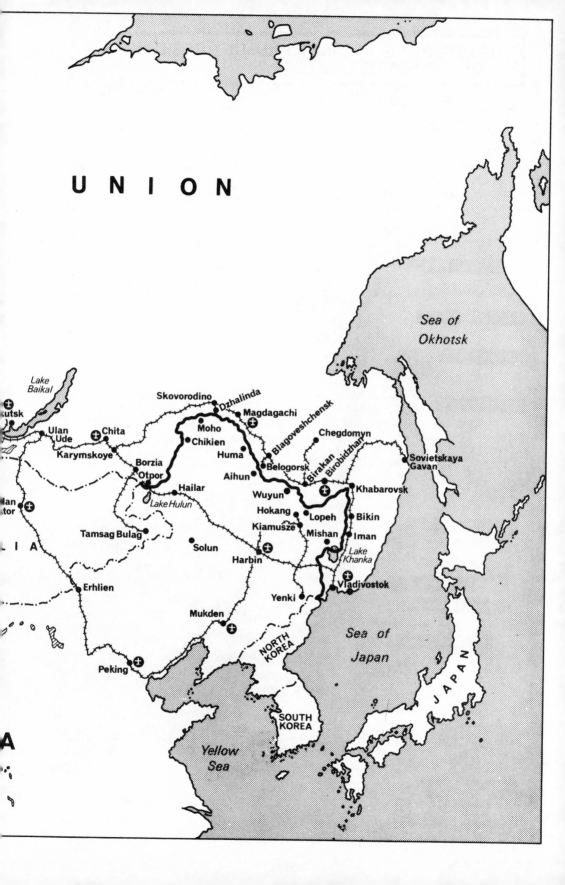

THE REPUBLICS AND AUTONOMOUS REGIONS OF THE SOVIET UNION IN 1970

North Sea

Arctic

North Cape

LATVIAN S.S.R.

ESTONIA S.S.R.

Baltic Sea

Karelian A.S.S.R.

Nenets N.O.

LITHUANIA S.S.R.

Part of the RSFSR

Komi A.S.S.R.

BELORUSSIAN S.S.R.

R U S S I A N

Khanty-Man

UKRAINIAN S.S.R.

Moscow

Komi-Permyak N.O.

MOLDAVIAN S.S.R.

Mary A.S.S.R.

Chuvash A.S.S.R.

Mordovian A.S.S.R.

Udmurt A.S.S.R.

S O V I E T

Black Sea

Tatar A.S.S.R.

Bashkir A.S.S.R.

Adyge A.O.

Abkhaz A.S.S.R.
N.Ossetian A.O.
S.Ossetian A.O.

Cherkess A.O.

Dagestan A.S.S.R.

Adzhar A.S.S.R.

Kara-Kalpak A.S.S.R.

GEORGIAN S.S.R.

ARMENIAN S.S.R.

Nakhichevan A.S.S.R.

Caspian Sea

AZERBAIDZAN S.S.R.

Nagorno-Karabakh A.O.

TURKMEN S.S.R.

KIRGI

Gorno-Badak

0 — 400
Miles

UZBEK S.S.R.

TADZHI

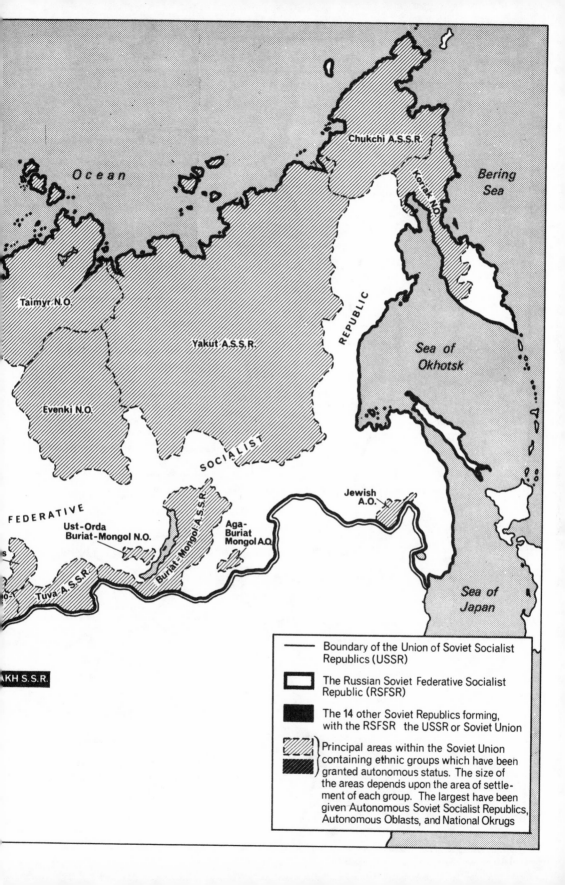

O c e a n

Taimyr N.O.

Evenki N.O.

Chukchi A.S.S.R.

Koriak N.O.

Bering Sea

Yakut A.S.S.R.

REPUBLIC

Sea of Okhotsk

S O C I A L I S T

FEDERATIVE

Jewish A.O.

Ust-Orda Buriat-Mongol N.O.

Buriat-Mongol A.S.S.R.

Aga-Buriat Mongol A.O.

Tuva A.S.S.R.

Sea of Japan

...KH S.S.R.

— Boundary of the Union of Soviet Socialist Republics (USSR)

☐ The Russian Soviet Federative Socialist Republic (RSFSR)

■ The 14 other Soviet Republics forming, with the RSFSR the USSR or Soviet Union

▨ Principal areas within the Soviet Union containing ethnic groups which have been granted autonomous status. The size of the areas depends upon the area of settlement of each group. The largest have been given Autonomous Soviet Socialist Republics, Autonomous Oblasts, and National Okrugs

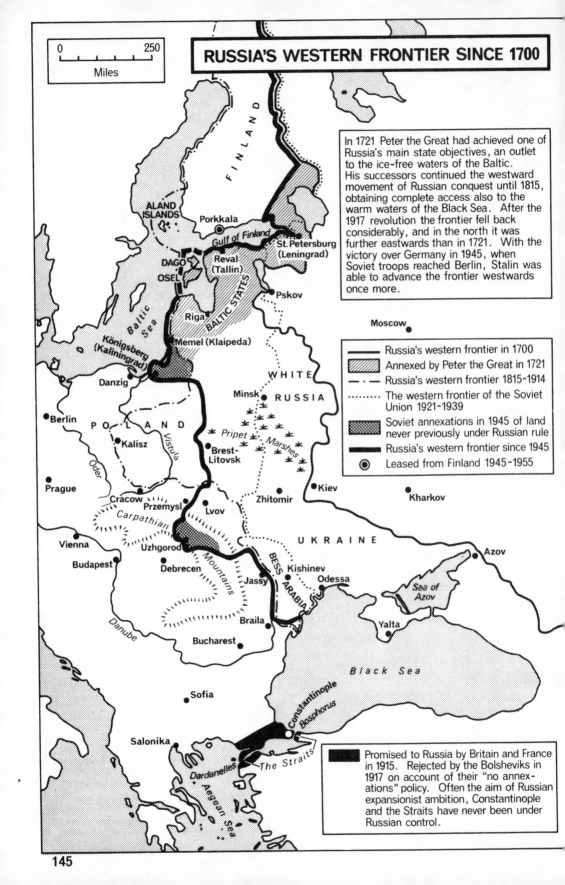

RUSSIA'S WESTERN FRONTIER SINCE 1700

0   250
Miles

In 1721 Peter the Great had achieved one of Russia's main state objectives, an outlet to the ice-free waters of the Baltic. His successors continued the westward movement of Russian conquest until 1815, obtaining complete access also to the warm waters of the Black Sea. After the 1917 revolution the frontier fell back considerably, and in the north it was further eastwards than in 1721. With the victory over Germany in 1945, when Soviet troops reached Berlin, Stalin was able to advance the frontier westwards once more.

ALAND ISLANDS

Porkkala

Gulf of Finland

St. Petersburg (Leningrad)

DAGO
OSEL

Reval (Tallin)

Pskov

Moscow

Riga

BALTIC STATES

Baltic Sea

Königsberg (Kaliningrad)

Memel (Klaipeda)

Danzig

WHITE

Minsk

RUSSIA

Berlin

P O L A N D

Vistula

Pripet

Marshes

Oder

Brest-Litovsk

Kiev

Kharkov

Prague

Cracow

Przemysl

Lvov

Zhitomir

Carpathian

Kalisz

— — Russia's western frontier in 1700

▨ Annexed by Peter the Great in 1721

—·— Russia's western frontier 1815-1914

········· The western frontier of the Soviet Union 1921-1939

▨ Soviet annexations in 1945 of land never previously under Russian rule

━━ Russia's western frontier since 1945

◉ Leased from Finland 1945-1955

Vienna

Uzhgorod

Mountains

U K R A I N E

Azov

Budapest

Debrecen

Jassy

BESS-ARABIA

Kishinev

Odessa

Sea of Azov

Braila

Yalta

Danube

Bucharest

Black Sea

Sofia

Constantinople

Bosphorus

Salonika

Dardanelles

The Straits

Aegean Sea

■ Promised to Russia by Britain and France in 1915. Rejected by the Bolsheviks in 1917 on account of their "no annexations" policy. Often the aim of Russian expansionist ambition, Constantinople and the Straits have never been under Russian control.

145

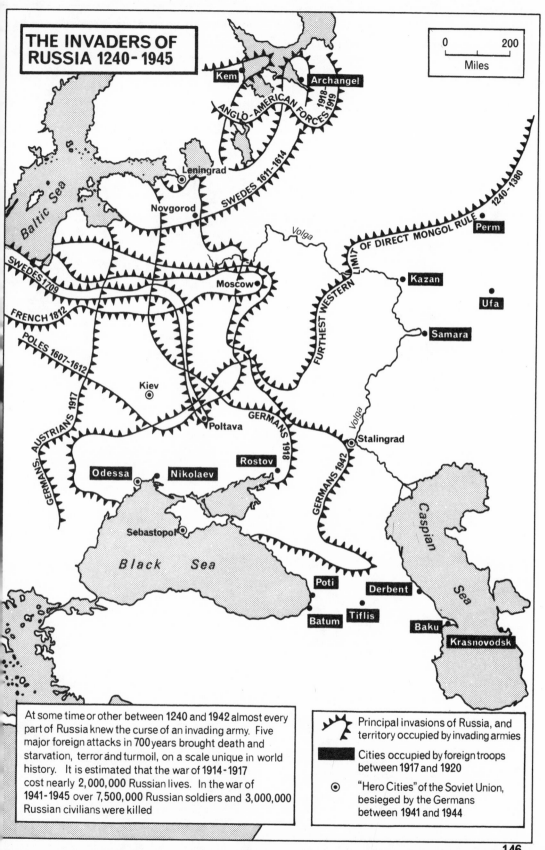

THE INVADERS OF RUSSIA 1240-1945

0   200
Miles

Kem

Archangel

ANGLO-AMERICAN FORCES 1918-1919

Leningrad

SWEDES 1611-1614

Novgorod

Volga

LIMIT OF DIRECT MONGOL RULE 1240-1380

Perm

SWEDES 1709

Moscow

FURTHEST WESTERN

Kazan

Ufa

FRENCH 1812

Samara

POLES 1607-1612

Kiev

AUSTRIANS 1917

GERMANS 1918

Poltava

Volga

Stalingrad

GERMANS,

Odessa

Nikolaev

Rostov

GERMANS 1942

Sebastopol

Caspian Sea

Black   Sea

Poti

Derbent

Batum

Tiflis

Baku

Krasnovodsk

At some time or other between 1240 and 1942 almost every part of Russia knew the curse of an invading army. Five major foreign attacks in 700 years brought death and starvation, terror and turmoil, on a scale unique in world history. It is estimated that the war of 1914-1917 cost nearly 2,000,000 Russian lives. In the war of 1941-1945 over 7,500,000 Russian soldiers and 3,000,000 Russian civilians were killed

Principal invasions of Russia, and territory occupied by invading armies

Cities occupied by foreign troops between 1917 and 1920

"Hero Cities" of the Soviet Union, besieged by the Germans between 1941 and 1944

146

Bibliography of Works Consulted

(i) ATLASES

Baratov, R. B. (and others), *Atlas Tadzhikskoi Sovetskoi Sotsialisticheskoi Respubliki* (Dushanbe and Moscow, 1968)

Bartholomew, John (ed), *The Times Atlas of the World*, 5 vols (London, 1959)

Bazilevich, K. V., Golubtsov, I. A. and Zinoviev, M. A., *Atlas Istorii SSSR*, 3 vols (Moscow, 1949–54)

Beloglazova, O. A. (ed), *Atlas SSSR* (Moscow, 1954)

Czapliński, Wladislaw and Ladogórski, Tadeusz, *Atlas Historyczny Polski* (Warsaw, 1968)

Droysens, G., *Historischer Handatlas* (Bielefeld and Leipzig, 1886)

Durov, A. G. (General editor), *Atlas Leningradskoi Oblasti* (Moscow, 1967)

Engel, Joseph, *Grosser Historischer Weltatlas* (Munich, 1962)

Grosier, L'Abbé, *Atlas Générale de la Chine* (Paris 1785)

Hudson, G. F. and Rajchman, Marthe, *An Atlas of Far Eastern Politics* (London, 1938)

Kalesnik, S. V. (and others), *Peterburg–Leningrad* (Leningrad, 1957)

Kosev, Dimiter (and others), *Atlas Po Bulgarska Istoriya* (Sofia, 1963)

Kubijovyć, Volodymyr, *Atlas of Ukraine and Adjoining Countries* (Lvov, 1937)

Kudriàshov, K. V., *Russkii Istoricheskii Atlas* (Leningrad, 1928)

Kovalevsky, Pierre, *Atlas Historique et Culturel de la Russie et du Monde Slave* (Paris, 1961)

McEvedy, Colin, *The Penguin Atlas of Medieval History* (London, 1961)

Penkala, Maria, *A Correlated History of the Far East* (The Hague and Paris, 1966)

Oxford Regional Economic Atlas: The USSR and Eastern Europe (Oxford, 1956)

Sochava, V. B. (Principal ed), *Atlas Zabaikalia* (Moscow and Irkutsk, 1967)

Taaffe, Robert N. and Kingsbury, Robert C., *An Atlas of Soviet Affairs* (London, 1965)

Terekhov, N. M. (senior editor), *Atlas Volgogradskoi Oblasti* (Moscow, 1967)

Toynbee, Arnold J. and Myers, Edward D., *Historical Atlas and Gazetteer* (London, 1959)

Voznesenski (and others), *Atlas Razvitiya Khoziastva i Kultury SSSR* (Moscow, 1967)

Westermann, Georg, *Atlas zur Weltgeschichte* (Braunschweig, 1956)

Zamyslovski, Igor E., *Uchebnii Atlas po Russkoi Istorii* (St Petersburg, 1887)

(ii) MAPS

Atanasiu, A. D., *La Bessarabie* (Paris, 1919)

Bazewicz, J. M., *Polska w Trzech Zaborach* (Warsaw, n.d.)

Bazileva, Z. P., *Rossiiskaya Imperia 1801–1861* (Moscow, 1960)

British G.H.Q., Constantinople, *Ethnographical Map of Caucasus* (Constantinople, 1920)

Fedorovskaya, G. P. (publisher), *Promyshlennost Rossii 1913; Promyshlennost Soyuza SSR 1940* (Moscow, 1962)

Filonenko, W. J., *Volkstumkarte der Krim* (Vienna, 1932)

Luchborskaya, E. P., *Rossiiskaya Imperia 1725–1801* (Moscow, 1959)

Stanford, Edward, *Sketch of the Acquisitions of Russia* (London, 1876)

Wyld, James, *Wyld's Military Staff Map of Central Asia, Turkistan and Afghanistan* (London, 1878)

(iii) ENCYCLOPAEDIAS, REFERENCE BOOKS AND GENERAL WORKS

Baedeker, Karl, *Russland* (Leipzig, 1912)
Cole, J. P., *Geography of the USSR* (London, 1967)
Florinsky, Michael T. (ed), *Encyclopaedia of Russia and the Soviet Union* (New York, 1961)
Katzenelson, Y. L. and Gintsburg, D. G. (eds), *Evreiskaya Entsiklopediya,* 16 vols (St Petersburg, 1906–13)
Kubijovyć, Volodymyr (ed), *Ukraine: A Concise Encyclopaedia* (Toronto, 1963)
Pares, Bernard, *A History of Russia* (London, 1926)
Parker, W. H., *An Historical Georgraphy of Russia* (London, 1968)
Sumner, B. H., *Survey of Russian History* (London, 1944)
Utechin, S. V., *Everyman's Concise Encyclopaedia of Russia* (London, 1961)
Zhukov, E. M. (ed), *Sovetskaya Istoricheskaya Entsiklopediya,* vols 1–12 (Moscow, 1961–69)

(iv) BOOKS ON SPECIAL TOPICS

Allen, W. E. D., *The Ukraine: A History* (Cambridge, 1940)
Allen, W. E. D. and Muratov, P., *Caucasian Battlefields: A History of the Wars on the Turco-Caucasian Border 1828–1921* (London, 1953)
Allilueva, A. S., *Iz Vospominanii* (Moscow, 1946)
Armstrong, John A. (ed), *Soviet Partisans in World War II* (Madison, 1964)
Armstrong, Terence E., *The Northern Sea Route* (Cambridge, 1952)
Avalishvili, Zourab, *The Independence of Georgia in International Politics 1918–1921* (London, 1940)
Baddeley, John F., *The Russian Conquest of the Caucasus* (London, 1908)
Baddeley, John F., *Russia, Mongolia, China,* 2 vols (London, 1919)
Caroe, Olaf, *Soviet Empire: The Turks of Central Asia and Stalinism* (London, 1953)
Chamberlin, William Henry, *The Russian Revolution 1917–1921,* 2 vols (New York, 1935)
Clark, Alan, *Barbarossa: The Russo-German Conflict 1941–1945* (London, 1965)
Conquest, Robert, *The Soviet Deportation of Nationalities* (London, 1960)
Cresson, W. P., *The Cossacks, their History and Country* (New York, 1919)
Dallin, Alexander, *German Rule in Russia 1941–1945* (London, 1957)
Dallin, David J., *The Rise of Russia in Asia* (London, 1950)
Dallin, David J. and Nicolaevsky, Boris I., *Forced Labour in Soviet Russia* (London, 1948)
Dixon, C. Aubrey and Heilbrunn, Otto, *Communist Guerilla Warfare* (London, 1954)
Dubnow, S. M., *History of the Jews in Russia and Poland* (Philadelphia, 1916–20)
Eudin, X. J. and Fisher, H. H., *Soviet Russia and the West 1920–1927: A Documentary Survey* (Stanford, 1957)
Fennell, J. L. I., *Ivan the Great of Moscow* (London, 1963)
Fennell, J. L. I., *The Emergence of Moscow 1304–1359* (London, 1968)
Fischer, Louis, *The Soviets in World Affairs,* 2 vols (London, 1930)
Fischer, Louis, *The Life of Lenin* (London, 1964)
Freund, Gerald, *Unholy Alliance: Russian-German relations from the Treaty of Brest-Litovsk to the Treaty of Berlin* (London, 1957)
Futrell, Michael, *Northern Underground: Episodes of Russian Revolutionary Transport and Communications through Scandinavia and Finland 1863–1917* (London, 1963)
Greenberg, Louis, *The Jews in Russia: The Struggle For Emancipation,* 2 vols (New Haven, 1944, 1951)

Höhne, Heinz, *The Order of the Death's Head: The Story of Hitler's S.S.* (London, 1969)

Indian Officer, An (anon), *Russia's March Towards India*, 2 vols (London, 1894)

Jackson, W. A. Douglas, *Russo-Chinese Borderlands* (Princeton, 1962)

Joll, James, *The Anarchists* (London, 1964)

Kamenetsky, Ihor, *Hitler's Occupation of Ukraine 1941–1944: A study of Totalitarian imperialism* (Milwaukee, 1956)

Kazemzadeh, F., *The Struggle for Transcaucasia* (New York, 1951)

Katkov, George, *Russia 1917: The February Revolution* (London, 1967)

Kennan, George, *Siberia and the Exile System* (New York, 1891)

Kerner, Robert J., *The Urge to the Sea: The Course of Russian History* (Berkeley and Los Angeles, 1946)

Kirchner, Walther, *Commercial Relations Between Russia and Europe 1400 to 1800* (Bloomington, Indiana, 1966)

Klyuchevskii, Vasilii Osipovich, *Peter the Great* (London, 1958)

Kochan, Lionel, *Russia in Revolution 1890–1918* (London, 1966)

Kolarz, Walter, *Russia and her Colonies* (London, 1952)

Krypton, Constantine, *The Northern Sea Route* (New York, 1953)

Lang, D. M., *A Modern History of Georgia* (London, 1962)

Leslie, R. F., *Reform and Insurrection in Russian Poland* (London, 1963)

Lias, Godfrey, *Kazak Exodus* (London, 1956)

Liubavskii, M. K., *Ocherk Istorii Litovsko-Russkovo Gosudarstva* (Moscow, 1910; Russian Reprint Series, The Hague, 1966)

Lorimer, F., *The Population of the Soviet Union: History and Prospects* (Geneva, 1946)

Lyashchenko, Peter I., *History of the National Economy of Russia to the 1917 Revolution* (New York, 1949)

Maksimov, S., *Sibir i Katorga,* 3 vols (St Petersburg, 1871)

Malozemoff, A., *Russian Far-Eastern Policy 1881–1904* (Los Angeles, 1958)

Manning, Clarence A., *Twentieth-Century Ukraine* (New York, 1951)

Mazour, Anatole G., *The First Russian Revolution, 1825: the Decembrist movement* (Stanford, 1961)

Mikhailov, V., *Pamiatnaya Knizhka Sotsialista-Revoliutsionera*, 2 vols (Paris, 1911, 1914)

Miller, Margaret, *The Economic Development of Russia 1905–1914* (London, 1926)

Mora, Sylvestre and Zwierniak, Pierre, *La Justice Sovietique* (Rome, 1945)

Nasonov, A. N., *Russkaya Zemlia* (Moscow, 1951)

Nikitin, M. N. and Vagin, P. I., *The Crimes of the German Fascists in the Leningrad Region: Materials and Documents* (London, 1947)

Nosenko, A. K. (ed), *V. I. Lenin 1870–1924* (Kiev, n.d.). A collection of photographs, with 2 maps

Obolenski, Prince Eugene, *Souvenirs D'Un Exilé en Sibérie* (Leipzig, 1862)

Owen, Launcelot A., *The Russian Peasant Movement 1906–17* (London, 1937)

Park, Alexander G., *Bolshevism in Turkestan 1917–1927* (New York, 1957)

Philippi, Alfred and Heim, Ferdinand, *Der Feldzug gegen Sowjetrussland 1941–1945* (Stuttgart, 1962)

Pierce, Richard A., *Russian Central Asia 1867–1917* (Berkeley and Los Angeles, 1960)

Pipes, Richard, *The Formation of the Soviet Union: Communism and Nationalism 1917–1923* (Cambridge, Massachusetts, 1954)

Platonov, S. F., *Ocherki Po Istorii Smuti v Moskovskom Gosudarstve* (Moscow, 1937)

Pospelov, P. N., *Istoriya Kommunisticheskoi Partii Sovetskovo Soyuza,* 6 vols (Moscow, 1964–68)

Pounds, Norman J. G., *Poland Between East and West* (Princeton, 1964)

Radkey, Oliver H., *The Agrarian Foes of Bolshevism* (New York, 1958)

Rapport du Parti Socialiste Revolutionnaire de Russie au Congres Socialiste International de Stuttgart (Ghent, 1907)

Reddaway, W. R., Penson, J. H., Halecki, O. and Dyboski, R. (eds), *Cambridge History of Poland*, 2 vols (Cambridge, 1941, 1950)

Reitlinger, Gerald, *The House Built on Sand: The Conflicts of German Policy in Russia 1939–1945* (London, 1960)

Riasanovsky, Nicholas V., *A History of Russia* (New York, 1963)

Rosen, Baron A., *Russian Conspirators in Siberia* (London, 1872)

Rostovtzeff, M., *The Iranians and Greeks in South Russia* (Oxford, 1922)

Salisbury, Harrison E., *The Siege of Leningrad* (London, 1969)

Schuyler, Eugene, *Peter the Great: Emperor of Russia,* 2 vols (London, 1844)

Schwarz, Solomon M., *The Russian Revolution of 1905* (Chicago, 1967)

Serge, Victor, *Memoirs of a Revolutionary 1901–1941* (London, 1963)

Seton-Watson, Hugh, *The Russian Empire 1801–1917* (London, 1967)

Shukman, Harold, *Lenin and the Russian Revolution* (London, 1966)

Simpson, Sir John Hope, *The Refugee Problem* (London, 1939)

Skazkin, S. D. (and others), *Istoriya Vizantii*, 3 vols (Moscow, 1967)

Slusser, Robert M. and Triska Jan F., *A Calendar of Soviet Treaties 1917–1957* (Stanford, 1959)

Squire, P. S., *The Third Department: The establishment and practices of the political police in the Russia of Nicholas I* (Cambridge, 1968)

Stephan, John J., *Sakhalin* (Oxford, 1971)

Sullivant, Robert S., *Soviet Politics and the Ukraine 1917–1957* (New York, 1962)

Sumner, B. H., *Peter the Great and the Ottoman Empire* (Oxford, 1949)

Sumner, B. H., *Peter the Great and the Emergence of Russia* (London, 1950)

Suprunenko, M. I. (and others), *Istoria Ukrainskoi RSR* (Kiev, 1958)

Tikhonov, Nikolai (and others), *The Defence of Leningrad: Eye-witness Accounts of the Siege* (London, 1944)

Treadgold, Donald W., *The Great Siberian Migration* (Princeton, 1957)

Trotsky, Leon, *My Life* (London, 1930)

Vernadsky, George, *The Mongols and Russia* (London, 1953)

Wheeler, G., *The Modern History of Soviet Central Asia* (London, 1964)

Woodward, David, *The Russians at Sea* (London, 1965)

Yarmolinski, Avram, *The Road to Revolution: A Century of Russian Radicalism* (London, 1957)

Yaroslavsky, E., *History of Anarchism in Russia* (London, 1937)

Zimin, A. A., *Reformy Ivana Groznovo* (Moscow, 1960)

(v) ARTICLES

Anon, 'How the Bear Learned to Swim', *The Economist* (London, 24–30 October 1970)

Bealby, John Thomas, Kropotkin, Prince Peter Alexeivitch, Philips, Walter Alison and Wallace, Sir Donald Mackenzie, 'Russia', *The Encyclopaedia Britannica* (Eleventh edition, London and New York, 1910)

Carsten, F. L., 'The Reichswehr and the Red Army 1920–1933', *Survey* (London, 1962)

Dziewanowski, M. K., 'Pilsudski's Federal Policy 1919–21', *Journal of Central European Affairs* (London, 1950)

Footman, David, 'Nestor Makno', *St Antony's Papers No. 6: Soviet Affairs No.* (Oxford, 1959)

Lobanov-Rostovsky, A., 'Anglo-Russian Relations through the Centuries', *Russian Review*, vol 7 (New York, 1948)

Parkes, Harry, 'Report on the Russian Caravan Trade with China', *Journal of the Royal Geographic Society*, vol 25 (London, 1854)

Stanhope, Henry, 'Soviet Strength at Sea', *The Times* (London, 25 January 1971)

Sullivan, Joseph L., 'Decembrists in Exile', *Harvard Slavic Studies,* vol 4 (The Hague, 1954)

Wildes, Harry Emerson, 'Russia's Attempts to Open Japan', *Russian Review,* vol 5 (New York, 1945)

Yakunskiy, V. K. 'La Révolution Industrielle en Russie', *Cahiers du Monde Russe et Sovietique* (The Hague, 1961)

Index

Compiled by the Author

Aaland Islands: ruled by Russia (1809–1917), 36

Abkhazia: annexed by Russia (1810), 48

Abo: annexed by Russia (1809), 47; Bolshevik propaganda enters Russia through (1903–14), 73

Aboukir (Egypt): bombarded by the Russian fleet (1798–1800), 45

Achinsk: a town of exile in Siberia, 54, 72; a Bolshevik leader in, at the time of the revolution (1917), 88

Aden: Soviet naval facilities at (1970), 141

Adrianople: battle at, and Treaty of (1829), 46, 51

Adriatic Sea: Slavs reach the shore of, 9; Russian naval activity against France in (1798–1800), 45

Afghanistan: a buffer state between Britain and Russia, 61

Ahwas (Persia): United States aid goes to the Soviet Union through (1941–5), 120

Aigun: Treaty of (1858), 60

Aix-la-Chapelle: conference of, 50

Akerman: claimed by the Ukrainians, 97

Akmolinsk: factories moved to (1940–42), 113; in Virgin Lands Region (established 1953), 136

Aktiubinsk: Ukrainians at (by 1937), 97; factories moved to (1940–42), 113; Virgin Lands campaign extended to (after , 1953), 136

Alans: settle north of Caucasus, 5; temporarily extend their settlements across the Caspian, 7; converted to Eastern Catholicism, 15; conquered by the Mongols of the Golden Horde, 21

Alaska: Russian settlement in (1784) and control of (1784–1867), 44

Albania: communist regime established in (1945), 133; China, not the Soviet Union, regarded as the source of all wisdom for (since 1961), 134

Albazin: Russian trading depot, founded (1665), 33; annexed by China (1720), 40

Aldan River: Soviet labour camp on, 111; Stalinist deportation of national groups to, 131

Aleppo: a border town of the Islamic world in 1000 AD, 15

Aleutian Islands: Russian, sold to the United States (1867), 44

Alexander I: annexes Finland (1809), 47; and the wars with France (1805–1815), 49; and the post-Napoleonic years, 50; establishes Congress Poland (1915), 52

Alexander II: assassinated, 55

Alexander Nevski: repulses Teutonic attack on Novgorod, 22

Alexander the Great, of Macedon: fails to subdue Scythians across Danube, 3

Alexandria: an important city in the Islamic world, 15; bombarded by the Russian fleet (1798–1800), 45; Soviet naval facilities at (1970), 141

Alexandropol: annexed by Russia (1828), 48; name changed to Leninakan, 139

Alexandrovsk: Bolshevik group in (1903–14), 73; attacked by anarchists (1918–20), 95; annexed to the Independent Ukraine (1918), 97

Alma Ata: Ukrainians at (by 1937), 98; Trotsky exiled to (1927), 113; industry at (1941–45), 121; a German plan for (1941), 122; Virgin Lands scheme extended to the north of (after 1953), 136; and the Soviet-Chinese border (1970), 143

Alps: part of the Roman Empire, 4, 5; reached by the Avars, 8; Slavs settle in the eastern regions of, 9

Amastris (Black Sea port): raided by the Goths, 5; under Roman Catholic control, 24

Ambarchik: a port on the Northern Sea Route, 112

Amderma: Kara Sea Expedition visits (1921), 105; and the Northern Sea Route, 112

Amisus: Greek colony on the Black Sea, 3; raided by the Goths, 5

Amur, River: northern boundary of the Mongol dominions in the Far East, 21; Russian settlements along, 33; Russian annexations in region of (1860), 60; Ukrainians settle along, 98; forms boundary of the Far Eastern Republic (1920–22), 106; Soviet labour camps on, 111; Jewish Autonomous Region established on (1934), 135

Anadyr: founded (1649), 33; on the Northern Sea Route, 112

Ananayev: anti-Jewish violence in, 69

Anapa: Cossack port on the Black Sea, 35; battle of (1791), 46; annexed by Russia (1829), 48; occupied by the Germans (1942), 128

Anarchists: exiled to Siberia, 55; their activities in European Russia, 56; their military successes in southern Russia (1917–20), 95

Ancona (Italy): bombarded by the Russian fleet (1798–1800), 45

Andizhan: annexed to Russia (1871), 61; linked to Moscow by railway (1915), 62; factories moved to (1940–42), 113

Andrusovo: Armistice of (1667), 31

Angara River: and Russian trade with China (1850–70), 59; Stalinist deportation of national groups to (1941–45), 131

Antioch (Syria): Viking settlers reach, 11; under Roman Catholic control, 24

Antonov-Ovseenko, Vladimir Alexandrovich: in Paris at the time of the revolution (1917), 88

Apollonia: Greek colony on the Black Sea, 3

Arabs: their settlement by 800 BC, 1

Aral Sea: Huns extend their rule to, 6; Mongols conquer region of, 21; Russian expansion south of (1865–95), 61; Ukrainian settlements in northern region of (by 1937), 98; Soviet Peoples' Republic of Khiva established on southern shore of (1917), 103

Archangel: founded (1584), 26; and the river systems of European Russia, 27; a shipbuilding centre (by 1800), 34; administrative centre of a Province established by Peter the Great, 38; industrial growth of (by 1860), 56; Bolshevik propaganda enters Russia through (1903–14), 73; occupied by British troops (1918–19), 91, 92, 94, 146; United States famine relief for Russia arrives at (1921), 102; Soviet labour camps established near, 109, 110; and the Northern Sea Route, 112; allied aid enters the Soviet Union through (1941–45), 121; a German plan for (1941), 122; Soviet naval strength at (1970), 141

Ardahan: siege of (1829), 46; ceded to Russia by Turkey (1878), 48, 61; ceded to Turkey by Russia (1921), 104

Argun, River: tin mines near, 106

Arkhangelskii monastery: 19

Armavir: revolutionary outbreak at (1905), 76; claimed as part of the Ukraine, 97; occupied by the Germans (1942), 124

Armenia: Viking settlers reach, 11; annexed by Russia (1828), 48; and the proposed Union of Border States (1919–20), 100; its brief independence (1918–20), 104; a Soviet Republic, 144

Armenians: their settlement by 800 BC, 1; under Islamic influence, 10; converted to Eastern Catholicism, 15; their growing discontent with Russian rule (by 1905), 68, 76

Ashkhabad: annexed by Russia (1881), 61; linked to Moscow by railway (1915), 62; occupied by British forces (1918–19), 103; allied aid enters the Soviet Union through (1941–45), 121

Assyrians: their settlement by 800 BC, 1

Astara: annexed by Russia (1813), 48; anti-Bolshevik revolt in (1920–21), 104

Astrabad: Persian town, annexed by Russia (1723–25), 37

Astrakhan: the principal town of the Mongol Khanate of Astrakhan, 25; conquered by Ivan IV (1556), 26; and the river systems of European Russia, 27; in area of peasants' revolt (1670–71), 32; revolt of Streltsy at (1705–08), 37; Bolsheviks active in (1903–14), 73; strikes in (1905), 76; Bolsheviks seize power in (1917), 91; famine in (1921), 102; Soviet labour camps near, 110; allièd aid enters the Soviet Union through (1941–45), 120, 121; a German plan for (1941), 122; Germans fail to reach (1941–43), 128

Atatürk, Kemal: his rejection of Armenian territorial claims gives him common cause with Lenin, 104

Athens: 3; raided by the Goths, 5; under Roman Catholic control, 24

Athos: raided by the Goths, 5

Attila the Hun: extends rule of the Huns to the Rhine, 6

Augustow: Germans occupy (1914), 81; Soviet Union annexes (1939), 114

Aurora (Russian cruiser): fires blanks at the Winter Palace, Petrograd (1917), 90

Auschwitz: German concentration camp at, 123

Austerlitz: Napoleon defeats the Russians at (1805), 49

Austria: Catherine the Great gives Russia a common frontier with, 41; a party to two partitions of Poland (1772, 1795), 42; Russia suppresses Hungarian revolt in (1849), 51; helps Russia suppress Polish revolt (1860), 53; signs trade agreement with Bolshevik Russia (1921), 101; helps to equip the Kara Sea Expedition (1921), 105; Russian refugees in (by 1930), 107; Soviet occupation zone in (1945–50), 133

Austria–Hungary: and European diplomacy (1872–1907), 63, 64; and Russian policy in the Balkans (1876–1914), 78, 79; Lenin allowed to leave (1914), 87

Avars: their European conquests, 8; their demise, 9; settled along the middle Danube, 10

Azef; exposed as a police spy, 72

Azerbaijan: and the proposed Union of Border States (1919–20), 100; its brief independence (1918–20), 104; a Soviet Socialist Republic, 144

Azov: principal town of the Crimean Khanate, 25; a principal town of the Don Cossacks, 35; Don Cossacks defeated at (1708), 37; battle of (1736), 46

Azov, Sea of: Greek and Scythian settlements on shores of, 3; river routes across Russia from, 27; naval battle in (1737), 46; anarchist headquarters on the shore of (1918–20), 95; German occupation forces driven from (1943–44), 129

Babylon: area of Assyrian settlement in 800 BC, 1; reached by nomads from central Asia, 2

Bagdad: part of the Islamic world, 10, 15

Bahrein: comes under British control (1867), 61

Baibert: battle of (1829), 46

Baikal, Lake: largely within the Mongol dominions, 21; early Russian settlements on, 33; Chinese territory extended towards (1720–60), 40; and the Siberian exile system (1648–1917), 54; and Russian trade with China (1850–70), 59; and the Trans-Siberian railway, 62; forms the western boundary of the Far Eastern Republic (1920–22), 106; Soviet labour camp near, 111; industry in the region of (1970), 137

Bakhchisaray: unsuccessful Russian attack on (1556–59), 26; battle of (1736), 46

Baku: Viking settlers reach, 11; temporarily annexed by Russia from Persia (1723–25), 37; large German community in (by 1914), 39; annexed by Russia (1806), 48; anarchists active in (1905–06), 55; industrial growth of (by 1860), 56; strikes in (before 1905), 68; industry in (by 1900), 71; political assassinations in, 72; secret Bolshevik printing press in, 73; revolutionary outbreak at (1905), 76; occupied by the Turks (1917–18), 85, 91; occupied by the British (1918–19), 92, 103, 104, 146; Soviet labour camps near, 110; United States aid reaches (1941–45), 120; a German plan for (1941), 122; its oilfields a major German military objective (1942), 124, 128; over half a million inhabitants (1959), 138

Bakunin, Mikhail Alexandrovich: exiled to Siberia, 54; his view of anarchism, 55

Balkans: raided by the Slavs, 8; Slav settlements in, 9; Turkish rule of, 49; Bismarck demarcates Austro-Russian line of influence in, 63

Balkhash, Lake: on the eastern boundary of the lands of the Golden Horde, 21; and Russian trade with China (1850–70),

59; Ukrainian settlements in the region of (by 1937), 98; anti-Bolshevik revolt in region of (1917–20), 103; Stalinist deportation of national groups to (1941–45), 131; industry to the north of (1970), 137

Balta: annexed by Russia (1793), 43; anti-Jewish violence in, 69

Baltic Sea: Goths settle along, 4; Goths extend their control to the Black Sea from, 5; reached by the Huns, 6; reached by the Slavs, 7; reached by the Avars, 8; Slav control established along part of southern shore of, 9; Kievan Russian trade across, 14; extension of German control along southern shore of, 20; Lithuanians rule from shore of, to Black Sea, 23; its shores entirely controlled by Roman Catholic rulers, 24; Tsar Fedor re-establishes Russian control on, 26; river routes across Russia from, 27; Russian trade on, 34; Russian westward expansion along (1721–1945), 35, 47; Jews expelled from the coastline of (1828, 1830), 51

Baltimore (USA): Ukrainians at, 99

Balts: their area of settlement by 800 BC, 1; by 200 AD, 4; increasingly discontented with Russian rule (by 1905), 68, 76; four million in Russia (1897), 74

Bandar Shah (Persia): United States aid enters Soviet Union through (1941–45), 120

Bar: Jews murdered in (1648–52), 31

Baranovichi: annexed by Russia (1795), 43

Barguzin: founded (1648), 33; and the Siberian exiles, 54; in the Far Eastern Republic (1920–22), 106

Barnaul: Ukrainians at (by 1937), 98; industry at (1941–45), 121; a German plan for (1941), 122; Virgin Lands campaign extended to (after 1953), 136 ·

Bashkirs: revolt against Russian rule (1708–11), 37; famine in homeland of (1921), 102; anti-Bolshevik uprising in (1917–20), 103; form an Autonomous Soviet Socialist Republic, 144

Basidu: British island near possible Russian railhead on Indian Ocean, 61

Batum: ceded to Russia by Turkey (1878), 48; anarchists active in (1905–06), 55; strikes in (before 1905), 68; Bolsheviks active in (1903–14), 73; revolution in (1905), 76; Turks advance on (1917), 85; Turks occupy (1918), 91; British occupy (1918–19), 92, 104, 146; Soviet aid to Republican Spain leaves from (1936–39), 101; a German plan to control (1941), 122

Baturin: revolt against Peter the Great in (1708), 37

Bavaria: German communists fail to seize power in, 108

Bayazit: occupied by Russia (1829), 46

Begovat: industry at (1941–45), 121

Belgium: Russian refugees from Bolshevism in (by 1930), 107

Belgorod: within area of peasants' revolt (1606–07), 29; trade fair at, 34; revolutionary outbreak at (1905), 76

Belgrade: Treaty of (1739), 46; and the defeat of Germany (1944–45), 130

Belogorsk: and the Soviet-Chinese border (1970), 143

Belomor Canal: largely built by forced labour, 109

Belozersk: within Kievan Russia, 13; Orthodox monastery established at, 16; Ivan IV seizes land in region of, 28

Belzec (Belzhets): German concentration camp at, 123

Bender: proposed Russian railway to Persian Gulf at, 61

Bendery: siege of (1770), 46

Berdiansk: attacked by anarchists (1918–20), 95; occupied by the Germans (1941–43), 128; Germans driven from (1943), 129

Berdichev: Jewish political activity in, 70

Berezov: founded (1593), 33

Bering Sea: Soviet labour camps on the shore of, 111

Berlin: colonized by the Germans, 20; Protocols of Zion published in (1911), 69; Russian students in, 70; Lenin in exile in (1907, 1912), 73; Treaty of (1878), 78; Lenin returns to Russia through (1917), 87; German communists try to seize power, but suppressed in, 108; entered by Soviet troops (1945), 113, 130; divided in Soviet, British, French and United States sectors (1945), 133

Berne (Switzerland): Lenin in exile in (1913–17), 73, 87

Bessarabia: annexed by Russia from Turkey (1812), 46, 50; peasant uprising in province of (1905), 75; Rumanian (from 1918), annexed by the Soviet Union (1940), 116; a German plan to control (1941), 122; Rumanian military government established in (1941), 123; reincorporated in the Soviet Union (1945), 133; a Soviet Republic, the Moldavian SSR (since 1945), 144

Bialystok (Belostok): Polish town, annexed by Prussia (1795), 43; becomes Russian (in 1815) and a centre of Polish revolt (1860), 53; anarchists active in (1905–06), 55; anti-Jewish violence in, 69, 75; political assassinations in, 72; and German war aims (1914), 80; Germans occupy (1915), 82; Red Army advances through, towards Warsaw (1920), 96; Soviet Union annexes (1939), 114; a part of Greater Germany, scene of a Jewish uprising, 123

Bikin: and the Soviet-Chinese border (1970), 143

Birobidzhan: capital of the Jewish Autonomous Region (since 1934), 135; and the Soviet-Chinese border (1970), 143

Bismarck: and European diplomacy (after 1872), 63, 64

Bitlis: Russian troops occupy (1915–16), 85; Armenian claims to (1918), 104

Black Sea: nomads from central Asia reach the shores of, 2; Greeks and Scythians settle by, 3; Roman rule on shores of, 4; the Huns extend their rule to, 6; Slavs extend their control to, 7; Avars control part of the northern shore of, 8; Slavs re-establish their control of part of the northern shore of, 9; Khazars control northern shore of, 10; Kievan Russian rule extended to the shores of (by 1054), 13; Kievan Russian trade across, 14; and the spread of Eastern Catholicism, 15; Russia fails to establish control on, 26; river routes across Russia from, 27; Cossacks settle on eastern shore of, 35; Peter the Great fails to establish Russian control of, 37; Catherine the Great establishes Russian territory on, 41; and the wars between Russia and Turkey (1721–1829), 46; Russian territorial expansion along the eastern shore of (1803–78), 48; Jews expelled from coastline of (1827, 1830), 51; controlled by anti-Bolshevik forces (1918–19), 92; Soviet naval strength in (1970, 141

Blagoveshchensk: Ukrainians at (by 1937), 98; in the Bolshevik-controlled Far Eastern Republic (1920–22), 106; on the Soviet border with China, 142, 143

Bobriki: changes name to Stalinogorsk, 139

Bobrov: conversions to Judaism in, 50

Bobruisk: annexed by Russia (1793), 43; special Gendarme detachment at, 51

Bodh Gaya: reached by nomads from central Asia, 2

Boguslav: annexed by Russia (1793), 43

Bohemia: a Roman Catholic State, 24

Bokhara: and Russian trade with China (1850–70), 59; annexed by Russia (1876), 61

Bolotnikov, Ivan Isayevich: leads peasants' revolt (1606–07), 29; Cossacks flee eastwards across the Urals after failure of revolt of, 33

Bolsheviks: abolish all special Cossack institutions (1920), 35; opposed by the Jewish Social Democratic Party (1917), 70; suppress the Socialist Revolutionary Party (1922), 72; and Lenin, 73; anti-war propaganda of (1915–17), 84; appeal in vain for an end to the war (March 1917), 86; urged by Lenin not to co-operate with Kerensky, 87; their leaders scattered in exile at the time of the revolution (1917), 88; defend Petrograd against General Kornilov (Aug 1917), 89; seize power in Petrograd (Oct 1917), 90; recognize independence of Estonia (1919), 93; advance on Warsaw (1920), 96; seek to control the Ukraine (1917–21), 97; forestall the proposed Union of Border States (1919–20), 100; extend their control to Central Asia (1917–36), 103; extend their rule in the Caucasus (1920–21), 104; send two sea expeditions to the Kara Sea (1920, 1921), 105; establish their control east of Lake Baikal (1920–22), 106; imprison over 80,000 Russians (1917–19), 107; imprison a further 750,000 Russians (1919–30), 109

Borisov: Jews murdered in (1648–52), 31; annexed by Russia (1793), 43; Napoleon retreats through (1812), 49

Borodino: Napoleon defeats the Russians at (1812), 49

Bosnia: and Russian policy in the Balkans (1876–1914), 78, 79

Braila: unsuccessful Russian attack on Turks at (1711), 37; siege of (1806), 46; Russian attack on (1828–29), 51

Brandon (Canada): Ukrainians at, 99

Bratsk: founded (1631), 33

Brazil: Ukrainians in (by 1937), 99; Russian refugees in (by 1930), 107

Bremen: unsuccessful seizure of power by German communists in, 108

Breslau (Wroclaw): annexed by Poland (1945), 133; anti-Soviet revolt in (1956), 134

Brest-Litovsk: conquered by the Lithuanians, 23; Jews murdered in (1648–52), 31; annexed by Russia (1795), 42, 43; special Gendarme detachment at, 51; anti-Jewish violence in, 69, 75; and German war aims (1914), 80; Austro-German army occupies (1915), 82; Treaty of (1917), 91, 97; annexed to the independent Ukraine (1918), 97; annexed by the Soviet Union (1939), 114

Briansk: conquered by the Lithuanians, 23; a part of Russia, a refuge for dispossessed landowners, 28; within area of peasants' revolt (1606–07), 29; trade fair at, 34; occupied by the Germans (1942), 119, 124; Germans driven from (1943–44), 129

Britain: Germanic tribes settle in, 7; Viking settlers reach, 11; and Russia's changing position during the Napoleonic wars, 49; Russian Jews emigrate to, 70; Russian trade with, 71; and Russia's Balkan policy (1876–1914), 78, 79; promises Constantinople to Russia (1915), 85; Lenin plans to return to Russia through (1917), 87; Russian war debts to (by 1917), 89; intervenes against the Bolsheviks (1918–19), 92, 93, 94; does not support Poles against Bolsheviks (1920), 100; signs trade agreement with Bolsheviks (1921), 101; helps to equip the Kara Sea Expedition (1921), 105; sends troops to Vladivostok (1918), 106; Russian refugees from Bolshevism in (by 1930), 107; Communist Party of, seeks freedom of action from Bolsheviks (1920), 108; Trotsky refused permission to settle in, 113

British Society of Friends: sends famine relief to Russia (1921), 102

Brody: Jewish refugees from Russia reach western Europe through (1890–1914), 70; Russian troops occupy, and mutiny at (1917), 89; occupied by Germany (1941), 123

Brusilov, Alexei Alexeyevich: advances against the Central Powers (1916), 83

Brussels: visited by Lenin, 73; communist propaganda disseminated in, 108

Bucharest: Treaty of (1812), 46; and the Russian war against Turkey (1806–12), 49; Russian attack on (1828–29), 51; Germans occupy (1916), 83; communism established in, 113

Budapest: Russians suppress national revolution in (1849), 51; communism established in, 113; and the defeat of Germany (1944–45), 130; anti-Soviet revolt in (1956), 134

Budini: possible Slav tribe named by Herodotus, 3

Bug, River (northern): a highway of trade for Kievan Russia, 14

Bug, River (southern): Scythian, Slav and Greek settlements on (by 300 BC), 3; a highway of trade in Kievan Russia, 14; incorporated into Russia by Catherine the Great (1791, 1793), 43

Bugarikhta: a town in the Tungus coal basin, 112

Bukhara: Soviet Peoples' Republic established in (1917), 103; industry at (1941–45), 121

Bukharin, Nikolai Ivanovich: in New York at the time of the revolution (1917), 88

Bukovina: annexed by the Soviet Union from Rumania (1940), 116

Bulavin, Kondraty Afanasevich: leads revolt of Don Cossacks (1707–08), 37

Bulgar: principal town of the Volga Bulgars, pays tribute to Kievan Russia, 13; a trading centre, 14

Bulgaria: Mongols raid, 22; and European diplomacy (1890–1907), 64; ritual murder charge against Jews in, 69; and Russian policy in the Balkans (1876–1914), 78, 79; Russian refugees in (by 1930), 107; strongly anti-communist (by 1926), 108; Soviet army advances through (1944–45), 130; deportation of citizens of, to Siberia (1945–46), 132; communist regime established in (1945), 133; appears to accept Soviet guidance with equanimity (since 1945), 134

Bulgars: settle along lower reaches of the Don, 9; driven by the Khazars westwards to the Danube, 10; settle in the Balkans, 12; converted to Eastern Catholicism, 15; under Turkish rule, 49

Bulun: a town in the Lena coal basin, 112

Burgas: acquired by Bulgaria from Turkey (1885), 78

Bushire (Persia): proposed Russian railway to Persian Gulf at, 61; allied aid to the Soviet Union goes through (1941–45), 120

Buturlinovka: claimed as part of the Ukraine, 97

Byzantium: area of Greek settlement in 800 BC, 1; reached by nomads from Asia, 2; under Persian and then Athenian control, 3; under Roman rule, 4, 6; capital city of the Eastern Roman Empire, 8, 9, 10; *see henceforth index entry for* Constantinople

Byzantine Empire *or* Byzantium: trades with the Khazar Kingdom, 10; Viking settlers reach, 11; part of, pays tribute to Kievan Russia, but subsequently reconquered, 13

Calchedon: Greek colony on the Sea of Marmara, 3

Calgary (Canada): Ukrainians at, 99

Callatis: Greek colony on the Black Sea, 3

Canada: sends troops to intervene against the Bolsheviks (1918–19), 94, 106; Ukrainian settlements in (by 1937), 99

Canton (China): Russian trade with (1850–70), 59; Moscow establishes Communist Party cell in (1920–24), 142

Carcine: Greek colony on the Black Sea, 3

Carlsbad: conference of, 50

Carpathian Mountains: reached by nomads from central Asia, 2; Scythian and Slav settlements in foothills of, 3; Roman control extended to, 4; Goths control eastern and southern foothills of, 5; controlled by the Huns, 6; Slavs extend their settlements to the southern and western slopes of, 7; Avar rule extended to, 8; Slavs settle in northern regions of, 9; crossed by the Mongols, 22; Russian army reaches eastern foothills of (1914), 81; Soviet Union annexes area in western foothills of (1945), 145

Caspian Sea: reached by nomads from central Asia, 2; Scythian settlements on, 3; Roman rule extended to, 4; the Huns extend their rule to, 6; largely controlled by the Khazars, 10; area paying tribute to Kievan Russia extends to, 13; Kievan Russian trade across, 14; Mongols rule northern shores of, 21; Russian rule reaches northern shores of, 26; Cossacks settle along shore of, 35; Russian expansion along the western shore of (1805–19), 48; Russian expansion east of (1865–95), 61; controlled by anti-Bolshevik forces (1918–19), 92; Ukrainian settlements by, 98; United States aid enters the Soviet Union through (1941–45), 120; Germans fail to reach (1941–43), 128

Castro, Fidel: invites Soviet Union to set up missiles in Cuba (1962), 140

Catherine the Great: divides Peter the Great's Provinces into smaller units, 38; invites German agricultural colonists to settle in Russia (1762), 39; Russian territorial expansion under (1762–96), 41, 42, 43

Cattaro (Kotor): occupied by Russian forces (1800–07), 45

Caucasus Mountains: Georgian settlements south of (by 800 BC), 1; reached by nomads from central Asia, 2; Scythian settlements on northern slopes of, 3; Roman control extended to, 4, 5; the Huns extend their control to the northern slopes of, 6; Khazars extend their rule to, 10; Mongols control northern slopes of, 22; Russian rule extended to the northern slopes of, 26; Russian control of completed (by 1878), 48; their brief period of independence from Russia (1918–20), 104; Germans fail to capture oilfields of (1942), 124, 128; industry in (1970), 137

Ceylon: Soviet fishing agreement with (1970), 141

Chalus (Persia): United States aid to Soviet Union passes through (1941–45), 120

Changsa (China): Moscow establishes communist group in (1920–24), 142

Chechen-Ingush: deported by Stalin to Siberia, 128, 131

Cheliabinsk: Ukrainians at (by 1937), 98; occupied by anti-Bolshevik forces (1918–19), 103; factories moved to (1940–42), 113; a German plan for (1941), 122; over half a million inhabitants (1959), 138

Chelmno: German concentration camp at, 123

Cherdin: uprising in (1648–50), 32

Cheremkhovo: coal mines at, 61; factories moved to (1940–42), 113

Cherkassk: a town in the Don Cossack administrative region, 35; Don Cossack revolt in region of (1707–08), 37

Chernigov: a town in Kievan Russia, 13; Orthodox monastery established at, 16; and the Russian principality of, 17; conquered by the Mongols, 22; conquered by the Lithuanians, 23; conquered by the Principality of Moscow, 25; within area of peasants' revolt (1606–07), 29; annexed by Poland (1618), 30; regained by Russia (1667), 31; trade fair at, 34; peasant discontent and serfdom in the Province of (by 1860), 58; Jewish political activity in, 70; peasant uprising in Province of (1905), 75; much fought over (1917–21), 97; occupied by the Germans (1942), 123; Germans driven from (1943–44), 129

Chiang Kai Shek: early Soviet aid to (1923–41), 142

Chernovtsy: annexed to the Independent Ukraine (1918), 97; German army driven from, by Soviet troops (1944), 129; reincorporated in the Soviet Union (1944), 133

Chernyshevski, Nikolai Gavrilovich: exiled to Siberia, 54

Chersonese: Greek colony on the Sea of Marmara, 3

Chicago (USA): Ukrainians at, 99

Chicherin, Boris Nikolaevich: in London at the time of the revolution (1917), 88

Chimkent: factories moved to (1940–42), 113

China: in 800 BC, 2; the northward and westward expansion of (1720–60), 40; Russian trade with (1850–60), 59; and Russian expansion in the Far East (1858–60), 60; and the European powers (1898–1904), 65; Kazakhs flee from Russia to (1916–32), 103; Russian refugees from Bolshevism (by 1930), 107; Albanians aligned with (since 1961), 134; Jewish Autonomous Region borders on (since 1934), 135; its relations with Russia (1860–1970), 142; its border with Russia (in 1970), 143

Chinese: 300,000 in the Bolshevik-controlled Far Eastern Republic (1920–22), 106

Chita: Trans-Siberian railway reaches (by 1899), 62; political assassinations at (1904–07), 72; Far Eastern Republic proclaimed at (1920), 106; Soviet labour camps near, 111; and the Soviet-Chinese border (1970), 143

Chitral: annexed by Britain (1895), 61

Chkalov: *for earlier index entries see* Orenburg: Virgin Lands campaign extended to (after 1953), 136

Chistiakovo: names changed to Torez, after the French communist leader, 139

Christianity: Goths converted to, 5; Kievan Russia adopts, 13; the spread of, leading to the division of the Slav world, 15

Chudovo: Germans occupy (1941), 126; Soviet partisans active near (1941–42), 127

Chungking (China): Russian trade with (1850–70), 59; Soviet air units defend against Japanese attack (1941), 142

Chuvash: a non Slav tribe, revolting against Russian rule, 29; form an Autonomous Soviet Socialist Republic, 144

Cleveland (USA): Ukrainians at, 99

Comintern: its propaganda largely ineffective (1919–27), 108; a village named after (Komintern), 139

Congress Poland: established by Alexander I (1815), 52; revolts against Russia (in 1831), 52, and (1860), 53

Constantinople: *for earlier index entries see* Byzantium; Viking settlers reach, 11; Varangarians lead an expedition against (in 860 AD), 12; a trading centre for Kievan Russian goods, 14; the centre of Eastern Catholicism in 1000 AD, 15; under Roman Catholic control in 1261, 24; Russian Jews flee to, 70; promised to Russia by Britain and France (1915), 85, 145; Russian refugees from Bolshevism in (by 1930), 107

Copenhagen: attacked by Russia (1710–21), 37; Lenin in exile in (1910), 73

Corfu: occupied by Russia (1800–07), 45

Corinth: raided by the Goths, 5

Corlu (Turkey): occupied by Russia (1829), 46, 51

Corrective Labour Camps: in European Russia (1917–57), 109, 110; east of the Urals (1918–58), 111

Cossacks: attack Moscow, 29; advance through southern Poland (1648–1652), 31; their movements and settlement (1500–1916), 35; compulsory settlement of, in the Far East, 60; active in anti-Bolshevik intervention (1918–19), 92; *see also index entry for* Don Cossacks

Cracow: a town in Poland, 17; annexed by Austria (1795), 42; an independent Republic, attacked by Russia (1846), 51; Polish rebels flee to (1831), 52; Lenin in exile in (1912), 73; Lenin arrested in (1914), 87; Polish (from 1918), the Germans occupy (1939), 114, 123; the Germans driven from (1944–45), 130; anti-Soviet revolt in (1956), 134

Craiova: occupied by Russia (1807), 46, and again (1828–29), 51

Crimea: Greek and Scythian settlements in, 3; Romans extend their control to, 4; reached by the Huns, 6; unsuccessful Russian attack on, 26; Peter the Great unable to drive Turks from, 37; annexed by Catherine the Great, 41; Anglo-French and Turkish attacks on (1854–55), 51, 61; anarchists' victory in (1920), 95; and the proposed Union of Border States (1919–20), 100; occupied by the Germans (1942), 119; a German plan to control (1941), 122; Germans driven from (1943–44), 129

Crimean Khanate: established by the Mongols on the shores of the Black Sea and Sea of Azov, 23; Russians fail to conquer (1711), 37

Crimean Tatars: deported by Stalin to Siberia, 128, 131

Croatia: a Roman Catholic State, 24

Croats: a western Slav tribe, 12; converted to Roman Catholicism, 15

Cuba: crisis over Soviet missiles in (1962), 140

Czechoslovakia: signs military assistance Treaty with Soviet Union (1935), 101; Russian refugees in (by 1930), 107; Sudeten Germans flee from (1945–46), 132; under communist control (1948), 133; anti-Soviet revolt in (1968), 134

Czechs: a western Slav tribe, 12

Czenstochowa: a centre of Polish revolt against Russia (1860), 53; anti-Jewish violence in, 69; Germans occupy (1914), 81

Czernowitz: occupied by Russia, the scene of mutinies in the Russian army (1917), 89

Daghestan: annexed by Russia (1819, 1859), 48

Dago: Baltic island, ruled by the Teutonic Knights, 20; taken by Russia from Sweden (1721), 36, 47; and German war aims (194), 80

Danes: their early settlements, 5

Danube, River: crossed by nomads from Asia, 2; crossed by Scythians, 3; controlled by the Romans, 4; Goths drive the Romans from northern bank of, 5; reached by the Huns, 6; reached by the Slavs, 7; largely controlled by the Avars, 8; crossed by the Slavs who extend their settlement to the Adriatic and the Balkans, 9; Bulgars settle along lower reaches of, 10; Slav settlements along, 12; the southern boundary of Kievan Russia reaches (by 1050), 14; reached by the Mongols (in 1300), 21; and Russian policy in the Balkans (1876–85), 78

Danzig (Gdansk): a Hansa town on the Baltic, 20; under Catholic control, 24; under Communist control (since 1945), 36; annexed by Prussia from Poland (1793), 42; Russian refugees in (by 1930), 107; a part of Greater Germany (1939–45), 123; anti-Soviet revolt in (1956), 134

Decembrist uprising (1825): 50

Decius: Roman Emperor, defeated by Goths, 5

Dedovichi: German reprisals against Russian civilians in (1941–43), 126

Denikin, Anton Ivanovich: defeated by a joint Bolshevik-Anarchist army (1919), 95; advances northwards from the Ukraine (1919), 97; his base in the Kuban (1919), 100; his activities in the Caucasus (1919), 104

Denmark: Russia allies with, against Sweden (1700), 47; Russian refugees from Bolshevism in (by 1930), 107

Derbent: a town paying tribute to Kievan Russia, 13; temporarily annexed by Russia from Persia (1723–25), 37; annexed by Russia (1806), 48; part of the Terek Peoples' SSR (1918–19), 104; occupied by British interventionist forces (1919), 146

Derevlians: a Slav tribe south of the Pripet marshes, 12

Detroit (USA): Ukrainians at, 99

Deulino: Russian territorial losses at armistice of (1618), 30

Dibrivki: anarchists defeat Austrians at (1918), 95

Dikson: Kara Sea Expedition visits (1921), 105; on the Northern Sea Route, 112

Diushambe: Soviet Peoples' Republic established in region of (1917), 103; name changed, first (1929) to Stalinabad, then (1961) to Dushanbe, 139; and the Chinese-Soviet border (1970), 143

Djask: comes under British control (1899), 61

Dmitri: defeats the Mongols of the Golden Horde, 25

Dnieper, River: and the Slavs (in 800 BC), 1; Scythians control lower reaches of after 600 BC, 3; Sarmatians settle along, 4; controlled by the Goths, 5; controlled by the Huns, 6; Slavs extend their control throughout the length of, 7; controlled by the Avars, 8; Slavs re-establish their control of, 9; Khazars control lower reaches of, 10; Vikings settle along, 11; a principal highway of trade in Kievan Russia, 14; Cossacks settle along, 35; Cossack revolt in region of (1708), 37; anarchist activity in region of (1917–20), 95; Soviet labour camps on, 110; Germans control (1942), 119; Germans driven from (1943–44), 129

Dniepropetrovsk: over half a million inhabitants (1959), 138

Dnieprostroi: occupied by the Germans (1942), 119

Dniester, River: and the Slavs (by 800 BC), 1; Scythians control lower reaches of after 600 BC, 3; Sarmatians reach eastern bank of, 4; controlled by the Goths, 5; controlled by the Huns, 6; controlled by the Slavs, 7; controlled by the Avars, 8; Slavs re-establish their control of, 9; Bulgars settle along lower reaches of, 10; a principal highway of trade in Kievan Russia, 14; Catherine the Great extends Russia's western frontier to, 41, 43; German army driven back across (1944), 129

Dno: and the siege of Leningrad (1941–43), 126; Soviet partisans active near (1941–42), 127

Dolonnor (China): Soviet military advance to, against Japanese (1945), 142

Don, River: and the Slavs (by 800 BC), 1; Slav, Scythian and Greek settlements on (by 300 BC), 3; Sarmatian settlements on, 4; Goths extend their control to, 5; Huns extend their control to, 6; Slavs control upper reaches of, 7; Avars extend their control to, 8; Slavs re-establish control of upper reaches of, 9; controlled by the Khazars, 10; within the area paying tribute to Kievan Russia, 13; a principal highway of trade, 14; and the river system of European Russia, 27; peasants' revolt along (1670–71), 32; agricultural produce in region of (by 1800), 34; Cossacks settle along, 35; Cossack revolt in region of (1707–08), 37; famine in region of (1921), 102; Germans advance in region of (1942), 124

Donbass: factories evacuated from (1940–42), 113

Don Cossacks: revolt against Russian rule, 32; form an autonomous administrative district in Tsarist Russia (1790–1916), 35; revolt of (1707–08), 37; prominent in fight against Bolsheviks (1919), 100; famine in homeland of (1921), 102

Donets, River: a highway of trade for Kievan Russia, 14; peasants' revolt along (1670–71), 32; coal basin of, developed (from 1860), 56

Dorostol: a town paying tribute to Kievan Russia, 13

Dorpat: ruled by the Teutonic Knights, 20; annexed by Russia from Sweden (1721), 47; special Gendarme detachment at, 51; Bolshevik influence in (1917), 89

Dostoevsky, Fedor Mikhailovich: exiled to Siberia, 54

Dresden: colonized by the Germans, 20; Russians advance through (1812), 49; Bolshevik activity in (1903–14), 73; part of the Russian zone of occupation of Germany (1945), 133

Dubno: annexed by Russia (1795), 43; Austrians occupy (1915), 82

Dudinka: Kara Sea Expedition visits (1921), 105; on the Northern Sea Route, 112

Dusiata: anti-Jewish violence in, 69, 75

Dvina, River: Slav settlements on (by 600 BC), 2; (by 200 AD), 4; Goths reach southern bank of, 5; controlled by the Huns, 6; upper reaches of controlled by the Slavs, 7, 9, 10; a highway of trade for Kievan Russia, 14; mouth of, and lower reaches, controlled by the Teutonic Knights, 20; Russians control mouth of (1721), 36; Russians hold the line of, against German attack (1916), 83; Germans control (1942), 119

Dvina River, Northern: and the river systems of European Russia, 27; Ivan IV seizes lands along the whole course of, 28; anti-Bolshevik forces occupy over 200 miles of (1918–19), 94; Soviet labour camps established on, 110

Dvinsk (Daugavpils): Jewish political activity in, 70; political assassinations in, 72; Bolshevik activity in (1903–14), 73; strikes at, (1905), 76; Bolshevik influence in (1917), 89; Poles capture from Russia, and give to Latvia (1919), 100; occupied by the Germans (1941–45), 123

Dzerzhinsky, Feliks Edmundovich: in Moscow at the time of the revolution (1917), 88

Dzhalinda: and the Soviet-Chinese border (1970), 143

Dzhezkazgan: labour camps at, 111

Dzhulfa: Bolsheviks occupy (1921), 104

East Berlin: anti-Soviet revolt in (1953), 134

East Galicia: occupied by the Poles (1919), 100

East Germany: anti-Soviet revolt in (1953), 134

East Rumelia: and Russian policy in the Balkans (1876–85), 78

Eastern Roman Empire: established, 6, 7; its rule extended from the Alps to the Caucasus, 8; Slavs penetrate into Balkan lands of, 9; becomes known as the Byzantine Empire, 10; see henceforth index entry for Byzantine Empire

Edessa (Syria): Viking settlers reach, 11; under Roman Catholic control, 24

Edmonton (Canada): Ukrainians at, 99

Egypt: British occupation of (1882), 61; Soviet fishing agreement with (1970), 141

Ekaterinenstadt: principal town of the Volga Germans, 39; name changed to Marx, 139

Ekaterinburg: and Russian industry (by 1900), 71; name changed to Sverdlovsk, 139; for subsequent index entries see Sverdlovsk

Ekaterinodar: revolutionary outbreak at (1905), 76; claimed as part of the Ukraine, 97; name changed to Krasnodar, 139

Ekaterinoslav: large Cossack settlement in, 35; Alexander I establishes military colonies in Province of (1810–25), 50; anarchists active in (1905–06), 55; peasant discontent in the Province of (1827–60), 57; serfdom in (by 1860), 58; peasant rioting common in (1902–04), 68; anti-Jewish violence in, 69; Jewish political activity in, 70; industry in (by 1900), 71; political assassinations in, 72; Bolsheviks active in (1903–14), 73; peasant uprising in Province of (1905), 75; revolution in (1905), 76; occupied by German troops (1918), 91; attacked by anarchists (1918–20), 95; annexed to the Independent Ukraine (1918), 97

Ekibastuz: coal mines at, 62; in Virgin Lands Region (established 1953), 113

Elbe, River: Germanic tribes settle along, 4, 5; controlled by the Huns, 6; Slav settlement reaches eastern bank of, 7; Avars extend their rule to, 8; Slavs establish control of southern reaches of, 9, 10; falls under German rule, 20

Eletz: within area of peasants' revolt (1606), 29

Elgen: Soviet labour camps at, 111

Elizavetgrad: anti-Jewish violence in, 69; Jewish poverty in, 70; anarchist conference in (1919), 95; renamed Kirovo, 139

Elizavetpol: annexed by Russia (1804), 48; occupied by the Turks (1917–18), 104; name changed by Stalin to Kirovabad, 139

Emba: Ukrainians at, 97

Emba, River: Russian fortress line constructed along, 61

Engels: large German community in (1918–41), 39

Enos: occupied by Russia (1829), 46, 51; promised to Russia by Britain and France (1915), 85

Erivan: annexed by Russia (1828), 48; special Gendarme detachment at, 51; controlled by anti-Bolshevik forces (1918–19), 92, 104; over half a million inhabitants (1959), 138

Ermak, Timofeevich: leads Cossacks east of the Urals, 35

Erzerum: Russian troops occupy (1829), 46; Russian troops occupy (1916), 83, 85; Armenian claims to (1918), 104

Essen (Germany): unsuccessful seizure of power by German communists in, 108

Estonia: taken by Russia from Sweden (1721), 36; peasant uprising in (1905), 75; the growing national aspirations of (1917), 89; anti-Bolshevik forces driven back to (1919), 93; and the proposed Union of Border States (1919), 100; signs non-aggression Pact with Soviet Union (1932), 101; Russian refugees in (by 1930), 107; annexed by the Soviet Union (1939), 115, 116; population movements from (1939–46), 132; reincorporated in the Soviet Union (1945), 133; a Soviet Republic (since 1945), 144

Euphrates, River: and the Assyrians by 800 BC, 1; crossed by nomads from central Asia, 2; reached by the Mongols, 21; Russians occupy upper reaches of (1916), 85

Fano (Italy): Russian naval squadron bombards (1798–1800), 45

Faroe Islands: Viking settlers reach, 11

Fedor, Russian Tsar: regains Russia's access to the Baltic Sea, 26; his death marks the end of the Rurik dynasty, 29

Fergana: factories moved to (1940–42), 113

Fili: Germans produce armaments at, near Moscow (1922–33), 101

Finland: annexed by Russia (1809), 36, 50; achieves independence (1917), 91; active against the Bolsheviks (1918–19), 94; and the proposed Union of Border States (1919), 100; signs non-aggression Pact with Soviet Union (1932), 101; Russian refugees in (by 1930), 107; attacked by the Soviet Union (1939–40), 115; Soviet annexations from (1940), 116; troops from, fight with the Germans on the Russian front (1941), 118; and the siege of Leningrad (1941–43), 126

Finland, Gulf of: Swedes attack Republic of Novgorod from, 18; Teutonic Knights control southern shore of, 20; the Principality of Moscow reaches, 25; the Swedes drive the Russians from, 30; Russians re-establish their control of (1721–1809), 36; anti-Bolshevik forces in (1919), 93; and the siege of Leningrad (1941–43), 126

Finns: their early settlements, 4, 5; increasingly discontented by Russian rule (by 1904), 68; their national aspirations dissatisfied (1914), 84; seek independence (1917), 89; intervene against the Bolsheviks (1918–19), 92, 93

Fischhausen: Baltic port, ruled by Teutonic Knights, 20

Fokshani: battle of (1789), 46; Russian attack on (1828–29), 51

Forced Collectivization: Kazakh's flee from (1932), 103; area of (1929–38), 113

'Forest Brethren': terrorist group (active 1905–06), 55

Formosa (Taiwan): annexed by Japan from China (1895), 66

Fort Alexandrovsk: name changed, first to Fort Uritsk, then to Fort Shevchenko, 139

Fort Ross: Russian trading post near San Francisco (founded 1811), 44

Fort William (Canada): Ukrainians at, 99

Fort Wrangel: Russian fort on the Pacific coast of Alaska (founded 1834), 44

France: Germanic tribes settle in, 7; Viking settlers reach, 11; Russia attacks Mediterranean possessions of (1798–1800), 45; and European diplomacy (1872–1907), 63, 64; allied to Russia (from 1894), 79; promises Russia Constantinople (1915), 85; Lenin plans to return to Russia through (1917), 87; Russian war debts to (by 1917), 89; intervenes against Bolsheviks (1918–19), 92, 93, 106; Ukrainian anarchist leader finds refuge in (1920), 95; supports Poles against Bolsheviks (1920), 100; signs military assistance Treaty with Soviet Union (1935), 101; Russian refugees in (by 1930), 107

Frankfurt: Russians advance through (1812), 49

Franks: defeat the Huns at Orléans, 6; converted to Roman Catholicism, 15

Franz-Ferdinand: assassinated at Sarajevo (1914), 79

Frunze: *for earlier index entries see* Pishpek: factories moved to (1940–42), 113

Galich: Orthodox monastery established at, 16; Ivan IV seizes lands in region of, 28

Galicia: A Russian Principality, 17; conquered by the Mongols, 22; a Roman Catholic region under Lithuanian control, 24; occupied by the Germans (1942), 119; largely reincorporated into the Soviet Union (1945), 133

Gallipoli Peninsula: allied attack on (1915), 83

Ganges, River: crossed by nomads from central Asia, 2

Gatchina: occupied by anti-Bolshevik forces (1919), 93; under German military rule (1941), 123

Gävle: Swedish town attacked by Russia (1710–21), 37

Gdov: uprising in (1648–50), 32; occupied by anti-Bolshevik forces (1919), 93; German reprisals against Russian civilians in (1941–43), 126; Soviet partisans near (1941–42), 127

Gelon: Greek colony on the Don, 3

Gendarme Districts: during the reign of Nicholas I, 50

Geneva (Switzerland): Russian students in, 70; Bolshevik newspaper printed in, 73; communist propaganda disseminated in, 108

Genghis Khan: Mongol westward conquests after the death of, 21

Geokchie: anti-Bolshevik revolt in (1920–21), 104

Georgia: annexed by Russia (1801), 48; and the proposed Union of Border States (1919–20), 100; its brief independence (1918–20), 104; a Soviet Republic, 144

Georgians: their settlements by 800 BC, 1; increasingly discontented by Russian rule (by 1905), 68, 76

Germans: their area of settlement by 800 BC, 1; by 200 AD, 4; by 400 AD, 5; by 550 AD, 7; converted to Roman Catholicism, 15; many settle in Russia (1760–1860), 39; two million in Russia (by 1897), 74

Germany: and European diplomacy (1872–1907), 63, 64; Russian trade with, 71; and European diplomacy (before 1914), 78, 79; Lenin returns to Russia through (1917), 87; occupies the Ukraine (March–Dec 1918), 97; obtains military training facilities in the Soviet Union (1922–33), 101; helps to equip the Kara Sea Expedition (1921), 105; Russian refugees in (by 1930), 107; Trotsky refused permission to settle in, 113; invades Poland (1939), 114; territorial extent of (on 22 June 1941), 117; invades the Soviet Union (1941), 118; defeated 1944–45), 130; flight of seven million German refugees to (1945–46), 132; occupied by Britain, France, the United States and the Soviet Union (1945), 133

Gildendorf: German collective farm in the Soviet Union, 39

Gogland Island: Germans fail to capture (1941–43), 126

Golden Horde: tribe of, converted to Islam, 21; its rule in southern Russia, 22; defeated by Prince Dmitri of Moscow, 25

Goldinski Island: Soviet-Chinese military clash on (1968), 135

Gomel: Jews murdered in (1648–52), 31; anti-Jewish violence in, 69; Jewish political activity in, 70; political assassinations in, 72; annexed to the independent Ukraine (1918), 97; occupied by the Germans (1942), 119; Germans driven from (1944), 129

Gori, annexed by Russia (1801), 48

Gorky: *for earlier index entries see* Nizhni Novgorod: a German plan for (1941), 122; a German military objective (1942), 124; over half a million inhabitants (1959), 138

Goths: their settlements by 200 BC, 4; their rule extended to the Black Sea by 200 AD, 5; defeated by the Huns, 6; settle in the Crimea, 7, 8, 9

Gotland: Baltic Island, ruled by the Teutonic Knights, 20

Grand Duchy of Lithuania, *see* Lithuania

Grand Duchy of Warsaw: established by Napoleon (1807), 49; largely annexed by Russia (1815), 50

Greece: Slavs settle in, 9; Russia opposes Greek revolt against Turks in (1815–25), 50; and Russian policy in the Balkans (1876–1914), 78, 79; Russian refugees in (by 1930), 107; unsuccessful communist intervention in civil war of, 113

Greeks: their settlement by 800 BC, 1; their Black Sea colonies

by 300 BC, 3; under Roman rule, 4; converted to Eastern Catholicism, 15; under Turkish rule, 49

'Green Ukraine': Amur region known as, because of Ukrainian settlements, 98

Greenland: Viking settlers reach, 11

Grodno: a town conquered by Kievan Russia, 13; incorporated in Lithuania, 23; Jews murdered in (1648–52), 31; annexed by Russia (1795), 43; anarchists active in (1905–06), 55; peasant discontent and serfdom in (by 1860), 57, 58; Jewish political activity in, 70; agricultural workers strike in Province of (1905), 75; German army occupies (1915), 82; seized by Poland from Lithuania (1920), 96; Soviet Union annexes (1939), 114, 116

Grozny: annexed by Russia (1859), 48; heavy industry in (by 1900), 71; revolution at (1905), 76; part of the Terek Peoples' SSR (1918–20), 104; its oilfields a major German military objective (1942), 124, 128

Gruzino: Germans occupy (1941), 126

Guliai Pole: anarchist headquarters at (1918–20), 95

Gumbinnen (East Prussia): Russians defeat the Germans at (1914), 81

Gümüsh Tepe (Caspian Sea): Viking settlers reach, 11

Gümüshane (Eastern Turkey): occupied by Russia (1829), 46

Gunib: Russian victory at (1859), 61

Gurev: a centre of Cossack settlement, 35; occupied by anti-Bolshevik forces (1919), 92; Ukrainians at (by 1937), 97; United States aid enters the Soviet Union through (1941–45), 120

Gurganj: Khazar town on the Oxus river, 10

Guru (Tibet): Tibetans defeated by the British at (1904), 65

Gus: Ivan IV seizes land in region of, 28

Gzhatsk: trade fair at, 34

Haji-Bey: Black Sea port, ruled by the Lithuanians, 23; ruled by the Ottoman Empire, 31; *for subsequent references see index entry for* Odessa

Hamburg: a Hansa town, 20; German communists try to seize power in, but suppressed, 108

Hami: annexed by China (by 1764), 40; and Russian trade with China (1850–70), 59

Hangö: Lenin lands at, on way to Petrograd (1917), 86, 87; United States famine relief arrives at (1921), 102; leased by the Soviet Union from Finland (1940), 115

Hankow (China): defended by Soviet air units against Japanese attack (1941), 142

Hanover: Russia allies with, against Sweden (1714), 47

Hanseatic League: its Baltic influence, 20

Hapsal: ruled by the Teutonic Knights, 20

Harbin: Mongol town, under Chinese control (by 1720), 40; linked to Russia by railway (by 1903), 62, 67; and the Chinese-Soviet border (1970), 143

Havana (Cuba): crisis provoked by Soviet missiles near (1962), 140

Hawaiian Islands: Russians fail to obtain trading foothold in (1820), 44

Helsingfors (Helsinki): part of Russia (1809–1917), 36, 47; a large German community in (by 1914), 39; strikes in (1905), 76; seized by Finnish Bolsheviks (1917), 100; United States famine relief for ·Russia arrives at (1921), 102; a German plan for (1941), 122

Heraclea: Greek colony on the Black Sea, 3; under Roman control, 4, 6, 7; raided by the Goths, 5

Herodotus: names possible Slav tribes north of Black Sea, 3

Hitler, Adolf: and the Soviet partisans, 127

Holland: Russian refugees from Bolshevism in (by 1930), 107

Holy Roman Empire: extends its control to the River Oder, 20; raided by the Mongols, 22

House of Chaghtai: a branch of the Mongol dominions, 21

House of Hulagh: a branch of the Mongol dominions, 21

Hungary: Mongols raid, 22; a Roman Catholic State, 24; Russian refugees in (by 1930), 107; Hungarian communists seize power only briefly in (1919), ₁08; Soviet army advances through (1944–45), 130; population movements from (1939–46), 132; under communist control (1945), 133; anti-Soviet revolt in (1956), 134

Huns: settle north of Caspian Sea, 5; extend their rule from the Rhine to the Oxus, 6; their waning strength, 7; settled along the eastern shore of the Sea of Azov, 8; form Khanate of Great Bulgaria, 9; *see henceforth index entry for* Bulgars

Iasika: Russians advance to, in war against Turkey (1806–12), 49

Iceland: Viking settlers reach, 11

Igarka: Kara Sea Expedition visits (1921), 105; Soviet labour camp at, and revolt of (1948), 111; on the Northern Sea Route, 112

Ili, River: Virgin Lands campaign extended to (after 1953), 136

Ilmen, Lake: Germans reach western shore of (1941), 126

Ilomanets: a town in the Republic of Novgorod, 18

Iman: Ukrainians at (by 1937), 98; and the Soviet-Chinese border (1970), 143

India: British expansion in, towards central Asia (1876–1895), 61; Soviet fishing agreement with (1970), 141

Indian Ocean: reached by the Mongols, 21; British influence extended in, 61; Soviet naval influence in (1970), 141

Indigirka, River: Stalinist deportation of national groups to (1941–45), 131

Indonesia: Soviet fishing agreement with (1970), 141

Indus, River: crossed by nomads from central Asia, 2

Ingria: conquered by Sweden, but regained by Russia, 26, 36 47

Iona: Viking settlers reach, 11

Ionian Islands: occupied by Russia (1800–07), 45

Iraq: Soviet fishing agreement with (1970), 141

Irbit: trade fair at, 34

Irkutsk: founded (1652), 33; a town of exile, 54; and Russian trade with China (1850–70), 59; political assassinations in, 72; factories moved to (1940–42), 113; and the Soviet-Chinese border (1970), 143

Irtysh, River: and the river systems of the Urals and European Russia, 27; Cossacks reach (1581), 35; and the Siberian exile system, 54; and Russian trade with China (1850–70), 59; Ukrainian settlements on the upper reaches of, 98; Soviet labour camps on, 111; Stalinist deportation of national groups to (1941–45), 131; industry along the upper reaches of (1970), 137

Isfahan (Persia): proposed Russian railway through (before 1907), 61; allied aid to Soviet Union goes through (1941–45), 120

Iskra: publishing centres of, 73

Islam: its influence paramount in the lands south of the Caspian, 10; Mongols of the Golden Horde converted to, 21

Ismail: sieges of (1791, 1806), 46; Russian attacks on Turkey launched from (1806–12), 49; special Gendarme detachment at, 51; claimed by the Ukrainians, 97

Issyk Kul, Lake: Kazakhs flee into China past, 103; Stalinist deportation of national groups to region of (1941–45), 131

Istros: Greek colony on the Black Sea, 3

Italy: and European diplomacy (1872–1907), 63, 64; Russian war debts to (by July 1917), 89; intervenes against the Bolsheviks (1918), 92, 94, 106; signs trade agreement with Bolshevik Russia (1921), 101; Russian refugees in (by 1930), 107; alleged revolutionary activity prepared against, inside Russia, 108; troops from, fight with the Germans on the Russian front (1941), 118

Itil: the Khazar capital, near the mouth of the Volga, 10; Viking settlers reach, 11; pays tribute to Kievan Russia, 13; a trading centre, 14

Ivan the Terrible: Novgorodians flee eastwards across the Urals from (1478), 33

Ivan IV: crowned 'Tsar of all the Russias' in 1547, 26; expropriates land throughout European Russia, 28

Ivangorod: the Principality of Moscow's port on the Gulf of Finland, 25; annexed by Sweden (1617), 30; regained by Russia (1721), 47

Ivanovo: strikes in (1885–1903), 68; Bolsheviks active in (1903–14), 73

Izborsk: a town in Kievan Russia, 13; attacked by the Teutonic Knights, 18

Izhevski: industry at (by 1800), 34

Ishma, River: a trade route of Novgorod, 19

Izium: cannibalism at, 102

Japan: and Russian expansion in the Far East (1850–90), 60, 66; defeats Russia in the Far East (1904–05), 67; Russian war debts to (by July 1917), 89; intervenes against Bolsheviks (1918–19), 92, 106

Jarrow: Viking settlers reach, 11

Jassy: unsuccessful Russian attack on Turks at (1711), 37; Treaty of (1791), 46; Russian attack on (1806–12), 49; Bolshevik propaganda enters Russia through (1903–14), 73; a Bolshevik leader at, at the time of the revolution (1917), 88; Russian soldiers mutiny at (1917), 89

Jerusalem: and the Jews in 800 BC, 1; part of the Islamic world, 15

Jewish Pale of Settlement: Jews restricted to, 68, 69; poverty in, 70

Jews: their settlement (by 800 BC), 1; over 100,000 murdered by the Cossacks (1648–1652), 31; Russia acquires 1,000,000 following the annexation of eastern Poland (1772–95), 42; Russia acquires a further 300,000, following the annexation of much of the Grand Duchy of Warsaw (1815), 49; expelled from the Baltic and Black Sea coastlines (1827, 1930), 51; exiled to Siberia if they failed to pay their taxes for three years running, 54; confined to the Pale of Settlement, 68; five million in Russia (1897), 74; welcome Germans as liberators from Tsarist tyranny (1914–17), 84; 25,000 in the Far Eastern Republic (1920–22), 106; wartime deaths (1939–45), 130; flight of, into Russia (1941), 132; Autonomous region of, in the Soviet Far East (since 1934), 135, 144

Judaism: Khazar Khan converted to, 10

Justinian: Roman Emperor, uses Avars to subdue the Slavs, 8

Kabarda: annexed by Russia, 41

Kachuga: shipbuilding at (from 1937), 112

Kaffa: Crimean port, under Roman Catholic control, 24; occupied by Russia (1771), 46

Kairouan: part of the Islamic world, 15

Kalgan (China): and Russian trade with China (1850–70), 59; Soviet military advance to, against Japanese (1945), 142

Kalisz: large German community in (by 1914), 39; Napoleon retreats through (1812), 49; a centre of Polish revolt against Russia (1860), 53; and German war aims (1914), 80; Germans occupy (1914), 81; part of Greater Germany (1940–45), 123; the most westerly town of Tsarist Russia (not ruled by Russia since 1914), 145

Kalmyks: deported by Stalin to Siberia, 128, 131

Kaluga: a town in the Principality of Moscow, 25; within area of peasants' revolt (1606–07), 29; industrial growth in the region of (by 1860), 56; peasant discontent in the Province of (1827–60), 57; serfdom in (by 1860), 58; Bolsheviks seize power in (1917), 91

Kama, River: part of the trade routes of Novgorod, 19; Ivan IV seizes lands along, 28; rapid industrial growth on (in the 1860's), 56; and Russian trade with China (1850–70), 59

Kamchatka: criminals and political prisoners sent to, 66

Kamen: and the Northern Sea Route administration, 112

Kamenets: Jews murdered in (1648–52), 31; annexed by Russia (1793), 43; Bolshevik propaganda enters Russia through (1903–14), 73; on Soviet side of Polish-Soviet frontier (1921–39), 96; much fought over (1917–21), 97

Kamenev, Lev Borisovich: in Siberia at the time of the revolution (1917), 88

Kamennyi monastery: 19

Kammin: Baltic port within the Holy Roman Empire, 20

Kandalakskaya: occupied by anti-Bolshevik forces (1918–19), 94; Soviet labour camps near, 109

Kara (eastern Siberia): gold mines at, worked by convict labour, 62; political exiles at, 72; communist labour camps compared with, 109

Kara (northern Siberia): visited by the Kara Sea Expedition (1921), 105

Kara Sea: river routes across Russia from, 27; Bolsheviks send two expeditions by sea to (1920, 1921), 105; Soviet labour camp region borders on, 111

Karaganda: coal mines at, 62; Soviet labour camps at, 111; factories moved to (1940–42), 113; a German plan for (1941), 122; Virgin Lands campaign extended to (after 1953), 136

Karasubazar: battle of (1737), 46

Karelia: taken by Russia from Sweden (1721), 36, 47; Soviet Labour camps in (1920–36), 109

Kargopol: Ivan IV seizes land in region of, 28; uprising in (1648–50), 32

Karpino: and the siege of Leningrad (1941–43), 126

Kars: battle of (1829), 46; ceded to Russia by Turkey (1878), 48, 61; revolutionary outbreak at (1905), 76; Turks occupy (1918), 91; annexed by Turkey (1921), 85, 104

Kashgar: and Russian trade with China (1850–70), 59; British want to extend their influence to, 65; and the Chinese-Soviet border (1970), 143

Kazakhstan: many Volga German farmers deported to (1927–33), 39; many Ukrainians settle in, 98; flight of Kazakhs from (1916–32), 103; Stalinist deportation of national groups to (1941–45), 131; Virgin Lands Region in (established 1953), 136

Kazalinsk: Russian line of forts constructed east of, 61

Kazan: dispossessed landowners settle in, 28; a shipbuilding and industrial centre (by 1800), 34; administrative centre of a Province established by Peter the Great, 38; peasant discontent in Province of (1827–60), 57; and Russian trade with China (1850–70), 59; peasant uprising in Province of (1905), 75; Bolsheviks seize power in (1917), 91; anti-Bolshevik force seizes control of (1919), 92, 146; Germans train in tank warfare secretly at (1922–33), 101; famine in (1921), 102; Soviet labour camps to the north and south of, 110; a German plan for (1941), 122; a German military objective (1942), 124; over half a million inhabitants (1959), 138

Kazan Khanate: adjoins Principality of Moscow, 25; conquered by Ivan IV (1552), 26

Kazvin (Persia): United States aid to Soviet Union passes through (1941–45), 120

Kem: occupied by Finnish troops (1918–19), 92, 94, 146; Soviet labour camps near, 109

Kem, River: and Russian trade with China (1850–70), 59

Kemerovo: labour camps at, 111; Virgin Lands campaign extended to (after 1953), 136

Kennedy, President John F: and Soviet missiles in Cuba (1962), 140

Kerch: battle of (1774), 46; strikes in (before 1905), 68; annexed to the Independent Ukraine (1918), 97

Kerensky, Alexander Fedorovich: Lenin urges Bolsheviks not to co-operate with (1917), 87

Kergedan: Ivan IV seizes land in region of, 28

Kerman (Persia): proposed Russian railway through, 61

Kexholm: annexed by Sweden (1617), 30; regained by Russia (1721), 47

Khabarovo: and the Northern Sea Route, 112

Khabarovsk: founded (1858), 60; Trans-Siberian railway reaches (by 1915), 62; Ukrainian settlement at (by 1937), 98; in the Bolshevik-controlled Far Eastern Republic (1922), 106; on the Soviet border with China, 142, 143

Khanty: and Russian trade with China (1850–70), 59

Khanka, Lake: annexed by Russia (1860), 60; and the Soviet-Chinese border (1970), 143

Khaqans: conquered by the Mongols, 21

Kharkov: in heavily populated area of Russia (1724), 38; anarchists active in (1905–06), 55; peasant rioting common in the Province of (1902–04), 68; heavy industry in (by 1900), 71; Bolsheviks active in (1903–14), 73; peasant uprising in

Province of (1905), 75; a Bolshevik leader in, at the time of the revolution (1917), 88; occupied by German troops (1918), 91; occupied by anti-Bolshevik Russian forces (1919), 92; anarchists active at, 95; annexed to the Independent Ukraine (1918), 97; famine in (1921), 102; alleged communist subversive activity in, 108; area of forced collectivization (1929–38), 113; occupied by the Germans (1941), 118, 119, 121, 123, 124, 128; a German plan for (1941), 122; Germans driven from (1943), 129; over half a million inhabitants (1959), 138

Khazars: reach eastern shore of the Caspian Sea, 8, 9; extend their rule along the Volga and to the Black Sea, 10; Viking settlers reach land of, 11; the Varangarians protect the Slavs from, 12; pay tribute to Kievan Russia, 13; and the trade routes of Kievan Russia, 14

Kherson: annexed by Russia from Turkey (1774), 43; peasant rioting common in Province of (1902–04), 67; Jewish poverty in, 70; Bolshevik activity in (1903–14), 73; peasant uprising in Province of (1905), 75; occupied by the Germans (1942), 119

Khiva: annexed by Russia (1873), 61; Soviet Peoples' Republic established in (1917), 103

Khmelnitski, Bogdan: leads the Cossacks against the Polish army, and against the Jews (1648–52), 31, 69

Khodzhent: name changed to Leninabad, 139

Kholm (near Lublin); annexed to the Independent Ukraine (1918), 97

Kholm (near Novgorod): Soviet partisans active near (1941–43), 127; Germans driven from (1943–44), 129

Kholmogory: Ivan IV seizes land in region of, 28

Khorram Shah (Persia): United States aid to the Soviet Union goes through (1941–45), 120

Khotan: annexed by China (by 1764), 40; and Russian trade with China (1850–70), 59; Britain wants to extend its influence to, 65

Khotin: siege of (1788), 46

Kiakhta: and the Siberian exiles, 54; and Russian trade with China (1850–70), 59

Kielce: and German war aims (1914), 80

Kiev: Viking settlers at, 11; becomes the capital of the Varangarians, 12; the principal town of Kievan Russia, 13; as a trading centre, 14; a centre of Eastern Catholicism, 15; principal town of a Russian Principality, 17; Orthodox monastery established at, 16; within the area of Mongol overlordship, 21, 22; conquered by the Lithuanians, 23; under Roman Catholic control, 24; annexed by Russia (1667), 31; Cossack revolt in region of (1708), 37; administrative centre of a Province established by Peter the Great, 38; anarchists active in (1905–06), 55; its growth (by 1860), 56; peasant discontent and serfdom in (by 1860), 57, 58; trade unions in, infiltrated by Tsarist secret police (by 1903), 68; ritual murder charge against a Jew in, 69; Jewish political activity in, 70; Bolshevik activity in (1903–14), 73; peasant uprising in Province of (1905), 75; revolution at (1905), 76; occupied by German troops (1918), 91; occupied by anti-Bolshevik Russians (1919), 92; anarchists in, 95; occupied by the Poles (April–June 1920), 96, 100; much fought over (1917–21), 97; factories evacuated from (1940–41), 113; occupied by the Germans (1941), 118, 119, 124; a German plan for (1941), 122; German SS Headquarters at (1941–44), 123; Germans driven from (1944), 129, 130; one million inhabitants (by 1959), 138; a 'Hero City' of the Soviet Union, 146

Kievan Rus: a mingling of Slav and Scandinavian culture, 12; its growth (by 1054), 13

Kilia: siege of (1791), 46

Kingisepp: German reprisals against Russian civilians in (1941–43), 126

Kirishi: Germans occupy (1941), 126

Kirgizia: famine in (1921), 102

Kirov, Serghei Mironovich: in the Caucasus at the time of the revolution (1917), 88

Kishinev: large German community in (by 1914), 39; its growth (by 1860), 56; anti-Jewish violence in, 69; Jewish political activity in, 70; political assassinations in, 72; secret Bolshevik printing press in, 73; Rumanian (from 1918), annexed by the Soviet Union (1940), 116; reincorporated in the Soviet Union (1945), 133

Kodak: annexed by Russia, 31

Kodiak: Russian settlement in Alaska, 44

Kokand: and Russian trade with China (1850–70), 59; annexed by Russia (1871), 61; anti-Bolshevik revolt in region of (1917–20), 103; factories moved to (1940–42), 113

Kokchetov: in Virgin Lands Region (established 1953), 136

Kolchak, Admiral Alexander Vasilievich: sets up anti-Bolshevik regime at Vladivostok (1918), 106

Kollontai, Alexandra Mikhailovna: in Sweden at the time of the revolution (1917), 88

Kolomea: part of the West Ukrainian Republic (1918), 97

Kolomna: strikes in (1905), 76

Kolpashevo: and Russian trade with China (1850–70), 59

Kolyma, River: early Russian settlements on, 33; Soviet labour camps on, 111; coal basin on, 112, 137; Stalinist deportation of national groups to (1941–45), 131

Kolymskaya: labour camps at, 111

Komarov: Russians defeat the Germans at (1914), 81; part of the Ukrainian Peoples' Republic (1917), 80

Komsomolskaya Pravda Island: on the Northern Sea Route, 112

Koniecpol: Jewish uprising against the Germans in, 123

Königsberg: ruled by the Teutonic Knights, 20; part of Prussia, 31; annexed to the Soviet Union (1945), 36, 133, 145; Bolshevik propaganda enters Russia through (1903–17), 73; Russian army fails to reach (in 1914), 81; becomes Russian (in 1945) and renamed Kaliningrad, 139

Konotop: anti-Jewish violence in, 69

Kopore: attacked by the Teutonic Knights (1223), 18

Korea: Russia fears British penetration of (after 1840), 60; and Japanese expansion in the Far East (1876–95), 66; Russian economic penetration of (1895–1904), 67

Koreans: conquered by the Mongols, 21; in the Bolshevik-controlled Far Eastern Republic (1920–22), 106

Kornilov, General Lavr Georgievich: his unsuccessful attack on Petrograd (Aug 1917), 89

Korsun: Jews murdered in (1648–52), 31

Koslov: uprising in (1648–50), 32

Kostroma: Orthodox monastery established at, 16; conquered by the Principality of Moscow, 25; Russian counter-attack against Poles gains troops from, 30; peasant discontent in the Province of (1827–60), 57; serfdom in (by 1860), 58

Kotlas: industry in (by 1900), 71; Soviet labour camps in the region of, 110; industry at (1941–45), 121; a German plan for (1941), 122

Kovda: labour camps at, 109

Kovel: Jews murdered in (1648–52), 31; annexed by Russia (1795), 43; area of Polish partisan activity against Russia (1831), 52; part of the Ukrainian Peoples' Republic (1917), 80; much fought over (1917–21), 97

Kovno (Kaunas): a town in Lithuania, 17; conquered by the Teutonic Knights, 20; reincorporated into Lithuania, 23; Jews murdered in (1648–52), 31; annexed by Russia (1795), 43; Polish revolt in the region of (1860), 53; anarchists active in (1905–06), 55; peasant discontent in the Province of (1827–60), 57; serfdom in (by 1860), 58; Jewish political activity in, 70; industry in (by 1900), 71; Bolshevik activity in (1903–14), 73; agricultural workers strike in Province of (1905), 75; and German war aims (1914), 80; German army occupies (1915), 82; Lithuanian (from 1919), annexed by the Soviet Union (1940), 116; annexed by Germany (1941), 123; reincorporated into the Soviet Union (1945), 133

Kozhevnikov Bay: on the Northern Sea Route, 112

Kozelsk: Ivan IV seizes land in region of, 28

Krasnik: Polish rebels flee into Austria from (1831), 52; a centre of Polish revolt against Russia (1860), 53; Russians defeat the Germans at (1914), 81

Krasnodar: occupied by the Germans (1943), 123, 128

Krasnovodsk: annexed by Russia (1869), 61; linked to Tashkent and Moscow by railway (by 1915), 62; revolutionary outbreak

at (1905), 76; occupied by British forces (1917–19), 103, 146; United States aid enters the Soviet Union through (1941–45), 120, 121; a German plan for (1941), 122

Krasnoyarsk: founded (1628), 40; Stalin in exile at, 54; Socialist Revolutionaries in exile at, 72; Ukrainian settlers at (by 1937), 98; Soviet labour camps near, 111; and the Northern Sea Route administration, 112; factories moved to (1940–42), 113; a German plan for (1941), 122; Virgin Lands campaign extended to (after 1953), 136; and the Soviet-Chinese border (1970), 143

Krasnoye Akdeiski: German military headquarters at (1941–42), 127

Kremenchug: Jewish poverty in, 70

Kremlin (Moscow): held by Government troops during the uprising of 1905, 77

Krevo: Russian soldiers mutiny in (1917), 89

Krivichians: an eastern Slav tribe, 12

Krivoi: industry in (by 1900), 71; occupied by the Germans (1942), 119; Germans driven from (1943–44), 129

Kropotkin, Prince Pyotr Alexeevich: and the Russian anarchists, 55

Krushchev, Nikita Sergeyevich: and the rehabilitation of deported peoples (1957), 131; blames 'Jewish individualism' for failure of Jewish Autonomous Region in the Soviet Far East, 135; establishes Virgin Lands Region (1953), 136; agrees to withdraw Soviet missiles from Cuba (1962), 140

Kuba: anti-Bolshevik revolt in (1920–21), 104

Kuban: annexed by Russia, 41; base for anti-Bolshevik army of Denikin (1919), 100; famine in (1921), 102

Kuban, River: Scythian and Greek settlements along, 3; a highway of trade for Kievan Russia, 14; Cossacks settle along, 35; German advance to (1941–42), 128

Kuibyshev: for earlier index entries see Samara: Soviet labour camps established in region of, 110; factories moved to (1940–42), 113, 121; over half a million inhabitants (1959), 138

Kulikovo: Mongols of the Golden Horde defeated at, 25

Kulja (Kuldzha): annexed by China (by 1764), 40; and Russian trade with China (1850–70), 59; and the Soviet-Chinese border (1970), 143

Kuma, River: Germans advance to (1941–42), 128

Kureika: Stalin in exile at, 54, 88

Kurile Islands: recognized by Russia as Japanese (1875), 60, 66

Kurgan: a town of exile in Siberia (before 1914), 54; factories moved to (1940–42), 113

Kurland: annexed to Russia by Catherine the Great, 41; peasant uprising in (1905), 75; and German war aims (1914), 80

Kurland: annexed to Russia by Catherine the Great, 41; peasant uprising in (1905), 75; and German war aims (1914), 80

Kursk: within Kievan Russia, 13; within area of peasants' revolt (1905–06), 29; uprising in (1648–50), 32; trade fair at, 34; peasant discontent in Province of (1827–60), 57; serfdom in (by 1860), 58; peasant uprising in Province of (1905), 75; anarchist conference at (1918), 95; anti-Bolsheviks occupy (1919), 97; occupied by the Germans (1941), 118, 123, 124; Germans driven from (1943), 129

Kushka: linked to Moscow by railway (1915), 62

Kustanai: in Virgin Lands Region (established 1953), 136

Kustenje: battle of (1828), 46, 51

Kutais: annexed by Russia (1804), 48; serfdom in the Province of (by 1860), 58; ritual murder charge against Jews in, 69; peasant uprising in (1905), 75; entered by the Bolsheviks (1920–21), 104

Kutchuk Kainardji: Treaty of (1774), 46

Kutno: German army occupies (1914), 81

Kutrigar Huns: settle along the lower Don, 7

Kuwait: comes under British control (1899), 61

Kuznetsk: renamed Stalinsk, 139

Kwangchuwan: French port on the China coast, 65

Ladoga: Viking settlers at, 11; within Kievan Russia, 13; Orthodox monastery established at, 16; attacked by the Swedes (1313), 18; Ivan IV seizes lands to the east of, 28; occupied by Sweden (1613), 30

Ladoga, Lake: Swedes attack Novgorodians across (1284, 1313)

18; river routes across Russia from, 27; Ivan IV seizes lands to the south and east of, 28; Swedish conquests in region of, 30; a Soviet labour camp established at, 109; and the siege of Leningrad (1941–43), 126

Ladozhskoye Ozero: a lakeside town, crucial for the defence of Leningrad (1941–43), 126

Laibach: conference of, 50

Lakhta: and the siege of Leningrad (1941–42), 126

Lampozhnia: town founded by the Republic of Novgorod, 19

Lanchow (China): and Russian trade with China (1850–70), 59; defended by Soviet air units (1941), 142

Lapland: a Roman Catholic region (by 1300), 24; part of, annexed by Russia from Sweden (1809), 47

Laptev Sea: Soviet labour camp region borders on, 111; Northern Sea Route goes through, 112

Latakia (Syria): Soviet naval facilities at (1970), 141

Latvia: taken by Russia from Sweden (1721),·36; the growing national aspirations of (1917), 89; intervenes against the Bolsheviks (1918–19), 92; and the proposed Union of Border States (1919), 100; signs non-aggression Pact with Soviet Union (1932), 101; Russian refugees in (by 1930), 107; annexed by the Soviet Union (1939), 115, 116; population movements from (1943–46), 132; reincorporated into the Soviet Union (1945), 133; a Soviet Republic (since 1945), 144

Lausanne (Switzerland): Lenin in, 73

Laz: their settlement by 800 BC, 1

Lednovo: and the siege of Leningrad (1941–43), 126

Leipzig (Germany): Russian students in, 70; Bolshevik activity in (1903–14), 73

Lemnos: raided by the Goths, 5

Lena, River: early Russian settlements along, 33; and the Siberian exile system, 54; Soviet labour camps on, 111; coal basin along the lower reaches of, 112, 137; Stalinist deportation of national groups to (1941–45), 131

Lenin, Vladimir Ilich: his political activity (before 1917), 73; returns to Russia from exile (1917), 86, 87, 88; goes into hiding in Finland (1917), 89; returns to Petrograd (Oct 1917), 90; established Third Communist International (1919), 108; towns and villages named after, 139

Lenin (Russian icebreaker); leads Kara Sea Expeditions (1920, 1921), 105

Leningrad: Soviet aid to Republican Spain leaves from (1936–39), 101; factories evacuated from (1940–41), 113; besieged by Germany (1941–43), 118, 126; a German plan for (1941), 122; Soviet partisans south of (1941–42), 127; three million inhabitants (by 1959), 138; Soviet naval forces based on (1970), 141; a 'Hero City' of the Soviet Union, 146

Lenkoran: annexed by Russia (1813), 48, 61; anti-Bolshevik revolt in (1920–21), 104

Lethbridge (Canada): Ukrainians at, 99

Lhasa (Tibet): conquered by China (1780), 40; British troops enter (1904), 65

Libau: taken by Russia from Poland (1795), 36, 42, 43; industrial growth of (after 1860), 56; Jewish political activity in, 70; revolution at (1905), 76; and German war aims (1914), 80; German army occupies (1914–15), 82

Lida: annexed by Russia (1795), 43; annexed by Germany (1941), 123

Liegnitz: attacked by the Mongols, 22

Lindisfarne: Viking settlers reach, 11

Lipetsk: Germans train pilots secretly at (1922–33), 101

Lisbon: Viking settlers reach, 11

Lithuania: Russian monasteries in, 16; controls Russian province of Polotsk, 17; attacks Republic of Novgorod, 18; extends its rule to Black Sea, 23; a Roman Catholic kingdom, 24; peasants flee from serfdom in, to become Cossacks, 35; annexed by Russia (1795), 41, 43; intervenes against the Bolsheviks (1918–19), 92; and the proposed Union of Border States (1919), 100; Russian refugees in (by 1930), 107; annexed to the Soviet Union (1940), 116; population movements from (1939–46), 132; reincorporated into the Soviet Union (1945), 133; a Soviet Republic (since 1945), 144

Litvinov, Maksim Maksimovich: in London at the time of the revolution (1917), 88

Liubech: a town in Kievan Russia, 13

Livonia: peasant uprising in Province of (1905), 75

Lodz: Polish town, annexed by Prussia (1793), 42; part of Russia, and anti-Jewish violence in, 69, 75; Jewish political activity in, 70; revolution in (1905), 76; and German war aims (1914), 80; Germans defeat Russians at (1914), 81; Polish (from 1918), occupied by Germany (1939), 114; part of Poland, and anti-Soviet revolt in (1956), 134

Lomza: Polish town annexed by the Soviet Union (1939), 114

London: Russian Jews flee to (1880–1905), 70; Lenin in exile in (1907), 73; Lenin plans to return to Russia through (1917), 87; Russian Bolshevik leaders in (1917), 88

Lovat, River: a highway of trade in Kievan Russia, 14

Lozovaya: attacked by anarchists (1918–20), 95

Lublin: Jews murdered in (1648–52), 31; annexed by Austria from Poland (1795), 42, 43; Russian (after 1815), and a centre of Polish revolt against Russia (1860), 53; revolution in (1905), 76; and German war aims (1914), 80; Russian army advances into Austria from (1914), 81; Polish (since 1918), Red Army fails to capture (1920), 96; occupied by Germany (1939), 114, 116; Jewish uprising against Germans in, 123

Luga: Tsarist troops disarmed at (1917), 86; occupied by anti-Bolshevik forces (1919), 93; German reprisals against Russian civilians in (1941–43), 126; Soviet partisans active near, 127; Germans driven from (1943–44), 129

Lugansk: large German community in (by 1914), 39; industry in (by 1900), 71; annexed to the Independent Ukraine (1918), 97; name changed to Voroshilov, 139; for further index entries see Voroshilov

Lunacharsky, Anatoli Vasilevich: in Switzerland at the time of the revolution (1917), 88

Lüneburg: a Hansa town, 20

Lutsk: becomes part of Russia (1795), 41, 43; a Polish town (since 1921), annexed by the Soviet Union (1939), 114; annexed by Germany (1941), 123

Lvov (Lemberg): a principal town of the Kingdom of Poland, 23; under Roman Catholic control, 24; Jews murdered in (1648–52), 31; annexed by Austria from Poland (1772), 42, 43; Bolshevik propaganda enters Russia through (1903–14), 73; Russians occupy (1914), 81; Russians driven from (1915), 82; Russians fail to retake (1916), 83; second Russian offensive against, unsuccessful (1917), 89; Red Army fails to capture (1920), 96; part of the West Ukrainian Republic (1918), 97; occupied by the Poles (1919), 100; annexed by the Soviet Union (1939), 114, 116; occupied by the Germans (1941), 118, 119; Jewish uprising against the Germans in, 123; Germans driven from (1944), 130; reincorporated into the Soviet Union (1945), 133

Macedonia: and Russian policy in the Balkans (1876–85), 78

Magadan: principal town of the Kolyma River forced labour area, 111

Magdagachi: and the Soviet-Chinese border (1970), 143

Magnitogorsk: many Ukrainians settled at (by 1937), 98; a German plan for (1941), 122; over a quarter of a million inhabitants (1959), 138

Magyars: settle along the middle Danube, 12; converted to Roman Catholicism, 15

Maikop: annexed by Russia (1864), 48; revolutionary outbreak at (1905), 76; occupied by the Germans (1942), 124, 128

Maimaichin: under Chinese control, 40; and Russian trade with China (1850–70), 59

Majdanek: a German concentration camp, 123

Makhachkala: part of the Terek Peoples' SSR (1918–19), 104; Germans fail to reach (1941–43), 128

Makhno, Nestor Ivanovich: controls large area of southern Russia (1918–20), 95

Maklakovo: and the Northern Sea Route administration, 112

Malaya Vishera: Nicholas II's train halted at (1917), 86; Germans occupy (1941), 126

Malo Yaroslavets: under German military rule (1942), 123

Manchester (USA): Ukrainians at, 99

Manchuria: area of growing Russian influence (after 1895), 67; liberated from Japan by Soviet troops, and returned to China (1945), 142

Manfredonia (Italy): bombarded by the Russian fleet (1798–1800), 45

Mangalia: occupied by Russia (1810, 1828), 46

Mangazeia: founded (1601), 33

Mannerheim, General: active against the Bolsheviks (1918–19), 94; defeats Finnish Bolsheviks (1918), 100

Mannerheim Line: Finnish defences, broken by the Soviet Army (1940), 115

Manych, River: German advance to (1941–43), 128

Marienwerder: ruled by the Teutonic Knights, 20

Mariupol: occupied by German troops (1918), 91; attacked by anarchists (1918–20), 95; annexed to the Independent Ukraine (1918), 97; name changed to Zhdanov, 139

Marseilles: Russian students in, 70

Mary: a non-Slav tribe, revolting against Russian rule (1606–07), 29; famine in homeland of (1921), 102; an Autonomous Soviet Socialist Republic, 144

Masurian Lakes (East Prussia): Russians defeated by the Germans at (1914), 81

Mauritius: Soviet fishing agreement with (1970), 141

Mazepa, Ivan Stepanovich: leads Cossack revolt (1708), 37

Mazovians: a Slav tribe north of the Pripet marshes, 12

Medes: their settlement by 800 BC, 1

Mediterranean Sea: reached by nomads from central Asia, 2; Vikings penetrate to, 11; Eastern Catholicism, Roman Catholicism and Islam established around, 15; Mongol conquests reach eastern shores of, 21; Roman Catholicism extends its control in east of, 24; Russian naval activity against France in (1798–1800), 45; and Soviet naval strength, (1970), 141

Medyn: Ivan IV seizes land in region of, 28

Megri: anti-Bolshevik revolt in (1920–21), 104

Melitopol: anti-Jewish violence in, 69, 75; annexed to the Independent Ukraine (1918), 97; occupied by Germany (1941), 123

Memel: ruled by the Teutonic Knights, 20; under communist rule (since 1945), 36, 133, 145

Memphis (Egypt): reached by nomads from central Asia, 2

Merv: annexed by Russia (1884), 61; linked to Moscow by railway (1915), 62

Mesembria: Greek colony on the Black Sea, 3

Meshed (Turkey): proposed Russian railway through, 61

Meskhetians: deported by Stalin to Siberia (1944), 131

Messina (Sicily): bombarded by the Russian fleet (1798–1800), 45

Mexico: Trotsky in exile in, and assassinated (1940), 113

Mezen, River: Soviet labour camps established at the mouth of, 110

Michael Romanov: crowned Tsar (1613), 29; liberates Moscow and Novgorod from Polish and Swedish control, 30

Midia (Turkey): occupied by Russia (1829), 46, 51; to have been part of a 'Big Bulgaria' (1878) 78; promised to Russia by Britain and France (1915), 85

Mikhailovsk: Russian settlement in Alaska (founded 1799), 44

Milan (Italy): a centre of Roman Catholicism in 1000 AD, 15; occupied by the Russians in the war against France (1798–99), 49

Military Colonies: established by Alexander I, 50; revolts in, 52

Mineralnye Vody: revolution in (1905), 76; claimed as part of the Ukraine, 97

Minin and Pozharsky: organize Russian counter-attack against Poles (1611–12), 30

Minsk: conquered by the Lithuanians, 23; Jews murdered in (1648–52), 31; becomes part of Russia (1793), 41, 42, 43; anarchists active in (1905–06), 55; peasant discontent and serdom in (by 1860), 57, 58; trade unions in, infiltrated by Tsarist secret police (by 1903), 68; anti-Jewish violence in, 69, 75; Jewish political activity in, 70; agricultural workers

strike in Province of (1905), 75; German army fails to reach (1915), 82; occupied by anti-Bolshevik forces (1918–19), 92; occupied by the Poles (1920), 96; occupied by the Germans (1941), 118, 119; a German plan for (1941), 122; Jewish uprising against the Germans in, 123; Germans driven from (1944), 130; over half a million inhabitants (1959), 138

Minusinsk: a town of exile in Siberia, 54, 72

Mir: annexed by Russia (1795), 43; occupied by Germany (1941), 123

Mitava (Mitau): under Roman Catholic control, 24; annexed by Russia (1795), 43; industrial growth of (by 1860), 56; Jewish political activity in, 70; industry in (by 1900), 71; and German war aims (1914), 80; German army enters (1915), 82

Mlava: a centre of Polish revolt against Russia (1860), 53; and German war aims (1914), 80; Germans occupy (1914), 81

Mogilev: Polish invasion of Russia launched from (1610), 30 Alexander I establishes military colonies in Province of (1810–25), 50; peasant discontent and serfdom in Province of (by 1860) 57, 58; anti-Jewish violence in, 69; Jewish political activity in 70; the Tsar's military headquarters at (1915–17), 84, 86 German SS headquarters at (1942), 123

Mogochin: shipbuilding at (after 1937), 112

Molotov: for earlier index entries see Perm: Soviet labour camps established near, 110; factories moved to (1940–42), 113; city of over half a million inhabitants (1959), 138

Monasteries: their foundation and spread within Russia, 16 and the eastern colonization of Novgorod, 19

Mongolia: under Soviet occupation (1945–46), 142; and the Soviet-Chinese border (1970), 143

Mongols: attack the Novgorodian town of Torzhok (1238), 18 their Empire (by 1300), 21; their conquest of Russia, 22, 146 driven from Russia by the Muscovites, 25; under Chinese control (by 1720), 40; 250,000 in the Bolshevik-controlled Far Eastern Republic (1920–22), 106

Montenegro: and European diplomacy (1890–1907), 64; and Russian policy in the Balkans (1876–1914), 78, 79

Montpellier: Russian students at the university of, 70

Montreal (Canada): Ukrainians at, 99

Moravians: a western Slav tribe, 12

Mordva: a non-Slav tribe, revolting against Russian rule, 29

Moshchny Island (Gulf of Finland): Germans fail to capture (1941–43), 126

Moscow: Orthodox monastery established at, 16; its conquests and expansion (by 1533), 25; and the rivers of European Russia, 27; Ivan IV seizes land in, 28; uprising in (1648–50) 32; peasants flee from serfdom in, to become Cossacks, 35 administrative centre of a Province established by Peter the Great, 38; Napoleon advances towards (1812), 49, 146 railway to St Petersburg from patrolled by a special Gendarme squadron (from 1846), 51; Anarchist group meets in (1840–80), 55; the industrial growth of (by 1860), 56; peasant discontent in the Province of (1827–60), 57; serfdom in the Province of (by 1860), 58; and Russian trade with China (1850–70), 59; and the opening of the Trans-Siberian and Asian railway systems, 62; strikes in (1885–1903), 68; Jews expelled from (1891), 69; Jewish political activity in, 70; and Russian industry (by 1900), 71; political assassinations in, 72 Bolsheviks active in (1903–14), 73; revolution in (1905), 76, 77 anti-war agitation at (1917), 84; secret police headquarters at burnt (1917), 86; Bolsheviks seize power in (1917), 91; alleged subversive communist activity in, 108; Soviet labour camp to the north of, 110; factories evacuated from (1940–42), 113 Treaty of, with Finland (1940), 115; a German plan for (1941) 122; a German military plan to attack from the east (1942) 124; five million inhabitants (by 1959), 138; twice occupied by the invaders of Russia (1612, 1812), 146

Mozdok: claimed as part of the Ukraine, 97; part of the Terek Peoples' SSR (1918–20), 104

Mozyr: Jews murdered in (1648–52), 31; annexed by Russia (1793), 43

Msta, River: and the river systems of European Russia, 27

Mukden (China): and the Soviet-Chinese border (1970), 143

Munich: Lenin in, 73
Munschengratz: Treaty of (1833), 51
Muraviev, Nikolai Nikolaevich: advocates Russian expansion in the Far East, 60
Murmansk: Lenin plans to return to Russia through (1917), 87; occupied by British troops (1918–19), 91, 92, 94; Kara Sea Expedition stops at (1921), 105; labour camp near, 109; and the Northern Sea Route, 112; allied aid enters the Soviet Union through (1941–45), 121; a German plan for (1941), 122
Murom: within Kievan Russia, 13; anti-Jewish violence in, 69, 75
Muromski monastery: 19
Murom-Riazan: a Russian Principality, 17; conquered by the Mongols, 22
Mus: occupied by Russia (1829), 46; occupied by Russia (1916), 83; Armenian claims to (1918), 104
Mylga: Soviet labour camp at, 111

Nachichevan: annexed by Russia (1828), 48
Naissus: Roman city in the Balkans, 4, 7; raided by the Goths, 5; for subsequent references see index entry for Nish
Nanking (China): Soviet air units defend against Japanese attack (1941), 142
Naples: bombarded by the Russian fleet (1798–1800), 45; Russia opposes national revolution in (1815–25), 50
Napoleon I: and Russia, 49, 146
Narva: ruled by the Teutonic Knights, 20; taken by Russia from Sweden (1721), 36, 37, 47; industrial growth of (after 1860), 56; revolution at (1905), 76; Bolshevik influence in (1917), 89; anti-Bolshevik forces advance on Petrograd from (1919), 93; Soviet partisans attack the Germans near (1941–42), 127
Narym: founded (1596), 33; a town of exile in Tsarist times, 54, 72; a Bolshevik leader in, at the time of the revolution (1917), 88; Soviet labour camp at, 111
Nebolchi: a town in the Republic of Novgorod, 18
Nerchinsk: founded (1659), 33, 40; in the Bolshevik-controlled Far Eastern Republic (1920–22), 106
Nerchinskii Zavod: and the Siberian exiles, 54
Neuri: possible Slav tribe named by Herodotus, 3
Nevel: Jews murdered in (1648–52), 31; Germans driven by the Soviet army from (1943–44), 129
New Archangel (Sitka): Russian settlement in Alaska (founded 1804), 44
New York (USA): Russian Bolshevik leaders in (1917), 88; Ukrainians at, 99
Nezhin: anarchists active in (1905–06), 55; anti-Jewish violence in, 69
Nicaea: raided by the Goths, 5
Nicholas I: Russia during his reign (1825–1855), 51; restricts Polish liberties, 52
Nicholas II: and the 1905 revolution, 76; lives in increasing isolation at his military headquarters (1916–17), 84; tries in vain to return to Petrograd (1917), 86
Nicomedia: raided by the Goths, 5
Niemen, River: a highway of trade for Kievan Russia, 14; mouth of controlled by Teutonic Knights, 20; Soviet Union controls mouth of (after 1945), 36; Catherine the Great extends Russian frontier to the eastern bank of (by 1796), 41
Nikolaev: Alexander I establishes military colonies in Province of (1810–25), 50; special Gendarme detachment at, 51; its growth (by 1860), 56; strikes in (before 1905), 68; Jewish poverty in, 70; industry in (by 1900), 71; revolution at (1905), 76; bombarded by the Turks (1915), 85; occupied by German troops (1918), 91, 146; annexed to the Independent Ukraine (1918), 97; in the Soviet Union (from 1919), occupied by the Germans (1942), 119, 128; Germans driven from (1943–44), 129
Nikolaevka: anti-Jewish violence in, 69
Nikolaevskii Station (Moscow): held by Government troops during the uprising of 1905, 77
Nikolaevsk-na-Amure: founded (1850), 60, 66; in the Bolshevik-controlled Far Eastern Republic (1920–22), 106

Nikopol: occupied by Russia (1829), 46; attacked by anarchists (1918–20), 95; occupied by Germany (1941), 123
Nish: Mongols raid in region of, 22; annexed by Serbia from Turkey (1878), 78
Niuvchim: industry at (by 1800), 34
Nizhnekolymsk: founded (1644), 33; a port of the Northern Sea Route, 112
Nizhneudinsk: a town of exile in Siberia, 64
Nizhni Novgorod: Orthodox monastery established at, 16; conquered by the Principality of Moscow, 25; dispossessed landowners flee to, 28; Russian counter-attack against Poles launched from (1611), 30; trade fair at, 34; terrorist activity in region of (1905–06), 55; industrial growth in the region of (by 1860), 56; peasant discontent in the Province of (1827–60), 57; serfdom in (by 1860), 58; anti-Jewish violence in, 69; political assassinations in, 72; secret Bolshevik printing press in, 73; peasant uprising in Province of (1905), 75; revolutionary outbreak at (1905), 76; name changed to Gorky, 139; for subsequent index entries see Gorky
Nizhni-Tagilsk: industry at (by 1800), 34
Noginsk: a town in the Tungus coal basin, 112
Nordvik: on the Northern Sea Route, 112
Norrköping (Sweden): attacked by Russia (1710–21), 37
North Korea: under Soviet occupation (1945–47), 142
Norway: signs trade agreement with Bolshevik Russia (1921), 101; Trotsky in exile in, 113
Norylsk: Soviet labour camp at, 111; in the Tungus coal basin, 112
Nöteborg: taken by Russia from Sweden (1721), 47
Novaya Ladoga: and the siege of Leningrad (1941–43), 126
Novaya Uda: Stalin in exile at, 54
Novaya Zemlya: Soviet labour camp at, 111, 112
Novgorod: Viking settlers at, 11; ruled by the Varangarians, 12, 13; a principal trading centre (by 1050), 14; a centre of Eastern Catholicism, 15; Orthodox monastery established at, 16; the principal town of the Republic of Novgorod, 17, 18; the eastern trade and colonization of, 19; branch trading station of the Hanseatic League established at, 20; outside the area of Mongol conquests, 21; incorporated in the Principality of Moscow, 25; and the river systems of European Russia, 27; Ivan IV seizes lands to the east of, 28; occupied by Sweden (1613), 30; uprising in (1648–50), 32; Alexander I establishes military colonies in Province of (1810–25), 50; peasant discontent in the Province of (1827–60), 57; serfdom in (by 1860), 58; anti-Bolshevik forces fail to capture (1919), 93, 94; occupied by the Germans (1941), 118, 126; Soviet partisans active near (1941–42), 127; Germans driven from (1943–44), 129
Novi Pazar: and Russian policy in the Balkans (1876–85), 78
Novgorod-Seversk: a Russian Principality, 17; conquered by the Mongols, 22
Novocherkassk: industry in (by 1900), 71; political assassinations in, 72; occupied by German troops (1918), 91
Novogrudok: annexed by Russia (1795), 43
Novo Radomsk: Germans occupy (1914), 81
Novorzhev: Soviet partisans active near (1941–42), 127
Novosibirsk: Ukrainians at (by 1937), 98; occupied by anti-Bolshevik forces (1918–19), 103; Northern Sea Route Committee headquarters (1920–25), 112; factories moved to (1940–42), 113, 121; a German plan for (1941), 122; over half a million inhabitants (1959), 138; and the Soviet-Chinese border (1970), 143
Novorossiisk: large German community in (by 1914), 39; annexed by Russia (1829), 48; strikes in (before 1905), 68; revolution in (1905), 76; bombarded by the Turks (1914), 85; occupied by anti-Bolshevik forces (1919), 92; claimed as part of the Ukraine, 97; United States famine relief arrives at (1921), 102; a German plan for (1941), 122; occupied by the Germans (1942), 128; Germans driven from (1943), 129
Novy Port: on the Northern Sea Route, 112
Nyda: Kara Sea Expedition visits (1921), 105
Nystad: Treaty of (1721), 47

Ob, River: lower reaches of form part of the trade route system of the Republic of Novgorod (by 1450), 19; Russian rule extended along, 26; and the river systems of the Urals and European Russia, 27; early Russian settlements on, 33; and the Siberian exile system, 54; and Russian trade with China (1850–70), 59; Ukrainian settlements on the upper reaches of (by 1937), 98; Kara Sea Expedition visits lower reaches of (1921), 105; Soviet labour camps on, 111; industry on the upper reaches of (1970), 137

Obodrichi: a western Slav tribe, 12

Obski Gorodok: founded (1585), 26

Ochakov: siege of (1788), 46

Ochrid: a centre of Eastern Catholicism, 15

Oder, River: Germanic tribes settle along, 4, 5; controlled by the Huns, 6; Slav settlements along, 7; controlled by the Avars, 8; controlled by the Slavs, 9, 10; becomes part of the Holy Roman Empire, under German rule, 20

Odessa: a main Russian shipbuilding centre, on the Black Sea, 34; large German community in (by 1914), 39; annexed by Russia from the Turks (1791), 41, 43; special Gendarme detachment at, 51; anarchists active at (1905–06), 55; a principal port for imports and exports (by 1860), 56; strikes in (before 1905), 68; anti-Jewish violence in, 69, 75; Jewish political acitivity in, 70; industry in (by 1900), 71; Bolshevik activity in (1903–14), 73; revolution in (1905), 76; Turkish bombardment of (1914), 85; occupied by German troops (1918), 91; occupied by French troops (1918–19), 92, 146; anarchists in (1918), 95; annexed to the Independent Ukraine (1918), 97; Soviet aid for Republican Spain leaves from (1936–39), 101; United States famine relief arrives at (1921), 102; occupied by the Germans (1941), 118, 119, 121; a German plan to control (1941), 122; German SS headquarters at (1941), 123; Germans driven from (1944), 129; Soviet naval forces based on (1970), 141

Odessus: Greek colony on the Black Sea, 3; for further index entries see, first Haji-bey and then Odessa

Oka, River: and the river systems of European Russia, 27; dispossessed landowners settle along, 29

Okhotsk: founded (1649), 33, 40

Okhotsk, Sea of: early Russian settlements on, 33

Okhta: strike at (1917), 86

Olbia: Greek colony on the Black Sea, 3; controlled by the Khazars, 10; Viking settlers reach, 11

Old Kodiak: Russian settlement in Alaska, 44

Oleg: Varangarian ruler, establishes his capital at Kiev, 12

Olekminsk: Ukrainians at, 98

Olevsk: annexed by Russia (1793), 43

Olonets: a town in the Republic of Novgorod, 18; anti-Bolshevik forces fail to capture (1918–19), 94

Oman: comes under British control (1895), 61

Omsk: founded (1716), 40; a town of exile in Siberia, 54; political assassinations in (1904–07), 72; Ukrainians at (by 1937), 98; occupied by anti-Bolshevik forces (1918–19), 103; and the Northern Sea Route administration, 112; factories moved to (1940–42), 113; a German plan for (1941), 122; Virgin Lands scheme extended to (after 1953), 136; over half a million inhabitants (by 1959), 138

Onega: occupied by anti-Bolshevik forces (1918–19), 92, 94

Onega Bay: labour camps on, 109

Onega, Lake: in the Republic of Novgorod, 18; anti-Bolshevik forces reach northern shores of (1918–19), 94; Soviet labour camps established at the northern shores of (1920–36), 109; Finns occupy the western shore of, during the siege of Leningrad (1941–43), 126

Onega, River: within the Republic of Novgorod, 18, 19; and the river systems of European Russia, 27; Soviet labour camps established on, 110

Opochka: attacked by the Lithuanians (1213), 18; Soviet partisans active against the Germans in (1941–42), 127

Ordzhonikidze, Grigori Konstantinovich: in exile in Siberia at the time of the revolution (1917), 88

Ordzhonikidze: for earlier entries see Vladikavkaz: Germans fail to capture (1941–43), 128

Orel: dispossessed landowners settle in, 28; within area of peasants' revolt (1906–07), 29; a heavily populated area of Russia (by 1724), 38; centre of an Anarchist group (1840–80), 55; industrial growth in the region of (by 1860), 56; peasant discontent and serfdom in (by 1860), 57, 58; peasant poverty in Province of (by 1904), 68; peasant uprising in Province of (1905), 75; occupied by anti-Bolshevik forces (1919), 92; Denikin fails to capture (1919), 97; occupied by the Germans (1941), 118, 123, 124; Germans driven from (1943), 129

Orenburg: Cossacks settle in, 35; and Russian trade with China (1850–70), 59; Bolsheviks seize power in (1917), 91; famine in (1921), 102; anti-Bolshevik revolt in region of (1917–20), 103; name changed to Chkalov, 139; for subsequent index entries see Chkalov

Oreshek: attacked by the Swedes, 18

Orléans: Huns defeated by the Franks at, 6

Orsha: Jews murdered in (1648–52), 31

Orsk: industry at (1941–45), 121

Osel: Baltic Island, ruled by the Teutonic Knights, 20; taken by Russia from Sweden (1721), 36, 47; and German war aims (1914), 80

Ossetia: annexed by Russia (1806), 48

Ostrov: uprising in (1648–50), 32; Soviet partisans active against the Germans in (1941–42), 127

Otpor: and the Soviet-Chinese border (1970), 143

Ottawa (Canada): Ukrainians at, 99

Ottoman Empire: Russia fails to capture Jassy and Braila from (1711), 37; joins Russia against France, bombarding French controlled ports in the Mediterranean (1798–1800), 45; its five wars with Russia (between 1721 and 1829), 46; and European diplomacy (1872–1907), 63, 64; and Russian policies in the Balkans (1876–1914), 78, 79; and the war with Russia (1914–17), 83

Oxus, River: crossed by nomads from central Asia, 2; Huns extend their rule to, 6; Khazars rule from the Black Sea to, 10; within the Mongol dominions, 21; and Russian trade with China (1850–70), 59

Pakistan: Soviet fishing agreement with (1970), 141

Palanga: Baltic port, annexed by Russia (1795), 43; area of Polish partisan activity against Russia (1831), 52

Paleostrovskii monastery: 19

Palermo (Sicily): bombarded by the Russian fleet (1798–1800), 45

Palestine: Russian Jews emigrate to, 70

Pamir: annexed by Russia (1895), 61

Pamplona: Viking settlers reach, 11

Panfilov: and the Soviet-Chinese border (1970), 143

Panticapaeum: Greek colony on the Black Sea, 3

Paris: Viking settlers reach, 11; Alexander I advances to (1812), 49; Russian students in, 70; Lenin in exile in (1908–12), 73; Lenin plans to return to Russia through (1917), 87; a Bolshevik leader returns to Russia from (1917), 88; communist propaganda disseminated in, 108

Paris Peace Conference: Poles defy (1919), 100

Paul, Tsar: sends Cossack army to invade India (1801), 49

Pavlodar: Ukrainians at, 98; in Virgin Lands Region (established 1953), 136

Pavlovsk: conversions to Judaism in (1796–1825), 50

Peasant discontent: near Vologda, under Alexander I, 50; in the Province of Pskov, under Nicholas I, 51; throughout Russia, 56; and serfdom, 57; before the 1905 revolution, 68; in 1905, 75

Pechenegs: the Varangarians protect the Slavs from, 11; pay tribute to Kievan Russia, 13

Pechora, River: part of the trade route system of the Republic of Novgorod, 19; and the river systems of European Russia, 27; dispossessed landowners settle along, 28; coal basin to the east of, 112; Stalinist deportation of national groups to (1941–45), 131

Peking: and Russian trade with China (1850–70), 59; linked to Russia by Railway (1903), 62; Moscow establishes communist

Party cell in (1920–24), 142; and the Soviet-Chinese border (1970), 143

Penjdeh: annexed by Russia (1885), 61

Penza: in area of peasants' revolt (1670–71), 32; peasant discontent in the Province of (1827–60), 57; serfom in (by 1860), 58; industry in (by 1900), 71; political assassinations in, 72; peasant uprising in Province of (1905), 75; Bolsheviks seize power in (1917), 91; famine in (1921), 102

Peregonovka: anarchist victory at (1919), 95

Perekop: battle of (1771), 46

Peresechen: a town conquered by Kievan Russia, 13

Pereyaslavl: a town in Kievan Russia, 13; Orthodox monastery established at, 16; chief town of the Principality of, 17; captured by the Mongols, 22; annexed by Russia from Poland, 31; anti-Jewish violence in, 69

Perm: Russian Principality of, conquered by Moscow, 25; industrial growth in the region of, 56; peasant discontent in the Province of (1827–60), 57; serfdom in (by 1860), 58; and Russian trade with China (1850–70), 59; and Russian industry (by 1900), 71; uprising in (1905), 76; controlled by anti-Bolshevik forces (1918–19), 92, 146; famine in (1921), 102; name changed to Molotov, 139; *for subsequent index entries see* Molotov

Permiaks: a nomadic, heathen tribe west of the Urals, 16

Pernau: taken by Russia from Sweden (1721), 36

Perovsk: and the Russian line of forts in Central Asia (1854–64), 61; name changed, first to Ak-Mechet, then to Kzyl-Orda, 139

Persia (Iran): Viking settlers reach, 11; Russian annexations from (1723), 37; Russian and British spheres of influence in (1907), 61; Russians advance through, to counter Turkish attacks (1915–16), 85; United States aid enters the Soviet Union through (1941–45), 120

Persian Gulf: British influence in (from 1867), 61; United States aid reaches the Soviet Union through (1941–45), 120

Persians: control Black Sea colonies before 500 BC, 3

Peter the Great: encourages Russian industrial growth, 34; wars of, and revolts against (1695–1723), 37; establishes Provincial divisions inside Russia, 38; and the incorporation of the Baltic Germans in Russia, 39; and the Great Northern War against Sweden (1700–21), 47; his annexations in western Russia (1721), 145

Petrograd: Nicholas II unable to reach (1917), 86; the return of the Bolshevik leaders to (1917), 88; Bolshevik influence in (1917), 89; the October Revolution in (1917), 90, 91; anti-Bolsheviks fail to capture (1919), 93, 94, 100; United States famine relief arrives at (1921), 102; alleged communist subversive activity in, 108; *see henceforth index entry for* Leningrad

Petropavlovsk (Kazakhstan): in Virgin Lands Region (established 1953), 136

Petropavlovsk (Siberia): a port on the Northern Sea Route, 112

Petrovsk: a town of exile in Siberia, 54; in the Far Eastern Republic (1920–22), 106

Petrozavodsk: industry at (by 1800), 34; anti-Bolshevik forces fail to reach (1918–19), 94; Soviet labour camp established near (by 1936), 109; Finns advance towards, and occupy (1941–42), 126

Petsamo: Soviet Union obtains rights in region of (1940), 115

Pevek: a port on the Northern Sea Route, 112

Peza, River: a trade route of Novgorod, 19

Phanagoria: Greek colony at mouth of the Kuban river, 3; under Roman rule, 6; controlled by the Khazars, 10

Phasis: Roman settlement on the Black Sea, 4, 6, 7, 10

Philadelphia (USA): Ukrainians at, 99

Piatigorsk: revolution in (1905), 76

Pilten: ruled by the Teutonic Knights, 20

Pinega: Ivan IV seizes land in region of, 28; occupied by anti-Bolshevik forces (1918–19), 94

Pinsk: conquered by the Lithuanians, 23; Jews murdered in (1648–52), 31; large German community in (by 1914), 39; incorporated in Russia (1793), 41, 42; part of the Ukrainian

Peoples' Republic (1917), 80; Austro-German army occupies (1915), 82; annexed by Poland from Lithuania (1921), 96; annexed by the Soviet Union (1939), 114, 116; reincorporated in the Soviet Union (1945), 133

Piotrkow: large German community in (by 1914), 39; German army occupies (1914), 81

Pishpek: anti-Bolshevik revolt at (1917–20), 103; name changed to Frunze, 139; *for subsequent index entries see* Frunze

Pityus: Roman settlement on the eastern shore of the Black Sea, 4; raided by the Goths, 5

Plevna: Russians defeat Turks at (1876), 78

Plotsk: German army occupies (1914), 81; Poles defend from the Red Army (1920), 96

Podlesia: annexed by Russia, 41

Podolia: annexed by Russia (1793), 41, 43; peasant discontent and serfdom in (by 1860), 57, 58; agricultural workers strike in Province of (1905), 75; and the proposed Union of Border States (1919), 100

Pogost-na-more: a town in the Republic of Novgorod, 18

Pokrovsk: a Bolshevik leader in exile at, at the time of the revolution (1917), 88; name changed to Engels, 139

Poland: Mongols raid, 22; unites with Lithuania, 23; a Roman Catholic State, 24; invades Russia and reoccupies Moscow, 30; peasants flee from serfdom in, and become Cossacks, 35; partitioned by Russia, Austria and Prussia (1768–95), 42, 43; revolt in, suppressed by Russia (1831), 51; rebels from, exiled to Siberia, 54; and German war aims (1914), 80; Russia's promises of autonomy to (1914), 84; the increasing national aspirations of (by 1917), 89; intervenes against the Bolsheviks (1918–19), 92; and the Russo-Polish war, (1920), 96; and the Ukraine (1920), 97; and the proposed Union of Border States (1920), 100; signs non-agression Pact with Soviet Union (1932), 101; Russian refugees in (by 1930), 107; strongly anti-communist (in the 1930's), 108; attacked by Germany and Russia (1939), 114; population movements from (1939–46), 132; a communist regime established in (1945), 133; anti-Soviet revolt in (1956), 134

Poles: a western Slav tribe, 12; Kievan Russia extends its territory to the borderlands of, 13; converted to Roman Catholicism, 15; increasingly discontented by Russian rule (by 1905), 68, 76; eight million in Russia (1897), 14

Polianians: a Slav tribe settled near Kiev, 12

Polochane: a Slav tribe north of the Pripet marshes, 12

Pologi: anarchist headquarters at (1918–20), 95

Polotsk: a town in Kievan Russia, 13; Orthodox monastery established at, 16; principal town of a Russian Principality, 17; conquered by the Mongols, 22; conquered by the Lithuanians, 23; Jews murdered in, 31; Jewish political activity in, 70

Poltava: conquered by the Lithuanians, 23; annexed by Russia, 31; trade fair at, 34; Cossack leader Mazepa defeated at (1708), 37; serfdom in the Province of (by 1860), 58; peasant rioting common in the Province of (1902–04), 68; political activity in, 70; political assassinations in, 72; Bolsheviks active in (1903–14), 73; peasant uprising in Province of (1905), 75; occupied by German troops (1918), 91; anarchist headquarters at (1918–20), 95; part of the Independent Ukrainian State (1917), 97; famine in (1921), 102; occupied by Germany (1941), 123

Ponoy, River: northern boundary of the Republic of Novgorod, 18

Porkkala (Finland): leased by the Soviet Union (1945–55), 145

Porkhov: a town in the Republic of Novgorod, 18; German reprisals against Russian civilians in (1941–43), 126

Port Arthur: Russian port in China, linked to Russia by railway (1903), 62, 65; captured by Japan (1905), 67; under Soviet rule (1945–55), 142

Port Said (Egypt): Soviet naval facilities at (1970), 141

Posiet Bay: Chinese territory, annexed by Russia (1860), 60

Posnan: Polish town, annexed by Prussia (1793), 42; part of Poland (1918–39 and since 1945), scene of anti-Soviet revolt (1956), 134

Potemkin (Russian battleship: crew seize control of (1905), 76

Poti: battles of (1809, 1829), 46; annexed by Russia (1804), 48; strikes in (before 1905), 68; Turks advance on (1917), 85; occupied by the Germans (1918), 104, 146; Germans fail to reach (1941–43), 128

Potsdam (Germany): conference at (1945), 113

Povorotnyi, Cape: Chinese territory, annexed by Russia (1860), 60

Prague: in the Holy Roman Empire, 20; Lenin in exile in (1912), 73; communist propaganda disseminated in, 108; communism established in (1948), 113; within Greater Germany (1939–45), 117; and the defeat of Germany (1944–45), 130; anti-Soviet revolt in (1968), 134

Predvinsk: shipbuilding at (after 1937), 112

Preslav: a Slav town in the Balkans, 12; within the area paying tribute to Kievan Russia, 13

Preslavets: a town paying tribute to Kievan Russia, 13

Pribilov Islands: Russian, sold to the United States (1867), 44

Prince Albert (Canada): Ukrainians at, 99

Prinkipo (Turkey): Trotsky in exile at, 113

Pripet Marshes: early Slav settlements in, 1, 4; controlled by the Goths, 5; controlled by the Huns, 6; controlled by the Slavs, 7; controlled by the Avars, 8; Slavs re-establish their control of, 9, 10; within Kievan Russia, 14; Polish, annexed by Russia (1793 and 1795), 42, 43; Germans hope to extend their territory towards (1914), 79; Polish army advances to (1920), 97; Russian army occupies Polish part of (1939), 114; occupied by the Germans (1941), 118, 119; Soviet army reaches (1944), 129

Prostitutes: exiled to Siberia, 54

Proudhon, Pierre Joseph: 'Property is theft', 55

Provedeniya Bay: on the Northern Sea Route, 112

Provinces of Russia: the boundaries, as established by Peter the Great, 38; as redrawn by Catherine the Great, 41; in 1900 (74)

Prussia: a Roman Catholic region, 24; Catherine the Great gives Russia a common frontier with, 41; a party to three partitions of Poland (1772, 1793, 1795), 42; Russia allies with, against Sweden (1714), 47; helps Russia suppress Polish revolt (1860), 53

Pruth, River: a highway of trade in Kievan Russia, 14; Russians fail to drive Turks from (1711), 37

Przemysl (Peremyshl): a town conquered by Kievan Russia, 13; a Polish town, Jews murdered in (1648–52), 31; annexed by Austria (1772), 43; Russians occupy (1914), 81; 81; Russians driven from (1915), 82; part of the West Ukrainian Republic (1918), 97; Polish (since 1921), annexed by the Soviet Union (1939), 114, 116; annexed by Germany (1941), 123

Pskov: a town in Kievan Russia, 13; Orthodox monastery established at, 16; frequently attacked by Teutonic Knights, 18, 20; conquered by the Principality of Moscow, 25; uprising in (1648–50), 32; peasant uprising in province of (1826–27), 51; peasant discontent and serfdom in the Province of (by 1860), 58; political assassinations in, 72; Bolsheviks active in, 73; agricultural workers strike in Province of (1905), 75; Nicholas II put under arrest at (1917), 86; occupied by German troops (1918), 91; occupied by the Germans (1941), 118, 119, 123, 126; Soviet partisans active near (1941–42), 127

Pskov, Lake of: western shore of reached by the Teutonic Knights, 20; Soviet partisans active against the Germans along eastern shore of (1941–42), 127

Pudozhskoi: a town in the Republic of Novgorod, 18

Pushkin, Alexander Sergeevich: urges the Siberian exile, 'keep your patience proud', 54

Pushkinskiye Gori: Soviet partisans near (1941–42), 127

Pustozersk: town founded by the Republic of Novgorod, 19; and the river systems of European Russia, 27

Putilov works (near Petrograd): strike in, suppressed by the army (1916), 84; further strike at (1917), 86

Qatar: comes under British control (1892), 61

Radek, Karl: in Switzerland at the time of the revolution (1917), 88

Radimichians: an eastern Slav tribe, 12

Radishchev, Alexander Nikolaevich: exiled to Siberia, 54

Radomsk: a centre of Polish revolt against Russia (1860), 53

Rakovsky, Christian: in Rumania at the time of the revolution (1917), 88

Razin, Stenka: leads peasants' revolt (1670–71), 32; peasants' flee eastwards across Urals after failure of revolt of, 33

Regina (Canada): Ukrainians at, 99

Republic of Novgorod: a Russian Principality, 17; styled 'Sovereign Great Novgorod', 18; unconquered by the Mongols, 21, 22; unconquered by the Lithuanians, 23; conquered by the Principality of Moscow, 25

Resht: Persian town, annexed by Russia (1723–25), 37

Reval (Tallin): and German eastward expansion (by 1500), 20; Roman Catholic control in, 24; taken by Russia from Sweden (1721), 36, 37, 47, 145; industrial growth of (after 1860), 56; strikes at (1905), 76; Germans hope to annex (1914), 79; Bolshevik influence in (1917), 89; United States famine relief arrives at (1921), 102; annexed by the Soviet Union (1939), 115, 116; a German plan for (1941), 122; German SS headquarters in, 123; reincorporated into the Soviet Union (1945), 133

Revolution of 1905: prelude to (1894–1904), 68; 75, 76, 77

Revolution of 1917: 86, 87, 88, 89, 90, 91

Rezhitsa: Tsarist troops move on Petrograd from (1917), 86

Rhine, River: within the Roman Empire, 4; Germanic tribes control eastern bank of, 5; controlled by the Huns, 6

Riabaya Mogila: battle of (1770), 46

Riazan: conquered by Kievan Russia, 13; conquered by the Principality of Moscow, 25; an industrial centre (by 1800), 34; in the most heavily populated area of Russia (in 1724), 38; industrial growth in the region of (by 1860), 56; peasant discontent in the Province of (1827–60), 57; serfdom in (by 1860), 58; peasant poverty in Province of (by 1904), 68; peasant uprising in Province of (1905), 75; a German plan for (1941), 122

Riga: and German eastward expansion (by 1500), 20; and Russian exports of timber and grain from (by 1800), 34; taken by Russia from Sweden (1721), 36, 37, 47, 145; large German community in (by 1914), 39; Napoleon advances near (1812), 49; anarchists active in (1905–06), 55; an industrial centre (by 1860), 56; strikes in (before 1905), 68; Jewish political activity in, 70; industry in (by 1900), 71; Bolshevik activity in (1903–14), 73; revolution in (1905), 76; Germans hope to annex (1914), 79, 80; German army fails to reach (1915), 82; Tsarist troops move on Petrograd from (1917), 86; Bolshevik influence in (1917), 89; occupied by German troops (1918), 91; Treaty of (March 1921), 96; United States famine relief arrives at (1921), 102; annexed by the Soviet Union (1939), 116; occupied by the Germans (1941), 118, 119; a German plan for (1941), 122; Jewish uprising against the Germans in, 123; Germans driven from (1944), 130; reincorporated into the Soviet Union (1945), 133; over half a million inhabitants (1959), 138

Rochester (USA): Ukrainians at, 99

Roman Catholicism: established in western Europe, 15; extends its control eastwards, 24

Roman Empire: extends its rule to western shore of the Caspian Sea, 4

Romanov: uprising in (1648–50), 32

Romanovs: rule Russia (1613–1917), 29

Rosenberg, Alfred: draws up plan for partition of the Soviet Union (1941), 122

Rostock: a Hansa town on the Baltic, 20; under communist control (since 1945), 36; anti-communist revolt in (1953), 134

Rostov (Old Rostov): within Kievan Russia, 13; Orthodox monastery established at, 16

Rostov-on-Don: anti-Jewish violence in, 69; Bolsheviks in (1903–14), 73; revolution in (1905), 76; occupied by German troops (1918), 91; occupied by anti-Bolshevik forces (1919), 92, 146; claimed as part of the Ukraine, 97; Soviet aid to Republican Spain leaves from (1936–39), 101; famine in (1921), 102; occupied by the Germans (1941), 118, 120, 121, 123, 124, 128; a German plan for (1941), 122; Germans driven from

(1943), 129; over half a million inhabitants (1959), 138

Rote Fahne: a German collective farm in the Soviet Union, 39

Rovno: annexed by Russia (1795), 43; revolution at (1905), 76; part of the Ukrainian Peoples' Republic (1917), 80; German army fails to reach (1915), 82; a Polish town (since 1921) annexed by the Soviet Union (1939), 114

Rumania: and European diplomacy (1872–1907), 63, 64; Russian sailors seek refuge in (1905), 76; and Russian policy in the Balkans (1876–1914), 78, 79; occupied by Germany and Austria (1916), 83; unsuccessful Russian attack on (1917), 89; intervenes against Bolsheviks (1918–19), 92; Ukrainian anarchist leader finds refuge in (1920), 95; reluctant to join Soviet Union in anti-German alliance (1939), 101; Russian refugees in (by 1930), 107; strongly anti-communist (in the 1930's), 108; Soviet annexations from (1940), 116; sends troops to fight with the Germans on the Russian front (1941), 110; establishes a military government over Bessarabia (1941), 123; Soviet army advances through (1944–45), 130; population movements from (1939–46), 132; under communist control (1945), 133; pursues foreign policy relatively independent from that of Soviet Union (since 1968), 134

Rurik: Varangarian ruler, leads expedition against Constantinople, 12; Kievan Russia ruled by the descendants of, 13

Rushchuk: sieges of (1771, 1811), 46

Ruza: uprising in (1648–50), 32

Rykov, Aleksei Ivanovich: in Siberia at the time of the revolution (1917), 88

Ryukyu Islands: annexed by Japan from China (1874), 66

Rzhev: German SS headquarters at (1942), 123

Sabirian Huns: settle at the mouth of the Volga, 7

Sakhalin: transferred to Russia from Japan (1875), 60; Japan annexes southern half of (1905), 67

St Lawrence Island: Russian, sold to the United States (1867), 44

St Louis (USA): Ukrainians at, 99

St Macarius: trade fair at, 34

St Petersburg: industry at (by 1800), 34; territory of, taken by Russia from Sweden, 36, 37; becomes the seat of the Russian Government (1712), 38; large German community in (by 1914), 39; Alexander I establishes military colonies in Province of (1910–25), 50; Decembrist uprising in (1825), 51; anarchist group meets in (1840–80), 55; industrial growth of (by 1860), 56; peasant discontent in the Province of (1827–60), 57; serfdom in the Province of (by 1860), 58; assassinations in (1902–04), 68; many Jews deported from (1891), 69; Jewish charitable institutions in, 70; political assassinations in, 72; Bolsheviks active in, 73; 'Bloody Sunday' in (1905), 76; Bolsheviks seize power in (1917), 84; see henceforth index entries Petrograd and Leningrad

Samara: founded (1586), 26; in area of peasants' revolt (1670–71), 32; Bashkir revolt in region of (1708–22), 37; centre of an Anarchist group (1840–80), 55; peasant discontent in the Province of (1827–60), 57; and Russian trade with China (1850–70), 59; political assassinations in (1903–14), 73; peasant uprising in Province of (1905), 75; revolution in (1905), 76; controlled by anti-Bolshevik forces (1919), 92, 146; famine in (1921), 102; alleged subversive communist activity in, 108; name changed to Kuibyshev, 139; for subsequent index entries see Kuibyshev

Samarkand: conquered by the Mongols, 20; and Russian trade with China (1850–70), 59; annexed by Russia (1868), 61; linked to Moscow by railway (1915), 62; anti-Bolshevik revolt in region of (1917–20), 103; factories moved to (1940–42), 113; a German plan for (1941), 122

Samsun: Black Sea port, under Roman Catholic control, 24

San Francisco (USA): Russian trading post founded to the north of (1811), 44

San Stephano: Treaty of (1878), 78

Sarai: Mongols of the Golden Horde establish their capital at, 21, 22; part of the Mongol Khanate of Astrakhan, 25

Sarajevo: assassination at (1914), 79

Saratov: founded (1590), 26; rebels march through, on way to Moscow (1606–07), 29; in area of peasants' revolt (1670–71), 32; an industrial centre (by 1800), 34; conversions to Judaism in (1796–1825), 50; peasant discontent in the Province of (1827–60), 57; serfdom in (by 1860), 58; peasant rioting frequent in Province of (1902–04), 68; ritual murder charge against Jews in, 69; political assassinations in, 72; Bolsheviks active in (1903–14), 73; peasant uprising in Province of (1905), 75; strikes in (1905), 76; Bolsheviks seize power in (1917), 91; Germans train secretly in chemical warfare at (1922–33), 101; famine in (1921), 102; occupied by anti-Bolsheviks (1918–19), 103; area of forced collectivization (1929–38), 113; a German objective (1942), 124; over half a million inhabitants (1959), 138

Sarkel: a town on the Don, part of Kievan Russia, 13; a trading centre, 14

Sarmatians: rule from the Dniester river to the Caspian Sea, 4; defeated by the Goths, 5

Saskatoon (Canada): Ukrainians at, 99

Save the Children Fund: sends famine relief to Russia (1921), 102

Schlüsselburg: a large German community in (by 1914), 39; industrial growth of (by 1860), 56; Germans make armaments secretly at (1922–33), 101; and the siege of Leningrad (1941–43), 126

Schwerin: colonized by the Germans, 20

Scranton (USA): Ukrainians at, 99

Scythians: reach north shore of Black Sea, 2; settle between River Danube and Caspian Sea, 3

Sebastopol: annexed by Russia from the Turks, 41; Russian naval expedition to the Mediterranean leaves from (1798), 45; anarchists active in (1905–06), 55; political assassinations in, 72; revolution at (1905), 76; bombarded by the Turks (1914), 85; annexed to the Independent Ukraine (1918), 97; United States famine relief arrives at (1921), 102; besieged by the Germans (1941), 118; conquered by the Germans (1942), 124; German SS headquarters at (1942–43), 123, Germans driven from (1943–44), 129; a 'Hero City' of the Soviet Union, 146

Sebezh: Jewish political activity in, 70

Sech: Cossack headquarters, annexed by Russia (1667), 31; large Cossack settlement in region of, 35; burnt to the ground by Peter the Great (1708), 37

Sedlits: anti-Jewish violence in, 69, 75; Jews rebel against the Germans in, 123

Seg, Lake: labour camps at, 109

Selenga: a town of exile in Siberia, 54

Semender: Viking settlers at, 11

Semipalatinsk: industry at (by 1800), 34; Chinese territory extended towards (1720–60), 40; and Russian trade with China (1850–70), 59; Virgin Lands campaign extended to (after 1953), 136; and the Soviet-Chinese border (1970), 143

Serbia: Mongols raid, 22; and European diplomacy (1890–1907), 64; and Russian policy in the Balkans (1876–1914), 78, 79; sends anti-Bolshevik force to Murmansk (1918–19), 92, 94

Serbs: a western Slav tribe, 12; converted to Eastern Catholicism, 15; under Turkish rule, 49

Severians: an eastern Slav tribe, 12

Seville (Spain): Viking settlers reach, 11

Shamil: defeated by the Russians at Gunib (1859), 61

Shanghai (China): Moscow establishes communist Party cell in (1920–24), 142

Shenkursk: Ivan IV seizes land in region of, 28

Shilka, River: iron ore near, 106

Shumla: siege of (1774), 46; battle of (1810), 49

Shusha: anti-Bolshevik revolt in (1920–21), 104

Shushenskoye: Lenin in exile at, 54

Siberia: Ivan IV extends Russian rule east of the Urals to, 26; Russian expansion in, 33; Cossacks defeat Mongols in (1581), 35; Volga Germans deported to (1941), 39; and the exile system of Tsarist Russia, 54; controlled by anti-Bolshevik forces (1918–19), 92; Stalinist deportation of national groups to (1941–45), 131

Silesians: a Slav tribe on the Elbe river, 12

Silistria: siege of (1774), 46; occupied by Russia (1828–29), 51; annexed by Rumania from Turkey (1878), 78

Simbirsk: in area of peasants' revolt (1670–71), 32; industrial growth at (by 1800), 34; peasant discontent in the Province of (1827–60), 57; serfdom in (by 1860), 58; anti-Jewish violence in, 69, 75; and Russian industry (by 1900), 71; political assassinations in, 72; peasant uprising in Province of (1905), 75; famine in (1921), 102

Simferopol: anti-Jewish violence in, 69, 75; occupied by German troops (1918), 91

Sinkiang: Britain seeks influence in (before 1907), 65; Soviet-Chinese conflict of interest in (since 1921), 142

Sinope: Greek colony on the Black Sea, 3

Siskoi monastery: 16

Skadovsk: Germans occupy (1941), 123

Skobelev: anti-Bolshevik revolt in region of (1917–20), 103

Slavgorod: Ukrainians at, 98

Slavs: their area of settlement by 800 BC, 1; by 600 BC, 2; by 300 BC, 3; by 200 AD, 4; recognize Goth overlordship by 400 AD, 5; under Hun domination, 6; their rule extended to the Baltic and the Danube, 7; largely subjugated by the Avars, 8; throw off Avar control and penetrate into the Balkans, 9, 10; their area of settlement by 880 AD, 12; and the growth of Slavophilism and anti-semitism in Russia, 69

Slonim: a town in Lithuania, 23

Slovakia: Slovak communists fail to seize power in, 108

Slovaks: a western Slav tribe, 12

Slovenes: a western Slav tribe, 12

Slovianians: a northern Slav tribe, 12

Slutsk: annexed by Russia (1793), 43

Smela: anti-Jewish violence in, 69

Smolensk: a town of Kievan Russia, 12, 13; within the Eastern Catholic world, 15; capital of a Russian Principality, 17; within the area of Mongol overlordship, 21, 22; under Roman Catholic control, as part of Lithuania, 23, 24; conquered by the Principality of Moscow, 25; annexed by Poland (1618), 30; regained by Russia (1667), 31; administrative centre of a Province established by Peter the Great, 38; and Napoleon's invasion of Russia (1812), 49; peasant discontent and serfdom in the Province of (by 1860), 57, 58; political assassinations in, 72; Bolshevik activity in (1903–14), 73; Bolsheviks seize power in (1917), 91; Germans train pilots secretly at (1922–33), 101; alleged communist subversive activity in, 108; occupied by the Germans (1941), 118, 124; German SS headquarters at, 123; Germans driven from (1943–44), 129

Smolny Institute (Petrograd): Lenin establishes his headquarters at (Oct 1917), 90

Smorgon: Jewish political activity in, 70; Russian soldiers mutiny in (1917), 89

Sochi: revolutionary outbreak in (1905), 76; claimed by Ukrainian nationalists, 97

Socotra (Indian Ocean): Soviet naval facilities at (1970), 141

Sofia: unsuccessful Bulgarian communist uprising in, 108; communism established in, 113; and the defeat of Germany (1944–45), 130

Sokal: a Polish town, annexed by the Soviet Union (1939), 114

Solikamsk: uprising in (1648–50), 32; industry at (by 1800), 34; Cossack march across the Urals begun from (1581), 35

Solovetski island (White Sea): monastery on, 16; Soviet labour camp on, 109

Solvychegodsk: town founded by the Republic of Novgorod, 19; Ivan IV seizes land in the region of, 28; uprising in (1648–50), 32

Sosva, River: Part of the eastern trade route system of the Republic of Novgorod, 19

South Yemen: Soviet fishing agreement with (1970), 141

Sovetskaya Gavan: a port on the Northern Sea Route, 112

Soviet Union, *see index entry for* Union of Soviet Socialist Republics

Spain: Viking settlers reach, 11; Russia opposes national revolution in (1815–25), 50; Soviet aid to Republican forces in (1936–39), 101; Russian refugees from Bolshevism in (by 1930), 107; Communist Party of, seeks freedom of action from Bolsheviks (1920), 108; troops from, fight with the Germans on the Russian front (1941), 118

Spaso-Kamenni monastery: 16

Spasskoi: a town in the Republic of Novgorod, 18

Stalin, Josef: deports Volga Germans to Siberia (1941), 39; his birthplace in Georgia (1879), 48; writes to his sister-in-law from Siberia (1913), 54; in Siberia at the time of the revolution (1917), 88; territorial annexations by, 113; deports Crimean Tatars and others to Siberia (1941–45), 128, 131; towns and villages named after, 139

Stalingrad (now Volgograd): *for earlier index entries see* Tsaritsyn: Soviet labour camps in the region of, 110; a German plan for (1941), 122; a principal German objective (1942), 124, 128; battle of (1942), 125; over half a million inhabitants (1959), 138

Stalino: German SS headquarters at (1942), 123; German offensive to the east of (1942), 124, 128; over half a million inhabitants (1959), 138

Stalinsk: factories moved to (1940–42), 113

Stanislavov (Stanislau): a Polish town, annexed by Austria (1772), 43; captured by the Russians (1917), 89; part of the West Ukrainian Republic (1918), 97; Polish (from 1921), annexed by the Soviet Union (1939), 114

Staraya Rusa: attacked by the Ukrainians (1253), 18; under German military rule (1941), 123, 126; Soviet partisans active near (1941–42), 127

Staritsa: Ivan IV seizes land in the region of, 28

Starodub: dispossessed landowners flee to, 28; annexed by Poland, 30; regained by Russia, 31; anti-Jewish violence in, 69

Staro-Konstantinov: annexed by Russia (1793), 43; Jewish rebellion against Russian military service laws in (1827), 70

Stavropol: Cossack settlements at, 35; political assassinations at, 72; revolutionary outbreak at (1905), 76; claimed as part of the Ukraine, 97; occupied by the Germans (1943), 120, 123, 128; Virgin Lands scheme extended to the east of (after 1953), 136; name changed to Toliatti, 139

Stettin (Szczecin): under communist control, as part of Poland (since 1945), 36, 133; anti-Soviet revolt in (1956), 134

Stockholm: attacked by Russia (1710–21), 37; Lenin in exile in (1910), 73; Lenin returns to Russia through (1917), 87; Russian Bolshevik leaders in (1917), 88; communist propaganda disseminated in, 108

Stolbova: Russian territorial losses at the Peace of (1617), 30

Stralsund: a Hansa town on the Baltic, 20

Streltsy: set up Cossack style Government in Astrakhan (1698), 37

Stretensk: and the Siberian exiles, 54

Stuttgart: Russian students in, 70; Lenin in exile (1907), 73

Stutthof: German concentration camp at, 123

Sudan: Soviet fishing agreement with (1970), 141

Suez Canal: and Russian trade with the Far East (by 1875), 59

Sukhona, River: a trade route of Novgorod, 19; and the river systems of European Russia, 27

Sukhumi: annexed by Russia (1810), 48

Sukhumkale: battle of (1809), 46

Surchinsk: in the Bolshevik-controlled Far Eastern Republic (1922), 106

Surgut: founded (1594), 26, 33; a town of exile, 54

Suvalki: Polish town, annexed by Prussia (1795), 43; Polish partisan activity against Russia in region of (1831), 51; revolution at (1905), 76; and German war aims (1914), 81; Germans occupy (1914), 81; Polish (since 1921), annexed by Germany (1939), 114

Suzdal: within Kievan Russia, 13; Orthodox monastery established at, 16; conquered by the Principality of Moscow, 21; Ivan IV seizes land in region of, 28

Sverdlov, Yakov Mikhailovich: in Siberia at the time of the revolution (1917), 88

Sverdlovsk: *for earlier index entries see* Ekaterinburg: Soviet labour camps established near, 110; factories moved to (1940)

42), 113, 121; a German plan for (1941), 122; over half a million inhabitants (1959), 138

viatoslav: ruler of Kievan Russia, tribute paid to by non-Slav regions, 13

vir, River: a trade route of the Republic of Novgorod, 19; and the river systems of European Russia, 27; Soviet labour camps established along, 109, 110

virstroi: labour camps at, 109

vobodny: Ukrainians at, 98

weden, Kingdom of: 16; attacks the Republic of Novgorod, 18; Roman Catholic, 24; deprives Russia of access to the Baltic Sea (1583), 26; invades Russia and occupies Novgorod, 30, 146; Russia wrests control of Gulf of Finland from (1721–1809), 36; Russia's territorial gains from (1700–1809), 47; Lenin returns to Russia through (1917), 87; Russian refugees in (by 1930), 107

wedes: their settlements by 200 AD, 4

wedish Red Cross: sends famine relief to Russia (1921), 102

witzerland: return of the Bolsheviks to Russia from (1917), 87, 88; Russian refugees from Bolshevism settle in (by 1930), 107

yracuse (USA): Ukrainians at, 99

yr Daria, River: Virgin Lands campaign extended to upper regions of (after 1953), 136

yria: Viking settlers reach, 11

ysola, River: and the river systems of European Russia, 27

abriz: part of the Islamic world, 10, 15; proposed Russian railway through, 61; Russians occupy (1916), 83, 85; Turks occupy (1918), 91; Russians annex (1945–48), 113

aganrog: founded by Peter the Great as a Russian naval base, but lost to the Turks, 37; annexed by Catherine the Great, 41; special Gendarme detachment at, 51; claimed as part of the Ukraine, 97; occupied by the Germans (1942), 119, 123, 124; Germans driven from (1943), 129

ambov: in area of peasants' revolt (1670–71), 32; peasant discontent in the Province of (1827–60), 57; serfdom in (by 1860), 58; peasant poverty in Province of (by 1904), 68; industry in (by 1900), 71; political assassinations in, 72; peasant uprising in Province of (1905), 75

anais: Greek colony on the Don, 3; under Roman rule, 4; controlled by the Khazars, 10; Viking settlers reach, 11; ruled by the Mongols, 22; under Roman Catholic control, 24

annenberg (East Prussia): Russians defeated by the Germans at (1914), 81

annu Tuva: annexed by the Soviet Union (1944), 142

anzania: Soviet fishing agreement with (1970), 141

ara: founded (1594), 33; Cossacks settle in, 35; Ukrainians at, 98; and the Northern Sea Route administration, 112

arki: Caspian port, annexed by Russia, 41

arnopol: a Polish town, annexed by Austria (1772), 43; annexed by Russia (1801–15), 50; Polish rebels flee to (1831), 52; Russians occupy (1914–15), 82; Russian troops mutiny at (1917), 84, 89; part of the West Ukrainian Republic (1918), 97; Polish (since 1921), annexed by the Soviet Union (1939), 114; annexed by Germany (1941), 123

arnow: an Austrian town, Russians occupy (1914), 81; Polish (from 1918), Germans occupy (1939), 114, 116; Jewish uprising against Germans in, 123

arsus: a centre of Eastern Catholicism, 15

ashkent: annexed by Russia (1865), 61; linked to Moscow by railway (1915), 62; political assassinations in, 72; Ukrainians at, 98; under Bolshevik control (1917), 103; factories moved to (1940–42), 113; a German plan for (1941), 122; over half a million inhabitants (1959), 138; and the Soviet-Chinese border (1970), 143

avda, River: and the river systems of the Urals and European Russia, 27

azovskoye: Kara Sea Expedition visits (1921), 105

eheran (Persia): proposed Russian railway through (before 1907), 61; allied conference at (1943), 113; United States aid to Soviet Union goes through (1941–45), 120

elavi: anti-Bolshevik revolt in (1920–21), 104

Temnikov: a centre of industrial growth (by 1800), 34

Terek Peoples' Soviet Socialist Republic: its brief existence (1917–18), 104

Terek, River: a highway of trade for Kievan Russia, 14; Russian rule extended to, 26; Cossacks settle along, 35; Soviet labour camps near, 110; Germans occupy upper reaches of (1941–43), 128

Ter-Petrosian, Semyon Arshakovich (Kamo): in the Ukraine at the time of the revolution (1917), 88

Tetukha Bay: zinc at, 106

Teutonic Knights: Baltic settlement of, 16; continually attack the Republic of Novgorod, without success, 18, 22; their descendants incorporated into Russia (1721), 39

Thaelmann: a German collective farm in the Soviet Union, 39

Theodosia (Feodosia): Roman settlement on the Black Sea, 4; special Russian Gendarme detachment at, 51; revolution at (1905), 76

Thorn: ruled by the Teutonic Knights, 20

Tibet: conquered by China (1780), 40

Tiflis: within the area of the authority of Eastern Catholicism by 1000 AD, 15; large German community in (by 1914), 39; annexed by Russia (1801), 48; anarchists active in (1905–06), 55; peasant discontent in the Province of (1827–60), 57; serfdom in (by 1860), 58; strikes in (before 1905), 68; peasant assassinations in, 72; peasant uprising in (1905), 75; Turks advance on (1917), 85; Turks occupy (1918), 91; British occupy (1918–19), 92, 104, 146; a German plan for (1941), 122; over half a million inhabitants (1959), 138

Tigris, River: and the Assyrians by 800 BC, 1

Tikhvin: occupied by Sweden (1613), 30; important Russian trade fair at (1700–1800), 34; occupied by the Germans (1941), 118, 126; Soviet partisans active near (1941–42), 127

Tiksi: a port on the Northern Sea Route, 112

Tilsit: Peace of (1807), 49

Tisza-Eszla (Hungary): ritual murder charge against Jews in, 69

Tiumen: founded (1586), 26, 33; shipbuilding at (from 1937), 112

Tmutorokan: a Slav town on the Black Sea, 12; part of Kievan Russia, 13

Tobol, River: and the river systems of the Urals and European Russia, 27; early Russian settlements on, 33

Tobolsk: founded (1587), 26, 33, 40; a town of exile in Siberia, 54; and Russian trade with China (1850–70), 59; Soviet labour camps near, 111; industry at (1941–45), 121

Tomi: Greek colony on the Black Sea, 3

Tomsk: founded (1604), 33, 40; a town of exile, 54, 72; Ukrainians at (by 1937), 98; Soviet labour camps near, 111; and the Northern Sea Route administration, 112; a German plan for (1941), 122

Tornea: annexed by Russia (1809), 47

Toronto (Canada): Ukrainians at, 99

Torzhok: attacked by the Mongols (1238) and by the Lithuanians (1245), 18; does not fall under Mongol control, 22

Tosno: anti-Bolshevik forces fail to capture (1919), 93; Germans occupy (1941), 126; Soviet partisans active near (1941–42), 127

Totma: Ivan IV seizes land in region of, 28; uprising in (1648–50), 32

Trade routes: of Kievan Russia, 14

Transcaucasian Federative Republic: its brief existence (1917), 104

Trans-Siberian railway: and the Siberian exiles, 54; and the development of Siberia (by 1917), 62; Ukrainian settlements along, 98; and the spread of Soviet rule to Central Asia (1917–36), 103; goes through the Bolshevik-controlled Far Eastern Republic (1920–22), 106; Soviet labour camps on, 111; administrative centres of the Northern Sea Route on (from 1920–25), 112; Jewish Autonomous Region of Birobidjan on, 135

Transylvania: a Roman Catholic region by 1000 AD, 24

Trapezus: Greek colony on the Black Sea, 3; controlled by Rome, 4; raided by the Goths, 5; see henceforth Trebizond

Trebizond: a Byzantine port on the Black Sea, 10; a trading

centre for Kievan goods going to India, 14; occupied by Russia (1829), 46; Armenian claims to (1918), 104

Trelleborg: Lenin returns to Russia through (1917), 87

Treviso: Russian campaign in Italy begins at (1798), 49

Troitski-Gledinskii monastery: 19

Troitski-Sergievski monastery: 16

Troki: annexed by Russia (1795), 43; a centre of Polish revolt against Russia (1860), 53

Troppau: conference of, 50

Trotsk: Germans manufacture poison gas secretly at (1922–33), 101

Trotsky, Lev Davidovich: describes life in Siberia (before 1917), 54; in New York at the time of the revolution (1917), 88; returns to Petrograd, and is arrested (1917), 89; and the Bolshevik seizure of power in Petrograd (1917), 90; and the defence of Petrograd (1919), 93; exiled, 113

Tsaritsyn: founded (1589), 26; in area of peasants' revolt (1670–71), 32; a shipbuilding centre, 34; large Cossack settlement in, 35; anti-Jewish violence in, 69, 75; industry in (by 1900), 71; Bolsheviks active in (1903–17), 73; strikes in (1905), 76; famine in (1921), 102; name changed to Stalingrad, 139; *for subsequent index entries see* Stalingrad (now Volgograd)

Tsarskoye Selo: special Gendarme detachment at, 51; Protocols of Zion published in, 69; troops disarmed at (1917), 86

Tsingtao: German port on the China coast, 65

Tskhinvali: anti-Bolshevik revolt in (1920–21), 104

Tuapse: Black Sea coastal town, claimed as part of the Ukraine, 97; Bolsheviks advance into the Caucasus from (1920), 104; Germans fail to capture (1941–43), 128

Tula: dispossessed landowners settle in, 28; within area of peasants' revolt (1606–07), 29; an industrial centre (by 1800), 34; in the most heavily populated area of Russia (in 1724), 38; conversions to Judaism in (1796–1825), 50; centre of an anarchist group (1840–80), 55; industrial growth in the region of (by 1860), 56; peasant discontent and serfdom in Province of (by 1860), 57, 58; industry in (by 1900), 71; peasant uprising in Province of (1905), 75; strikes in (1905), 76; Germans make armaments secretly at (1922–33), 101; Soviet labour camps in region of, 110; German SS headquarters at (1942), 123; Germans driven from (1943), 129

Tunguska, River: and the Siberian exile system, 54

Tura: Ukrainians at, 98

Tura, River: and Russian trade with China (1850–70), 59

Turgai: Ukrainians at, 98

Turinsk: a town of exile in Siberia, 54

Turkestan-Siberian railway (Turksib): and the spread of Soviet rule to Central Asia (1930–36), 103

Turkey: signs Treaty of Kars with the Bolsheviks (1921), 104; Russian refugees in (by 1930), 107; alleged revolutionary activity prepared against, inside Russia, 108; Germans fail to reach Caucasus frontier of (1941–43), 128

Turks: settle on the eastern shore of the Aral Sea, 8, 9, 10

Turnovo: occupied by Russia (1810), 46

Turov: Russian Principality of, 17; conquered by the Mongols, 22; conquered by the Lithuanians, 23; Russians advance against Poles through (1654–55), 31; annexed by Russia (1793), 43

Turukhansk: founded (1619), 33; Stalin in exile at, 54; political exiles at, 72; a Bolshevik leader in, at the time of the revolution (1917), 88; Kara Sea Expedition visits (1921), 105; Soviet labour camp at, 111

Tver: Orthodox monastery established at, 16; peasant discontent in the Province of (1827–60), 57; serfdom in (by 1860), 58; political assassinations in, 72; Bolsheviks active in (1903–14), 73; strikes at (1905), 76; name changed to Kalinin, 139

Tyras: Greek colony on the Black Sea, 3

Udskii: founded (1679), 33

Ufa: industrial growth in region of, 34, 56; political assassination in (1903), 68, 72; and Russian industry (by 1900), 71; Bolsheviks active in (1903–14), 73; strikes in (1905), 76; controlled by anti-Bolshevik troops (1919), 92, 146; famine in (1921), 102; anti-Bolshevik revolt in region of (1917–20), 103; a German plan for (1941), 122; over half a million inhabitants (1959), 138

Ukhta: Soviet labour camps at, 109

Ukraine: a part of the Roman Catholic world (by 1462), incorporated into Lithuania, 24; a part of Russia, but increasingly discontented with Russian rule (by 1905), 68, 76; 22 million Ukrainians (in Russia, 1897), 74; under German influence (1917–18), 80; national aspirations dissatisfied by Russian promises (1914), 84; the increasing national aspiration of (by 1917), 89; troops of, active in anti-Bolshevik intervention (1918–19), 92; successful anarchist activity in (1917–20), 95; its changing frontiers (1917–21), 97; and the proposed Union of Border States (1919), 100; famine in (1921), 102; occupied by the Germans (1941), 119; a German plan for (1941), 122; population movements from (1939–46), 132

Ukrainian Soviet Socialist Republic: boundary of (1921), 97; boundary of (since 1945), 144

Ulan Bator: capital of Mongolian Peoples' Republic, 143

Uman: battle of (1738), 46; secret Bolshevik printing press in, 73; Poles fail to capture (1920), 97

Umea: Swedish port, attacked by Russia (1710–21), 37

Union of Border States: proposed establishment of (1919), 100

Union of Soviet Socialist Republics (Soviet Union): and the Ukraine, 97; diplomacy of (1920–40), 101; formally annexes the Far Eastern Republic (1922), 106; the Republics and Autonomous Regions of (since 1945), 144

United States of America, The: and Russian territorial settlement in Alaska (1784–1867), 44; two million Russian Jews emigrate to (1880–1914), 70; Russian war debts to (by July 1917), 89; intervenes against the Bolsheviks (1919), 92, 94, 106; Ukrainian settlements in (by 1937), 99; sends famine relief to Bolshevik Russia (1921), 101; Russian refugees from Bolshevism in (by 1930), 107; sends aid to the Soviet Union (1941–43), 120; and Soviet missiles in Cuba (1962), 140

Ural Mountains: Russian monastic colonization to the west of, 16; Novgorod trade routes to the west and east of, 19; Mongols conquer the southern area of, 21; Russian rule extended east of, 26; and the river systems of European Russia, 27; Russian expansion and settlement east of (1478–1710), 33; Cossacks cross to the east of, 35; Chinese annexations reach to within 500 miles of (by 1764), 40; places of exile to the east of (1648–1917), 54; industrial growth in (by 1860), 56; and Russian industry (by 1900), 71; Ukrainian settlements east of, 97; Soviet labour camps in, 110; industry in (1941–45), 121; a German plan for (1941), 122; Stalinist deportation of national groups to the east of (1941–45), 131; industry in (1970), 137

Ural, River: and the river systems of European Russia, 27; Cossacks settle along, 35; revolt of Bashkirs in region of, 37

Uralsk: large Cossack settlement in, 35; Ukrainians at (by 1937), 98; factories moved to (1940–42), 113; Virgin Lands campaign extended to (after 1953), 136

Urdzhar: and the Soviet-Chinese border (1970), 143

Uritsky, Mikhail Solomonovich: in Sweden at the time of the revolution (1917), 88

Urmia, Lake: under Russian control (1916), 83

Urumchi: annexed by China (by 1764), 40; independent (since 1946), 143

Usa, River: and the river systems of European Russia, 27

Ussuri, River: Russia annexes eastern bank of (1860), 60

Ust Ishim: and the Northern Sea Route administration, 111

Ustiug: Orthodox monastery established at, 16

Ustkamenogorsk: founded (1720), 40

Ust-Nem: town founded by the Republic of Novgorod, 19

Ust Port: on the Northern Sea Route, 112

Ustye: Germans fail to capture (1941–43), 126

Utigar Huns: settle north of the Caucasus, 7

Uzbekistan: Stalinist deportation of national groups to (1941–45), 131

Uzhgorod: annexed to the Independent Ukraine (1918), 97; annexed to the Soviet Union (1945), 133, 145

Valaam: Orthodox monastery on island of, 16

Valence: Viking settlers reach, 11
Valka: Bolshevik influence in (1917), 89
Van: Armenian claims to (1918), 104
Van, Lake: under Russian control (1916), 83; Armenian claims to (1918), 104
Varangarians: mould the Slavs into a coherent federation, 12
Varna: siege of (1829), 46, 51
Varzuga: Ivan IV expropriates land in region of, 28
Vasa: annexed by Russia (1809), 47
Vasilkov: centre of the Decembrist uprising (1825), 51
Velikie Luki: a border town of the Republic of Novgorod, 18; occupied by the Germans (1942), 119
Veliki Ustiug: town founded by the Republic of Novgorod, 19; Ivan IV seizes land in region of, 28; uprising in (1648–50), 32
Verkholensk: Trotsky in exile at, 54; Socialist Revolutionary Party exiles at, 72
Verkhoyansk: political exiles at, 72
Verny: anti-Bolshevik revolt at (1917–20), 103
Viatchians: an eastern Slav tribe, 12
Viatka: Russian Principality conquered by the Mongols, 22; conquered by the Principality of Moscow, 25; serfs sold as iron factory workers in, 50; terrorist activity in region of (1905–06), 55; industrial growth in the region of (by 1860), 56; famine in (1921), 102; name changed to Kirov, 139
Viazma: conquered by the Lithuanians, 23; a part of Russia under Ivan IV, who seizes land in region of, 28; within area of peasants' revolt (1606–07), 29; occupied by Poland (1611–13), 30; Russian army advances against Poles from (1654), 31; Napoleon advances to Moscow through (1812), 49; under German military rule (1942), 123
Vidin: battles of (1811, 1828), 46
Vienna: conference of, 50; Russian students in, 70; Bolshevik activity in (1903–14), 73; Lenin passes through, on way to Switzerland (1914), 87; communist propaganda disseminated in, 108; within Greater Germany (1938–45), 117; and the defeat of Germany (1944–45), 130, 133
Vikings: settle along the Dnieper and the Volga, 11
Vilkoviski: annexed by Russia (1795), 43; Germans defeat the Russians at (1914), 81
Vilna: a principal town of Lithuania, 23, 24; Jews murdered in (1648–52), 31; becomes part of Russia (1795), 41, 42, 43; area of Polish partisan activity against Russia (1831), 52; Polish revolt in the region of (1860), 53; anarchists active in (1905–06), 55; its growth (by 1860), 56; peasant discontent and serfdom in the Province of (by 1860), 57, 58; Jewish political activity in, 70; Bolshevik activity in (1903–14), 73; agricultural workers strike in Province of (1905), 75; strikes at (1905), 76; and German war aims (1914), 80; Germans occupy (1915), 82; Russian counterattack on, unsuccessful (1917), 89; seized by Poland from Lithuania (1920), 96; dispute over (1919–20), 100; annexed by Lithuania (1939), 114; annexed by the Soviet Union (1939), 116; annexed by Germany (1941), 123; Germans drive from (1944), 130; reincorporated into the Soviet Union (1945), 133
Viluisk: a town of Siberian exile, 54
Vinland: Viking settlers reach, 11
Vinnitsa: Jews murdered in (1648–52), 31; annexed by Russia (1793), 43; Germans driven from, by Soviet forces (1944), 129
Virgin Lands Region: established by Krushchev (1953), 136
Visby (Wisby): a trading centre for the Baltic Sea, 14; ruled by the Teutonic Knights, 20
Vistula, River: Slav settlements along by 800 BC, 1; controlled by the Goths, 5; controlled by the Huns, 6; controlled by the Slavs, 7; controlled by the Avars, 8; Slav control re-established along, 9, 10; a highway of trade for Kievan Russia, 14; mouth of controlled by Teutonic Knights, 20; the Poles halt advance of the Red Army at (Aug 1920), 96
Vitebsk: conquered by the Lithuanians, 23; Jews murdered in, 31; Russian, and peasant discontent in the Province of (1827–60), 57; serfdom in (by 1860), 58; Jewish political activity in, 70; political assassinations in (1904–07), 72; occupied by the Germans (1942), 119, 123
Vladikavkaz: a Bolshevik leader in, at the time of the revolution

(1917), 88; part of the Terek Peoples' SSR (1918–20), 104; name changed to Orzhonikidze, 139; for subsequent reference see Ordzhonikidze
Vladimir: Orthodox monastery established, at, 16; uprising in (1648–50), 32; peasant discontent in the Province of (1827–60), 57; serfdom in (by 1860), 58
Vladimir: ruler of Kievan Russia, marries a sister of the Byzantine Emperor, 13
Vladimir Monomakh: briefly reunites Kievan Russia, 17
Vladimir-Suzdal: a Russian Principality, 17; conquered by the Mongols, 22
Valdivostok: founded (1860), 60; linked to Moscow by the Trans-Siberian railway, 62; Ukrainians at (by 1937), 98; anti-Bolsheviks at (1918–22), 106; Soviet labour camps established near, 111; terminus of the Northern Sea Route from Murmansk, 112; United States aid enters the Soviet Union through (1941–45), 121; Soviet naval strength at (1970), 141; and the Soviet-Chinese border (1970), 143
Volga, River: crossed by nomads from Asia, 2; Scythian settlements reach western bank of, 3; Slavs settle along upper reaches of, 4, 5, 7, 9, 12; Huns control lower reaches of, 6, 7; largely controlled by the Khazars, 10; Vikings settle along, 11; almost entirely within the area ruled by or paying tribute to Kievan Russia, 13; a principal highway of trade, 14; active Russian monastic colonization along upper reaches of, 16; falls under Mongol domination, 21; falls entirely under Russial rule (by 1598), 26; and the river systems of European Russia, 27; dispossessed landowners settle along, 28; peasants' revolt along (1670–71), 32; Russian industrial growth on (by 1800), 34; and revolts against Peter the Great, 37; industrial growth on upper reaches of (by 1860), 56; and the river route from Moscow to Irkutsk (1850–70), 59; Bolshevik activity along (1903–17), 73; famine in region of (1921), 102; Soviet labour camps on, 110; factories moved east of (1940–42), 113; a German military objective (1942), 124, 128; Virgin Lands scheme extended to eastern bank of (after 1953), 136; industry on (1970), 137; railways east of (by 1959), 138; and the invaders of Russia (1240–1945), 146
Volga Bulgars: pay tribute to Kievan Russia, 13
Volga German Republic: established (1918), disbanded (1941), 39
Volga Germans: deported by Stalin to Siberia, 128, 131
Volhynia: a Russian Principality, 17; conquered by the Mongols, 22; annexed by Russia from Poland (1795), 43; serfdom in the Province of (by 1860), 58; agricultural workers strike in Province of (1905), 75; Germans hope to incorporate into Germany (1914), 79; and the proposed Union of Border States (1919), 100
Volhynians: a Slav tribe south of the Pripet marshes, 12
Volkhov: and the siege of Leningrad (1941–43), 126
Volkhov, River: a highway of trade in Kievan Russia, 14; in the Republic of Novgorod, 18, 19
Volodarsky, Mosei Markovich: in New York at the time of the revolution (1917), 88
Vologda: in the Republic of Novgorod, 18, 22; conquered by the Principality of Moscow, 25; Ivan IV seizes land in region of, 28; serf rebellion in region of (1812–13), 50; anti-Jewish violence in, 69; 75; strikes at (1905), 76; industry at (1941–45), 121; a German plan for (1941), 122
Volokolamsk: Orthodox monastery established at, 16; part of the Republic of Novgorod, 18
Vorkuta: Soviet labour camps in the region of, 110, 111; in the Pechora coal mining area, 112; a German plan for (1941), 122
Voronezh: founded (1586), 26; within area of peasants' revolt (1606), 29; uprising in (1648–50), 32; a shipbuilding centre, 34; a centre of Cossack settlement, 35; Cossack revolt in region of (1707–08), 37; peasant discontent in the Province of (1827–60), 57; serfdom in (by 1860), 58; peasant poverty in (by 1904), 68; Bolsheviks active in (1903–14), 73; peasant uprising in Province of (1905), 75; strikes in (1905), 76; Bolsheviks seize power in (1917), 91; anti-Bolsheviks fail to capture (1919), 97; Germans driven from (1943), 129

Voroshilov: *for earlier index entries see* Lugansk: occupied by the Germans (1942), 119

Vyborg: under Roman Catholic control, 24; industry at (by 1800), 34; part of Russia (1721–1917), 36, 37, 47; large German community in (by 1914), 39; industrial growth of (in the 1860's), 56; strike at (1917), 86; Finnish (from 1917), ceded to Russia by Finland (1940), 115, 116; annexed by Russia (1945), 133

Vychegda, River: a trade route of Novgorod, 19; and the river systems of European Russia, 27

Vym, River: a trade route of Novgorod, 19

Vymskii–Arkhangelskii monastery: 19

Wakhan: given to Afghanistan by Russia and Britain (1905), 61

Warsaw: capital city of the Kingdom of Poland, 23; under Russian rule (1815–1915), contained a large German community, 39; annexed by Prussia (1795), 42; becomes Russian (1815), and centre of Polish revolt against Russia (1831), 52; again a centre of Polish revolt (1860), 53; anarchists active in (1905–06), 55; factory development in (by 1860), 56; Jewish political activity in, 70; industry in (by 1900), 71; political assassinations in, 72; revolution in (1905), 76; Germans hope to annex (1914), 79, 80; Germans occupy (1915), 82; Poles defend from attack by the Red Army (June 1920), 96; communism established in (1945), 113; occupied by Germany (1939), 114, 116; Jewish uprising against Germans in (1942), 123; anti-Soviet revolt in (1956), 134

Weihaiwei: British port on the China coast, 65

West Ukrainian Republic: established (Nov 1918), 97

White Huns: settle along the Oxus River, 6, 7

White Russia (Belorussia): annexed by Catherine the Great, 41, 43; occupied by the Poles (1919), 100; occupied by the Germans (1942), 119; a Soviet Republic (since 1945), 144

White Sea: Orthodox monastery on an island in, 16; Principality of Moscow extends its control to, 25; river routes across Russia from, 27; Ivan IV seizes lands along the shore of, 28; controlled by Britain (1918–19), 91, 92, 94; Soviet labour camps established on, 109, 110

Windau: taken by Russia from Poland (1795), 36, 43

Winnipeg (Canada): Ukrainians at, 99

Winter Palace (Petrograd): seized by the Bolsheviks (1917), 90

Wismar: a Hansa town on the Baltic, 20; under communist control (since 1945), 36

Wrangel, Pyotr Nikolaevich: defeated by a joint Bolshevik-Anarchist army (1920), 95; based on the Crimea, 100

Wrangel Island: Soviet-Canadian dispute over (1921–45), 112

Wuhan (China): Moscow establishes communist Party cell in (1920–24), 142

Xanten (Germany): ritual murder charge against Jews in, 69

Yadrin: in area of peasants' revolt (1670–71), 32

Yakutsk: founded (1632), 33, 40; a town of exile, 54, 72; and the Lena coal basin, 112

Yalta: anarchists active in (1905–06), 55; annexed to the Independent Ukraine (1918), 97; annexed by Germany (1941), 123; allied conference at (1945), 113

Yalu, River: Russia fears British expansion in the region of (after 1840), 60; Soviet troops advance to, against Japanese (1945), 142

Yalutorovsk: a town of exile in Siberia, 54

Yama: attacked by the Teutonic Knights, 18

Yamburg: occupied by anti-Bolshevik forces (1919), 93

Yangtse, River: within the Mongol dominions, 21

Yarkand: annexed by China (by 1764), 40; and Russian trade with China (1850–70), 59; Britain wants to extend its influence to, 65

Yaroslav: ruler of Kievan Russia, in whose reign the first Russian legal code was compiled, 13; the division of Kievan Russia after his death, 17

Yaroslavl: Russian counter-attack against Poles draws troops from, 30; peasant discontent in the Province of (1827–60), 57; serfdom in (by 1860), 58; strikes at (1905), 76; Polish (from 1918), Germans occupy (1939), 114

Yaungulbene: Bolshevik influence in (1917), 89

Yellow River: Eurasian nomads move westwards from, 2; seen as possible southern boundary of Russian territorial zone in China (1900), 65

Yemen: Soviet fishing agreement with (1970), 141

Yenisei, River: early Russian settlements on, 33; and the Siberian exile system, 54; Ukrainian settlements on the upper reaches of (by 1937), 98; Kara Sea Expedition visits lower reaches of (1921), 105; Soviet labour camps on, 111; industrial development of (by 1970), 137

Yeniseisk: founded (1619), 40; and Russian trade with China (1850–70), 59; a town of exile, 72

Yorktown (Canada): Ukrainians at, 99

Younghusband, General Francis: leads British military expedition to Lhasa, 65

Yudenich, General Nikolai Nikolaevich: fails to capture Petrograd (Sept 1919), 93, 100

Yugoslavia: Russian refugees in (by 1930), 107; strongly anti-communist (by 1926), 108; German population of flees to Germany (1945–46), 132; communist regime established in (1945), 133; Soviet control of foreign, economic and domestic policy rejected (since 1949), 134

Yurev: a town conquered by Kievan Russia, 13

Yuzovo: name changed to Stalino, 139

Zaison: and the Soviet-Chinese border (1970), 143

Zakataly: occupied by the Turks (1917–18), 104

Zakopane: Lenin in exile in (1913), 73

Zamosc: Jews murdered in (1648–52), 31; a centre of Polish revolt against Russia (1860), 53

Zaporiye: and the siege of Leningrad (1941–43), 126

Zaporozhe: occupied by the Germans (1942), 119; Germans driven from (1943), 129

Zaporozhian Cossacks: join revolt of Don Cossacks (1707), 37

Zbarazh: Jews murdered in (1648–52), 31

Zeya, River: gold fields of, 106

Zhigansk: a town in the Lena coal basin, 112

Zhitomir: conquered by the Lithuanians, 23; Russian (since 1793), acquired (by 1914) a large German community, 39; annexed by Russia (1793), 42, 43; anti-Jewish violence in, 69, 75, Jewish communal charity in (before 1914), 70; political assassinations in (1903–07), 72; occupied by German troops (1918), 91; much fought over (1917–21), 97; annexed by Germany (1941), 123; Germans driven from (1944), 129

Zinoviev, Grigori Yevseevich: in Switzerland at the time of the revolution (1917), 88

Zirians: a nomadic heathen tribe west of the Urals, 16

Zlatoust: strikes in (1905), 76; Germans build armaments secretly at (1922–33), 101

Zungar Kalmuks: China conquers central Asian lands of (1724–64), 40

Zurich (Switzerland): Russian students in, 70; Bolshevik activity in (1903–14), 73